YEATS ANNUAL No. 3

Under its new editor, *Yeats Annual No. 3* has been expanded in scope and now includes contributions from a much wider range of international Yeats scholars. Essays by Antony Coleman, Robert Fraser, R. A. Gilbert, Christopher Murray, Ruth Nevo, William H. O'Donnell, Edward O'Shea and Donald Masterson, and Michael J. Sidnell stand alongside George Barker's new poem, "Ben Bulben Revisited". Topics covered by the essayists include Yeats, Synge and the Georgians; Jack B. Yeats's sketches of rehearsals of "The Hour Glass" at the Lower Camden Street Theatre; Yeats and A. E. Waite; Yeats and Schopenhauer; Portraits of Yeats (with a checklist); the big house, Yeats and the Irish context; Yeats, George Barker and the idea of Ireland; and the Ellis–Yeats edition of Blake's *Works*.

Graham Hough and James Lovic Allen open a new forum on "mastering what is most abstract" in *A Vision*, while Ronald W. Schuchard and Elizabeth Ingli James assess the Yeats collections at Emory and Reading Universities respectively. A. Norman Jeffares, John S. Kelly, Colin Smythe and others contribute shorter notes. Many of the contributions to this volume draw upon unpublished materials.

Richard Burton, Richard Cave, Karen Dorn, Ian Fletcher, Ellic Howe, Patrick Parrinder, Marjorie Perloff, Michael Sidnell and Richard Taylor contribute extended reviews of new editions and studies (including the new edition of Yeats's *Poems*). By special arrangement the new location register of literary manuscripts at Reading University is tapped for its Yeats listings. The volume is lavishly illustrated with sixteen pages of plates, including many little-known photographs.

The editor

Warwick Gould is Lecturer in English Language and Literature at The Royal Holloway College, University of London. He is co-editor (with Phillip L. Marcus and Michael J. Sidnell) of *The Secret Rose, Stories by W. B. Yeats: a Variorum Edition* and is currently working with collaborators on *The Collected Letters of W. B. Yeats*, *Volume II*, and on two volumes in the new Macmillan *Collected Edition of the Works of W. B. Yeats*, *Early Essays* and *The Celtic Twilight and The Secret Rose*.

In the same series

YEATS ANNUALS Nos 1, 2
Edited by Richard J. Finneran

THOMAS HARDY ANNUALS Nos 1, 2
Edited by Norman Page

O'CASEY ANNUALS Nos 1, 2, 3
Edited by Robert G. Lowery

Further titles in preparation

YEATS ANNUAL No. 3

Edited by Warwick Gould

First published 1985

Published by
THE MACMILLAN PRESS LTD
Houndmills, Basingstoke, Hampshire RG21 2XS
and London
Companies and representatives
throughout the world

Typeset by
Wessex Typesetters
Frome, Somerset

Printed in Hong Kong

British Library Cataloguing in Publication Data
Yeats annual.—No. 3
1. Yeats, W. B.—Societies, periodicals, etc.
821'.8   PR5907
ISBN 0-333-32457-9
ISSN 0278-7687

Contents

"MASTERING WHAT IS MOST ABSTRACT": A FORUM ON *A VISION*

REVIEWS

Contents vii

List of Abbreviations

The works listed below are cited in the texts by abbreviation and page number. Some individual essays use additional abbreviations, as explained in the appropriate notes.

Au   *Autobiographies* (London: Macmillan, 1955).

AV[A]   *A Critical Edition of Yeats's* A Vision (1925), (eds) George Mills Harper and Walter Kelly Hood (London: Macmillan, 1978).

AV[B]   *A Vision* (London: Macmillan, 1962).

E&I   *Essays and Introductions* (London and New York: Macmillan, 1961).

Ex   *Explorations*, sel. Mrs W. B. Yeats (London: Macmillan, 1962; New York: Macmillan, 1963).

L   *The Letters of W. B. Yeats* (ed.) Allan Wade (London: Rupert Hart-Davis, 1954; New York: Macmillan, 1955).

LDW   *Letters on Poetry from W. B. Yeats to Dorothy Wellesley*, intro. Kathleen Raine (London and New York: Oxford University Press, 1964).

LMR   *Ah, Sweet Dancer: W. B. Yeats Margot Ruddock, A Correspondence* (ed.) Roger McHugh (London and New York: Macmillan, 1970).

LRB   *The Correspondence of Robert Bridges and W. B. Yeats* (ed.) Richard J. Finneran (London: Macmillan, 1977; Toronto: Macmillan of Canada, 1978).

LTSM   *W. B. Yeats and T. Sturge Moore: Their Correspondence, 1901–1937* (ed.) Ursula Bridge (London: Routledge & Kegan Paul; New York: Oxford University Press, 1953).

LTWBY   *Letters to W. B. Yeats* (eds) Richard J. Finneran, George Mills Harper and William M. Murphy (London: Macmillan; New York: Columbia University Press, 1977).

Mem   *Memoirs* (ed.) Denis Donoghue (London: Macmillan, 1972; New York: Macmillan, 1973).

Myth   *Mythologies* (London and New York: Macmillan, 1959).

SS	*The Senate Speeches of W. B. Yeats* (ed.) Donald R. Pearce (London: Faber & Faber, 1961).
UP1	*Uncollected Prose by W. B. Yeats*, vol. 1 (ed.) John P. Frayne (London: Macmillan; New York: Columbia University Press, 1970).
UP2	*Uncollected Prose by W. B. Yeats*, vol. 2 (eds) John P. Frayne and Colton Johnson (London: Macmillan, 1975; New York: Columbia University Press, 1976).
VP	*The Variorum Edition of the Poems of W. B. Yeats* (eds) Peter Allt and Russell K. Alspach (New York and London: Macmillan, 1957).
VPl	*The Variorum Edition of the Plays of W. B. Yeats* (eds) Russell K. Alspach (London and New York: Macmillan, 1966).
VSR	*The Secret Rose: Stories by W. B. Yeats; A Variorum Edition* (eds) Phillip L. Marcus, Warwick Gould & Michael J. Sidnell (Ithaca: Cornell University Press, 1981).
Wade	Allan Wade, *A Bibliography of the Writings of W. B. Yeats*, 3rd .edn, rev. Russell K. Alspach (London: Rupert Hart-Davis, 1968).

Editorial Board

Notes on the Contributors

James Lovic Allen is Professor of English at the University of Hawaii at Hilo, where he has taught since 1963. He is the author of many articles on Yeats, and his *Yeats's Epitaph: a Key to Symbolic Unity in his Life and Work* is reviewed in this volume.

George Barker's most recent collection of poems is *Anno Domini* (Faber, 1983).

Richard Burton is a graduate of Oxford, and is currently completing a doctoral thesis at The Royal Holloway College, University of London, on the accommodation of science in the development of W. B. Yeats.

Richard Allen Cave is a lecturer at Bedford College, University of London. He is the editor of *Hail and Farewell* and *The Lake* and author of *The Novels of George Moore*.

Antony Coleman formerly Professor of English at the Universities of Heidelberg and Alexandria, is the editor of the Revels edition of *The Provoked Wife* and co-editor, with Antony Hammond, of *Poetry and Drama, 1570–1700: Essays in Honour of Harold F. Brooks*. He is currently preparing a monograph on Irish painting, and a study of the Big House.

Karen Dorn's *Players and Painted Stage: The Theatre of W. B. Yeats* has just been published by Harvester Press and her study of D. M. Thomas will be published shortly. She has taught at the Universities of Maryland and Cambridge and is currently working on a study of W. B. Yeats's broadcasts.

Ian Fletcher is Professor Emeritus of the University of Reading and Professor of English at the Arizona State University at Tempe. The author of numerous articles on Yeats and other figures of the *fin de siècle*, he is the editor of *The Collected Poems of Victor Plarr* and *The Collected Poems* of *Lionel Johnson*: the last is noticed in this volume. He is currently preparing the Ellis and Yeats manuscripts for publication.

Robert Fraser who has lectured at the Universities of Ghana and Leeds, has recently completed a doctoral thesis on the poetry of George Barker at The Royal Holloway College, University of London. He has published four books on Commonwealth literature, including *The Novels of Ayi Kwei*. He is currently preparing a monograph on A. E. Housman.

R. A. Gilbert is a leading Bristol bookseller, specialising in Hermetica, and in associated fields. His *The Golden Dawn, Twilight of the Magicians* and his other recent books including *A. E. Waite: a Bibliography* are noticed in this volume. He is currently working on a biography of A. E. Waite.

Graham Hough is Professor Emeritus of English of the University of Cambridge and the author of *The Last Romantics*. His *W. B. Yeats's Mystery Religion* was published by Harvester in 1984 and his co-edition, with Eric Warner, of *Strangeness and Beauty*, is noticed in this volume.

Ellic Howe's authoritative *The Magicians of the Golden Dawn: a Documentary History of a Magical Order* is well known. His books include, *Urania's Children: the Strange World of the Astrologers* and *The Black Game: British Subversive Operations Against the Germans during the Second World War*.

Elizabeth Ingli James is a graduate of Oxford and works at the Library, University of Reading.

A. Norman Jeffares is Professor of English at the University of Stirling and is the author of numerous standard studies and editions of W. B. Yeats and other writers. His *Anglo-Irish Literature* (Macmillan History of Literature Series) was published in 1982 and his *New Commentary on the Poems of Yeats* is reviewed in this volume. His *Selected Poems of W. B. Yeats* was published in 1984.

John S. Kelly is a fellow of St. John's College, Oxford, and is the General Editor of *The Letters of W. B. Yeats*. Volume I, which he has co-edited with Eric Domville, is now in the press.

Donald Masterson is Professor of English at the State University of New York at Oswego. He is preparing a critical study of Blake's *Songs of Innocence and of Experience*.

Christopher Murray is a lecturer in the department of English at University College, Dublin. He is the editor of *Selected Plays of Lennox Robinson* and author of *Robert William Elliston, Manager*.

Ruth Nevo is Renée Lang Professor of Humanities and Chairman of the English Department, Hebrew University of Jerusalem. She is the author of *The Dial of Virtue, Tragic Forms in Shakespeare* and *Comic Transformations in Shakespeare*. She is currently working upon a study of Yeats and other thinkers of his time.

William H. O'Donnell is Associate Professor of English at Pennsylvania State University and the editor of *The Speckled Bird*. His *Guide to the Prose Fiction of W. B. Yeats* is reviewed in this volume. He is currently editing Yeats's *Prefaces and Introductions* for the new Macmillan *Collected Works*.

Edward O'Shea is Professor of English at the State University of New York at Oswego. He is the author of *Yeats as Editor* and has just completed a descriptive catalogue of Yeats's personal library.

Patrick Parrinder is Reader in the English department of Reading University and is the author of *Authors and Authority*. He is currently working upon a book on Joyce.

Marjorie Perloff is Professor of English at the University of Southern California and the author of *Rhyme and Meaning in the Poetry of Yeats* and *Poetics of Indeterminacy: Rimbaud to Cage*. She is working on a series of essays on postmodernism and lyric and on a book on "The Futurist Moment" in poetry and painting.

Ronald W. Schuchard is Associate Professor of English at Emory University and is currently editing, with John S. Kelly, volumes III and IV of the *Letters of W. B. Yeats*.

Michael J. Sidnell is Professor of English at Trinity College, University of Toronto. He is the co-editor of *Druid Craft: the Writing of the Shadowy Waters*: co-editor of *The Secret Rose, Stories by W. B. Yeats: A Variorum Edition*. His *Dancing Death: a History of the Group Theatre* was published by Faber in 1984. He is currently preparing a book on Yeats and modern poetry and editions of Yeats's manuscripts.

Olympia Sitwell is currently engaged in newspaper research in London.

Colin Smythe, whose publishing firm has a unique interest in Irish and Anglo-Irish Literature, is currently preparing a new edition of *A Bibliography of the Writings of W. B. Yeats* for Oxford University Press and a bibliography of Lady Gregory's writings (to be published as part of the final volume of the *Coole Edition* of her works). He is co-editor, with Ann Saddlemyer, of *Lady Gregory Fifty Years After* (to be published in 1985).

David C. Sutton has done research on Yeats and the Irish Ballad tradition, and has worked as a librarian at Trinity College, Dublin, the Polytechnic of Central London and at the University of Reading.

Richard Taylor is Professor of English at the University of Bayreuth, and is author of *The Drama of W. B. Yeats, Irish Myth and the Japanese No*. His *Reader's Guide to the Plays of W. B. Yeats* was published in 1984, and he is now working upon the publishing history and textual criticism of Pound's *Cantos*.

List of Plates

Plates 1–5 are reproduced from a copy of the John Camden Hotten facsimile of *The Marriage of Heaven and Hell* in Yeats's library (courtesy Miss Anne Butler Yeats); Plates 6, 12b, 13a & b, 14 are reproduced by courtesy of the Library, University of Reading; Plate 9 is reproduced by permission of the Glasgow City Art Gallery (Kelvingrove); Plates 10, 11a & b are reproduced from photographs by Michael Foley – present location of the originals is unknown; Plates 12a and 16 are reproduced by courtesy of Emory University; Plates 15a & b are reproduced from photographs by Professor A. Norman Jeffares.

Editor's Note

Shortly before this volume went to press, Professor F. S. L. Lyons, FBA, died after a short illness. Formerly Provost of Trinity College, Dublin, Leland Lyons was widely known as the author of many standard works such as *Ireland since the Famine* and *Charles Stewart Parnell*.

At the time of his death, Leland Lyons had drafted 100 pages of his biography of W. B. Yeats, after nearly ten years of preparatory labour. Yet from one point of view, all of his other books could be seen as preparation for what would have been one of the great modern biographies. Leland Lyons had shown from the epigraph of *Ireland since the Famine* – ". . . More substance in our enmities/Than in our love" – to the last sentences of *Culture and Anarchy in Ireland, 1890–1939* how much Yeats's thought had offered him a perspective upon the period, one characterized by

> an anarchy in the mind and in the heart . . . which forbade not just unity of territories, but also "unity of being", an anarchy that sprang from the collision within a small and intimate island of seemingly irreconcilable cultures, unable to live together or to live apart, caught inextricably in the web of their tragic history
>> Out of Ireland have we come.
>> Great hatred, little room,
>> Maimed us at the start.

With this third issue, *Yeats Annual* has a new editor and a new format, which offers some new features which it is intended will continue. Shorter Notes, biographical, bibliographical, source-related and textual are welcomed, and it is hoped to offer space for the reprinting of fugitive poems and prose pieces, and for readers' correspondence and queries. "Mastering what is most abstract" inaugurates an occasional forum upon *A Vision*, to which contributions are also invited. While George M. Harper's study of the making of *A Vision* proceeds, and while a new edition of the 1937 text for the new Macmillan *Collected Edition* is in progress (under the editorship of Walter K. and Connie Hood), scholarly comment is especially welcome, but critical evaluation of *A Vision* in a variety of contexts is also too urgently needed to be delayed.

By special arrangement with the national Location Register of Twentieth-Century English Literary Manuscripts and Letters at the University of Reading, we publish a preliminary listing of Yeats MSS holdings in the British Isles, which will be annually updated. The bibliography, also a new feature with this issue, will be an annual feature in future. It is also intended to follow our first two "Significant Research Collections" with further descriptive accounts of collections of particular interest to Yeats scholars on both sides of the Atlantic. It is hoped that these surveys and the Location Register listings will make the compilation of the urgently needed catalogue of Yeats MSS easier. The regular listing of Dissertation Abstracts (reprinted by the courtesy of the publishers of *Dissertation Abstracts International*) has been held over until No. 4 because of shortage of space. Next year it is also intended that a more comprehensive listing of European dissertation abstracts will be included.

My first debt as editor is to my predecessor, Richard Finneran, whose energy and enthusiasm led to the realisation of *Yeats Annual*, his own conception, in the first issues. My second is to the distinguished team of editorial advisers listed above upon whose advice I have relied, as well as to others such as Martin Dodsworth, Professor Joan Grundy, Professor George Mills Harper, Dr John Harwood, Professor Graham Hough, the late Professor F. S. L. Lyons, FBA, Professor Phillip L. Marcus and Dr M. K. Schuchard. Miss Deirdre Toomey has had a shaping role at every stage of the production of this volume: her judgement and assistance have been invaluable. I am also indebted to the many potential contributors who overwhelmed me with contributions.

It is the aim of *Yeats Annual* to represent the best work in the field from around the world. Contributions to No. 5 (1986) should reach me at the latest by 31 March 1985, at

English Department
The Royal Holloway College (University of London)
Egham Hill
Egham
Surrey TW20 0EX
UK   WARWICK GOULD

Acknowledgements

I am indebted to Miss Anne Yeats and to Mr Michael B. Yeats for permission to use both unpublished and published materials by W. B. Yeats included in this volume, and to Colin Smythe, on behalf of Anne de Winton and Catherine Kennedy, for permission to use unpublished material by Lady Gregory, and on behalf of Mrs Diarmuid Russell to quote from the unpublished correspondence of George Russell, as well as for much advice and assistance. I am grateful to John D. Barrett, the editorial board of *Prompts*, and the Irish Theatre Archive for permission to re-use material first published in a different form in that journal, and to Michael Schmidt, the Carcanet Press and *PN Review* for permission to reprint George Barker's "Under Ben Bulben".

The cover design, adapted from Thomas Sturge Moore's designs for H. P. R. Finberg's translation of *Axël* (1925), is reproduced in this form by permission of Miss Riette Sturge Moore, to whom I owe an especial debt of thanks.

Imogen Taylor and Linda Shaughnessy of A. P. Watt & Co., Julia Steward and Frances Arnold of The Macmillan Press, and Kim Scott-Walwyn of Oxford University Press were particularly helpful during the preparation of this volume.

Librarians whose kindness and helpfulness made the preparation of this book a pleasant task include Miss Angela Carter of The Royal Holloway College Library, Steven Clews of The University of London Library, Michael Bott and Dr J. Edwards of The University of Reading Library, the staff of The Bodleian Library, Oxford, Dr Margaret Nickson of the Dept of Manuscripts, British Library, and the staff of The British Library, Reference Division and Newspaper Library, Colindale.

For bibliographical assistance I am indebted to Professor Jacqueline Genet, Dr Maurice Harmon, Professor Frank Kinahan, Professor Heinz Kosok, Robert G. Lowery, Dr Colin McDowell, Dr Rosamund McGuinness, Robert Melbourne, Professor Maureen Murphy, Anne and Patrick Rafroidi, Colin Smythe, Deirdre Toomey and Kathleen Wales, as well as to all of the other contributors to this volume. My colleagues at The Royal Holloway College and Valerie Murr have also been of much assistance to me.

WARWICK GOULD

ARTICLES

"The One Deep Student": Yeats and A. E. Waite

R. A. Gilbert

With the usual combination of malice and perceptiveness that typified his spiteful mind, Aleister Crowley threw together as his fictional opponents in his novel *Moonchild*, "Gates" and "one Arthwait" to represent the two opposing paths within the Golden Dawn. In reality these two were Yeats, the Magician, and A. E. Waite, the Mystic, but their ways had seemingly parted in 1903 and there was no obvious reason for Crowley to link them. Or was there?

Arthur Edward Waite was a minor poet, self-taught scholar of the occult and a major, if unrecognised, mystic. He was born in Brooklyn, in 1857, the illegitimate child of Emma Lovell, "an educated English-woman of the upper middle-class",[1] and of Charles Waite, a Connecticut sea-captain. At the age of two years he was brought back to England with his infant sister after the death of his father, and raised in genteel poverty in suburban London with a minimum of schooling and a morbid enthusiasm for the Roman Catholic Church to which his mother had been converted. In 1874 his sister died and he began to lose his faith, to write verse and to develop his critical interest in occultism and the byways of spirituality. He made an unsatisfactory marriage, in 1888, that had the effect of pushing him ever deeper into both his occult studies and his writing, and in time he found his way into the Hermetic Order of the Golden Dawn.[2] His later career was one of increasing concern with his own secret Order, the Fellowship of the Rosy Cross, and of ever-deepening gloom over his inadequate income as a writer. He left London in 1920 for the Kent coast where he died in 1942, still writing and convinced that he was the principal "exponent in poetical and prose writings of sacramental religion and the higher mysticism, understood in its absolute separation from psychic and occult phenomena".[3]

Waite's whole approach to the supernatural was that of the mystic and he defined the distinction between the occultist and the mystic, in terms that were unusually clear for him, in "The Life of the Mystic", an article that he wrote for the first issue of *The Occult Review*:

3

a very clear differentiation now exists between the terms "occult" and "mystic", and it is one also which it is necessary to recognise, though, fundamentally . . . the two words are identical, differing only in that one of them is of Latin and the other of Greek origin. By the occultist we have come to understand the disciple of one or all of the secret sciences; the student, that is to say, of alchemy, astrology, the forms and methods of divination, and of the mysteries which used to be included under the general description of magic. The mystic is . . . perhaps more difficult to describe, except in the terminology of some particular school of thought; he has no concern with the study of the secret sciences; he does not [p30] work on materials or investigate forces which exist outside himself; but he endeavours, by a certain training and the application of a defined rule of life to re-establish correspondence with the divine nature from which, in his belief, he originated, and to which his return is only a question of time, or what is commonly understood as evolution. The distinction between the occultist and the mystic, however much the representative of physical science at the present day might be disposed to resent the imputation, is, therefore, loosely speaking, . . . the distinction between the man of science and the man of introspection. . . . It may be said more fully, in the words of the late Edward Maitland, that the occultist is concerned with "transcendental physics, and is of the intellectual, belonging to science," while the mystic "deals with transcendental metaphysics, and is of the spiritual, belonging to religion" . . . on the one hand there are the phenomena of the transcendental produced on the external plane, capable of verification and analysis, up to a certain point; and, on the other, there is the transcendental life. "That which is without corresponds with that which is within," says the most famous Hermetic maxim; indeed the connection suggested is almost that of the circumference with the centre, and if there is a secret of the soul expressed by the term mysticism, the phenomena of the soul manifesting on the external plane must be regarded as important; but these are the domain of occultism.[4]

This is in striking contrast to Yeats's attitude at the same period, which is expressed forcefully in his plea to his fellow members of the Golden Dawn:

> Because a Magical Order differs from a society for experiment and research in that it is an Actual Being, an organic life holding within itself the highest life of its members now and in past times, to weaken its Degrees is to loosen the structure, to dislimn, to disembody, to dematerialize an Actual Being . . .[5]

And, further,

We have no choice but to remain a Magical Order, whose organization is a Talisman, or to become wholly a mere society for experiment and research, with an organization empty of magical significance . . .[6]

And yet it was through magic, not through mysticism, that Waite met Yeats.

Waite was initiated into the Golden Dawn in January 1891, ten months after Yeats's own initiation, the ceremony being held at Stent Lodge, Forest Hill, the home of S. L. MacGregor Mathers, where Yeats had received his introduction to magic. Waite's course into the Order was a familiar one: from Spiritualism to Theosophy, by way of Éliphas Lévi, and a desire for something at once more Western and less anti-Christian than the spurious wisdom of the Mahatmas. Unlike most of his fellow-initiates, however, Waite – or Frater Sacramentum Regis as he was known in the Order – became rapidly dissatisfied, leaving early in 1893 to further his career as an occult scholar and to found his short-lived but remarkable journal, *The Unknown World*. Three years later he was "re-admitted by ballot",[7] probably helped by a successful series of alchemical translations that included *The Hermetic Museum Restored and Enlarged* and *The Hermetic and Alchemical Writings of Paracelsus*. He played no active part in the affairs of the Golden Dawn, did not enter the Second Order, the Rosae Rubeae et Aureae Crucis, until 1899 and kept his head down during the squalls of the next two years. In 1903 he showed his hand.

The Order had lacked a formal Constitution for over two years – since the expulsion of Mathers – and every attempt to formulate one had failed. Finally, a third General Meeting was held in May 1903 at which J. W. Brodie-Innes's[8] attempt to impose his own Constitution (with himself as Chief) was rejected at Waite's instigation. In the chaos that ensued Waite effectively divided the Order, taking with him "those who regarded the Golden Dawn as capable of a mystical instead of an occult construction"[9] together with the Order's properties, leaving the magicians in charge of Brodie-Innes and Dr Felkin.[10]

Despite the fundamental difference of emphasis, the Holy Order of the Golden Dawn under the obedience of the Independent and Rectified Rite, as Waite's faction grandly called itself, remained on friendly terms with Felkin's Stella Matutina, helped by a genuine desire to reach a *modus vivendi* which resulted in the Concordat drawn up by Felkin and Waite in 1907. Long before this Yeats, who had, of course, taken the magical path, had suggested "that the two parties although independent of each other should use a common Temple of the Outer Order and common head quarters for the Inner"[11] although Waite had rejected the idea: "I understood that both sides had tacitly abandoned this idea as unworkable; at any rate this is how we on our part continue to view it."[12] Yeats did not approve of the division but he recognised that some of his friends did not want magic, and he made no effort to dissuade Pamela Colman Smith from staying with Waite and helping him to develop the new Tarot cards that were such a radical break with tradition.[13]

Nor does he seem to have objected to the printed rituals issued to members in 1910; indeed, he may have been unwittingly instrumental in bringing them about. From 1904 to 1909 the Independent and Rectified Rite used a modified version of the Order rituals while Felkin held his followers to the originals, but both parties became seriously alarmed when Aleister Crowley threatened to publish the rituals in his journal *The Equinox*. Yeats thought that prior publication of the rituals, translated into Latin, might secure copyright for them and he wrote to the Society of Authors for their opinion on this course of action.[14] Nothing came of the Latin project but it seems to have inspired Waite to rewrite the modified rituals and to have them printed – with the financial and literary help of Felkin who agreed to pay part of the cost and to make appropriate alterations in the copies printed for his magicians.[15]

There was, however, no further co-operation between the two Orders, for Felkin's followers were not entirely happy with Waite's ceremonies and by 1912 Felkin was receiving new rituals from the astral plane and promoting bizarre ideas about the astral beings with whom he believed himself to be in contact. These ideas began increasingly to affect Waite's members as well as his own, to such a degree that in 1914, for this and other reasons, Waite closed down the Isis–Urania Temple and brought the Independent and Rectified Rite to an end.[16]

In the same year Felkin was carrying his astral fantasies to the lengths of actively seeking for the material tomb of the mythical Christian Rosenkreuz, an occupation that had increasingly obsessed him since his meeting with Rudolf Steiner in 1910, and one that neither Yeats nor Waite could take seriously. It is possible that "The Mountain Tomb" (*VP* 311) is concerned not only with the burial of the Imagination but is also an oblique attack on the follies of Dr Felkin; if this *is* the case, then Waite's comment on the poem, in *The Occult Review*,[17] is heavily ironic: "Mr. W. B. Yeats occupies the place of honour [in *The Quest*, of April 1913] with some verses on the Mountain Tomb, which are Rosicrucian in their refrain, but much too cryptic in motive for one to understand why."

Much less cryptic were Yeats's motives for seeking advice from Waite, early in 1914, on the origin of the doctrine of the Astral Light (the all-pervading Universal Medium of the occultists): Waite was already an acknowledged authority on Éliphas Lévi, the French occultist who coined the term, and had published three major translations of Lévi's work[18] – all of which were known to Yeats and at least one of which, *Transcendental Magic*, he possessed. Waite's letter[19] was scarcely helpful for he said nothing constructive that did not appear in his recently published translation of *The History of Magic*, added a sneer at Steiner and

C. W. Leadbeater and concluded by saying "I would help you if I could on this side of the question, [the possible Eastern source of the doctrine] but it is one for a reliable eastern student, on the understanding that he is not a Theosophist."

The letter may not have helped Yeats, but it did serve to remind him of Waite's reputation as an interpreter – the only one in England – of the ideas of the French mystic, Louis Claude de Saint-Martin,[20] and it was in this capacity that Yeats remembered Waite twenty years later in his essay *Louis Lambert*; "I think it probable that Éliphas Lévi found his 'Astral Light' not, as he said, in Saint-Martin, where the one deep student of that eighteenth-century mystic known to me has searched for it in vain, but in *Louis Lambert*" (*E&I* 440).

And the question about the astral light was not the first occasion of Yeats's seeking Waite's advice. In 1903, when the strife within the Golden Dawn was approaching boiling-point, he asked Waite to supper to discuss the unpublished papers of William Stirling, the author of that odd book *The Canon*[21] Waite recorded the visit, and his impressions of Yeats, in his enormous diary for 1903:[22]

This is how it fell out yesterday [January 19th] and in its way it was curious. I reached 18 Woburn Buildings through a desponding slough of roadway and an atmosphere which held mud in solution. I rang the bell. Brother Devil descended to receive me looking gaunt in the gaslight and distorted in the mist which came in with me from the street. He escorted me up to the top floor where a fire burnt in a common open range provided with an oven and in this the dinner plates were warming. The cloth was laid upon the table towards the window end of the room. I observed a flagon of Funchal wine partially emptied. A vast female[23] was preparing the meal in a room which opened towards the back part of the house and is, I believe, on ordinary occasions the poet's bedroom. It is not worth while to particularise but by 8.30 p.m. I took advantage of the engagement, which I had already pleaded, to avoid an encounter with the admirable Lady Gregory and to hear more than might be reasonable concerning the old Irish romances and the wonders of the heroic period towards which I have but slight attraction. In the meantime we talked to lengthy hours of many matters. The poet adverted to the fact that I had recently published a very successful book of verse and was anxious to see my still more recent work on the Kabalah.[24] He told me that the unfortunate Frater ———— of the House of the Hidden Stairs[25] had suddenly lost his wife and he evidently found that this was irreparable otherwise than in the conventional way for she had looked after him most faithfully in the periodic fits of drink-craving which came over him. This scandal I had not heard previously.

He was also most interested to learn that I was looking up the old

Graal legends in connection with the Knightly Orders – news which must have reached him as soon as ever I had made known the fact to our study-group and I suppose through the Frater Elliott.[26] He expressed satisfaction and explained a scheme of literary criticisms which he had in view and into which a study of the Graal must enter, but it was necessary that the scholar should precede him. He agreed with me that the German Grail legends must be later than the others, and has offered through Lady Gregory to make me acquainted with Miss Jessie L. Weston[27] of Parsifal and Wagner fame. He explained that he was seeking to create an ideal for the aristocratic classes particularly in Ireland where the peasantry have theirs in folklore.[28] We both agreed that allegory in fiction was a product of the middle classes and was typically bourgeois. Bourgeoisérie is his enemy and is mine. As regards the author of the Canon he told me that his name was Stirling. He has promised to lend me the book, at which I glanced as we talked and he waits for my opinion on the pile of MS. which has been put into his hands as the literary remains of the author. I have promised to give him an opinion whether there is anything which calls for publication.

Two days later he recorded in his diary his impressions of Yeats as a man and as a poet:

There is one thing which strikes me – perhaps it has occurred to others – about the Frater Diabolus – and that is the entire absence in him of that geniality which is such a marked characteristic of his country-men. His type externally is that of the Irish peasant: he is dark, lean, pallid, tall, gaunt, big-boned, lanky in arm & leg: he walks with straight knees and a peculiar stalk. He is not actually discourteous but has no affability. Perhaps he has more sincerity than distinguishes his people generally; certainly he has a whole-hearted earnestness in literature and he believes really in the kind of aboriginal occultism which he understands. Of things mystical he has, I should say, no knowledge. He is the same in poetry; he has the incantating charm and the elfin melancholy; but of the depths or the heights, nothing. I do not speak of his nationalist aspirations except to say that I suppose they *are* aspirations. From any serious standpoint, they could not surely be worth a thought.

Clearly, Waite saw Yeats not only as a supporter of the opposing camp in the Golden Dawn but as opposite in every way, for he accepted poetry as truly great only when it contained profound mystical insights, he was politically Conservative and physically the antithesis of Yeats, being short and rather stout. And he treated Yeats's earnestness in a somewhat cavalier fashion, for when the manuscripts duly arrived, on 10 February,

Waite did nothing with them and returned them virtually unread. He probably suggested that the family should consider having them published at their own expense, for he records that Yeats told him that the family was "in poor circumstances" adding himself that it "was not a serious loss to the world" if they should not be published. He was equally scathing in his diary about *The Canon* itself: "If there ever was in the past, as the book suggests, a canon which covered and ruled all the arts, then the most desirable thing that could happen is that it should have been lost, which is what has occurred apparently, and the last thing that need be wished for is its recovery except as a matter of curiosity."

Yeats ought to have guessed Waite's reaction to *The Canon* for he would have known from Waite's published works of his hostility to the gnostic ideas, speculations on Christian origins and pagan "Cabalism" of the book. Waite was equally unimpressed by Yeats's Celtic enthusiasms – indeed, the whole Celtic world was alien to him, so much so that the chapters on the Celtic Church in his *Hidden Church of the Holy Graal* were prepared for him by Arthur Machen – and this, too, Yeats should have known for he had long been aware of Waite's attitude to fairy lore. This was expressed in *Elfin Music: An Anthology of English Fairy Poetry* which Waite had edited in 1888: "The original fairy of Frankish poetry and fiction was simply a female initiated into the mysteries and marvels of magic. . . . The immediate source of the conceptions which are at the base of English fairy poetry must be evidently sought in the romances and legends of early French chivalry" (p. xi).

These comments may well have inspired Yeats's own public derision of such fairies: "The personages of English fairy literature are merely, in most cases, mortals beautifully masquerading. Nobody ever believed in such fairies. They are romantic bubbles from Provence. Nobody ever laid new milk on their doorstep for them."[29] His own copy of *Elfin Music* is dated 4 August 1888, and although this is probably too late for him to have altered *Fairy and Folk Tales* (which appeared in September) in response to it, he may well have been shown the book at an earlier date by William Sharp who knew both Waite and Yeats personally, and who was closely involved with the Walter Scott Company, the publisher of both titles. Even if this was not the case, Yeats undoubtedly knew of Waite's work at this time for he drew upon *The Mysteries of Magic*, Waite's first translation of Éliphas Lévi, for the note in *Fairy and Folk Tales* concerning elementals, "Gods of the Earth", or "nature spirits".[30]

Utterly opposed to each other as they were in all things occult, each man evidently respected the other, for Waite's visit of 1903 was not the only one. Writing, in *Shadows of Life and Thought*, of contemporary poets, Waite recalled Yeats: "We used to see one another some years later on. It was often in secret circles, but occasionally I looked him up and occasionally he came to Ealing. It was not because I cared for his verse, though I cared enough, and not because he was drawn to mine. The password between us was MAGIA, seeing that when we first met I was still appraising the bits and pieces of occult schools, which – for all that I know – Yeats may never have left. More seriously, I was drawn to him because he also was soaked in faërie lore, and lived amongst it more even than myself" (p. 119). The visits to Sidmouth Lodge, Waite's home at Ealing from 1900 to 1920, whatever they were about, must have been between 1904 and 1908, for which years Waite's diaries are not available – there is no mention whatever of Yeats from 1909 onwards.

During these years of occasional meeting their ideas developed in their own distinctive ways. When each sought the other out it could only have been for the exchange of knowledge and experience gained on their diverging and ultimately irreconcilable paths within the Golden Dawn. Yeats's Way is summed up in his essay *Magic*:

> I believe in the practice and philosophy of what we have agreed to call magic, in what I must call the evocation of spirits, though I do not know what they are, in the power of creating magical illusions, in the visions of truth in the depths of the mind when the eyes are closed; and I believe in three doctrines, which have, as I think, been handed down from early times, and been the foundations of nearly all magical practices. These doctrines are –
> (1) That the borders of our mind are ever shifting, and that many minds can flow into one another, as it were, and create or reveal a single mind, a single energy.
> (2) That the borders of our memories are as shifting, and that our memories are a part of one great memory, the memory of Nature herself.
> (3) That this great mind and great memory can be evoked by symbols (*E&I* 28).

Waite's beliefs in the immanence of God and in the absolute necessity of seeking Divine Union are expressed most elegantly in his autobiography, but they are given also in somewhat pompous manner in his *Points of Contemplation Appertaining to the Grade of Neophyte* (1916) in which form his followers learned how his Order was set eternally over and against magic: "The fulfilment of earthly life is in that life which is eternal, and the sole purpose of man's sojourn in the material world is that he may attain union with the Divine." After instructions to the candidate the following Points are made:

> The Divine Being dwells immanently in the whole creation and testifies to the self-knowing spirit of man through the medium of the manifest world.
>   The world is therefore sacramental, the outward sign of an infinite grace and power abiding behind the vestures of material things, and

dispensing power and grace through all the channels according to man's capacity for reception.

The cosmic communication of the immanent GOD to man is through the channel of the senses, and for this reason these also are sacramental.

The first work of the seeker after Divine Things is the purification of his own nature, so that he may communicate worthily with the world and with GOD therein.

By the manifest nature of man is to be understood not only the body and its senses but the material mind, desires, emotions and will. Within these there lies the great world of the soul, and this world can open to the seeker who is properly prepared.

When the channels of communication – that is to say, sense and mind, desire and will – have been cleansed and sanctified, it is taught in the Doctrine and Symbolism of the Rosy Cross that there is a fuller communication between the GOD immanent in the universe and the DIVINE IMMANENCE in the soul of man. The soul is changed and renewed as by a second birth in time, and the world is transformed also, being seen under a new light, shining from within the soul.

Similar as these two Ways may appear when stripped of the verbiage, it is a similarity of appearance only; the two essences are quite distinct and their respective devotees can have no true common ground. So it was with Waite and Yeats; an undoubted mutual respect never led to real friendship and their meetings seem only to have reinforced their opposing views. Waite was undoubtedly one of those friends' friends of Yeats who were all "estranged" *(AV[A]* ix), and he evidently realised this: "Had we found one another more often, we might have become friends; but ever our paths diverged."[31] Each convinced of the other's wrongness, they yet respected each other, they read each other's books and certainly they spoke to one another. It is equally certain that they did not listen.

NOTES

1. A. E. Waite, *Shadows of Life and Thought: a Retrospective Review in the form of Memoirs* (1938) p. 15.
2. The Hermetic Order of the Golden Dawn was a secret Magical Order set up in 1887 by William Wynn Westcott, physician, Freemason and *soi-disant* Rosicrucian. He based the Order on a series of cypher manuscripts, allegedly of ancient date but probably forged in the 1880's, and developed a series of initiatory rituals with the help of S. L. MacGregor Mathers, a fellow-Rosicrucian more inventive than Westcott and driven by a mania for power. An inner Order specifically concerned with Magic was added in 1892 and it was to this that the more earnest members gravitated. The curious history of the Order is told in full by Ellic Howe in his book *The Magicians of the Golden Dawn* (1972) and more briefly in my own *The Golden Dawn: Twilight of the Magicians.* (1983)

Yeats's involvement in the Order is recounted in George Harper's *Yeats's Golden Dawn*. (1974)

 3. Waite's own description of himself; it forms part of his regular entry in *Who's Who* from 1910 to 1942.

 4. *The Occult Review*, I:1 (Jan. 1905) 29–30.

 5. *Is the Order of R. R. & A. C. to Remain a Magical Order?*, as reprinted in *Yeats's Golden Dawn*, by George Mills Harper (London: Macmillan, 1974) p. 261.

 6. Ibid., p. 264.

 7. Waite was No. 99 on the Order's roll. Comments on Waite's entry in the Order's Address Book read successively: "In abeyance", "Demitted 1893" and "Re-admitted by ballot, 17 Feb. 1896."

 8. John William Brodie-Innes (1848–1923) ("Sub Spe"), was an Edinburgh Lawyer who became President of the Scottish Lodge of the Theosophical Society. In 1891 he joined the Golden Dawn and from 1893 to 1897 was Imperator of the Amen-Ra Temple at Edinburgh. He maintained an ambivalent attitude to Mathers but consistently opposed the trend to mysticism that resulted in the schism of 1903. See *LTWBY, passim*.

 9. *Shadows of Life and Thought*, p. 228.

10. Dr Robert William Felkin ("Finem Respice"), was an Edinburgh Physician who worked as a medical missionary in Uganda in the late 1870s and achieved a reputation as an expert in tropical medicine. He entered the Golden Dawn in 1894 through the Amen-Ra temple but moved to London shortly afterwards and joined the Isis–Urania Temple. After the schism of 1903 he led the magical branch, the Stella Matutina, and set up the Amoun Temple. In 1915 he emigrated to New Zealand, where he had previously established a branch of his Order, and died there in 1922.

11. Stated by Waite in a letter to Felkin of 1 January 1904. The letter is in the "Private Collection" referred to by Ellic Howe, *op. cit.*

12. Ibid.

13. Pamela Colman Smith was an American artist who came to London in 1899, joined the Golden Dawn, as "Soror Quod Tibi id Aliis", and took Waite's part in 1903. She produced, under Waite's guidance, the Tarot cards that were published in December, 1909 together with Waite's *Key to the Tarot*. Waite thought that the symbols of the Tarot, "or some at least among them – were gates which opened on realms of vision beyond occult dreams. I saw to it therefore that Pamela Coleman [*sic*] Smith should not be picking up casually any floating images from my own or another mind" (*Shadows*, p. 185) Their Tarot pack was very much a joint venture.

14. Yeats wrote to Felkin on 11 June 1909 enclosing a copy of his letter to the Society of Authors. Both letters are in the "Private Collection".

15. Two letters to Felkin, from Helen Rand of 23 June 1910, and from Waite of 28 June 1910, are in the "Private Collection". They give details of the printing of the rituals and of the costs to be borne by each Order.

16. Waite's own account, in *Shadows of Life and Thought*, p. 229, is extremely brief: "In 1914 I put an end to the Isis–Urania or Mother Temple, owing to internecine feuds on the authenticity of documents." This, no doubt, covered both Felkin's dubious astral teachings and the claim by Marcus Worsley Blackden, Waite's former Co-Chief, that the spurious cypher rituals were not only genuine but probably ancient Egyptian.

17. Vol. XVII, no. 6 of June 1913, 359. Waite's comment was made in his regular, but unsigned, feature *Periodical Literature*, a review of contemporary esoteric journals.

18. *The Mysteries of Magic: a Digest of the writings of Éliphas Lévi with Biographical and Critical Essay* was published in 1886, a revised edition being issued in 1897. *Transcendental Magic, its Doctrine and Ritual* appeared in 1896, and *The History of Magic* in 1913. Eliphas Lévi's real name was Alphonse Louis Constant (1810–75).

19. The letter is dated 31 January 1914. It was published in *LTWBY* 279. Yeats's original letter to Waite has not survived – which is scarcely surprising in view of the manner in which Waite's papers were stored variously in cellars and woodsheds. At Ramsgate he

became alarmed at the dampness of the cellar and hung bundles of papers from the rafters – to no avail, for they still rotted.

20. Waite had written the only significant study and anthology of Saint-Martin (1743–1803) to be published in English: *The Life of Louis Claude de Saint-Martin the Unknown Philosopher and the Substance of his Transcendental Doctrine* (London 1901). It was highly regarded by the French Martinists and their leader, Papus (Gérard Encausse), awarded Waite the degree of Doctor of Hermetic Science. Papus also published articles by W. T. Horton in his journal *I.N.R.I.* and Horton, who was a friend of both men may well have shown Waite's book to Yeats in a fit of Martinist enthusiasm.

21. *The Canon: an exposition of the Pagan Mystery perpetuated in the Cabala as the Rule of all the Arts. With a Preface by R. B. Cunninghame Graham* (London, 1897). The book was published anonymously. Unpublished correspondence between Yeats and Rothenstein between 1898 and 1903 indicates that it was the latter who sought to interest Yeats in Stirling's book (which was still being advertised on the endpapers of Yeats's *The Tables of the Law, AND The Adoration of the Magi* (London: Elkin Mathews, 1904). Yeats was interested in Stirling's work, and was prepared to try to interest occult students such as Waite in them, but had "no great trust" in his ideas. Yeats described Stirling's death as a "terrible thing", but the cause of his death is not known.

22. The diary for 1903 comprises 250 quarto sheets bound up and lettered "Annus Mirabilis Redivivus". From 1909 to 1942 Waite used pocket diaries, all of which have survived save those for 1911 and 1914. There are four other quarto diaries surviving, apparently for the years 1904 to 1908, but the present custodians will not permit access to them.

23. Surely Mrs Old, "a tall, robust country-woman from somewhere a little to the east of Oxford", as Masefield recalled her, in *Some Memories of W. B. Yeats* (Dublin, Cuala, 1940, p. 14). Yeats's housekeeper, she was later to tell Masefield " 'I shall never forget the blessed days with Mr Yeats at Woburn Buildings, for, oh, they were blessed days' " (ibid.).

24. The two books were *A Book of Mystery and Vision* and *The Doctrine and Literature of the Kabalah*. Both appeared in 1902 but the exact dates of publication are not known.

25. Waite's euphemism for the Golden Dawn. It has not been possible to identify "the unfortunate Frater".

26. The study-group was within the *Societas Rosicruciana in Anglia*, a Masonic Rosicrucian Society that Waite had joined in 1902. Hugh Elliott was a fellow-member of both the SRIA and the Golden Dawn; after the schism of 1903 he joined Felkin's Stella Matutina.

27. Jessie Weston believed that the Holy Grail had its origin in the pre-Christian Mystery religions of the Near East, a point of view that Waite rejected utterly and over which he later clashed with Miss Weston in the pages of *The Quest*. It is unlikely that he really wished to meet her.

28. Waite evidently knew nothing of the Castle of Heroes. A full account is given in Lucy Shepard Kalogera, *Yeats's Celtic Mysteries* (Unpub. Ph.D thesis, Florida State University, 1977).

29. *Fairy and Folk Tales of the Irish Peasantry* (1888) p. xvi.

30. Ibid, p. 319. See also *The Mysteries of Magic* (1886) pp. 118–28. The translation is from *Dogme et Rituel de l'Haute Magie* (1856).

31. *Shadows of Life and Thought*, p. 119.

Yeats and Schopenhauer

Ruth Nevo

In his monumental volume on W. B. Yeats, Harold Bloom expressed disquiet concerning *A Vision*, the grand exfoliation of Yeats's symbolic system. The full of the moon, the Apollonian or individuating principle of Yeats's Great Wheel spinning between alternating states of conciousness, is, he says, "alas, occult . . . really fit stuff for Yeats's spooks to have instructed him in, and difficult to accept as being after all what it is, the center and repository of value in Yeats' system. What, in imaginative or human terms, does it come to, and what can it show us?"[1]

It is upon this question, or rather upon an answer to this question, that certain affinities between the thought of Yeats and of Schopenhauer can throw light. Yeats must have read *The World as Will and Idea, or Representation* quite soon after it was translated into English between 1883 and 1886[2] (when he was in his twenties) for in 1913, at the age of 48, he recalls having read him "as a young man" (*E&I* 347). Schopenhauer, I submit, was a powerful presence hovering among those "spooks". It is strange that this influence or affinity (noticed in passing by Thomas Whitaker in *Swan and Shadow*, in 1964)[3], has not been taken up in the criticism of Yeats, though the impression made upon Yeats by Nietzsche, Schopenhauer's disciple and adversary, has been so universally recognised as to have become a commonplace of Yeats studies. Perhaps the enchantment exercised upon Yeats, as indeed upon a whole generation of succeeding writers, by the young philosopher obscured the earlier, but no less long standing attachment. It is worth reviving then, for what it can reveal to us, chiefly, perhaps, because Nietzsche's own controversy with his precursor mirrors the perennial controversy of Yeats with himself upon the opposition between the primary and antithetical, or objective and subjective principles. In more immediately relevant terms, between the obligation to "resignation" or to "tragic joy".

Schopenhauer, Yeats wrote to Sturge Moore, "can do no wrong in my eyes – I no more quarrel with him than I do with a mountain cataract" (*LTSM* 117). But in fact it is as much by quarrelling with him, and in the name of an adverse, Nietzschean, principle, as by incorporating him,

15

that he exhibits the depth of his indebtedness. "I am always", he writes in a Diary entry of 1930, "in all I do, driven to a moment which is the realisation of myself as unique and free, or to a moment which is the surrender to God of all that I am. . . . could those two impulses, one as much a part of truth as the other, be reconciled, or if one or the other could prevail, all life would cease" (*Ex* 305). This major tenet in Yeats's thought itself adopts Schopenhauer's postulate that "universal conflict is essential to the phenomenon of the will"; that matter – all of life – "has its existence only in a struggle of conflicting forces".[4] But if, by 1930, Yeats could accept dualism, he was for most of his life torn by bi-polarity, by the incessant alternation in mode, mood, self-definition and priority between insurgent rival impulses, desires, convictions, evaluations. The overshadowing of Schopenhauer by Nietzsche in the critical perception of Yeats obscures a whole dimension of struggle in a life of struggle, and prevents us from seeing that there is a sense, which I hope will become apparent, in which the names of Nietzsche and Schopenhauer themselves name a primary Yeatsian opposition.

We find repeated references to Schopenhauer throughout Yeats's writings. In a letter to *The United Irishman* of 7 December 1901 he praises "An essay on poetry by Shelley and certain essays by Schopenhauer are probably the best things that have been written on the subject ["Literature and Conscience"] by modern writers." In the 1913 essay on "Art and Ideas" already referred to, Schopenhauer's dictum that "no man – so unworthy a thing is life seen with unbesotted eyes – would live another's life" (*E&I* 347) turns up among a series of personal reminiscences. In *Pages from a Diary* written in 1930 he mentions Schopenhauer as one of those abstract thinkers whose relation to "concrete reality" is such as to pass on "both the thought and the passion" (*Ex* 303) and he claims him as a believer in the rebirth of the soul in 1931, in the Notes to "The Resurrection" (*VPL* 934). Most interestingly for my present purposes, as I shall argue, in an essay called "The Holy Mountain", in which he discusses Indian piety, he succinctly summarises a Schopenhauerian duality. "The Spirit, the Self that is in all selves, the pure mirror, is the source of intelligence, but Matter is the source of all energy, all creative power, all that separates one thing from another, not Matter as understood by Hobbes and his Mechanists, . . . but interpreted with profound logic almost what Schopenhauer understood by Will" (*E&I* 461).

Though no explicit record exists of Yeats's first encounter with Schopenhauer, the 1913 essay is permeated by references to the period of his young manhood. "Two days ago" he was at the Tate Gallery to see paintings by Millais and Rossetti and "recovered an old emotion" (*E&I* 346). "The painting of the hair", in the Rossetti called up "memories of sketches of my father's on the margins of the first Shelley I had read, while the strong colours made me half remember studio conversations . . .". Potter's *Field Mouse* takes him back still further, into childhood, for "it had hung in our house for years". Finally, "I had learned to think in the midst of the last phase of Pre-Raphaelitism and now I had come to Pre-Raphaelitism again and rediscovered my earliest thought" (*E&I* 346). It is surely significant that it is in this context of "earliest thought" and of the Pre-Raphaelitism by which he was attracted in the eighties that Schopenhauer, apparently quite adventitiously, is recalled. It would be my guess that Yeats was reading Schopenhauer first during the late eighties, at the time of his involvement with the Theosophical Society. Schopenhauer's learned and eloquent treatise, grounded in evolutionary concepts and slanted towards Eastern mysticism, sponsored and gave credence to the synthesis of science, religion and philosophy by which Yeats was enchanted in the doctrines of Madame Blavatsky, and offered, moreover, the very comprehensive structure of thought which he needed to combat his father's sceptical rationalism, which was also, willy-nilly, his own. Richard Ellmann's account of the appeal of the Theosophical Society could apply almost without modification to the impact we may suppose *The World as Will and Idea* to have had upon the young Yeats. "The movement gathered force", says Ellmann, "because it attacked atheism and at the same time supported anti-clericalism; because it attacked science, yet was careful to use the weapons of scientific language and confirmation whenever possible . . . because it upheld fatalism, yet offered hope of progress; because it denounced modern man as fiercely as Nordau, but at the same time offered him the opportunity of becoming like a god. Spiritual evolution restored the hope which natural evolution had removed, and materialism was utterly condemned".[5]

Ernest Dowson had certainly read Schopenhauer before 1889, for he notes on the fifth of March of that year that "Plato on 'Love' still seems to me less convincing than Schopenhauer".[6] Another possible intermediary among Yeats's acquaintances at the time was Wilde: Yeats writes in *The Trembling of the Veil* "I saw a good deal of Wilde at that time – was it 1887 or 1888? – I have no way of fixing the date[7] except that I had published my first book, *The Wanderings of Oisin*, and that Wilde had not yet published his *Decay of Lying*." When Christmas dinner, to which Wilde had invited him, was over, Wilde had read to him from the proofs of *The Decay of Lying* the sentence, " 'Schopenhauer has analysed the pessimism that characterises modern thought, but Hamlet invented it. The world has become sad because a puppet was once melancholy' " (*Au* 134–5).

Whatever its inception, the Schopenhauer connection I believe can be shown to have been enduring and fundamental. And before I enter upon this task I would like to offer for consideration a striking circumstance, which may well be evidence of a persistent memory. I refer to a peculiarly haunting phrase (for Yeats) which occurs in a poem of 1920, and again in 1934.

"On a Picture of a Black Centaur by Edmund Dulac" is a poem which projects a cleavage within the psyche, in which dark, a powerful centaur, "horrible green parrots", dead bread of intellect and full-flavoured wine of instinct, soul and self play out the drama of inner conflict. Yeats composed it in 1920 and placed it in *The Tower* between "Leda and the Swan" and "Among School Children" (both, if you will, poems which reflect upon relations between Will and Idea or Representation). In it the strange phrase first appears:

> I, being driven half insane
> Because of some green wing, gathered old mummy wheat
> In the mad abstract dark and ground it grain by grain. . . .

In 1934, thinking about the contrary natures of his two children – Anne, who "always thinks of death", "the Mars–Venus personality", and Michael, Jupiter–Saturn, the Antithetical, "always thinking about life"[8] – Yeats wrote (then, and again at the end of the revised *A Vision*, where he announces the end of a cycle and the "gradual coming and increase of the counter-movement") the cryptic lines:

> Should Jupiter and Saturn meet
> O what a crop of mummy wheat! (*AV[B]* 302)

In the fourteen years between the two poems the image itself suffers a transformation from death to life, and becomes a marvellously condensed notation for all of Yeats's unceasing meditation upon the mysteries of cyclic resurrection. Can it be purely fortuitous that Schopenhauer, speaking of the atemporal, omnipresent, perdurable will to live has the following footnote?

> On 16 September, 1840, at a lecture on Egyptian Antiquities given at the Literary and Scientific Institute of London, Mr. Pettigrew exhibited some grains of wheat, found . . . in a grave at Thebes, in which they must have been lying for three thousand years. They were found in a hermetically sealed vase. He had sown twelve grains, and from them had a plant which had grown to a height of five feet, whose seeds were now perfectly ripe . . . in the same way, in 1830, Mr. Haulton produced at the Medical Botanical Society in London a bulbous root that had been found in the hand of an Egyptian mummy . . . at least two thousand years old. He had planted it in a flower pot, where it had at once grown up and was flourishing . . . (*Sch.* 1. 137)

"Mummy wheat" witnesses a very close kinship. And when Yeats is read in the light of that kinship "many crooked things are made straight", as Yeats put it in a passage which itself makes a Schopenhaurian claim: "If all our mental images," he says, ". . . are forms existing in the general vehicle of *Anima Mundi*, and mirrored in our particular vehicle, many crooked things are made straight" (*Myth* 352). It is also the case that the differences between them are as illuminating as the parallels. For always it will be Yeats's insistence upon the inalienable freedom of the artist's creativity which will distinguish his thought from the melancholy philosopher's ascetic resignation of all the things of this world, including the artist's creativity. Nevertheless the basic antinomy of being and knowing, Will and Idea, consciousness and experience permeates the thought of both; a fascination with forms of Vedic mysticism is shared by both; Saint and Artist are key figures for both; both see existence as an unappeasable warfare of contraries; and such topics as aesthetic detachment, the Wheel of recurrences, the mirror of mind, the stage managed life all appear in the web of their discourse, in many rich and wonderful transformations. In the scope of the present essay I can merely touch upon one or two of these themes, themselves intricately interrelated, and in the hope that I shall not pay too high a price in lucidity for the inevitable condensation.

I begin with a poem "Whence Had They Come?" from a series called "Supernatural Songs" in the volume *A Full Moon in March* which Yeats published in 1935:

> Eternity is passion, girl or boy
> Cry at the onset of their sexual joy
> 'For ever and for ever'; then awake
> Ignorant what Dramatis Personae spake;
> A passion-driven exultant man sings out
> Sentences that he has never thought;
> The Flagellant lashes those submissive loins
> Ignorant what that dramatist enjoins,
> What master made the lash. Whence had they come,
> The hand and lash that beat down frigid Rome?
> What sacred drama through her body heaved
> When world-transforming Charlemagne was conceived? (*VP* 560)

Yeats's questions – he is a very interrogative poet – are always interesting, and puzzling. Are these questions, for instance, psychological questions, or historical questions, or metaphysical questions? And upon what assumptions do they rest? His paradigms – lover, poet, ascetic or saint, world-conqueror – map out an area in which these rationalistically separated disciplines appear to dissolve or fuse. The masterful rhetoric of the poem brings together lover, artist, fanatic and emperor under a rubric which puts into question at one stroke the autonomy of all their activities and motivations. And this by subtly subverting the very notion of motivation as we have rationally understood the term. These personae, the questions intimate, are not autonomous, self-determining, intiating, originating beings. They are driven, they are carried forward by a motivating force outside themselves or their consciousness of themselves. They are presented as having found themselves when they are not indeed quite, or wholly or only themselves. Or possibly, precisely by not being wholly and only themselves have they found and defined themselves. "Man is nothing until he is united with an Image," Yeats said elsewhere. (*VPl* 749)

The metaphor of the theatre – they are "dramatis personae" – exactly delineates the strangeness of this union. The text they speak or act, these dramatis personae, is, it seems, already inscribed, yet the drama comes into being only through their actions. "Whence had they come" divides into two parts, the first dealing with passion and its apparently spontaneous intuitions: the second with action, whether self-directed or other-directed, capable of instituting far-reaching change in historical events. But the poem's formal structure, its tight couplets, rivet the two parts together, so that the idea is totalised, comprehensive: applicable to all that we do, feel or conceive.

Book III of *A Vision*, "the Soul in Judgment", provides a prose gloss on the passionate questioning of the poem: "The *Spirit* finds concrete events in the *Passionate Body*, but the names and words of the drama it must obtain . . . from some incarnate Mind, and this it is able to do because all spirits inhabit our unconsciousness. . . . the Dramatis Personae of our dreams" (*AV[B]* 226–7). But in a beautiful earlier poem of 1919 called "The Double Vision of Michael Robartes", we find again the theatre metaphor – a puppet theatre in this case – in all its baffling indeterminacy of agent and act, subject and object. It is Phase I on the Wheel that he begins with – the Phase of complete plasticity, or objectivity; or rather the interim moment "When the old moon is vanished from the sky / And the new still hides her horn". Then

> Under blank eyes and fingers never still
> The particular is pounded till it is man.
> When had I my own will?
> O not since life began.
>
> Constrained, arraigned, baffled, bent and unbent
> By these wire-jointed jaws and limbs of wood,
> Themselves obedient,
> Knowing not evil and good;

Obedient to some hidden magical breath.
They do not even feel, so abstract are they.
So dead beyond our death,
Triumph that we obey. (*VP* 382–4)

The anaphoric "themselves" (the blank eyes and fingers? or the wire-jointed jaws and limbs of wood?) pinpoints the recursive structure. The "I", the brooding consciousness pluralises into a universal "we", that obeys. But what or whom is obeyed, and what, or who obeys? The question, "When had I my own will?" like the question Whence? in the previous poem, is unsettling, portentous. The questions assume an extra-personal, suprapersonal power whose text is that which we act out even, or particularly, in our most intense and ecstatic and distinctively personal moments. Yet it leaves open the nature of that power, and even, since it is a question and not an answer, the certain knowledge of its existence. "I am full of uncertainty, not knowing when I am the finger, when the clay" (*Myth* 366).

The imagery of that sentence is sufficient reminder, if reminder be needed, that there is of course a theological answer to Yeats's questions. But Yeats, a profoundly religious mind, though heterodox, is of the great company of the post-enlightenment sceptics, those orphans of the spirit who were left with nothing but their own human resources by the Nietzschean death of God, indeterminately emancipated or disinherited. The received traditional answer therefore is not available to him; and if, in what has been called his "heroic humanism" Yeats embraces his condition: "We must hold to what we have that the next civilisation may be born, not from a virgin's womb, nor a tomb without a body, not from a void, but of our own rich experience" (*Ex* 437) it is precisely the unavailability of given answers that generates his deeply troubled, boldly speculative and indefatigable inquiring opus, and makes him, arguably, Irish nationalist though he be, *the* great English poet of the twentieth century. My point at present is that the awe so masterfully expressed in this poem before the intuition of an unfathomable, suprarational, uncontrollable Will realising itself through the representations of individual willing, is mediated by Schopenhauer, and nourished by Schopenhauer; a fruit, so to speak, of the very same soil. That just such an intuition, and just such a mediation has informed other great seminal twentieth century minds is the gist of Thomas Mann's essay, *Freud and the Future*, published as it happens, just one year after Yeats's poem. "Freud's description of the id and the ego", Mann there asks, "is it not to a hair Schopenhauer's description of the Will and the Intellect? A translation of the latter's metaphysics into psychology?" And then, pinpointing what he calls "the profound and mysterious contact between the two" Mann uses the same dramatic metaphor implicit in Yeats's poem. "In Schopenhauer's essay. *Transcendant Speculations on Apparent Design in the Fate of the Individual*, a pregnant and mysterious idea is developed," he says, and it is briefly this: "That precisely as in a dream it is our own will that unconsciously appears as inexorable objective destiny, everything in it proceeding out of ourselves and each of us being the secret theatre-manager of our own dreams, so also in reality the great dream that a single essence, the will itself, dreams with us all, our fate, may be the product of our inmost selves, of our wills, and we are actually ourselves bringing about what seems to be happening to us."[9] In the light of this passage, in the light of the convergence of Freud's dark, inaccessible domain of the id, "melting pot of seething excitations and contradictory impulses" (as Mann puts it) with Schopenhauer's "sinister kingdom of the will", of blind strife, primitive, irrational, volatile, indestructible, "knowing no values, no good and evil, no morality", Yeats's question

> Whence had they come,
> The hand and lash that beat down frigid Rome?
> What sacred drama through her body heaved
> When world-transforming Charlemagne was conceived? (*VP* 560)

dissolves into a profoundly menacing irony for our times. What happens to us is unmasked. And what we do, what we will, is the sinister face that appears.

There are further instances of the metaphor of the world as theatre in Yeats and Schopenhauer which will lead me conveniently into my next theme, the question of the artist versus the saint.

Teatrum mundi is an ancient commonplace, of course. We know it best perhaps in Shakespeare, in many hauntingly suggestive forms. In Pirandello it has its modern apotheosis, internalised, ironically inverted, indeterminate, with its own dark post-Schopenhauerian side. Basically the topos was Platonic. The phenomenal world is not reality, merely a copy or imitation, as the theatre is a copy or imitation. But Yeats, like Schopenhauer, was a devoted antagonist, not disciple, of Plato. When Plato "separates the Eternal Ideas from Nature and shows them self-sustained", he says, "he prepares the Christian desert and the Stoic suicide" (*AV[B]* 271). And Schopenhauer, for whom "the whole of nature is the phenomenon, and also the fulfilment of the will-to-live": who, despite his exposition of the inherent, inevitable and implacable misery of existence, devotes many pages to the refutation of the Stoic message, and whose Saint is Vedic not Christian, would surely have assented.

Schopenhauer's bleak account of the eternal recurrence of Idea in the manifestations of Will goes like this: "In the world," he says, "it is the same as in the dramas of Gozzi, in all of which the same persons always appear with the same purpose and the same fate. The motives and incidents certainly are different in each piece, but the spirit of the incidents is the same. The persons of one piece know nothing of the events of another, in which, of course, they themselves performed. Therefore, after all the experiences of the earlier pieces, Pantaloon has become no more agile or generous, Tartaglin no more conscientious, Brighella no more courageous, and Columbine no more modest" (*Sch* 183).

Yeats's elaboration of the metaphor is sprightlier, and the dissonance will enable us to see how the kinship between them is not identity, nor the congruence imitation. The subterranean dialogue between them that I am attempting to trace is just for this reason so fructifying. Yeats too begins from the notion of Eternal Recurrence in his *A Vision*, the book in which he articulated and systematised his intuitions concerning the nature of history, personality and creativity as constituted by, and through, a whirling spiral of dialectical contraries, for which the waxing and waning of the moon was his central symbol. "When I wish", he wrote, "for some general idea which will describe the Great Wheel as an individual life I go to the *Commedia dell'Arte* or improvised drama of Italy. The stagemanager, or *Daimon*, offers his actor an inherited scenario, the *Body of Fate* [elsewhere Yeats defines this concept as "the series of events forced upon a man from without"] and a *Mask* or rôle as unlike as possible to his natural ego, or *Will*, and leaves him to improvise through his *Creative Mind* the dialogue and details of the plot. He must discover or reveal a being which only exists with extreme effort, when his muscles are as it were all taut and all his energies active" (*AV[B]* 83–4).

So far so good. We note the wide margin Yeats leaves for differentiation, improvision, the creative principle. And we note the insistence upon the Masks as an anti-self, the opposite of all a man is in his daily life; the epitome of what he most desires, which Yeats says elsewhere, he would most abhor if he did not so desire it. But this is antithetical man – Yeats's figure for the artist, perceiver and shaper of images "that instinct may find its lamp" (*Ex* 274). For Schopenhauer, too, it is the artist who is the highest manifestation of that consciousness through which "the will, hitherto following its tendency in the dark with extreme certainty and infallibility, kindles a light for itself" (*Sch I* 150). Yeats's antithetical or subjective man discovers or creates an identity through struggle, in his given circumstances, with a predestined role which is conditioned upon what is to his own nature "of all things not impossible, the most difficult" (*Myth* 332, *Au* 194–5, *AV[B]* 83). A destiny at once loved and hated. It is an onerous task he sets his artist. Primary or objective man is what Yeats calls the polar opposite of the artist, he who seeks himself in identification with some inclusive other, larger than the self and external to it. It is his image of primary man that Yeats finds in "the *Commedia dell'Arte* in its decline. The *Will* is weak and cannot create a rôle, and so, if it transform itself, does so after an accepted pattern, some traditional clown or pantaloon" (*AV*[*B*] 84). Was not Yeats recalling Schopenhauer, with whom he says he can no more quarrel than with a mountain cataract, when he wrote that passage? It is tempting to think so because in fact he does quarrel, as has been noted and much that is great in his poetry arises from this dispute between lovers. It is upon the crucial matter of the will and its freedom that the quarrel hinges, and it is the divergence one from the other, in the very same theatre metaphor, that clarifies and illuminates the issue. Schopenhauer's metaphor is two dimensional; Yeats's four dimensional; his four faculties provide room for manoeuvre within the dialectical duality of losing and finding which structures his entire thought. "The human soul", he says, "is always moving outward into the objective world or inward into itself; and this movement is double because the human soul would not be conscious were it not suspended between contraries, the greater contrast the more intense the consciousness." In a Note to "The Cat and the Moon" he writes I "saw in the changes of the moon all the cycles: the soul realising its separate being in the full moon, then, as the moon seems to approach the sun and dwindle away, all but realising its absorption in God" (*VPl* 807).

Later, in the 1937 prolegomenon to *A Vision* alternation is condensed into antinomy: "Every action of man declares the soul's ultimate, particular freedom, and the soul's disappearance in God; declares that reality is a congeries of beings and a single being; nor is this antinomy an appearance imposed upon us by the form of thought but life itself, which turns, now here, now there, a whirling and a bitterness" (*AV*[*B*] 52). World-will and mind, then, for both Yeats and Schopenhauer stand to each other in the relation of stage-manager and actor in the Commedia dell'Arte. But what for Yeats is the Commedia dell'Arte in its decline, lacking the antithetical or subjective principle of strenuous, anguished, but free creativity, is, for Schopenhauer, all that there is. Schopenhauer's world-in-itself is an arena of blind, fierce and implacable struggle between forces striving to realise their potentialities, fighting for *lebensraum*. Inorganic nature, the creatures, each able to maintain its existence only by the incessant elimination of another's, human beings driven by insatiable desires, agitations, energies – all are curbed only by each other in perpetual contest. At some evolutionary moment appears mind or consciousness, in the service of the need for food or procreation, and with it the world as representation – the only world we can know. The whole course of time itself, of history, of pre-history is the production, or projection, of this consciousness. But for the individual consciousness itself only suffering can issue from the unending kinesis of will. Happiness is delusory because that which is desired is no other than the mere annulling of a deficiency or lack, or the stilling of a pain, which is immediately replaced either by a fresh need or desire or a "fearful life-destroying boredom, dreariness and emptiness" (*Sch I* 164). Only the Saint, by mortification of the will, can achieve transcendence over what Schopenhauer calls "this penal servitude of willing". And, but only briefly, the Artist, in his moments of disinterested contemplation when (I quote) "knowledge withdraws from its subjection to the will, throws off its yoke, and, free from all the aims of the will, exists purely for itself, simply as a clear mirror of the world. At such moments everything that moves our will and thus violently agitates us, no longer exists. Happiness and unhappiness have vanished; we are no longer the individual . . . we are the one eye of the world . . . the world as representation alone remains . . . the world as will has disappeared" (*Sch I* 152, 195–9).

Yeats too, eloquently describes the moment of poetic creativity, of poetic blessedness – "pure will-less knowing", in a number of poems, and, discursively, in his account of Phase 15. There the terms echo Schopenhauer's remarkably. The consonance is more than conceptual or verbal. It is rhythmic, melodic, for the listening ear. What is described is the full of the moon, symbol of the phase of complete Beauty, as he calls it, where

> Thought and will are indistinguishable, effort and attainment are indistinguishable; . . . nothing is apparent but dreaming *Will* and the Image that it dreams . . . Now contemplation and desire, united into one, inhabit a world where every beloved image has bodily form, and every bodily form is loved . . . as all effort has ceased, all thought has become image, . . . All that the being has experienced as thought is visible to its eyes as a whole, and in this way it perceives, not as they are to others, but according to its own perception, all orders of existence (*AV[B]* 135–6).

Thus each on the Artist. And the consonance runs on into their respective discriptions of the Saint, like a harmonic counterpoint: To Yeats's Saint "the total life has suddenly displayed its source. If he possess intellect he will use it but to serve perception and renunciation. His joy is to be nothing, to do nothing, to think nothing; but to permit the total life, expressed in its humanity, to flow in upon him, and to express itself through his acts and thoughts. He is not identical with it, he is not absorbed in it, for if he were he would not know that he is nothing, that he no longer even possesses his own body, that he must renounce even his desire for his own salvation, and that this total life is in love with his nothingness" (*AV[B]* 180–1). Schopenhauer's is one who has "overcome the world, in whom the will, having reached complete self-knowledge, has found itself again in everything, and then freely denied itself, and who then merely wait to see the last trace of the will vanish with the body that is animated by that trace. Then, instead of the constant transition from desire to apprehension and from joy to sorrow; instead of the never-satisfied and never-dying hope . . . the unquenched thirst of the

man who wills . . . we see an ocean-like calmness of spirit. . . . What
remains after the complete abolition of the will, is, for all who are still full
of the will, assuredly nothing. But . . . to those in whom the will has
turned and denied itself, this very real world of ours with all its suns and
galaxies, is – nothing" (*Sch I* 411–12).

For Schopenhauer, however, the Artist is no more than a faint
adumbration of the Saint. Whereas for Yeats, just as the primary
principle, that which serves, and the antithetical principle, that which
creates, are at opposite poles, so Saint and Artist are at opposite poles,
both dying each other's life, living each other's death, as he would have
put it. But he insists, again and again, upon the primacy of the artist's
will to create form, Apollonian lucidity of form, from the dross and flux of
life, the fury and the mire of human veins. Indeed Schopenhauer's *On the
Sublime* in conjunction with "Byzantium" allows us to perceive and
assess the strength of the rejection, in that poem, of the saint's way, its
affirmation of the artist's creativity which arises out of and transcends
the "dolphin-torn, the gong-tormented sea" of human temporality. Here
is a paragraph of Schopenhauer on the Sublime:

> If we lose ourselves in contemplation of the infinite greatness of the
> universe in space and time, meditate on the past millenia and on those
> to come; or if the heavens at night actually bring innumerable worlds
> before our eyes, and so impress on our consciousness the immensity of
> the universe, we feel ourselves reduced to nothing: we feel ourselves as
> individuals, as living bodies, as transient phenomena of will, like
> drops in the ocean, dwindling and dissolving into nothing. But against
> such a ghost of our own nothingness, there arises the immediate
> consciousness that all these worlds exist only in our representation,
> only as modifications of the eternal subject of pure knowing'.
> (*Sch I* 205)

The thrust and substance of Yeats's imagery remembers such a
passage, and others in chapter 39 of Book III, too many of which it would
be tiresome to cite. In "Byzantium" oceanic gnosis and "the golden
smithies of the Emperor" are Siamese twins, each other's doubles, and it
is the passionate struggle to repress, one, or the other, which expresses
itself in the violent verbs and staccato anaphoras of the final stanza.

In calmer mood, in a great poem on this very theme called
"Vacillation", Yeats announces his artist's manifesto:

I – though heart might find relief
Did I become a Christian man and choose for my belief
What seems most welcome in the tomb – play a predestined part.
Homer is my example and his unchristened heart. (*VP* 503)

The "playing of a predestined part" here set antithetically against "choosing" takes us back to our theatre metaphor. It is an extension, or specialisation, of the theatre metaphor that provides Yeats with his central trope for art's transcendence over temporality, and for the finding and composing of the unified self. That specialisation is dance, a symbol which Yeats pursued both in drama and lyric. His *Plays for Dancers*, which he derived from the Japanese Noh and which excited him more than any of his other plays, he regarded as the apex of his dramatic achievement – the "theatre's anti-self" (*Ex* 257), which he sought. The coupling of dancer and dance, self-contained, self-containing, symbolised supremely for him the art of arts – "predestinate and free, creation's very self" (*Au* 273).

Not that the dancer/dance relation is immune to the whirling and the bitterness of the antinomies. Choreography is stage-management too. And the question, "How can we know the dancer from the dance?" inscribes, Paul de Man has shown,[10] when read as a rhetorical one, a rejoicing at the totality of self-expression found by the dancer through the dance, but yields, when read literally, a fear of the loss of individuality as dancer disappears into the dance. When Yeats seeks an image to articulate the opposition between antithetical and primary civilisations it is just this reversibility that he uses:

> Those riders upon the Parthenon had all the world's power in their moving bodies, and in a movement that seemed, so were the hearts of man and beast set upon it, that of a dance; but presently all would change and measurement succeed to pleasure, the dancing-master outlive the dance. (*AV[B]* 276)

And even the ecstatic dancing girl in "The Double Vision of Michael Robartes", who had "outdanced thought" and "body perfection brought" no more than a figure "en abyme" since, after the "reward" of the visionary moment the speaker can but "make my moan" as for an unattainable Belle Dame, and then "arrange" it "in a song . . ." – distanced and separated by its very verbality from the imagined plenitude of the dance itself. We can now understand why the mysterious Thirteenth Cone, "that which is in every man, and called by every man his freedom" is characterised by the charismatic dance figure. "It becomes even conscious of itself . . . like some great dancer . . . dancing some primitive dance and conscious of his or her own life *and* of the dance" (my italics) (*AV[B]* 240).

Such transcendence of antinomy is reserved by Schopenhauer for the Saint in his unmoved stillness alone, and at the cost of all willing, labour or warfare. For Yeats, as for all artists, who must "spin a web out of their own bowels) the victory is an intellectual daily re-creation of all that exterior fate (Schopenhauer's Will) snatches away, and so that fate's antithesis" (*Au* 189).

On the snatching away, the ravages and decay and the wounds of the world's warfare, the destruction of form, of cities, of civilisation, Yeats the poet can be as eloquently inspired as was the superlative pessimist. But where Schopenhauer makes his peace with the wretchedness of existence, Yeats never does. Schopenhauer unifies his antinomies by totalising renunciation. Yeats, like Nietzsche, says "We begin to live when we conceive life as tragedy" (*Au* 189). But note, to live, not to die to the world, as Schopenhauer would have us do. It was no doubt his need to combat Schopenhauer's denial of life and the world, his own tendency temperamentally, which made him call Nietzsche "that strong enchanter" who filled him, he wrote, with a "curious astringent joy" (*L* 379). In Nietzsche Yeats found authentication for his artist's tragic joy, the means whereby again and again he challenged, and rejected the Saint's way of renunciation. But the rejection was never easy. The conception of a conscious and willing subject which wills itself into a condition of will-lessness could point, for him, alternately, both to Saint and to Artist. Many, perhaps most, of his poems are debates between self and soul, interior dialogues between Saint and Artist as he and Schopenhauer both conceived them, with but a hard-won victory going to the Artist. "We who are poets and artists", he wrote in *Anima Hominis*, "not being permitted to shoot beyond the tangible, must go from desire to weariness and so to desire again, and live but for the moment when vision comes to our weariness like terrible lightning, in the humility of the brutes. . . . Only when we are saint or sage, and renounce experience itself, can we, in the imagery of the Christian Cabbala, leave the sudden lightning and the path of the serpent and become the bowman who aims his arrow at the centre of the sun" (*Myth* 340). Yeats, unlike Schopenhauer, was irremediably split, strung between his polarities, "caught between the pull / Of the dark moon and the full". The unity of being his nature craves is defeated by a perpetual ambivalence, a perpetual oscillation of contraries. Gain or loss of self veer for him ceaselessly from the individual principle to the suprapersonal, or universal. He is artist to the end, but "Meru", written, like "Whence had they come?" in 1935, the poem with which I want to conclude, is a brilliantly imaginative rendering of the vision of Schopenhauer's Saint, and it is the Schopenhauerian reading which saves the poem from certain grave allegations which have been made about it.

Meru

Civilisation is hooped together, brought
Under a rule, under the semblance of peace
By manifold illusion; but man's life is thought,
And he, despite his terror, cannot cease

Ravening through century after century,
Ravening, raging, and uprooting that he may come
Into the desolation of reality:
Egypt and Greece, goodbye, and good-bye, Rome!
Hermits upon Mount Meru or Everest,
Caverned in night under the drifted snow,
Or where that snow and winter's dreadful blast
Beat down upon their naked bodies, know
That day brings round the night, that before dawn
His glory and his monuments are gone. (*VP* 563)

The crux for interpretation in this poem lies in the reading of the genitive "of" in its central lines: "ravening, raging, and uprooting that he may come / Into the desolation of reality". The line has been read as a positive evocation of Dionysian destruction, dismemberment, the loss of the individual shaping principle in some ecstatic abandon. Even Jeffares, soberest of Yeats's commentators, says no more of this poem than that "it envisages man as a destroyer of what he creates".[11] And Erich Heller and Frank Kermode among others have found here (and elsewhere) a dark Fascist underside or shadow in the mind of Yeats.[12] But it is precisely such shadows and their origins, that is the question in "Whence Had They Come?"; precisely such shadows that haunt all twentieth century minds, learned in the moral devastation that can breed in a quasi-Nietzschean worship of oceanic engulfment, a glorification of archaic turbulence, of the heroic, the boundless. No one was more haunted than Yeats by the approach of a "sinking in upon the moral being" (*AV*[*B*] 268) nor with more appalled trepidation. If in 1936 he would write to Ethel Mannin, "Every nerve trembles with horror at what is happening in Europe", and remind her of "the rough beast" of "The Second Coming" (*L* 850–1), it was as early as 1897, in "Rosa Alchemica" that he describes, in a remarkable passage, a presaging of horror:

> ... I was possessed with the phantasy that the sea, which kept covering [the house upon the promontory] with showers of white foam, was claiming it as part of some indefinite and passionate life, which had begun to war upon our orderly and careful days, and was about to plunge the world into a night as obscure as that which followed the downfall of the classical world. One part of my mind mocked this phantastic terror, but the other, the part that still lay half plunged in vision, listened to the clash of unknown armies, and shuddered at unimaginable fantaticisms, that hung in those grey leaping waves. (*VSR* 138)

Earlier, aesthetic or Nietzschean Yeats could contain or absorb or sublimate the horror. In *Per Amica* (1917) he writes: "He only can create the greatest imaginable beauty who has endured all imaginable pangs, for only when we have seen and foreseen what we dread shall we be rewarded by that dazzling, unforeseen, wing-footed wanderer" (*Myth* 332).

What then of "Meru?" There is a rough beast, fierce, savage, implacable, evoked by its violent verbs, driven, despite its terror, towards some inescapable apocalypse. But "man's life is *thought*", and it is therefore thought itself that must raven, rage and uproot, in a frenzy like that of Lear, in order to come into the desolation of *its own* reality. "The feeling of the sublime", says Schopenhauer, "arises through our being aware of the vanishing nothingness of our own body in the presence of a greatness which itself, on the other hand, resides only in our representation, and of which we, as knowing subject, are the supporters. Therefore, here as everywhere, it arises through the contrast between the insignificance and dependence of ourselves as individuals, as phenomena of will, and the consciousness of ourselves as pure subject of knowing. . . . Many objects of our perception excite the impression of the sublime; by virtue both of their spatial magnitude and of their great antiquity, and therefore of their duration in time, we feel ourselves reduced to nought in their presence, and yet revel in the pleasure of beholding them. Of this kind are very high mountains, the Egyptian pyramids, and colossal ruins of great antiquity" (*Sch I* 206). Such is the pleasure of the sublime. Whereas on Mt Meru what is represented is neither the sublime, nor a dreadfully desired black apocalypse, but a Schopenhauerian ascesis – a subjugation of the will but also of the masterful images of art and empire. The genitive "of" switches the functions of head and modifier indeterminately between its terms: desolation, reality; both, either, can take the major stress. The Saint, caverned in night beneath the winter's dreadful blast, knows and dismisses the world as will and as representation for the snowy vanishing that it is.

NOTES

1. Harold Bloom, *Yeats* (Oxford University Press, 1970) p. 240.
2. *The Word as Will and Idea*, trans. Haldane and Kemp, 1883–6. In Yeats's own library by 1920 were Schopenhauer's *The Art of Controversy and other Posthumous Papers*, selected and translated by T. Bailey Saunders, (London: Swan Sonnenschein, 1896) and *The Wisdom of Life, being the first part of Aphorismen zur Lebensweisheit*, translated by T. Bailey Saunders (London: Swan Sonnenschein, 1891). No evidence of Yeats's own use of the volumes can be adduced here, except that neither volume is annotated by him, although the second is annotated, possibly in his wife's hand. I am grateful to Edward O'Shea for this information.
3. T. Whitaker, *Swan and Shadow* (Chapel Hill, 1964) p. 94 and *passim*.
4. A. Schopenhauer, *The World as Will and Representation*, trans. E. F. J. Payne (New York: Dover Publications, 1969) vol. I, pp. 148–9. Henceforth *"Sch I"*.

5. Richard Ellmann, *Yeats: the Man and the Masks* (London: Macmillan, 1949) p. 60.

6. *The Letters of Ernest Dowson*, eds Desmond Flower and Henry Maas, (London: Cassell, 1967) p. 45.

7. Yeats's memory of his first encounter with Wilde involves the following (salient but irreconcilable) elements; a Christmas dinner apparently postdating the publication of *The Wanderings of Oisin* (out by 13 January 1889) *and* its review by Wilde (in *The Pall Mall Gazette*, XLIX:7587 (12 July 1889), after which meal Wilde reads from the proofs of *The Decay of Lying* (published in *The Nineteenth Century*, January 1889, and subsequently in *Intentions*, May 1891). While these facts seem to suggest Christmas 1889, Wilde at that date would have been unlikely to have been reading proof for *Intentions*. Christmas 1890 seems too late. However, two letters of 24 January 1889, to Katharine Tynan and John O'Leary, give evidence that Yeats had recently met Wilde, who was to try to get *The Wanderings of Oisin* for review in *The Pall Mall Gazette*. It would seem, therefore, that Christmas 1888 is in fact the most likely date for the meeting, by which time Yeats may well have had an advance copy of his book, and when Wilde could well have been correcting proofs of his essay for its first printing.
   Yeats had been at one of Lady Wilde's receptions in mid-December 1888 (*L* 97): it is possible that the invitation to Christmas dinner from her son came on that occasion. Much earlier, Wilde had written to William Ward that his mother's "last pessimist, Schopenhauer, says that the whole human race ought, on a given day, after a strong remonstrance, *firmly but respectfully* urged on God, to walk into the sea and leave the world tenantless, but of course some skulking wretches would hide and be left to people the world again, I'm afraid" (*Letters of Oscar Wilde*, ed. Rupert Hart-Davis, [London, Hart-Davis, 1962], 20). I am grateful to Warwick Gould for assistance with this note.

8. A. Norman Jeffares, *A Commentary on the Collected Poems of W. B. Yeats* (London: Macmillan, 1968) pp. 432–3.

9. Thomas Mann, "Freud and the Future" (1936) in *Essays of Three Decades*, trans. H. T. Lowe-Porter (New York: Knopf, 1947) p. 311.

10. Paul de Man, "Semiology and Rhetoric" in *Textual Strategies*, ed. Josué V. Harari (London: Methuen, 1979) p. 130–1. It is worth noting, in connection with "Among School Children" that the famous "great-rooted blossomer" also echoes, remarkably, a recurrent image in Schopenhauer's discussion of individuation in organic and inorganic nature, and of consciousness in man. For example: "The tree is an aggregate from the individual shooting fibre showing itself in every rib of the leaf, in every leaf, in every branch . . . only the whole is the complete presentation of an indivisible Idea . . . (*Sch I* 132) and again "The whole tree is only the constantly repeated phenomenon of one and the same impulse that manifests itself most simply in the fibre, and is repeated and easily recognizable in the construction of leaf, stem, branch and trunk" (*Sch I* 289).

11. Jeffares, *A Commentary on the Collected Poems of W. B. Yeats* (London: Macmillan, 1968) p. 434.

12. Erich Heller, *The Disinherited Mind* (London: Bowes & Bowes, 1952) finds the "terrible meaning" of *Meru* in the notion that he attributes to it: that "thought . . . stands between man and his desire for the spontaneity of innocence and the integrity of being" and "causes man to rave and rage and desolate his reality", to "destroy the cities of man so that, perhaps, they might be rebuilt after the images of pure aesthetic delight" (pp. 340–5 *passim*). Frank Kermode, in *The Sense of an Ending* (London: Oxford University Press, 1966) makes a similar but harsher claim: "The most terrible element in apocalyptic thinking is its certainty that there must be universal bloodshed; Yeats welcomed this with something of the passion that has attended the thinking of more dangerous, because more practical men" (pp. 108–9). Earlier, the accusing finger was that of Yvor Winters, *The Poetry of W. B. Yeats* (Denver, 1960) and it pointed in particular to *The Second Coming*: "We may find the beast terrifying, but Yeats finds him satisfying – he is Yeats's judgement upon all that we regard as civilised. Yeats approves of this kind of brutality" (p. 10). Harold Bloom, (whose reading of "Meru,"

Yeats, p. 419, is admirably just) nevertheless does accuse Yeats of bowing to a deterministic "dogma of process and entropy" (p. 278) and reaffirms Winters's conception of *The Second Coming*: "What I hear in the poem is exultation on the speaker's part as he beholds his vision, and this exultation is not only an intellectual one" (p. 321).

*Note:—*In addition to the books in Yeats's library mentioned *supra n.*2, he owned at the time of the 1920s catalogue of his books three further Schopenhauer volumes: *Counsels and Maxims*, translated by T. Bailey Saunders, (1892); *Studies in Pessimism, a series of essays*, translated by T. Bailey Saunders, (1892); *Essays*, n.d., but probably the Walter Scott edition of 1897 *et. seq.* I am grateful to Edward O'Shea for this information.

In the Automatic Script for June 2, 1918, Schopenhauer took his place in Phase II, alongside Carlyle (*AV*[*A*] xxxiii, 18 [notes]).

The Big House, Yeats, and the Irish Context

Antony Coleman

I

A. You have a country house. Are you a planter?
B. Yes, I have planted a great many oak trees, and ash, and some elm round a lough.
Swift, *A Dialogue in Hybernian style between A and B*.

Meanwhile, the country houses lit a chain of bonfires through the nights of late summer and autumn and winter and early spring. . . . People whose families had lived in the country for three or four hundred years realised suddenly that they were still strangers and that the mystery of it was not to be revealed to them – the secret lying as deep as the hidden valleys in the Irish hills, the barriers they had tried to break down standing as strong and immoveable as those hills, brooding over an age-old wrong. Elizabeth, Countess of Fingall, *Seventy Years Young* (London, 1937) p. 414.

Over two centuries separate these quotations, which establish the standpoint of this investigation of one aspect of Yeats's claim that all his art theories (by implication his literary practice) depend on "rooting of mythology in the earth", that aspect being the poems on Coole Park.[1] While his contribution to the genre of country-house poetry appears now a matter of critical consensus, critical evaluation of that contribution in the context of Irish writing in English is curiously lacking.[2]

Despite Daniel Harris's assertion that "Coole fused in one estate three aristocratic traditions: the ancient Irish legacy, the courtly beauty of the Renaissance and later the Anglo-Irish heritage" these poems are rather loosely rooted in Irish earth.[3] Comparison with the small handful of Irish poems addressing themselves to the theme (to be considered later) is inapt, as they exhibit a higher level of achievement, but three elements of the Irish context expose the distortion in Yeats's perspective – the failure to include the Gaelic tradition, the exaggeration of his claims for the Anglo-Irish addition to "the matter of Ireland", and the aversion of his

33

gaze from the social reality which Allingham explored in *Laurence Bloomfield in Ireland*.

II

When Yeats made his famous declamation to the Senate in 1925

> We against whom you have done this thing are no petty people. We are one of the great stocks of Europe. We are the people of Burke; we are the people of Grattan; we are the people of Swift. . .

he invoked three names of the eighteenth century, that century which saw the consolidation of an alien aristocratic class in all its stony arrogance.[4] Swift, Burke, Grattan compose a triad of *virtus*: theirs is an aristocracy of intellect. It was Burke who at century's end provided the severest indictment of the Ascendancy, the "no petty people" whom Yeats was celebrating. "Ascendancy" wrote Burke was

> a liberal distribution of places and pensions and other graces of government . . . wide indeed of the significance of the word. New *ascendancy* is the old *mastership*. It is neither more nor less than the resolution of one set of people in Ireland to consider themselves as the sole citizens of the commonwealth and to keep a dominion over the rest by reducing them to an absolute slavery under a military power, and thus fortified in their power, to divide the public estate . . . as a military booty, solely amongst themselves . . . I cannot conceive what mode of oppression in civil life, or what mode of religious persecution may not come within the methods of preserving an ascendancy . . . it signifies *pride* and *dominion* on the one part of the relation and on the other *subserviency* and *contempt*. . .[5]

The symbol of that "pride and dominion" was the Big House, a symbol which could not be invested with those genial and humane values, the theme of mutuality between *magister* and *minister* which Jonson had hymned in "To Penshurt". Between the Anglo-Irish exploiters and the Gaelic exploited the line was drawn – the Penal Laws with their savage clauses were the instruments by which the power gained by Cromwell's ferocious sword was maintained. Formal, reasonable, stately, the Big House spoke in a strange accent; it did not speak to the Gaelic heart. "Plantation" with its connotation of a natural growth, the sense of roots, is too gentle a word for the process of Anglo-Irish acquisition and exposes the irrelevance of the Jonsonian tradition. Penshurst was "rear'd with no mans ruine no mans grone". For Jonson the Sidney home was both *phenomenon* and *noumen*, both fact and symbol. And it could be both because it was based on accord between the rulers and the ruled, on the shared acknowledgement of rights and duties. By incorporating the local names, Gamage, Ashore, he elevates them to a mythic status, and asserts that native dignities have equal stature with the classic. He does more. He pictures the ancestral harmony as under threat from new forces whose symbols were the "proud ambitious heaps" then in course of building. The elegiac note in "To Penshurst" finds a poignant echo in the laments of the bardic poets as they too surveyed the destruction of an ancient tradition.

The Anglo-Irish heritage was – it is Jonah Barrington's phrase – "an ambiguous heritage".[6] It could not have been otherwise. The predicament of the Anglo-Irish, separated from "the meer Irish" by religion and language, bound to the English crown in loyalty, has been described as chronic ambivalence. By ambivalence is meant the condition of having two homes – one historic (Ireland), the other atavistic (England), two loyalties – one immediate (Anglo-Ireland), the other ultimate (Crown and Empire), and two cultures – one improvised (Anglo-Irish) the other absolute (English).[7] That improvised culture was a colonial one; the Anglo-Irish remained loyal to the forms and idiom of the motherland and the long roll call of these who found success in London from Congreve to Sheridan imitated (however much they enriched) the metropolitan norms. They were not innovators. At home their libraries contained the classics, books on geology, travel, history; their bent was towards the practical, the delimited. In this their instinct coincided with that of the age, and is most honourably illustrated in the person of Richard Lovell Edgeworth. But Edgeworth is not typical of his class and he himself has rehearsed the more genuine depiction of their "improvised culture". Writing in 1820 he observed that there was a distinction "about half a century ago [i.e. during the accepted heyday of the Anglo-Irish] between the manners and mental cultivation of a few families of the highest class of the aristocracy of Ireland and all the secondary class of gentry" and with that majority in mind continued:

> The fashion has passed away of those desperately tiresome, long formal dinners which were given two or three times a year by each family in the country to their neighbours, where the company had more than they could eat, and twenty times more than they should drink; where the gentlemen could talk only of claret, horses or dogs; and the ladies only of dress and scandal.[8]

Claret, horses and dogs. Here are Swift's planters at their lucrative ease, fit objects for ironic scrutiny by a Farquhar, a Sheridan. If Edgeworth approximates the fictive Allworthy, the Anglo-Irish gentry are variants of Squire Western. They were "averse to reflexion", as Barrington recalled and "the morning chase and evening conviviality composed the diary of their lives".[9] Family *pietas*, an indulgent estimate of her family and caste, underlies Elizabeth Bowen's later survey (a survey coloured by the ambivalence noted above), but she endorses the judgement that the Anglo-Irish were lovers of horses not books. Hers is an intriguing account. As writer she surveys with austere, if sympathetic, detachment the follies of her people. As the last representative of her house at Bowens Court she qualifies, in odd mixture of circumspection and approval, their imposed presence and later activity.

> . . . my family got their position and drew their power from a situation that shows an inherent wrong . . . having gained this position through an injustice, they enjoyed their position through privilege. But while they wasted no breath in deprecating an injustice it would not have been in their interest to set right, they did not abuse their privilege – on the whole they honoured it. . . . The security they had, by the eighteenth century, however ignobly gained, they did not use quite ignobly. They began to feel, and exert, the European idea – to seek what was humanistic, classic, and disciplined. It is something to subscribe to an idea, even if one cannot live up to it. These country gentlemen liked sport, drink and cardplaying very much better than they liked the arts.[10]

There is abundant evidence to refute the claim that the Anglo-Irish "honoured their privilege". The Big House was set apart from the village, behind great granite walls which secured its physical isolation, itself a manifestation, in F. S. L. Lyons's words, "of the intellectual and spiritual isolation in which they were condemned to live".[11] That condemnation was, from their coming, self-imposed, a matter of choice and inclination. For the Irish the land was both historic and atavistic home, their condition not one of spiritual and cultural dislocation (indeed their commitment to the *noumenal* would provide Synge with inspiration) but their lives, when examined by the nineteenth century novelists, exhibit both "subserviency and contempt" and pre-eminently despair, a despair generated by "the huge un-manageable evil" in whose shadow those lives were lived.[12] The lords of Ireland, Yeats's "no petty people", had failed to discharge the responsibilities of lordship; for AE their literature was "arid and empty of spiritual life."[13] The Anglo-Irish heritage is indeed relevant to the critical inspection of the Coole Park poems but not, I would suggest, in the gratulatory sense which has marked their commentary. Between MacNeice's dismissal of the Big House which "in most cases . . . maintained no culture worth speaking of – nothing but an obsolete bravado, an insidious bonhomie and a way with horses" and Day Lewis's fervid panegyric "the inherited aristocratic tradition offered style, the virtues of courtesy, lucidity, and self-possession as the basis – if not as a substitute for morality", Henn's summary seems modest, persuasive even; "The truth about the great houses of the South and West lies perhaps somewhere between Yeats's pictures of Coole Park . . . and MacNeice's 'snob idyllicism' " until we are alerted by his use of the word "chapel" that his is not an objective voice.[14] What all three omit, like Yeats himself, is the Gaelic tradition.

III

Douglas Hyde towards the conclusion of his *A Literary History of Ireland* tells how Teig Mac Daire MacBrody, last of the Irish classic poets, "was hurled over a cliff in his old age by a soldier of Cromwell who is said to have yelled at him with savage exultation, as he fell 'Say your rann now, little man' ".[15] The anecdote may be *ben trovato* (indeed by ascribing such literacy to a Cromwellian soldier almost certainly so); its survival bears witness to the strength of folk memory meditating on "an age-old wrong" in Lady Fingall's phrase, and the outrage offered the vernacular culture. With the coming of the "planters" the Gaelic order, its values, its existence was under a final, annihilating threat. Some elements survived in much attentuated form, traced in strong commitment by Daniel Corkery in *The Hidden Ireland*, but the blow struck was a mortal one.[16] From the end of the seventeenth century the prevailing note of the Irish poets is the elegiac. The culture whose destruction they mourned, stressed, above all, the imperative of *style*; embellishment, intricacy, elaboration distinguish both their graphic and written arts; in social organisation the mode was patriarchal; in intellectual orientation they favoured the concrete, the passional; they delighted in their local places, and their establishments of power, civility, and religion – the monasteries and "longports" of their spiritual and temporal leaders. Manus O'Donnell wrote, in 1532 of "Inmhain Druim Cliab mo croidhe" – "Drumcliffe beloved of my heart", and in him we have an exemplar of the high culture of the Gaelic order. Lord of Tirconnel, he was poet, scholar, and prince. As warrior-prince, he defended his lordship with success, in wily combination of policy and strength. His life held, more securely than Major Gregory's, the epic dimension. His obituary in *The Annals of the Kingdom of Ireland* describes him as

> a fierce, obdurate, wrathful and combative man towards his enemies . . . a mild, friendly, benign and hospitable man towards the learned, the poets, and the ollaves . . . skilled in many arts, gifted with a profound intellect, and the knowledge of every science.[17]

As patron-prince he encouraged the bardic order whose especial task was the celebration of the ancestral nobility of the historic Gaelic families: the relationship accepted and enacted was truly one of mutuality – the prince protecting, acknowledging, and rewarding the bards who recorded and praised his inherited dignities, but who also proposed criticism – often fierce, always feared, in the satiric form – when the prince fell short. As scholar-prince Manus compiled *Betha Colaim Chille (The Life of Columcille)* which includes a chapter "Of Columcille and the Poets of Erin" where the poets' power to assure "an eternity of remembrance" is urged – *Cormac cain buich neoid, nua a molta, crin a seoid*:

> Cormac the gentle conquered avarice
> Fresh are his praises, withered his wealth.[18]

A recent scholar has proposed that "Manus the Magnificent" is a Renaissance figure uniting in his person three contemporary versions of the idea of the Prince – Erasmus's *Institutio Principis Christianae* Macchiavelli's *Il Principe* and *Il Cortegiano* of Castiglione and, while the proposal does not compel an unqualified assent, it has, in one of its terms, more cogency than Corinna Salvadori's uncritical equation of Urbino and Coole.[19] What is of especial value in the proposal however, is its stress on the level of culture attained by Manus and his family at their castle at Lifford, itself the subject of an encomium by Tadhg Dall Ō Huiginn:

> A beloved dwelling is the castle of Lifford,
> homestead of a well-abounding encampment;
> forge of hospitality for the men of Ulster,
> a dwelling it is hard to leave.
> Beloved the delightful lofty building,
> its coverlets, its tables, its cupboards,
> its wondrous handsome firm walls,
> its smooth marble arches

and there is praise for Manus and his wife "dwelling as entertainers of guests" with time to give "to the books of fair poetry".[20] An element of idealised convention (possibly even conventionalised ideal) may be present here – the same no doubt is true of Jonson's encomium on Penshurst – but in the case of both poets the conviction that here were "lords dwelling" as lords should, hospitable, generous, and liberal cannot be in dispute. The planting on this Gaelic earth of "proud, ambitious heaps" and the social dislocation and cultural wreck to which they bore witness provides a major theme for the poetic historians of the following century. As late however as the beginning of the eighteenth century Aogān Ō Rathaille could celebrate, though possibly with some exaggeration, the continuation of hospitality traditional in the *caislean*:

I saw, said she, in that palace of music
speckled silks, sheer satin cloth;
blades being sharpened, mead for the sick.
Crowds for the great house merrily heading
harp tunes playing melodiously,
histories read by the learned and the wise

but the prevailing note, heard also in the poems of his great predecessor, Dāibhi Ō Bruadair is, to borrow Daniel Harris's comment on the Coole Park poems, "of embattled elegy".[21] The poetry they wrote encompassed both public and private occasions; the poets addressed themselves to discourse on matters of communal importance, chief of these being, given the times that were in it, the decline of native institutions. These poets are the eloquent voices of "The Dispossessed", and they could articulate an *indignatio* as *saeva* as that of Swift:

Cashel's company gone, its guesthouses and youth;
the gabled palace of Brian flooded with otters;
Ealla left leaderless, lacking royal Munster sons.
The deer has altered her erstwhile noble shape
since the alien raven roosted in Ros's fastness;
fish fled the sunlit stream and the quiet current
feathers of the swift bird-flock drift on the wind
tattered like a cat's fur in a waste of heather;
cattle deny the flow of milk to their calves
– since "Sir Val" walked into the rights of the gentle Carthy.[22]

The "Sir Val" of the concluding line was Sir Valentine Browne, whose father Sir Nicholas, descended of an Elizabethan planter family, had been Ō'Rathaille's patron (assuming that role from the Mac Carthys whose lands he held). In one of his latest poems he returned in loyalty to the Mac Carthys, ancestral patrons of his bardic family: "In the grave with this cherished chief I'll join those kings my people served before the death of Christ."[23] The arrogant boast of ancient lineage (a desperate pride of self), the emphasis on a personal, a feudal relationship, emphasises his inability to comprehend the new, impersonal forces, now agents of the cataclysmic changes he witnessed. Dearness of emotion gave noumenal force to the attachment to place and family, to the cherishing the memory of past glory, and the dogged refusal to accept the inevitable. It is an aspect of the Gaelic tradition for which Louis MacNeice found memorable expression:

in vain
the Norman Castle and the Tudor bribe;
the natives remained native, took their bribe
and gave their word and broke it. Thus today
some country house, up to its neck in weeds,

looks old enough to stand its ground beside
the bonegrey bog oak in the bog. The old
disorder keeps its pattern while the new
order has gone stagnant.[24]

Had Yeats addressed himself to this tradition, his Coole Park poems
would have attained both deeper and more persuasive moral resonance.
By ignoring it he simplified social circumstance, denied moral complexity in favour of an imposed, a factitious, harmony with consequent
discrepancy between "the earth" and "the mythology" on which it was
claimed to be founded. The Coole Park poems are icons and, like icons,
subserve a limited vision.

IV

*A poem occasioned by a view of Powers-court house, the improvements park etc.
Inscribed to Richard Wingfield*, published in Dublin in 1741, is a modest
performance, a minor addition to the verse letters of the century which
nonetheless possesses a two-fold value. Its confident assurance confirms
that after a period of roughness, greed, and panic, the Anglo-Irish were
attempting a new amenity, a cosmopolitan style, and in its use of an
English form it reveals the colonial dependence noted above. Not all
would make as opulent a gesture as Richard Wingfield, who is compared
by the anonymous author to "One late in print The Man of Ross". The
comparison is singular and leads one to question whether the author had
at all taken Pope's meaning. John Kyrle, the "Man of Ross" of the
"Epistle to Bathurst" is praised for the temperate measure of his life, for
avoiding "Grandeur" and "proud Courts" – a contrast to the extravagance of "Timon" in the "Epistle to Burlington" whose lavish ostentation
provides a truer equivalent to Wingfield's building. There is bland
allusion in *A poem occasioned* . . . to "the woe" that "late o'er pale Hibernia
past" but perhaps in the reference to the woods for "prospect and
defence" some sense that the smiling landscape contains a threat to its
security is present.[25]

The beauty of the setting, "the gilt profile and stately colonade" are
seen in direct relation to the merit and "Taste" being ascribed to
Wingfield.

Eden springs where late you found a Waste
Sketch'd in your House, the candid heart we view,
Its Grace, Strength, Order all reflecting you.[26]

Conspicuous by omission is treatment of the social dynamics of the state,
the nexus of interdependent relationships between landlord and tenant
composing a communal fabric. Rather perfunctorily, we are told that
"Benevolence"

Removes sharp Famine, Sickness and Despair;
Relieves the asking eye, the rising tear.[27]

Critical scrutiny of the social actuality is absent, if not precluded. Indeed it would not have been in the author's interest to inspect too closely the source of the funds making possible "the fluted Dorics (raising) the rich saloon". Introspection did not trouble the Anglo-Irish; indeed their focus on energy, the imperative of *will* accounts largely for the success of their enterprise. Their contribution to the "matter of Ireland" were accidental effects of their presiding aim which was *dominion*. If they assisted the survival of the Irish language it was because it was to be used as spiritual adjunct of the secular arm. (The first printed book in Irish was a Protestant catechism). If they excelled in oratory it was because through Parliament and the Courts their *dominion* was exercised. If they addressed themselves to the recovery of Celtic antiquities in the nineteenth century, it was to legitimise their pursuit of instinct over intellect. They were celebrants, accordingly, of heroic virtue in an age of innocence, and of an evasion through imaginative identification with the distant world of Celtic legend – an evasion of the decline of their order adumbrated in Gladstone's legislation. With his *Laurence Bloomfield in Ireland*, William Allingham had earlier rejected the easy certitudes exhibited in Wingfield's apologist. His intent was to cast a clear eye on the present social situation – the distrust between landlord and tenant exacerbated by the greed of the former and the hate of the latter, who meditated on injustice and who resorted, increasingly, to violence. Perhaps, as L. M. Cullen argues, the landlord is not central to the story.[28] Perhaps as Robert Welch argues, "For writers concerned about the state of the country it was all too easy to locate evil in the harsh system of oppression rather than trying to think of it as something inherent in human nature."[29] The perception of contemporaries, the observations of foreign visitors, the images proliferating in the nineteenth century novels all combine to qualify the element of revisionism present in such arguments. Lisnamoy, Allingham's fictive village, presents in microcosm the situation general in Ireland. That the landlords had failed in their social responsibilities and that their day was ending George Moore acknowledged frankly: ". . . in Ireland the passage direct and brutal of money from the horny hands of the peasant to the delicate hands of the proprietor is terribly suggestive of serfdom. In England the landlord lays out the farm and the farm buildings. In Ireland he does absolutely nothing. He gives the bare land to the peasant, and sends his agent to collect the half-yearly rent. . . I am an Irish landlord, I have done this, I do this, and I shall continue to do this, for it is as impossible for me as for the rest of my class to do otherwise: but that doesn't prevent me from recognising the fact that it is a worn-out system, no longer possible in the nineteenth century, and one whose end is nigh", and there is confirmation in the Swiss visitor, Moritz Bonn, who noted in 1902, ". . . we may find almost everywhere large demesnes with parks, garden and home-farm; but the landlord's house at the best was only an important centre of consumption and very rarely the central point of a great scheme of management embracing the entire property".[30]

Allingham pictures a desolate landscape:

> The cornstacks seen through rusty sycamores
> Pigs, tatter'd children, pools at cabin doors,
> Unshelter'd rocky hillsides, browsed by sheep
> Summer's last flowers that nigh some brooklet creep.
> Black flats of bog, stone fences loose and rough,
> A thornbranch in a gap thought gate enough
> And all the wide and groveless landscape round
> Moor, stubble, aftermath or newplough'd ground
> Where with the crows, white seagulls come to pick. . .[31]

Imperious in the landscape stands Lisnamoy House, home of Sir Ulick Harvey (whose shield carried a mailed arm and bore the motto *meis ut placet utens*):

> Lisnamoy House can see far summits rise
> In azure bloom, or cold on misty skies,
> Above the broad plantation set to screen
> Those dismal wastes of bog that stretch between;
> The Village, northward, only shows a spire
> As humbly conscious of the haughty Squire
> Whose Lady visits but the Vicar's wife . . .
> 　　　　　　　　　Groves
> Shut out from view a thousand vulgar fields
> Whose foison great Sir Ulick's grandeur yields.[32]

Here is no mutuality: arrogant self-confidence is Sir Ulick's defining trait. And it is a trait disconcertingly present in the Anglo-Irish (inherited from their eighteenth century progenitors) even as their *caste* approached its end. They persevered in their "aversion to reflexion", and "the lettered peace" which Yeats found in his "perfect country house" would not have raised a sympathetic echo in them.

Allingham tells how "a noble sprig" addressed Laurence Bloomfield at dinner:

> Come down to shoot the country, I presume?
> Good cocking in Sir Ulick's upper wood –
> Cover for grouse at Croghan, doocid good.

Queer fellows, though, the common fellows round
And every one a poacher – does your ground
Touch on the river?[33]

And he succeeds here in catching a tone, recording an attitude. His material was perhaps too intractable for poetic treatment – the novel form would have suited him better. The English novel with its focus on moral choice, itself an indication of an assured social system, was not relevant to the Irish situation where *race*, *language*, and *history* were presiding imperatives. (It required a Joyce to exploit the possibilities). But in his notation of "great Sir Ulick's grandeur" (no more than, in English terms, a small landowner) he finds a neat deflation. He also succeeds, most honourably, in articulating outrage at the central injustice:

Mark the great evil of a low estate;
Not Poverty, but Slavery – one man's fate
Too much at mercy of another's will.[34]

His liberal optimism, his faith in a peasantry at one with landlord in a benign paternalism were soon to be destroyed in the ferocities of the Land War, with peasant farmers acutely aware of a landlord's living on his estate "not to protect and assist his tenantry but because it was the only place in the wide world where he could obtain sufficient credit to subsist".[35] The land, its ownership and the relations of those who lived on it were the passionate concerns. The native "dispossessed" had never abandoned their sense of prior ownership; few of the later incumbents had honoured their places of dignity and privilege. Servility, at best a familiar address, (Thady in *Castle Rackrent* provides immediate illustration) marks one group; arrogance defines the other: "Tis unmisgiving pride that makes him frank / with humble folk, and dress beneath his rank."[36] Allingham had explored with both concern and insight a social reality from which Yeats resolutely averted his gaze; his unaccommodating intensity in the matter of Coole was gained at the expense of historic, of actual truth.

V

Aristocracy as elected myth has not been under consideration. Aristocracy as fact, as experienced in the Irish context has been the focus of attention. Yeats, of course, qualified his account of the Anglo-Irish heritage.[37] His claim is for the few not the many, a claim, however, qualified neither in "Coole Park, 1929" nor in "Coole Park and Ballylee, 1931", nor in his incidental references to the Big House in other poems.

The reservations I maintain find secure confirmation in the first section of "Meditations in Time of Civil War", entitled "Ancestral Houses". "The marvellous accomplishment" of the third section, "My Table", equates with the "certainty upon the dreaming air" of "Coole Park, 1929" – both passages celebrating a ceremonious tradition, high style, heroic value. Yeats's is a felt certitude in such value, the value of heroic life, passionate, sensuous, aristocratic living.[38] What he dismisses are the legitimate felt certitudes of others now engaged in a civil war to establish their own validity. Here lies explanation of his failure to be an Irish, a popular poet: unlike the Gaelic poets of the eighteenth century, he does not express his feelings in the idiom of national events – his mode of consciousness being English, he ignores significant implications in the Irish experience, an experience the stated subject of his meditations, "Time of Civil War".

Comparison with Joyce is relevant. Thomas Flanagan has discussed the manner in which both writers "came to accept [their] identity as . . . Irish writer[s]", and he isolates with devastating honesty Yeats's central dilemma:

> At the heart of Yeats's problem lay an issue which he addressed in a complex and subtle manner, in part because the issue was in itself complex, in part because it touched directly upon his own social identity, the issue of language. Instinct and logic alike suggested to him that the strong nourishing root of Irish culture was its Gaelic traditions, but he was reluctant to accept that these traditions were vested in the Irish language.[39]

"Meditations" is a superb instance of Yeatsian flight from a real to an imagined human situation. His psychic need for such flight, the splendour with which he often invested it, are not my present concern. My concern is with the impoverishment it imposes upon this occasion.

> Where slippered Contemplation finds his ease
> And Childhood a delight for every sense,

with its deployment of an obsolete diction – but interestingly drawn from his idealised century – is an index of a mind determined in its evasion of the actual, the "chain of bonfires" which Lady Fingall, in authentic aristocratic style, contemplated with insight, sympathy and humour. Contradiction abounds in the passage. "Bitter and violent men" are praised. Cromwellians? They were the builders. Bitter and violent men are, by implication, condemned. Free Staters? Republicans? They are the incendiaries. An innate vulgarity is revealed in the phrase "the inherited glory of the rich". Some sense that all was not high style in his memorialised caste is present in " 's but a mouse" but the emotional pressure, not qualified by irony, falls on praise of "a haughtier age". The events from 1916 to 1922 were a clear rejection of that haughtiness. By failing to acknowledge this, by not incorporating such tension and attempting balance or reconciliation, Yeats lessened his achievement. Richard Gill attends only to the Yeats perspective: "Divorced from the nagging injustices and complexities of its local history, the house came to represent a humane order of culture and civility, a state of community beyond the circumscription of nation or class", a divorce which Gill apparently endorses.[40] Divorce involves an attenuation of experience. Despite the assertion of grace, culture, a "dance-like glory" at Coole those "nagging injustices" were ghosts which refused to be ignored. In what locale, other than the purely imaginative, could community be found without "the circumscription of nation or class"? Time and place create the parameters of community.

The intention of "Coole Park 1929" is panegyric; the achievement is elegy. Coole Park had been sold to the Irish Free State in 1927. Like his Gaelic poetic predecessors of the seventeenth century, Yeats was unable to come to terms with the new order, itself a partial return to an earlier one. "In memory of Lady Gregory" provides a more appropriate title, the last line inviting such memory for "that laurelled head" as he sets her life and work in relation to the "Irish Renaissance" in which she played a part. Obituarists are not restricted by the test of objectivity. Still, there is something excessive in the chosen terms of praise. What is especially dismaying, however honourable the wish to commemorate his benefactress, (that Anglo-Irish incarnation of the Duchess at Urbino) are the omissions in the roll of fame. Sean O'Casey is a conspicuous absentee. Those present compose a strange company – a major statesman, a major poet, a major dramatist and two amateurs, one of politics, the other of art. Both Hugh Lane's donation of paintings (in the sphere of culture) and Shawe-Taylor's organisation of the 1902 Land Conference (in the sphere of politics) were worthy actions. They were not representative actions. George Moore, more certainly established than Yeats in the *caste* being memorialised, had written of earlier younger sons that they fell into the Kildare Street Club as into an oysterbed where they remained "spending their days drinking sherry, and cursing Gladstone".[41] One swallow, one Shawe-Taylor, even one Douglas Hyde, does not make a summer. To suggest, as George O'Brien does, that "The Anglo-Irish artistic achievement" found that achievement in "its finest hour", the age of Yeats, is disservice to both.[42] There was no age of Yeats, and his citation as spokesman and best representative of the Anglo-Irish would have astonished Edith Somerville who had her M. F. H. placed before her D. Litt. *honoris causa* on her memorial tablet.[43] Stubborn fact resists the blandishment of Yeats's seductive rhetoric. A Shawe-Taylor, a Hugh Lane are not energised despite their description as "impetuous men". Impetuousity is not all especially where feeling is profound. We can accept the transformation of Maud Gonne into "Cathleen Ni Houlihan" but Augusta Gregory with her homely figure, her barm-bracks, her lisp, her Victorian dress will not be transformed into a high priestess of culture. Her little plays are lively through charm, not power.

These are serious, even damaging, reservations. As meditation on a complex past the poem is weakened by concentration on the aristocratic few who assisted the development of a national literature. But the poem has a strength of tone and structure. It is framed between two superb images:

> A sycamore and lime-tree lost in night
> Although that western cloud is luminous

and

> When nettles wave upon a shapeless mound
> And saplings root among the broken stone

where human events, now distanced in time, are contemplated as part of a cosmic process, and the falling night is analogy for the spiritual dark encroaching upon, soon to extinguish the "dance-like glory" – Yeats's perception here, and acceptance of, such cosmic process, echoes that of Wordsworth in "A slumber" where the sense of personal loss is balanced by the insight that Lucy is now

> Rolled round in earth's diurnal course
> With rocks and stones and trees

There were few in the New State to concur with the sentiment. As L. M. Cullen strikingly reminds us ". . . the passing of the old regime was both unbloody and operated slowly but the disavowal of all it stood for was more vehement than in Russia or France and with few exceptions the leaders and public opinion alike in the new state were not prepared to care for the buildings, institutions or cultural aspirations of the old order".[44]

"Coole Park and Ballylee, 1931", written a year before Lady Gregory's death, is an altogether more commanding performance. The historical period it purports to enlarge upon is ample – Anglo-Norman dimension, Ascendancy apotheosis, Gaelic *continuum*. The tower, the cellar, the house introduce poet, singer and patroness all sharing a local habitation and linked in psychic relationship. The progression from the tower to the country house marked the security achieved by the Anglo-Irish after the Battle of the Boyne, from structures built for defence to structures where "lettered peace" might be possible.[45] Few unfortified dwellings are found before 1690, itself an index of the country's disturbed state. The achieved security too had insecure foundations and this is possibly reflected in the massiveness of the buildings, heavy with a masculine assertiveness (quite foreign to their Italian source of inspiration), put up between 1730 and 1750. These great houses – Carton, Westport, Russborough – sheltered the families of highest social consequence. From the colonnaded splendours of Speaker Connolly's house at Castletown to the plain granite boxes affronting the Irish landscape the distance is wide. It is to the more modest group that Coole Park belonged. The "bigness" was a matter of attitude not architecture. Yeats in characteristic simplification of history and experience, exaggerates the graciousness of life they enshrined. Further, he attempts to make sacred the purely secular:

> . . . gardens rich in memory glorified
> Marriages, alliances and families,

"Glorified" qualifies legalistic "alliances", a qualification not his conscious intent. He is dextrous, an adept rhetorician, with time and circumstance modifying his utterance; he was at least as aware as George Moore of the limitations of that "Ascendancy" whose apotheosis he hymns – an awareness present in his reduction of the Coole Park experience to equivalence with that of "some poor Arab tribesman and his tent". He cannot be denied a sense of humour, however shrill its accent on occasion. Criticism cannot be too severe, either, on his secularising the sacred; the "ceremony" of the imagination had been established by Wordsworth, confirmed by Keats and Shelley. If the human situation, however, was, for Yeats, the long memory, it was on these Coole Park occasions a selective memory. Lord Taafe in his *Observations on Affairs in Ireland from the Settlement to the Present Time* (1766) reported "That to distress their minds, damp their industry, and render their property precarious was deemed sound policy", having in view the legislative policy of Queen Anne and her successors.[46] When Yeats introduces Raftery to his poetic geography he adroitly sidesteps inconvenient historic fact. Raftery's is a diminished voice, a voice which haltingly echoes the cadences of a Dáibhi Ó Bruadair, and the voice was diminished through the agency of the *caste* whose praise is Yeats's present theme. Small point, accordingly, in affirming that in the West of Ireland Yeats found a "unity of culture" unless the term can be stretched to include both statement and negation.[47] Even Yeats is not flexible enough for that. His source for knowledge of Raftery was Douglas Hyde's *Love Songs of Connaught*, where an over-generous sympathy coloured judgement of the work (influenced also by a nineteenth century idealisation of the peasant at expense of the artisan), and where the age's demand for sentiment softened the rigour of the original. Hyde, need it be said, was no Coleridge. The Anglo-Norman dimension is even more irrelevant. What contribution there was can be subsumed under two heads, administration and economics, both topics slender of inspiration. To be fair one must acknowledge that the Anglo-Norman dimension is only sketchily present in the poem, indeed chiefly by implication in the joint title "Coole Park and Ballylee", and, by its secondary placing, of lesser importance. The poem's main emphasis falls on stanzas four and five, their burden Ascendancy's apotheosis.

The argument so far conducted denies to Yeats "rootedness", specifically rootedness in Irish soil. It is not an unfamiliar accusation; he has often been depicted as a magpie of sources, and a peacock in their use. He had access, admittedly, to the Irish tradition through the scholarly translations of the century. He had access to the oral tradition through mediation of Lady Gregory. The first looking-glass was distorted; the second he distorted, this last being Padraig Pearse's accusation. It is true he got from these sources what he needed for his purposes. Those purposes did not include fidelity to their originating occasions.

VI

Few poets after Yeats pay homage to The Big House although the theme continues to interest novelists – from Elizabeth Bowen the line goes forward to Jennifer Johnston, to Molly Keane where the nostalgia (by now *de rigeur*) is tempered by irony.

M. J. MacManus in *Rackrent Hall and other poems* employs buoyant rhythms to enact an indulgent scorn:

> Rackrent Hall was very old
> Walls of limestone and turrets strong,
> Built with the first adventurer's gold
> Built to outlive the centuries long
> But it hadn't the strength of a Fenian's song

and the great lady herself ("To Father Thady she gave a chapel / just like handing a child an apple") now lies in the graveyard

> Under a cross that sweeps the skies,
> And there among the nameless throngs
> Turlough O'Carolan, maker of songs[48]

O'Carolan lives in memory; the patrician is commemorated in stone. What consolation there was available to the folk came from their cherishing the accounts of past glory, indifferent as they were to what had been imposed. Two traditions then on the land – the older and

Gaelic, the new and Anglo-Irish – touching only in such contrived reduction as Yeats's schema of poet, peasant, and nobleman. A more just estimate is found of that dual inheritance in Michael Hartnett's poem "A Visit to Castletown House" with which this account aptly approaches its conclusion. The poem is the penultimate lyric in his collection *A farewell to English* in which he announced his intention to write henceforth in Irish.

> I have made my choice
> and leave with little weeping:
> I have come with meagre voice
> to court the language of my people.[49]

In "A Visit to Castletown House" (headquarters of the Georgian Society) Hartnett describes a concert he attended there:

> The avenue was green and long, and green
> light pooled under the fernheads; a jade screen
> could not let such liquid light in. . .
> The house was lifted by two pillared wings
> out of its bulk of solid chisellings
> and flashed across the chestnut-marshalled lawn[50]

Art, artifice, and nature. It is nature, he infers, that endures, establishes continuities, roots. During the interval he stepped

> into the gentler evening air
> and saw black figures dancing on the lawn,
> Eviction, Droit de Seigneur Broken Bones:
> and heard the crack of ligaments being torn
> and smelled the clinging blood upon the stones.[51]

Here is the Gaelic *continuum*. Ferocious loyalty bred of ferocity. Nature, history, emotion – a resonant triad. Its distance from Yeats's evasive "ceremony of innocence" endorses my opening charge that his Coole Park poems are loosely rooted in Irish soil.

NOTES

1. *LTSM*, 114.
2. See Daniel A. Harris, *Yeats: Coole Park and Ballylee*, (Baltimore & London: Johns Hopkins University Press 1974); Richard Gill, *Happy Rural Seat: the English Country House and the Literary Imagination* (New Haven, Conn.: Yale University Press, 1971).
3. Harris, op. cit., p. 53.
4. Donald R. Pearce (ed.), *The Senate Speeches of W. B. Yeats* (London: Faber, 1961) p. 99.

5. *The Writings and Speeches of Edmund Burke* (London: The Beaconsfield Edition, n.d. [?1901] VI, pp. 392–3. The passage occurs in "A Letter to Richard Burke, Esq., on Protestant Ascendancy in Ireland", which can be dated after 19 February, 1792. The letter is not reprinted in *The Correspondence of Edmund Burke* (CUP).

6. *Personal Sketches of his own Times* (London, 1827), II, p. 63.

7. L. P. Curtis, Jr., "The Anglo-Irish Predicament", *20th Century Studies*, 4 (November 1970) p. 61. The late Professor F. S. L. Lyons reminded me that the loyalty was not unconditional, and instances the activity of the Patriot Party after 1782. When the Ascendancy felt its position to be threatened, it qualified its commitment, and this, of course, was increasingly the case throughout the nineteenth century. I was grateful to him for this reminder.

8. *Memoirs of Richard Lovell Edgeworth* (London, 1820), II, pp. 375, 377–8.

9. *Rise and Fall of the Irish Nation* (Paris, 1833) p. 32.

10. *Bowen's Court* (London, 1942) pp. 32, 338–9; "The Big House", *The Bell*, (Dublin) I.i., (Oct. 1940) p. 73.

11. "The Twilight of the Big House", *Ariel*, I.3, (July 1970) p. 122.

12. Maurice Harmon, "Cobwebs before the Wind", in *Views of the Irish Peasantry*, Daniel J. Casey and Robert E. Rhodes (eds) (Hamden, Conn: Archon Books, 1977) p. 141.

13. H. G. Richardson and G. O. Sayles, *The Administration of Ireland 1172–1377* (Dublin: Stationery Office for the Irish Manuscripts Comm., 1963) p. 69. I adapt their comment on the Anglo-Norman period, and am grateful to Reverend Father Benignus Millett, O. F. M., who brought this study to my attention. "I read the Anglo-Irish literature of the last century before the Gaelic tradition was made known by the labour of scholars and I find it arid and empty of spiritual life", *Ireland Past and Present* (London: 1922) p. 10.

14. Louis MacNeice, *The Poetry of W. B. Yeats* (London: Faber, 1941, re-issued with a foreword by Richard Ellmann, 1967) p. 97; C. Day Lewis, "A Note on W. B. Yeats and the Aristocratic Tradition" in *Scattering Branches*, Stephen Gwynn (ed.) (London: Macmillan, 1940) p. 176; T. R. Henn, *The Lonely Tower* (London: Methuen, 1950) pp. 7, 8.

15. Op. cit., 1901, p. 517. The Gaelic literary achievement found a guarded response from Stephen Gwynn and Frank O'Connor. Gwynn wrote: "However much worth there is which survives of their work may be questioned; certainly it is not all high poetry", but he added "it is all educated work [written] for the learned" (*Irish Literature and Drama in the English Language* [London: 1936] p. 26). O'Connor while admitting "this is not a culture which appeals to me" also agrees "it was a real culture, a purely aristocratic culture" (The *Backward Look*, [1967] p. 86). For a better sense of the achievement see *The Pleasures of Gaelic Poetry*, (Sean MacRéamoin (ed.) [1982]), especially David Greene's magisterial essay, "The Bardic Mind" (pp. 37–62), where the skill of the bards in articulating a personal voice within an arduous discipline is demonstrated.

16. Daniel Corkery, *The Hidden Ireland*, (Dublin: Gill, 1925).

17. Op. cit., John O'Donovan (ed.) (Dublin: 1851), V, p. 1595.

18. Op. cit., A. O'Kelleher and G. Schoepperle (eds) (Chicago, 1918) p. 351.

19. Brendan Bradshaw, " 'Manus the Magnificent': O'Donnell as Renaissance Prince" in *Studies in Irish History*, Art Cosgrove and Donal McCartney (eds) (University College Dublin, 1979) p. 19. Bradshaw develops with excessive warmth an insight of Edmund Curtis in his *A History of Medieval Ireland* (2nd edn, 1938) p. 366. "Yeats found his Irish Urbino in Coole demesne. . . . As he and Lady Gregory spent their summer evenings reading about the brilliant company gathered centuries earlier in the Italian palace, they could not but realise that they were in an Irish Urbino", *Yeats and Castiglione* (Dublin, 1965) p. 22.

20. *The Bardic Poems of Tadhg Dall Ō Huiginn*, Eleanor Knott (ed.) (Irish Texts Soc., XXIII [1921] 1926) II, 24, ll. 1–4, 21–4, 15, 28.

I have to thank An tAthair Micheal Mac Craith O. F. M. for this reference.

21. *An Duanaire 1600–1900: Poems of the Dispossessed* (Mountrath: Dolmen, 1981) Seán

Ō Tuama and Thomas Kinsella (eds), p. 145, ll. 1–3, 9, 13–14; Harris, op. cit., p. 52.
22. *An Duanaire*, p. 163, ll. 5–7, 9–11, 17–20.
23. Op. cit., p. 167, ll. 27–8. Declan Kiberd in his useful "The Perils of Nostalgia: a Critique of the Revival" in *Literature and the Changing Ireland*, Peter Connolly (ed.) (Gerrards Cross: Colin Smythe, 1982) pp. 1–24, suggests these lines as the source of Yeats's
> And there is an old beggar wandering in his pride –
> His fathers served their fathers before Christ was crucified
> *(VP* 580, and see also 544).
24. *Tim was Away*, Terence Brown and Alec Reid (eds) (Dublin: Dolmen, 1974) pp. 1–2, ll. 30–9.
25. Op. cit., p. 5, l. 68.
26. Op. cit., p. 11, ll. 147–9.
27. Op. cit., p. 5, ll. 66–7.
28. *The Emergence of Modern Ireland 1600–1900* (London: 1981) p. 253.
29. *Irish Poetry from Moore to Yeats* (Gerrards Cross: Colin Smythe, 1980) p. 14.
30. *Parnell and his Island* (London: 1887) pp. 7–8; *Modern Ireland and Her Agrarian Problem* (London: 1906) p. 65. Moore states the traditional view of landlord–tenant relations, a view shared by Parnell, Davitt and Butt, and consistently supported by the evidence supplied in the several Reports of Parliamentary Commissions on the land question. This view has been the subject of lively debate since the publication in 1971, (in the Harvard Economic Series) of Barbara Lewis Solow's *The Land Question and the Irish Economy 1870–1903*. Her primary data source was the Reports, but she ignores the evidence which would impugn her revisionist thesis, nor does she substantiate her observation "Perhaps in terms of prices and acres and rents and evictions the Irish landlord did nothing seriously to restrain economic development in Ireland" (op. cit., p. 202). Also revisionist in tendency is Peter Roebuck's essay "Landlord Indebtedness in Ulster in the Seventeenth and Eighteenth Centuries" in *Irish Population, Economy and Society* (Oxford; Clarendon Press, 1981). A corrective will be found in *Irish Peasants, Violence, and Political Unrest 1780–1914* (Manchester: Manchester University Press, 1983). Of value, too, is Liam Kennedy's "Studies in Irish Econometric History", in *Irish Historical Studies*, xxiii: 91 (May, 1983), where he states "Alas for splendid new historical possibilities, the would-be revisionists have slipped on the humble issue of appropriate tests of significance" (op. cit., p. 195).
31. *Laurence Bloomfield in Ireland* (New York & London: Garland, 1979) p. 4, ll. 19–27.
32. Op. cit., pp. 14–15, ll. 214–20, 224–5.
33. Op. cit., p. 53, ll. 260–4.
34. Op. cit., p. 77, ll. 268–70. Two passages from Malcolm Brown's essay "Allingham's Ireland" in *Irish University Review*, 13:1 (Spring 1983), support the argument I am conducting. "*Laurence Bloomfield's* most striking quality is *lucidity*, reinforced by expert knowledge, a liberal moral sensitivity, and Chaucerian realistic detail. What could be more un-Irish? What could be more disgusting?" (op. cit., p. 10). Allingham shows the landed gentry and aristocracy as "vulgar, ignorant, cruel, stupid, bigoted, degenerate, tasteless" (ibid., p. 13).
35. W. T. H., *The Encumbered Estates of Ireland* (London: 1850) p. 9.
36. *Laurence Bloomfield in Ireland*, p. 23, ll. 24–5.
37. "Our upper class cares nothing for Ireland except as a place for sport", *VP* 836, also *Au* 201.
38. Peter Ure, *Yeats and Anglo-Irish Literature* (Liverpool: Liverpool University Press, 1974) p. 191.
39. "Yeats, Joyce, and the matter of Ireland" in *Critical Inquiry*, 2, 1975–76, p. 48.
40. *Happy Rural Seat*, p. 168.
41. *Parnell and his Island*, p. 31. China pisspots with Gladstone's face in the bowl were common in country house bedrooms.

42. "Seamus Heaney's Tradition", in *The Cambridge Quarterly*, VII:2 (1977) p. 177. Seamus Heaney has elaborated on the point that I am making: "Yeats and Lady Gregory seem to have assented to the Wildean paradox that nothing that actually occurs is of the slightest importance. They were intent in setting a faith in symbol against any sociological exploration, setting myth against history, ecstasy against irony, art against life", and he concludes, "Yeats created a magnificent and persuasive Ireland of the mind, but a partial one" ("A Tale of Two Islands" in *Irish Studies I*, [CUP 1980], P. J. Drudy (ed.), p. 5). I question Heaney's "persuasive".

43. My brother Ciaron Coleman alerted me to this juxtaposition.

44. L. M. Cullen, op. cit., p. 248.

45. The phrase occurs in Yeats's description of Penns in the Rocks, "the perfect country house, lettered peace and one's first steps out of doors into a scene umbrageous, beautiful (I take those words from Carlyle's description of my native country) (*LDW* 38–9).

46. Op. cit., p. 8. R. B. McDowell has commented: "Probably the most striking feature of Irish life in this century was 'the peculiar system by which the large majority of the people was kept in a state of carefully planned and well-preserved inferiority. . . . It is remarkable how the members of this proud community were able to ignore the existence of their helots" (*Irish Public Opinions 1750–1800* [London: Tucker, 1944] p. 10).

47. Harris, op. cit., p. 233.

48. Op. cit. (Dublin, 1941) p. 17, ll. 11–15, p. 18, ll. 15–16, p. 19, ll. 10–12.

49. Op. cit. (Dublin, 1975) p. 67, ll. 10–13.

50. Op. cit. p. 58, ll. 1–3, 9–11.

51. Op. cit. p. 59, ll. 4–8.

Code Breaking and Myth Making: the Ellis–Yeats Edition of Blake's *Works*

Donald Masterson and Edward O'Shea

There has been a great deal of critical interest in W. B. Yeats's and Edwin Ellis's three volume collaborative edition, *The Works of William Blake, Poetic, Symbolic and Critical*, the so-called Quaritch edition.[1] The reasons are evident enough. Yeats's interest in Blake was life-long, and the themes and aesthetics of both poets are clearly compatible, when the differences expressed by such critics as Hazard Adams have been acknowledged.[2] Furthermore, the Ellis–Yeats edition was the first to see Blake's symbolic system as a whole, giving much attention to the difficult prophetic books, works neglected and even scorned by earlier editors such as Swinburne and Rossetti. Finally, it was the first to print the text of *The Four Zoas*, albeit in a far from satisfactory fashion. For these reasons, the *Works* has been thoroughly discussed in a general way by a number of commentators. But opinions have differed rather widely as to the historical value this edition has for Blake scholarship. Focusing on its numerous textual errors, the editors' doubtful emendations of Blake's writings, and their penchant for arcane interpretations, one group of commentators tends to dismiss the *Works* as at best an interesting curiosity. Foremost among these is Northrop Frye. He charges that Ellis and Yeats "approached Blake . . . from the wrong side of Blavatsky", a wry comment bolstered by attacks on the weaknesses of Ellis and Yeats as editors and on their "over-schematized commentary full of false symmetries, which, itself more difficult to understand than Blake, is further confused by centrifugal expositions of Boehme and Swedenborg".[3] Kathleen Raine, in what seems to be a minority report, takes issue with at least the latter part of Frye's evaluation. Admitting to some problems in the commentary, she asserts nevertheless that "Ellis's and Yeats's work comes near to the underlying principle and intention of Blake's symbolic thought . . .", and she adds, "Blake would have condoned its mistakes, and probably set about adding to his all-embracing mythology whatever in Ellis and Yeats is not already there."[4] Deborah Dorfman, taking a more moderate view than either Frye or

Raine, presents what we regard as the most useful assessment of the *Works*. After acknowledging its obvious failings, Dorfman concludes that the edition did "sanction and provoke serious scholarship based on Blake's prophetic books", and she adds that Ellis's and Yeats's description of Blake's "system" was informed and accurate enough to encourage future "addition, qualification, documentation, and comparative studies".[5]

If one subscribes to Dorfman's view, then it is clear that the *Works*, excepting only the Gilchrist biography, is the nineteenth century's most significant contribution to Blake scholarship. Such being the case, the process by which the edition was made is of obvious scholarly interest. That process has already been examined in part by Ian Fletcher who has discovered and catalogued some of Ellis's and Yeats's working papers for the Blake edition.[6] Our intention here is at once more comprehensive and particular. Firstly, we will examine a cluster of supporting materials read and annotated by the two editors while preparing the *Works*. These include copies of Swedenborg's *Divine Love and Divine Wisdom*, his *Arcana Coelestia* and *Spiritual Diary* as well as Franz Hartmann's *The Life and Doctrines of Jacob Boehme*. Secondly, we will focus on a facsimile of one of Blake's best known works in the nineteenth century, *The Marriage of Heaven and Hell*, a facsimile heavily annotated by Ellis and Yeats, most likely as a working document used in formulating their ideas about Blake's mature mythology. Finally, we will illustrate how Yeats's four years labour on this edition served as a formative influence on his own poetry and mythmaking.

The Blake-related materials found in Yeats's private library in Dalkey include a copy of Emmanuel Swedenborg's *Divine Love and Divine Wisdom*[7] presented to Yeats by Ellis. Yeats carefully transcribed into this copy Blake's own annotations as found in the volume in the British Museum. But from the evidence of Yeats's library the most important source books for Ellis's and Yeats's understanding of Swedenborg were the first volume of his *Arcana Coelestia* (London, 1891) and the first three volumes of *The Spiritual Diary* (London, 1883), all heavily annotated by Yeats. For an understanding of Boehme, Ellis and Yeats turned to Franz Hartmann's compendium *The Life and Doctrines of Jacob Boehme* (London, 1891). The copy in Yeats's library is fully annotated almost throughout in pen and pencil of various colours by both men.

An item of even more striking interest is the rare John Camden Hotten facsimile of *The Marriage of Heaven and Hell* (1868).[8] The facsimile in Dalkey which, we speculate, originally belonged to Ellis, consists of 27 hand-coloured plates on 27 leaves. Seventeen plates have been annotated mostly in pencil by Ellis and Yeats, some very heavily, and in addition, the versos of two of the plates also contain full annotations. It is sometimes fairly easy to differentiate the hands in the facsimile – as on plate fifteen – where Yeats lists the Four Zoas in the right hand margin

and Ellis's annotations are in the left (see plate 1).[9] But on the more
fully-annotated pages, it is often difficult to differentiate two very similar
hands. In any case, we believe from Yeats's own testimony and from the
conclusions of Ian Fletcher that the annotations in the Hotten facsimile
were as completely a collaboration as the finished edition. Fletcher, after
presenting drafts of Ellis's and Yeats's work on the edition in which one
writer revises the other until it is impossible even to distinguish styles,
concludes: "... it seems important to remember that much of the
revision was done in the same room at the same time and that whose
hand held the pen is not always significant. The Yeats–Ellis commentary
was collaboration in the deepest sense".[10]

PLACING BLAKE IN THE THEOSOPHICAL TRADITION: ELLIS'S AND YEATS'S READING OF SWEDENBORG AND BOEHME

Close to the beginning of their collaboration on the *Works* Yeats wrote to
Ellis: "The reason I have not attacked Jerusalem and Milton is that the
Biblical part, so important to both books, is still a blank to me. I am
pushing on with Boehmen and Swedenborg reading, in the hope to find it
clear up." [11] Ellis and Yeats then discovered Swedenborg and Boehme as
they unravelled Blake. Frye's contention that the *Works* is also "a
centrifugal exposition of Boehme and Swedenborg" is an accurate one,
though he intends it as a criticism; we contend that Ellis's and Yeats's
reading of the two writers (along with a general knowledge of the
Cabala) provided them with a necessary point of entry into Blake's
system. Approaching Blake via these three authorities gave them the
confidence to attempt the edition in the first place, and it was not an
arbitrary decision, since Blake's *The Marriage of Heaven and Hell*[12] was, at
least in part, a satiric response to Swedenborg's *Heaven and Hell*. But in a
wider sense, agreement can be found in the Cabala, in Boehme, in
Swedenborg, and in Blake, that man's condition was fallen because
"disintegrated", and this view was recognised by Ellis and Yeats. In
Cabalistic doctrine this is expressed as the disjunction between the
Sefirot, the divine principles, and the lower world of creation, in
Swedenborg as the division of spirit from reason, and in Boehme as the
substitution of the human will for the divine, with the result that the once
androgynous Adam loses his sexual self-sufficiency and takes on a
corrupting physical form. In Blake's mature myth this "dis-integration"
is expressed through the Four Zoas and their emanations, and this myth
in turn is, as we shall see, a prominent feature of Ellis's and Yeats's
reading of *MHH*. If the Fall implies a dichotomy between the spiritual
and physical, these "worlds", though qualitatively different, are related
through "correspondences" (Swedenborg's term and Blake's) or "signa-

tures" (Boehme's). The physical world "reflects" or symbolises the higher spiritual order.

From the evidence of Yeats's library, it is clear that Blake's progressive disillusionment with Emmanuel Swedenborg was shared by Ellis and Yeats, though it is also true that Yeats at least continued to read Swedenborg carefully and to write about him some twenty years after the *Works* had been published,[13] just as Blake never entirely lost interest in him. Yeats makes effective use of his own transcriptions of Blake's annotations to Swedenborg's *Divine Love and Divine Wisdom* in his "The Necessity of Symbolism" in the *Works* to convey his thesis that Swedenborg as "corrected" by Blake could be the necessary antidote to modern scientific positivism, to the tyranny of the material world over the spiritual. As he quotes Blake's annotation approvingly in "The Necessity of Symbolism": "Study science till you are blind, study intellectuals till you are cold, . . . yet science cannot teach intellect much less can intellect teach affection" (*WWB*, I 240). It was also in Blake's annotations to *Divine Love and Divine Wisdom* that Yeats found an early expression of one of the themes of *MHH*. Countering Swedenborg's contention that Good is from God, Evil from Man, Blake writes "Good & Evil are here both Good & the two contraries Married" (*Erd* 604). Yeats does not quote this passage, but elsewhere in the essay he emphasises Blake's corrective to Swedenborg – that will and emotion are not evil but are a necessary part of the dialectic.

For Blake in *MHH*, Swedenborg is the precursor and "the Angel sitting at the tomb" that the risen Christ has vacated. "Swedenborg's writings are a recapitulation of all superficial opinions, and an analysis of the more sublime, but no further" (*Erd* 34, 43). And Crabb Robinson in his "Reminiscences" quotes Blake as saying of Swedenborg, "He was a divine teacher. He has done much good, and will do much. He has corrected many errors of Popery, and also of Luther and Calvin. Yet Swedenborg was wrong in endeavouring to explain to the rational faculty what reason cannot comprehend" (as quoted in *WWB*, I 143).[14] Yeats's own assessment was similar: presumably Swedenborg's early training as a scientist coloured his mysticism with rationality. As Yeats was later to represent Swedenborg in "Swedenborg, Mediums, and the Desolate Places (1914)": "He considered heaven and hell and God, the angels, the whole destiny of man, as if he were sitting before a large table in a Government office putting little pieces of mineral ore into small square boxes for an assistant to pack away in drawers" (*Ex* 33).

Ellis and Yeats also follow Blake in esteeming the writings of Jacob Boehme, the 17th-century German theosophist, more highly than those of Swedenborg. As Blake writes in *MHH*: "Any man of mechanical talents may, from the writings of Paracelsus or Jacob Behmen, produce ten thousand volumes of equal value with Swedenborg's" (*Erd* 43). Ellis and Yeats echo Blake's judgment in the Memoir to the *Works*

(*WWB*, I 23), but it is Yeats in his annotations to the first volume of
Swedenborg's *Arcana Coelestia* who makes the fullest and most particular
comparison of Swedenborg and Boehme, though it does not appear
directly in the *Works*. In the first chapter of *Arcana Coelestia* Swedenborg
glosses the story of the six days of creation in Genesis. His exegesis takes
the form of an account of the six states of the regeneration of man which
move from the primordial darkness of childhood through successive
states of increasing awareness of faith and love. Yeats comments
marginally: "comparison of this chapter with Boehme's shows how
much more Blake was indebted to Boehme than to Swedenborg for his
fundamentals".[15] And a page later: "This whole chapter shows how little
Swedenborg found where Boehme discovered the entire basis of modern
metaphysics. Swedenborg is at his weakest when face to face with
fundamentals. He is a moralist much more than a mystical philosopher.
His 'correspondences' are always much less suggestive than Boehme's
'signatures'." The reference to "Boehme's chapter" is difficult to
determine precisely, but Yeats may have in mind the chapter "The
Restoration of Nature" in Hartmann's *Life and Doctrines of Jacob Boehme*.[16]
Despite Hartmann's attempt in this compendium to "systematise"
Boehme's writings on this subject, his account of creation is much less
coherent than Swedenborg's, but it is also less morally charged and more
elemental, evocative, and "poetic", and this undoubtedly accounts for
Yeats's preference.

Yet another reason for Yeats deciding that Boehme was of greater
importance than Swedenborg in understanding Blake's intellectual
inheritance was Boehme's doctrine of the sovereign imagination. At
about the time that Ellis and Yeats were making the *Works*, Yeats had
concluded that Blake's notion of the imagination as the primary creative
faculty originated in Boehme, and even more specifically in a commentary added by Boehme's English disciple, William Law, to Boehme's *The
Way to Christ Discovered and Described* (Bath, 1775). Yeats carefully
transcribed Law's gloss on Boehme under the heading "Imagination as
understood by Boehme" in his own copy of *The Poems of William Blake*
which he edited independently of Ellis in 1893 as a general reader's
edition. This transcription reads in part: "its works [i.e. the imagination's] cannot be hindered because it *creates* and *substantiates* as it goes and
all things are possible to it. . . . It is the eternal ground *scene*, and subject
of both *good* and *evil*, and is therefore the Key of both Heaven and Hell".
Yeats was to refer to a phrase from this passage some forty years later
when he read in Denis Saurat's *Blake and Modern Thought* that Blake's
thinking was a last manifestation of "Le culte de la sensibilité" of the
18th century. In his own pencilled comment, Yeats took exception to
Saurat's assertion. His memory for dates and citations is typically only
approximate here: "The source of Blake's thought is not '*culte de la
sensibilite*' but 17th century theories about the sovereign powers of

imagination as summarized in an anonymous writer in I think 1740. It alone 'substantiates as it goes' . . . Blake's thought or style reverted to the 17th century." [17] The repetition of the phrase "substantiates as it goes" as applied to the creative imagination suggests that what Yeats has in mind is not an anonymous 18th century writer but rather Law's commentary which he had forgotten by the time he read Saurat's book. In any case, Yeats for over forty years continued to believe that Boehme, not Swedenborg, was a source or at least a precedent for Blake's revolutionary understanding of the importance of the imagination. This understanding is nowhere specifically discussed in the *Works*, but its elucidations of Blake's system presume it. We have seen that in reading and annotating Swedenborg and Boehme while making the *Works*, Ellis and Yeats were making comparisons between the authors, to the advantage of Boehme. But most of the annotations are specific attempts to root Blake's symbols or his myth in Swedenborg's and Boehme's writings. Where Swedenborg offers an anagogic account of the second day of creation in *Arcana Coelestia* and at Boehme's interpretation of it in Hartmann's compendium, Yeats suggests in his annotations a comparison to Chapter II of *The Book of Los*.[18] Insofar as all three passages represent "creation myths" and depict a general sundering of human life or male–female principles from undifferentiated creation ("chaos" or "Mysterium Magnum" to use Boehme's term), the comparisons seem apt. But the parallels are not pointed out in the Commentary[19] to *The Book of Los*, probably because they are too particular to be genuinely helpful, but they must have reinforced the editors' conviction that the writings of Blake, Boehme, and Swedenborg were intricately related and that the three men were working in the same general tradition, using similar methods.

It is indicative of Yeats's impatience with Swedenborg, shared by Blake in *MHH*, that his annotations to *Arcana Coelestia* break off abruptly and almost completely after Chapter II. This is not the case with Hartmann's *Life and Doctrines of Jacob Boehme* which Ellis and Yeats have annotated elaborately throughout. Both readers are initially skeptical and question Hartmann's scholarship[20] or Boehme's expression,[21] but as they begin seeing more and more associations with Blake's poetry, the scepticism disappears. Their annotations especially draw parallels between Boehme's writings and *The Book of Los*, *The Book of Urizen*, *The Four Zoas*, and *Jerusalem*, the same works Yeats and Ellis concentrated on in their reading of *MHH*. The two editors emphasise in their annotations the compatibility (as later critics have also done) between Boehme's cosmogony and Blake's, and their remarks in effect conflate both authors' accounts into one creation myth. To take an example, at Hartmann's account of Boehme's dialectical triad "contraction", "motion", and "anguish" which produces all creation, Yeats writes "All this in Urizen" [22] and in fact the first chapters of *The Book of Urizen* follow this pattern as Urizen "contracts, expands, and rotates".[23] This is one instance where the Commentary for *The Book of Urizen* in the *Works* follows the annotations closely. There Ellis and Yeats credit Boehme with establishing the pattern of the "three dark creations" which Blake follows (*WWB*, II 135), and they suggest through a chart (see Fig. 1) how Boehme's triad is compatible with the "head, heart, loins" correspondences which they see as so important in understanding all of Blake's work, including very prominently *MHH*.

As often as not Ellis's and Yeats's annotations to Swedenborg and Boehme focus on single images rather than larger parallels. Yeats says that in preparing the edition, he and Ellis made lists of all Blake's mythological characters and symbols and that Ellis turned them into a concordance.[24] This concordance does not seem to have survived, but one can see something of this same systematizing attempt in Yeats's annotation to Swedenborg's application of the Genesis account of the creation of the fish on the fifth day. Swedenborg writes: "*By creeping things which the waters bring forth*, are signified scientifics, which belong to the external man; by birds in general, rational and intellectual things, of which the latter belong to the internal man." Yeats here reminds himself to "quote" the passage "apropos of fish"[25] and then connects the reading, rather arbitrarily it seems, to plate 13 of *America* which in part depicts a predatory fish about to feed on a dead soldier. To apply Swedenborg's symbolism of the fish as representing "external man" to Blake's fish in *America* seems less than helpful or accurate, and to extend this symbolism to other representations of fish in Blake would be positively misleading, for Blake does not use the image with any complete symbolic consistency. (The fish attempting to break from the net in plate 22 of *MHH* has even been identified by another commentator as Swedenborg!)[26] What has encouraged Yeats here (and both men throughout the *Works*) to make these symbolic equivalents is his belief in what he would later call the "Anima Mundi", the reservoir of unconscious symbolism available to all men, whether Swedenborg, Blake, or a London medium. Though the precise term comes later in Yeats, the theory is expressed in the *Works* as the "great postulate" – "the underlying unity of all minds as portions of the one great mind or imagination, 'the body of God' " (*WWB*, I 327). This postulate, in its more colourful application, led Ellis and Yeats to attempt to conjure up Ololon, Urthona, and Orc by having subjects repeat their names in a trance (*WWB*, I 327). But it was the same belief that made Ellis and Yeats compile a concordance of Blake's symbols. While the doctrine of the "Anima Mundi" may be attractive in explaining the power of, for example, the image of the "rough beast" slouching towards Bethlehem to be born in Yeats's "Second Coming", it seems to fail in explaining more equivocal images and leads to a false and illusory consistency that is the major failing of the *Works*.

After we have acknowledged the tendency in the *Works* to enforce too much symbolic consistency in reading Blake in the light of Swedenborg and Boehme, we must also recognize Ellis's and Yeats's primary motivation for doing it. Nineteenth century critics tended to see Blake's poetry as esoteric, eccentric, and finally perhaps not worth the effort it demanded to be understood in all its detail. To Ellis and Yeats, faced with this attitude, it must have seemed reassuring that Blake spoke in the "universal language" of symbols, a language that could be substantiated in a long, continuing though "esoteric" theosophical tradition. If they were overly eager and overly systematic in seizing such symbolic correspondences, we can nevertheless understand their reason for doing so in the early 1890s.

THE ANNOTATIONS TO THE HOTTEN FACSIMILE OF *THE MARRIAGE OF HEAVEN AND HELL*

We have seen how the dedication of Yeats and Ellis to the mystical–theosophical tradition was the governing perspective in their preparation of the *Works*, especially in the writing of "The Symbolic System". This interest quite naturally led to a preoccupation with Blake's later poetry, that work which seemed to them most responsive to this tradition. In fact, it can accurately be said that the prophetic books were for Ellis and Yeats both a source of inspiration and a measure against which all of Blake's other work was judged. Such a perspective is everywhere evident in the edition, and, more specifically, is clearly apparent in the Hotten facsimile annotations. To some extent, the comments on this facsimile are directed toward an explication of *MHH* itself, and a number of these observations were eventually incorporated in the published commentary on this work. But taken as a whole, these annotations show that the two editors were mainly interested in relying on *MHH* as a means towards fuller understanding of the prophetic books, especially *The Four Zoas*, *Milton*, and *Jerusalem*. Our examination of these comments will, therefore, focus on those which most directly reveal Ellis's and Yeats's preoccupation with the prophetic books. We will not attempt a comprehensive review, which would require a separate study. But, before turning to these annotations, we would like to examine briefly two passages from the Commentary on *MHH* which pointedly illustrate our contention.

After a long paragraph of comparison betwen *MHH* and the prophetic books, Ellis and Yeats strongly imply their preference for the later works. Referring to "The Voice of the Devil" passage in *MHH*, they assert that:

Blake was here attempting to write his doctrines without the aid of the myth, using merely popular terms. His difficulty was insuperable. The

popular terms would not fit his ideas, and the attempt to employ them
in the new sense with parenthetical scraps of explanation has caused
such obscurity that anyone who does not know Blake well enough to
see what he intends to convey in spite of his method of conveying it,
will not see anything here but paradox (*WWB*, II 64–5).

The implication here is that, contrary to what previous critics had
thought, Blake's mythmaking in his later poetry eliminated the obscurity he might justly be charged with in earlier works such as *MHH*. No
doubt Ellis and Yeats had Swinburne's *William Blake* in mind when
taking this view. Like a number of his contemporaries, Swinburne much
admired *MHH*, calling it "the high water mark of [Blake's] intellect",
and "a work which we rank as about the greatest produced in the line of
high poetry and spiritual speculation".[27] But his opinion of the prophetic
books, notably *Jerusalem*, was hardly as enthusiastic. Of Blake's epic he
suggests that "one cannot imagine that people will ever read through
this vast poem with pleasure enough to warrant them in having patience
with it".[28] Swinburne obviously did not reckon with the patience Ellis
and Yeats were soon to demonstrate in their long labour on such poems.
The single most important goal of this labour was to verify the coherence
of Blake's canon, thereby refuting probably the most damaging charge
then brought against his work. The second excerpt from the Commentary on *MHH* demonstrates in a more particular way how they went
about doing so.

After the previously cited passage about Blake's undeveloped myth in
MHH, Ellis and Yeats offer an explication of what they call the
"contraries" in his work by comparing them to their "mythical
equivalents" in the later poetry:

Jehovah (after Christ's death)	The Divine Unity
(before)	Urizen in the South
Christ	Los, or Imagination
The Heaven formed from what was stolen from the Abyss	Golgonooza, or Art
The Devil	Orc

They conclude by admitting that these are "not exact equivalents, but
sufficiently nearly so for the tracing of Blake's ideas from one form of
expression to another" (*WWB*, II 65). As tentative and idiosyncratic as
this comparison may seem to us now, it represents the first diligent
attempt to formulate a coherent view of Blake's evolving myth.
Moreover, this scheme, with its fourfold symmetry and the inclusion of
Urizen, Los, and Orc, points to the major breakthrough made by these
editors in presenting Blake's cosmology – the introduction of the Four

Zoas and the elaboration of this myth. An important working record of this endeavour can be seen in the annotations to the Hotten facsimile, and a useful place to begin examination of these comments is with reference to Ellis's and Yeats's scheme just cited.

On plate six of the facsimile, the initials W. B. Y. are prominently printed in the upper left margin, perhaps to indicate Yeats's special responsibility for this section's explication. If so, then some of the ideas underlying the "contraries" and "mythical equivalents" presented in the Commentary were probably first developed by Yeats on this page. The phrase in the above-mentioned scheme from the Commentary, "The Heaven formed from what was stolen from the Abyss", a near repetition of a line in *MHH*, seems to have intrigued Yeats, no doubt due to his uncertainty concerning the meaning of "the Abyss". A comment in the upper right margin of plate six evidences his interest in determining what Blake meant by this term: "The Abyss-material not the mental – hence the generation world, not the new regeneration." The identification of the "material" world of "Generation" with the Abyss and its juxtaposition with the "mental" realm of "regeneration", though certainly speculative, nonetheless offers an interesting example of Yeats's attempt to look through *MHH* to the prophetic books, notably *Milton* and *Jerusalem*. These later works provided Ellis and Yeats with the particulars of Blake's fourfold vision, in this case the state of generation. Thus the contrary of the Abyss, Heaven, one of the "popular" terms that troubled their reading of *MHH*, is understood by these editors as an early equivalent of Golgonooza, Los's city of art, first mentioned in *The Four Zoas* but fully described in *Milton* and *Jerusalem*.

Such was the editors' approach in most of the annotations to the Hotten facsimile, but a full page of observations on the verso of plate four, facing plate five, offers one of the few extended comments related primarily to an issue in *MHH* itself. Reacting to the passage concerning *Paradise Lost* and *The Book of Job*, Ellis and Yeats remark:

> It indeed appeared to Milton that his Satan (desire) was what was cast out.
>
> But from Job we learn that the outcast was Reason (Milton's Messiah) was cast out of the first heaven, i.e. imagination and formed *a* heaven – that is held up a picture of the desirable he aimed at which was purely a reproduction of the material (abyss) without imaginative truth, & was therefore the mechanical, exterior furniture – heaven of the conventional historical churches.

Awkwardly phrased as this annotation is, it still offers useful commentary on one of the most controversial sections in *MHH*. Ellis and Yeats agree with Blake that in *Paradise Lost* Milton fails to recognize that desire is directly allied with imaginative creation and at odds with conventional moral codes. Milton's Messiah, who Blake equates with Reason, the restrainer of Desire, is identified by the two men as the false deity of the "material" world whose sterile and "mechanical" image of heaven mirrors the Abyss into which man has fallen. This heaven is also that of the "historical churches", which, given Ellis's and Yeats's preoccupation with *Milton* and *Jerusalem*, is probably a reference to the Twenty Seven Churches, Blake's symbols for dogmatic Christianity as described in these poems. Even when compared to recent commentary on this passage from *MHH*, this gloss offers worthwhile insights into Blake's ideas on morality and the poetic imagination.[29] So too does the annotation following the one just cited:

> Also – that the exit of Satan was not a casting out but was the inspired desire of Christ that he took with the rest of him into incarnation, & which enabled him to use generation or mortal life as a step to the formation of regeneration or the mental delights of the true imaginative heaven in the bosom of God which is the bosom of man.

The famous phrase from *MHH*, "all deities reside in the human breast", obviously prompted Ellis and Yeats to expand this idea by observing that "the true imaginative heaven" can be found in "the bosom of God which is the bosom of man", a statement succinctly capturing a central Blakean notion. But their identification of Satan with the "inspired desire of Christ", although provocative, is not warranted even by the ironic vocabulary of *MHH*. Had the editors been more familiar with Satan as he appears in the prophetic books, the personification of error and eternal death, perhaps they would have been wary of such an association. The annotation, however, offers some useful insights on Blake's doctrine, far more than a related passage from the Commentary on *MHH*:

> The limiter (who is really Satan as Reason) believes the force of desire that it controls to have been actually cast out. But the Devil, as the delighter, says that the mobility of God is distinguished from his eternity, that this mobility is Christ, that it fell, or went out into the void which then became nature, and, on returning, that it formed the joys of heaven from that which it took from the energy, or "eternal hell" outside (*WWB*, II 63–4).

One can readily see why the *Works*, filled with muddled and inaccurate passages like this, has been attacked by scholars. In reply to this criticism, we can only reiterate our contention that the edition's value lies not in its often uncertain analysis of Blake's work, but in its frontal assault on a system previously thought inpenetrable by most of Ellis's and Yeats's contemporaries.

One of the most interesting examples in the Hotten facsimile of the way *MHH* was used to penetrate Blake's myth appears on plate fifteen in a hand that is unquestionably Yeats's (see Plate 1). Down the right hand margin, Yeats jotted the names Urizen, Luvah, Urthona, and Gnomes. This plate contains the section called "The Printing House in Hell," and each of these figures is associated with a creature found in a chamber of that house. Urizen is seen as corresponding to the Dragon Man, Tharmas to the Viper, Luvah to the Eagle, Urthona to the Lions, and the Gnomes to the Unnamed Forms. It is difficult to understand why Yeats made these associations, but they do demonstrate the extent to which he felt compelled to expand Blake's myth into contexts which now seem highly dubious. One possible explanation for such speculative comparisons is that Yeats was engaged in the research and perhaps the writing of "The Symbolic System" at the time he made these annotations. Although overly-schematised and needlessly complex, this long essay nonetheless offered some valuable insights into the cosmogony of the prophetic books. One passage from this essay may help explain Yeats's "discovery" of the Zoas in *MHH*:

> It must always be remembered that the Zoas exist in everything. Blake held the doctrine of the macrocosm, and microcosm, and would gladly have assented to the saying of Paracelsus: "He who tastes a crust of bread tastes all the stars and all the heavens."[30] There is no grass blade of the field, no pebble of the brook, in which he could not have found the Zoas and some of their correspondences (*WWB*, I 260–1).

Throughout "The Symbolic System," Yeats doggedly pursues such correspondences, providing numerous charts, tables, and diagrams to support his explanations. It does not seem all that surprising, then, that in discovering this new territory, so to speak, he would be looking for agreement between *MHH* and Blake's later work a bit too overzealously.

The Hotten facsimile annotation just cited was not developed in "The Symbolic System", but Ellis and Yeats considered it important enough to include in the commentary on *MHH*. The Unnamed Forms of the fifth chamber are here identified as the "Gnomes of Palamabron", an association that they probably made because in later works, notably *Milton* and *Jerusalem*, Palamabron is paired with Rintrah, a figure first seen in *MHH*. In any case, Ellis and Yeats acknowledge that these Gnomes "are not part of the four-fold humanity", their term for the Blakean construct which particularly fascinated them. Of the figures that are so associated, Urthona is given the most attention. For some reason, the original identifications made in the annotation were changed in the commentary. Here the Dragon man is not seen as a precursor of Urizen; Urthona is assigned this role, and the comment made about the latter exemplifies the free-wheeling speculation for which the *Works* is notorious:

> The Dragon-Man of the cave is not said to be Urthona, but we perceive him to be a nameless form of this Zoa, joined with his spectre, who divided in the early pages of "Jerusalem." The caves he clears are the dens that Urizen explores afterwards. He is the porter of the Northern Bar in "Thel." (*WWB*, II 69)

An idiosyncratic reading of this sort illustrates what we regard as both the weakness and strength of the overall approach in the *Works*. Although recognising the significance of *MHH* and the works preceding it, Ellis and Yeats, for the most part, regarded these writings as "mere poetry" and suffered them only to the extent that they cast light on the prophecies that followed. Such tendentiousness naturally produced glosses like this one, which pay minimal heed to the text at hand and serve rather more as a springboard for fanciful leaps into the poetry which really interested them. At the same time, the persistence of these editors in such practice, if it did not always produce wisdom, sometimes resulted in significant elaborations of Blake's myth. One of these advances is suggested on the next page of the Hotten facsimile, plate sixteen (see Plate 2).

This plate begins with a passage that obviously would have attracted the attention of these editors: "The Giants who formed this world into its sensual existence and now seem to live in it in chains are in truth the causes of its life & the sources of all activity." A comment in the margin reads: "These giants are the 4 Zoas." Speculative though this annotation is, one can readily see why the association was made. With their reference to creation and their mention of giant forms from which all experience generates, these lines strongly suggest the myth Blake was to articulate in *The Four Zoas*. In fact, Ellis and Yeats were confident enough in their detective work to further pursue it in the design at the top of the plate. This illustration presents five seated figures, two on each side of a larger bearded form. Those flanking this figure are turned inward toward him, while he stares directly at the reader. All are swathed in heavy garments.[31] Once again, in rigorously schematic fashion, the annotators identify the left hand figure as Luvah, the next as Tharmas, the figure to the right of the central form as Urthona, and the last as Urizen. "Man Bound" is their identification of the middle form. A glance at Ellis's brief discussion of this design in a section of the *Works* called "Blake the Artist" tells us, as we would expect, that "Man Bound" is Albion, the Ancient Man who first appears in *The Four Zoas*. Ellis further identifies these figures as the "five senses in darkness", an interesting comment considering the emphasis in *MHH* on sensory perception. None of these identifications from the Hotten facsimile was included in the Commentary on *MHH*.

Not adverse to drawing forced parallels between the Dragon Man in *MHH* and the Porter of the Northern Bar in *Thel*, they discard arguably useful (considering when they were made) insights concerning the origins of the Zoas myth.

Other annotations, however, on plate sixteen were developed in a profitable fashion. Over the name of each Zoa, Ellis and Yeats also placed one of the corresponding elements. Luvah is associated with air, Tharmas with water, Urthona with earth, and Urizen with fire. These correspondences were thoroughly developed in one of the more readable and engaging sections of "The Symbolic System" where Yeats expounds upon the characteristics of the Zoas. His observations on Urizen and Luvah are especially interesting:

> Urizen is "The Prince of Light." In his good aspect of thought, not yet withdrawn from Divine Love and inspiration, he would be the warm and light-giving beams of fire; but as we have him most constantly in Blake, he is its cold light, its beam long separated from the source. Luvah is the regent of air and of the breath, whereby the physical body gets the least material, because least opaque of its corporeal ingredients, – the symbol of its wayward feeling, and the vehicle whereby it sighs its sorrows. . . . As the son is centre of the Divine Triad, Father, Son, and Holy Spirit, so Luvah stands between unfallen Urizen and Tharmas, and air between fire and water (*WWB*, I 257)

When one compares Yeats's obviously committed analysis of the Zoas myth with the view of predecessors like Swinburne that the "jumbled worlds of Tharmas and Urthona" produce the "apparent madness of final absurdity",[32] then Yeats's sensitivity to Blake's vision is readily evident. This section of "The Symbolic System" illustrates other characteristics of the Zoas, their compass point, their body parts, their position on the globe (Zenith, Nadir, etc.), and their states. The extent to which this information has been helpful to Blake scholars can best be judged by comparing it to a similar schema in Northrop Frye's *Fearful Symmetry*. Although identifying Urizen's element as air and Luvah's as fire, Frye's chart shows basic similarities with Yeats's scheme, although it is more informed and complete.[33] In examining these two studies, written more than a half century apart, one can more fully appreciate the previously cited assessment of the *Works* by Dorfman; it did indeed encourage future "addition and qualification".

Glances at other plates in the Hotten facsimile reveal further evidence of Ellis's and Yeats's commitment to the explication of Blake's later poetry. On the top of plate three, for instance, they note: "Edom is the body – one of the 5 senses, one of the 7 kings of Asia – in the place where Adam was new-created." This comment was prompted, no doubt, by Blake's reference to Edom on this plate: "Now is the dominion of Edom, & the return of Adam into Paradise." Remembering a subsequent allusion to Edom early in *Jerusalem*, Ellis and Yeats in the *Works* launch into a three paragraph discussion of Blake's use of the term in this poem. Their discussion concludes, not surprisingly, by suggesting a possible source in the Cabala: "The Kabalists tell of seven early worlds destroyed before this world began. They call these seven worlds Edom. Blake uses the idea contained in this myth without repeating it or endorsing it" (*WWB*, II 63). Once again, the method in the *Works* is made plain – a preoccupation with Blake's mature mythmaking and a disposition toward seeing the mystical–theosophical tradition as a basis for his vision.

A number of similar annotations on the first few plates of the Hotten facsimile are worthy of attention, but, given the limitations of our study, we will examine only one more group of comments before turning to "A Song of Liberty", which, as we shall see, deserves special consideration.

Without question, the most attentively-annotated page in the Hotten facsimile is "The Argument" (see Plate 3). It is covered with comments, and the facing page continues these remarks. Unique in their attention to the design as well as the text, these annotations include speculation on the identity of the figures in the illustration and on the significance of its colours. In addition, Ellis and Yeats again find correspondence with *Jerusalem* as well as note Blake's debt to Boehme and Swedenborg. For example, we find this comment in the upper right margin: "Blake before he knew Bohmen and Swedenborg." The annotators are responding to adjacent lines: "Once meek, and in a perilous path, / The just man kept his course along / The vale of death." They no doubt see the "just man" as Blake, who was "once meek" (not wrathful or prophetic) before he was inspired by these two visionaries. We have fully explored Ellis's and Yeats's insistence on Boehme and Swedenborg as sources for Blake's thinking, so further elaboration is unnecessary. It is interesting to note, however, that this gloss may have been too dubious even for them, for no such speculation appears in the *Works*.

Another unpublished but noteworthy observation was made at the top of the plate: "This argument is (J. B. Y.) a description of the fall (with correspondences) see Jerusalem p 26." We speculate that J. B. Y. is a reference to Yeats's father, John Butler Yeats,[34] but the reference to *Jerusalem* is self-evident. Plate twenty-six divides the first two chapters of the poem and presents the following boldly lettered statements: "SUCH VISIONS HAVE APPEARED TO ME AS I MY ORDERED RACE HAVE RUN JERUSALEM IS NAMED LIBERTY AMONG THE SONS OF ALBION" (*Erd* 171). The first of these proclamations is the probable focus of Ellis's and Yeats's reference. Very likely, they regard

Blake as the speaker, and "SUCH VISIONS" include the one depicted
on this plate in *MHH*. The "fall", of course, refers to the account from
Genesis, which the editors think "The Argument" comments on, a
determination they seem to have arrived at more through attention to
the design than the text. For instance, they note at the bottom of the
plate: "The upper figure is the biblical satan & so is the red part of the
lower figure. The blue out of which he comes is Blake-Satan. The black
(earth) on which the girl stands is Blake-Satan." Recent commentators
on this design have noted that the upper figure "suggests Satan in
serpent form tempting Eve"[35] supporting at least part of Ellis's and
Yeats's interpretation. The remainder of the annotation, needless to say,
seems dubious, especially the identification of Blake with Satan.
Nonetheless, they pursue this association in a still questionable but more
substantive comment on the verso of plate one facing "The Argument".
They begin by assessing the design as a whole:

> The picture is a glyph – The blue & green are air & water (Luvah as
> Blake's "Satan" or reason gives consciousness of passion, – (the red
> ball, – the holy ghost,) to innocence, natural instinctive bodily
> tendency.) In a word gives consciousness to instinct. In the fall of man
> the *discovery* of that fall was itself a marriage of Heaven (mind,
> Knowledge) & Hell (physical energy).

Among other observations, this note alters and expands the
Blake–Satan idea by suggesting that Luvah, one of the Zoas, is Blake's
equivalent of the biblical Satan. As such, he is associated with reason,
the power that restrains instinctual energies by creating self-
consciousness. Ellis's and Yeats's mistake is to see Luvah in Urizen's
role, for the latter figure is the notorious tyrant of the prophetic books,
pre-figured in *MHH* as the Satan of *The Book of Job*. Apparently, they
were not yet able to keep their devils or their Zoas straight. One also
wonders why the Holy Ghost is seen as "the conciousness of passion", or,
for that matter, the marriage of heaven and hell as the "discovery" of
man's divided self. The ready answer is that these comments and most of
the others on these two pages are necessarily tentative at this preliminary
stage in the preparation of the *Works*. None were included in the
Commentary on *MHH*.

The latter third of the Hotten facsimile contains few annotations,
probably because Ellis and Yeats found little on these plates to provoke
speculation about the prophetic books. But, as we have noted, "A Song
of Liberty" stimulated much interest. Two of the three plates are heavily
annotated, mostly with comments pointing toward the later works. This
prose poem, which Blake added to *MHH* close to the time he was
composing his political prophecies like *America*, naturally reflects the
declamatory tone of such poems and was probably more to Ellis's and

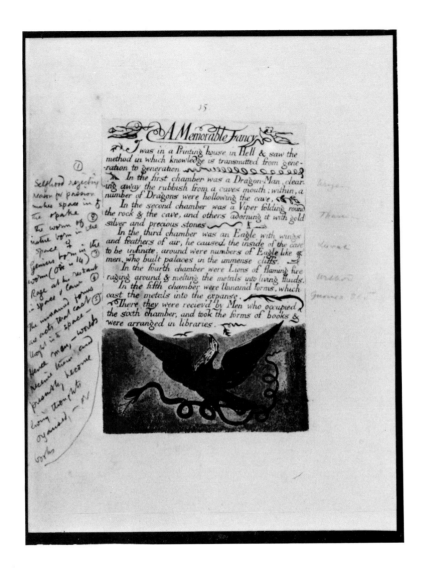

1 *The Marriage of Heaven and Hell* (plate 15, John Camden Hotten facsimile 1868).

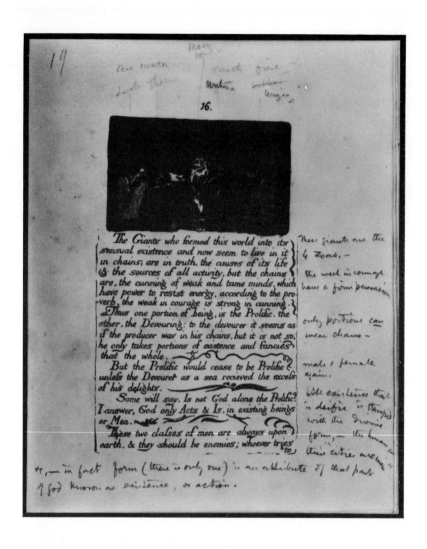

16.

The Giants who formed this world into its
sensual existence and now seem to live in it
in chains; are in truth, the causes of its life
& the sources of all activity, but the chains
are, the cunning of weak and tame minds, which
have power to resist energy, according to the pro-
verb, the weak in courage is strong in cunning.
    Thus one portion of being, is the Prolific, the
other, the Devouring: to the devourer it seems as
if the producer was in his chains, but it is not so,
he only takes portions of existence and fancies
that the whole.
    But the Prolific would cease to be Prolific &
unless the Devourer as a sea received the excess
of his delights.
        Some will say, Is not God alone the Prolific?
I answer, God only Acts & Is, in existing beings
or Men.
        These two classes of men are always upon
earth. & they should be enemies; whoever tries

These giants are the
4 Zoas, –

the weak in courage
have a firm persuasion

only portions can
mean chains –

male & female
again.

All existence that
is desire is stamped
with the divine

form, – the human
their cities are ...

handwritten marginal note at bottom: He, – in fact form (there is only one) is an attribute of that part
of god known as existence, or action.

2 *The Marriage of Heaven and Hell* (plate 16, John Camden Hotten facsimile 1868).

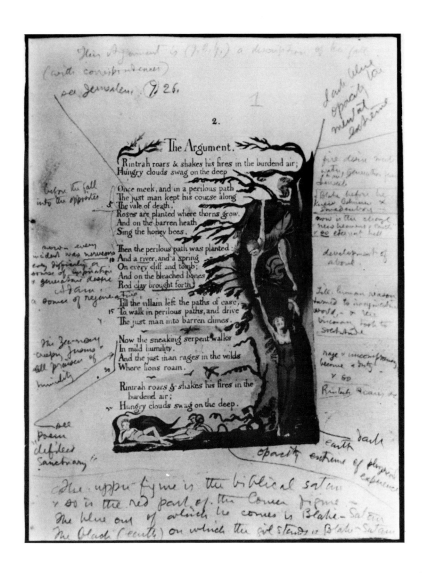

The upper figure is the biblical satan
& so is the red part of the Corner figure
The blue out of which he comes is Blake-Satan
The black (earth) on which the girl stands is Blake-Satan

2.

The Argument.

Rintrah roars & shakes his fires in the burden'd air;
Hungry clouds swag on the deep

Once meek, and in a perilous path
The just man kept his course along
The vale of death.
Roses are planted where thorns grow.
And on the barren heath
Sing the honey bees.

Then the perilous path was planted:
And a river, and a spring
On every cliff and tomb;
And on the bleached bones
Red clay brought forth.

Till the villain left the paths of ease,
To walk in perilous paths, and drive
The just man into barren climes.

Now the sneaking serpent walks
In mild humility.
And the just man rages in the wilds
Where lions roam.

Rintrah roars & shakes his fires in the
burden'd air;
Hungry clouds swag on the deep.

---

3   *The Marriage of Heaven and Hell* (plate 2, John Camden Hotten facsimile 1868).

*hurl'd the new born wonder thro' the starry
night.*
11. The fire, the fire, is falling!
12. Look up! look up! O citizen of London
enlarge thy countenance: O Jew, leave coun
ting gold! return to thy oil and wine: O
African! black African! (go. winged thought
widen his forehead.)
13. The fiery limbs, the flaming hair, shot
like the sinking sun into the western sea.
14. Wak'd from his eternal sleep, the hoary
element roaring fled away;
15. Down rush'd beating his wings in vain
the jealous king; his grey brow'd councel-
-lors, thunderous warriors, curl'd veterans,
among helms. and shields, and chariots
horses, elephants: banners, castles, slings
and rocks,
16. Falling, rushing, ruining! buried in
the ruins, on Urthona's dens.
17. All night beneath the ruins, then
their sullen flames faded emerge round
the gloomy king.
18. With thunder and fire: leading his
starry hosts thro' the waste wilderness

4   *The Marriage of Heaven and Hell* (plate 26, John Camden Hotten facsimile 1868).

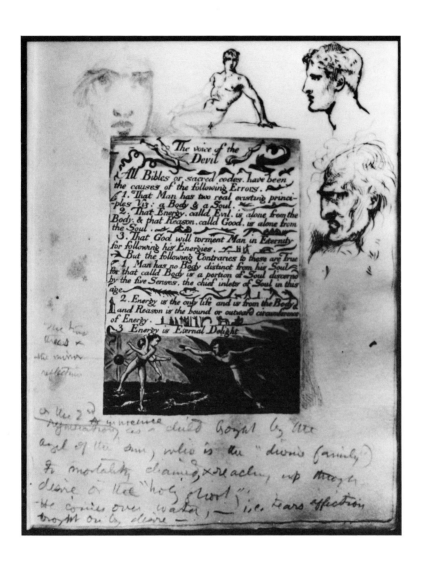

5 *The Marriage of Heaven and Hell* (plate 4, John Camden Hotten facsimile 1868).

6 W. B. Yeats: studio portrait photograph by Chancellor, Dublin, 1902 (courtesy Department of English, University of Reading).

7   W. B. Yeats: John Singer Sargent, 1908, charcoal (private collection, USA in 1970), (ex.coll. John Quinn).

8 W. B. Yeats: Augustus John, 1907, etching.

9   W. B. Yeats: Augustus John, 1930, oil, 48″ × 30″ (coll. Glasgow City Art Gallery [Kelvingrove] no. 1817).

10   Jack B. Yeats: *Rehearsing Willies Wise Man FAYS LITTLE THEATRE* (photograph
by Michael Foley).

11a Jack B. Yeats: *John Quinn and Russell at Fays Theatre Dublin* (photograph by Michael Foley).

11b Jack B. Yeats: *John Quinn at Rehearsal in Fays Little Theatre* (photograph by Michael Foley).

12b   W. T. Horton: *The Soul and Evil* (University of Reading).

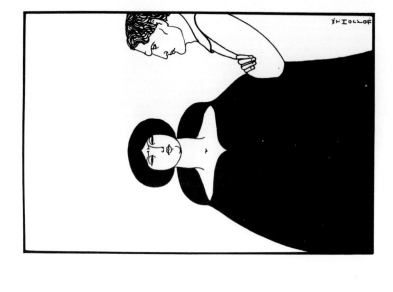

12a   W. T. Horton: *Aspiratus*, inscribed by Horton "to W. B. Yeats
in affection and deep gratitude 1896"

13a   W. T. Horton: *God Lights the Stars His Candles* (University of Reading).   13b   W. T. Horton: *The Spirit and the Soul* (University of Reading).

14 John Butler Yeats: chalk drawing, Charles Elkin Mathews, signed and dated "July 2nd 1894" (University of Reading).

15a Yeats's birthplace: George's Ville, No 15, Sandymount Avenue: capstone of gatepost (photograph by A. Norman Jeffares).

15b Yeats's birthplace: George's Ville, No 15, Sandymount Avenue (photograph by A. Norman Jeffares).

on a child's death

You shadowy armies of the dead
Why did you take the starlike head
The faltering feet, the little hand?
For purple kings are in your band
And there the heads of poets bend;
Why did you take the faltering feet?
She had much need of some fair thing
To make love spread his quiet wing
Above the tumult of her days
And shut out our foolish blame & praise.
She has her squirrel & her birds
But these have no sweet human words
And cannot call her by her name:
Their love is but a woodland flame.
You wealthy armies of the dead
Why did you take the starlike head?

WBY.
Sept 5.
1893.

16   W. B. Yeats: "On A Child's Death", holograph, signed and dated "Sept. 5 1893".

Yeats's taste than the often dry irony that troubled their readings on previous plates of *MHH*. Moreover, the opening lines of the "Song", with its references to the "Eternal Female" and the "Shadows of Prophecy", doubtless renewed the editors' enthusiasm for unearthing seeds of Blake's myth in *MHH*. They recognised the unique character of these last three plates and stressed this point in the Commentary: "The 'Song of Liberty,' though issued from Blake's press under the same cover with the 'Marriage of Heaven and Hell,' is really a separate book" (*WWB*, ii 74). A bit later in the Commentary, after discussing some of the "Song's" verses in detail, Ellis and Yeats add: "We have passed a barrier in going from the last book [*MHH*] to this one, and everything reads in its true order now" (*WWB*, ii 75). By "true order" they apparently mean the outlines of Blake's "system" which we have seen them trying to elucidate. Now confident in their position, they continue to explicate the "Song", continuously using it to clarify their ideas about *The Four Zoas*, *Milton* and *Jerusalem*. Several concepts contained in this explication and in other sections of the *Works* appear in the Hotten facsimile. Presumably, the ideas were first tested there. By far the most significant is the "head, heart, loins" triad, referred to several times.

A brief catalogue of Ellis's and Yeats's references to this triad in "A Song of Liberty" shows how much it dominated their thinking. In the upper part of plate twenty-five we find the following scheme:

lake river sea
Head heart loins
of
water

This note comments on the adjacent lines: "The Shadows of Prophecy shiver by the lakes and rivers and mutter across the ocean!" Just below this annotation, Ellis and Yeats offered another triad:

France Spain Rome
Luvah heart loins
heart reason loins
[cancelled]

Here they are responding to the call: "France rend down thy dungeon; Golden Spain burst the barriers of old Rome." Another note in the right margin elaborates further on these lines: "Rome is loins acting tyrannically as head." Continuing on to the next plate (twenty-six), we find a more involved annotation (see Plate 4):

hurls through [the] starry night, or through intellect,
the complex desire, or son, that has both male & female

elements, being born of heaven & hell – head is down
now, – the fire falls from loins to head, (night).

The Orc-like figure with "flaming hair", the "new born wonder" is
the focus of Ellis's and Yeats's attention. Finally, in Yeats's hand, a
variation of the triad is offered: Loins $\begin{cases} \text{head} \\ \text{heart} \\ \text{Loins} \end{cases}$ [erased]. This note, in
the left margin next to verses 11 and 12, seems to be a revision of a parallel
one in the right margin. There the words heart and loins are written
twice but cancelled. "Head", written next to the line "Look up! look up!
O citizen of London" is not deleted. We can only guess at why these and
other revisions were made, and the Commentary for the "A Song of
Liberty", containing only one unenlightening reference to this triad, is
not much help in clarifying the overall significance of the head, heart,
loins scheme. But, turning to "The Symbolic System", we find that
Yeats considered this trope as nothing less than the key to Blake's entire
myth. There Yeats goes to great length to trace the "various subdivisions" of what he terms "the triad of personal life – head, heart, loins, or
of thinking, emotional, and instinctive existence" (*WWB*, I 260). Ellis
and Yeats found the triad on plate thirty-four of *Milton* where Blake
associates head, heart, and loins with three of the four states of being.[36]
But they are not content merely to represent "states of being".
Conversant as they were with the mystical–theosophical tradition, they
saw the triad as the fundamental pattern of all creation, whether cosmic
or personal (artistic). As Yeats puts it in "The Symbolic System":

> This poetic genius or central mood in all things is that which creates
> all by affinity – worlds no less than religions and philosophies. First, a
> bodiless mood, and then a surging thought, and last a thing. This triad
> is universal in mysticism, and corresponds to Father, Son, and Holy
> Spirit. In Swedenborg it is divided under the names celestial,
> spiritual and natural degrees; in the Kabala as Neschamah, Ruach
> and Nesphesch, or universal, particular and concrete life. In
> Theosophical mysticism we hear of the triple logos – the unmanifest
> eternal, the manifest eternal, and the manifest temporal; and in Blake
> we will discover it under many names and trace the histories of the
> many symbolic rulers who govern its various subdivisions.
> [*WWB*, I 241.]

Here "mood", "thought", and "thing" correspond to "heart", "head",
and "loins" and more speculatively to Luvah, Urizen, and Tharmas.[37]
The association of "mood", "thought", and "thing" with Father, Son,
and Holy Ghost does not follow the traditional doctrine of the procession
of the persons of the Trinity nor does the notion of Luvah as the first

parent power square with Blake, but it is good Romantic doctrine that the creative act begins with an emotion or mood, a formulation that Yeats at least was pursuing in poem and essay at about the time that he and Ellis were making the *Works*.[38]

When one realises the importance of the "head, heart, loins" triad in Ellis's and Yeats's understanding of Blake and the degree to which they generalise it, it can provide an explanation of other annotations in the Hotten which may not specifically use the terminology but do follow the overall scheme. One such annotation is the gloss for plate two of *MHH* which we have already examined in another context:

> The picture is a glyph – The blue & green are air & water (Luvah as Blake's "Satan" or reason gives consciousness of passion, – (the red ball, – the holy ghost,) to innocence, natural instinctive bodily tendency.) In a word gives consciousness to instinct.

Discounting for the moment the confusing association of Luvah with Satan–Reason, we find the same elements here as in the passage just quoted from "The Symbolic System":

HEART	HEAD	LOINS
[Hotten Luvah (gives) facsimile]	Reason, consciousness (to) of passion	Innocence, natural instinctive bodily tendency
[Symbolic System] A bodiless mood (then)	a surging thought (then)	a thing

Here the confusion of Luvah with Satan–Reason is both an illustration of the danger of "reading Blake backwards", that is reading *MHH* in the light of the later prophetic works where Satan is associated with Urizen while in *MHH* he is "energy" and "Eternal Delight", and of attempting to match too rigidly a conceptual scheme with a "glyph". For in plate two of *MHH*, the upper figure is "giving" the lower figure an object, but the notion of "giving" confuses the sense of "simultaneity" that the quotation from "The Symbolic System" conveys. The annotator of the facsimile seems to recognise this problem, for below the annotation just quoted ("The picture is a glyph . . .") he writes more consistently: "The moment passions appear, reason (opposite) appears. In a word, – the moment the forbidden fruit was eaten Satan (reason) was created and brought into existence and made Satanic." We can see from this illustration that though the "head, heart, loins" formula does not appear insistently in the annotations on the facsimile until "A Song of Liberty", the basic tripartite scheme informs Ellis's and Yeats's thinking about *MHH* from the very beginning of their reading.

Once Ellis and Yeats had decided that "head, heart, loins" was the basic schema for understanding Blake, it required some detailed knowledge of his work and some imaginative contrivance to organise most of his canon into a unified but highly schematised plan. No matter that the triad of head, heart, loins did not quite parallel Blake's fourfold vision, Yeats skirted the problem ingeniously. For instance, Dorfman notes that within each of Blake's prophetic poems "the chapters or sections are assigned aspects such as the heart of the head, the loins of the head, and so on; the fourth of any series is seen as a bringing together or realization of the preceding three".[39] We also notice that on a chart in "The Symbolic System" into which Yeats fits most of the prophecies, he adds a fourth body part, the womb, not the "stomach and intestines terrible" named on plate thirty-four of *Milton*. Apparently, this last anatomical correlative offended Yeats's aesthetic sensibilities, and so, taking his usual license, he "improved" Blake's system. A glance at his chart, however, shows telling gaps in the scheme under "womb" (see Fig. 1).

In our view, the annotations to "A Song of Liberty" and those found elsewhere in the Hotten facsimile are ground-breaking efforts, efforts that eventually resulted in the construction of an intriguing but finally unsound interpretative structure in the *Works*. That structure soon collapsed under the weight of more clear-headed and informed views of Blake's poetry. Yet, as we have shown, the ruins of Ellis's and Yeats's "system" at least offered a foundation upon which later Blakeans could construct sounder readings. Moreover, Yeats's own poetry which was in its formative stage while he laboured on Blake, continued to be influenced even into maturity by elements of Blake's vision. Others have detailed these influences, and we will briefly examine a particular correspondence found in the Hotten facsimile in the final part of our study, so no extensive parallels need be drawn here. Yet, one striking example of the profound effect Yeats's work with Blake had on his own mythmaking should be mentioned.

More than thirty years after completing the *Works*, Yeats was still relying on its formulations as resources for his own visionary system. His symbol of the gyres, for instance, took shape as he was reading the prophetic books.[40] But, a more interesting example of Blake's influence, from our point of view, was provided by George Mills Harper in a recent paper on Yeats's automatic script. Harper, using some of the key terms from the script, has constructed a chart which shows remarkable similarities to the one Yeats used to outline Blake's system.[41] As we might expect, Yeats's conception is fourfold, but instead of the Four Zoas, he personalised the scheme by substituting himself, Iseult Gonne, Maud Gonne, and a combination of George Yeats and Lady Gregory as central figures. Eleven sets of correspondences which Yeats develops are identified by Harper, six of which closely resemble those associated with the Zoas in the *Works*. Prominent among these is the head, heart, loins triad, related respectively to the four women Yeats names.[42] Obviously still searching for the appropriate fourth element in this scheme, Yeats ambivuously identifies his own body part as "Fall". This continued uncertainty is of little consequence. What does matter is that during the period of his greatest achievement as a poet, Yeats was still drawing on a "system" he learned while preparing the *Works*.

THE MAKING OF THE BLAKE EDITION AND YEATS'S OWN POETRY: "THE TWO TREES" AS AN EXAMPLE

Though the making of the *Works* occupied a great deal of the energies of both Ellis and Yeats from 1888 to 1892, there was some time for other work. Yeats continued to write poetry during this period, and it is not surprising to find the almost total absorption of his Blake studies overflowing into his strictly creative work. A poem of this period that shows the mark of Blake and more particularly of the Blake edition is "The Two Trees". It has often been remarked by critics that "The Two Trees" owes much to the Cabala and to Blake,[43] but it would be more accurate to say that it is a byproduct of the *edition of Blake* in which Ellis and Yeats apply their understanding of the Cabala, Swedenborg, and Boehme to an interpretation of Blake's system.

The symbolism of "The Two Trees" is difficult, even confusing, because Yeats in this poem is working with so many generally compatible but still slightly discrepant sources and equivalents. The glass or mirror suggests an immediate, popularly-derived symbolism of egotistical self-absorption, but that of the two trees comes from a more esoteric source (the Cabala ultimately), and as we shall see, these popular and esoteric symbolisms work together uneasily in the poem. One solution, our own, is to read both images as esoteric symbols.

As an indication of how complex the associations of "The Two Trees" are, we can refer to an annotation on plate four of the Hotten facsimile of *MHH* (see Plate 5). In Blake's illustration, two figures face each other, the one at the left holds a child over water with the sun at his back, the other, fastened at its foot, reaches towards them out of fire. One gloss, in the left margin, identifies the figures as "The two trees and the mirror reflection". Now this clearly cannot be meant as a primary identification, for human figures are not trees. Even the Commentary to *MHH* in "Blake the Artist" in the *Works* identifies the figures as Los and Orc (*WBB*, II 351),[44] but the more surprising indentification shows the complex associationism at work here and suggests a basis for Yeats's "Two Trees" in the Blake edition. In fact, discussions of the motifs of the two trees and the mirror recur throughout the *Works*. Yeats (presumably) explicates the symbol of the mirror at length in section two of "The Symbolic System", and there are long treatments of the two trees symbol elsewhere in "The Symbolic System" and in the "Memoir" (*WWB*, I 292, 318–19; II 232).

In Yeats's poem "The Two Trees" the poet-persona cautions his beloved to gaze on the "holy tree" growing in her own heart rather than the dark tree reflected in her glass. The "holy tree" bears "trembling flowers" in its "ignorant" leaves; the dark tree harbours only "The ravens of unresting thought" in its broken branches, and some of the antinomies of the poem seem fairly clear from a first reading: emotion vs. intellect, innocent spontaneity contrasted to destructive self-absorption. Critics have variously identified the two trees as the Sephirotic Tree of Life and the Tree of the Knowledge of Good and Evil of the Cabala, or alternately, the Tree of Life (Sephiroth) and its reflection, the infernal poisonous Qliphoth, or Tree of Death.[45] In some depictions, the Tree of Knowledge grows beneath the Tree of Life as a kind of counter image, and these explanations are generally helpful in identifying the symbolism of the *trees* in the poem, though they tell us less about the "glass" or mirror as an independent image. Here the *Works* can help considerably, but it also extends our understanding of the two trees symbolism beyond the references to the Cabala.

In Hartmann's compendium of Boehme's writing, Yeats found the notion that the "tree of temptation" might grow within the human personality, ("Beloved, gaze in thine own heart", Yeats writes in "The Two Trees"), and in Swedenborg, in a passage marked by Yeats, that the temptation represented by the Tree of Knowledge was to found knowledge of God on sense data or scientific demonstration, what Blake would damn as "natural religion".[46] As Swedenborg glosses the biblical prohibition against eating of the fruit of the Tree of Knowledge:

> These words . . . signify that it is allowable to obtain a knowledge of what is true and good by means of every perception derived from the Lord, but not from self and the world, or to inquire into the mysteries of faith by the sense or from science, for in this case the celestial principle is destroyed.[47]

The polarities here might be roughly translated into the context of "The Two Trees" as a call for intuition over abstract impersonal inquiry, emotion (the claims of the heart) over reason. Yeats states this in more strictly Blakean terms in "The Symbolic System" when he writes:

> It [the Tree of Knowledge] grows from under the heel of Urizen, or from the lower and nether regions of his mind. The front is always emanative, and the back spectral. Orc climbs up it as a serpent, seeking thereby to obtain power over men and deceive them by pretending that his earth-born energy, expressing itself in religion, and in legality, and in hypocrisy . . . springs from the zenith to which

he mounts. . . . The Tree of Life is the current of life when seeking
God, and the tree of Good and Evil is the same current seeking the
world (*WWB*, I 318).

Yeats's identification of the Tree of Good and Evil with "seeking the
world" suggests a more compatible symbolism for the glass or mirror of
the poem. To regard the mirror as simply a symbol of egotistical
self-absorption, presumably to be countered by looking beyond the self
to the "objective" world – is a plausible notion but one not finally borne
out by the poem. In fact "The Two Trees" says just the reverse. For the
woman gazing in the glass does not see her own deformed image, surely
an anti-romantic notion for a poet who valued physical beauty as much
as Yeats did, but rather the counter-image of the "Tree of Life", the dark
spectral image of "The Tree of Knowledge". The mirror symbolism of
the Cabala and of Yeats's understanding of Blake as explained in "The
Symbolic System" can help us here. In the Cabala, the mirror is
"Binah", the female principle, the font of nature; in Blake "the vegetable
glass of Nature" (*WWB*, I 247). Yeats's Commentary also explains that
the mirror, once a manifestation of God's own contemplation of himself,
was transformed by reason (Urizen) into "that hard stepmother we call
Nature", "the delusive goddess Nature" or the fallen world of emanation
(*WWB*, I 248–9). As Yeats embellishes the identification, when the
masculine and feminine principles "become spectres or selfhoods, the
mirror [nature] in its turn, grow spectrous, and is changed into a
'vortex,' seeking to draw down and allure. It ceases to be a passive
maternal power and becomes destroying" (*WWB*, I 249).[48]
    In these terms, the beloved of "The Two Trees" is cautioned *not*
against vanity or self-absorption, simply understood, but rather against
dissipating her self-possession by too much attention to the world of
"outer weariness / Made when God slept in times of old". The alternatives are much the same as those of Yeats's much later poem "A Prayer
for my Daughter" which is also a companion poem in respect to the
general symbols of tree and mirror. In that poem Yeats's daughter is
urged to develop an inwardness that is not the narcissistic inwardness of
the "looking glass" (in the more conventional use of the mirror image),
but a self-sufficiency and an independence rooted in the deepest
self-knowledge. Once this is done, Yeats writes, "The soul recovers
radical innocence / And learns at last that it is self-delighting, / Self-
appeasing, self-affrighting, / And that its own sweet will is Heaven's
will".
    Yeats's prolonged study of Blake while making the 1893 edition with
Ellis inevitably then had a very particular impact on his own creative
work. Not only did it spark single poems like "The Two Trees", but it
provided him with an enlarged repertoire of symbols that he would
repeat and refine for the rest of his life. In addition, the "diagrammatic",

systematising approach, most evident in "The Symbolic System", was a precedent for his own attempt at an all-encompassing psychological and historical system some thirty years later in *A Vision*.

Even today, almost a century after the *Works* was published, most Blake critics still feel compelled to attack the edition.[49] But does such a reaction serve a useful purpose any longer? The erratic text of the *Works* has long since been corrected by subsequent editions, notably Erdman's, and Northrop Frye has taught us to read Blake without necessarily having to rely on the mystical and occult tradition which, perhaps inevitably, sent Ellis and Yeats down some bizarre bypaths as they made their way through his poetry. What should be emphasized now is that *Works* stands at the beginning of modern Blake scholarship: it takes Blake seriously, it takes him whole, it stresses his firm continuity with the past rather than his eccentricity. It is also the most significant body of evidence for another continuity between Yeats and the tradition which he and Ellis formed out of Blake, Boehme, and Swedenborg.

NOTES

1. *The Works of William Blake, Poetic, Symbolic and Critical*, Edwin J. Ellis and William Butler Yeats (eds) 3 vols (London: Bernarcd Quaritch, 1893). In the text, references to this edition will appear hereafter as *Works*, citations as *WWB*.
2. Adams's recent essay, "The Seven Eyes of Yeats", in *William Blake and the Moderns*, Robert J. Bertholf and Annette S. Levitt (eds) (Albany: SUNY Press, 1982) pp. 3–14, offers a useful reassessment of the Blake/Yeats relationship as discussed in his well known study *Blake and Yeats: the Contrary Vision* (Ithaca: Cornell University Press, 1955).
3. Northrop Frye, "Yeats and the Language of Symbolism", *Fables of Identity* (New York: Harcourt Brace & World, 1963) pp. 231–2.
4. Kathleen Raine, "Yeats's Debt to William Blake", *Defending Ancient Springs* (London: Oxford University Press, 1969) p. 73.
5. Deborah Dorfman, *Blake in the Nineteenth Century* (New Haven, Conn.: Yale University Press, 1969) p. 226.
6. Ian Fletcher, "The Ellis–Yeats–Blake Manuscript Cluster", *The Book Collector* 21 (1972) 72–94.
7. The edition Blake annotated was *The Wisdom of Angels concerning Divine Love and Divine Wisdom* (London: M. Sibley, 1788); Yeats transcribed Blake's annotations into *Angelic Wisdom concerning The Divine Love and concerning The Divine Wisdom* (London: Swedenborg Society, 1883).
8. William Blake, *The Marriage of Heaven and Hell* (London: William Blake, c. 1790–3; rept London: J. C. Hotten, 1868). Textual references to this reprint edition will appear as "Hotten facsimile". We are grateful to Professor David Erdman for making this identification for us.
9. We would like to thank Mary Jo O'Shea for making the photographic reproductions; they are published with the permission of Michael Yeats and Anne Yeats.
10. Fletcher, p. 94.
11. Fletcher, p. 90.
12. Subsequent references to this work will appear as *MHH*; references to *MHH* as text will be to *The Complete Poetry and Prose of William Blake*, rev. edn, David V. Erdman,

commentary Harold Bloom (Berkeley: University of California Press, 1982). In-text citations to this standard edition will be made as *Erd.*

13. Yeats was reading and marking the two volumes of Swedenborg's *The Principia* after 1912. See also Yeats's "Swedenborg, Mediums and the Desolate Places" (1914) in *Ex.*

14. The Morley edition of Robinson's "Reminiscences" varies somewhat from Yeats's presentation: " 'He was a divine teacher; he has done much and will do much good; he has corrected many errors of Popery, and also of Luther and Calvin.' Yet he also said that Swedenborg was wrong in endeavouring to explain to the *rational* faculty what the reason cannot comprehend;" *Henry Crabb Robinson on Books and their Writers,* Edith J. Morley (ed.) (London: J. M. Dent, 1938) I, 327.

15. (London: Swedenborg Society, 1891) p. 5. Yeats's library contains vol. I only. This and subsequent annotations by Yeats are quoted with permission of Michael Yeats and Anne Yeats.

16. Hartmann's chapter "The Restoration of Nature" glosses many of the same passages from *Genesis* as Swedenborg's first chapter in *Arcana Coelestia* using the same anagogic method.

17. Yeats's comment appears at the bottom of p. 32 in his own copy of Denis Saturat's *Blake and Modern Thought* (London: Constable, 1929).

18. At p. 1, paragraph 8 of the *Arcana* Yeats has written: "Compare second book of Los"; in Hartmann, *The Life and Doctrines of Jacob Boehme, The God Taught Philosopher* (London: Kegan Paul, Trench, Trubner, 1891) p. 128 at par. 1 his annotation reads "Compare Book of Los, Chapter 2 and the differentiation of the 'element.' Compare Blake's Dark Hermaphrodite."

19. Subsequent textual references to the individual commentaries to Blake's works in the volume II of *Works* will be made as "Commentary."

20. Hartmann, p. 21. At the phrase "A third translation", Yeats, apparently, has written: "no, it was only edited by Law. The translation was spurious".

21. Hartmann, p. 69; at the phrase "so as to become revealed" Yeats writes: "Out into what? If there is an out unity is dead."

22. Hartmann, p. 76; the comment is at the top of the page.

23. See S. Foster Damon, "The Book of Urizen". *A Blake Dictionary* (Providence: Brown University Press, 1965).

24. See Yeats's inscription in Lady Gregory's copy of *WWB* in the Berg Collection; for a transcription see *Yeats as Editor* (Dublin: Dolmen Press, 1975) p. 28.

25. Swedenborg, *Arcana,* p. 18, par. 40.

26. *The Illuminated Blake,* annotated by David V. Erdman (Garden City: Anchor Books, 1974) p. 15.

27. Algernon Charles Swinburne, *William Blake: a Critical Essay* (1867; rpt. New York: Benjamin Blom, 1967) p. 204.

28. Swinburne, p. 276.

29. Harold Bloom's commentary in Erdman's *Complete Writings* follows Ellis and Yeats in recognising that Blake saw in *Paradise Lost* "a falsification of the relation between human desire and the idea of Holiness", p. 897. Northrop Frye, in *Fearful Symmetry* (1947); rpt. Boston: Beacon Press, 1967, p. 118), echoes Ellis's and Yeats's comment to the effect that "without imaginative truth" man forms a false image of heaven. He notes in his commentary on *MHH* that "The essential truth of religion can be presented only in its essential form, which is that of imaginative vision."

30. This quotation from Paracelsus appears as the epigraph to Yeats's *Poems* (1895 *et seq.*).

31. For further discussion of this plate, see Erdman, *Illuminated Blake,* p. 113.

32. Swinburne, pp. 196–7.

33. Frye, *Fearful Symmetry,* pp. 277–8.

34. William M. Murphy in *Prodigal Father: the Life of John Butler Yeats* (Ithaca and London: Cornell University Press, 1978) p. 67, describes J. B. Y.'s enthusiasm for Blake's work which he shared in conversations with Edwin Ellis. Perhaps this annotation points to J. B. Y. as the source for this reading of "The Argument".

	Head.			Heart.		
	Head.	Heart.	Loins.	Head.	Heart.	Loins.
MILTON.	The Descent of Milton.			Descent of Ololon.		
	Palamabron and Satan change places.	Rest in Heaven.	War between Satan and the Divine Family.	Lucifer — The fixing of Satan into personality.	Moloch is impatient.	Elohim creat Adam a Fainted.
JERUSALEM.	The first winter comes—Vala and Jerusalem embrace on the Lily of Havalah.			The Divine Family try to bring Albion back Eden by force.		
VALA.	The Birth of the Spectre and of Los and Enitharmon.	The building of the Mundane Shell.	The contests of Urizen and Tharmas with their Emanations.	The fixing of Urizen into a sevenfold personality.	Orc is conceived and his birth from the heart of Enitharmon is described.	Urizen wand with globe fire. The forms round b (compare " U zen," chap. and 8).
SONS OF LOS and AMERICA & EUROPE.	Africa. The growth of religious laws and philosophies.			Asia. The growth of the pleasurable life of the bo		
URIZEN.	Urizen becomes a selfhood in Heaven.	Urizen covers himself with the Opaque and so hides from Eternity. He is separated from Los.	Urizen changes and tosses in agony.	Los fixes the changes and gives a human personality to Urizen. He fixes the changes into seven states.	Enitharmon comes from the breast of Los. Chaos is divided up into spaces.	Orc is born Los and E tharmon.
THEL.				The Lily speaks to Thel.	The Cloud speaks.	The wor speaks.
BOOK OF LOS.				Los divides the selfhoods from himself and fixes them as upper and lower, outer and inner.	Los organises the void into element.	Los sleeps in waters of vegeta tion (the mor body).
TIRIEL.	Tiriel's emanation dies; he curses his sons; they drive him away.	He wanders as an old man to the garden of Har and Heva.	He rests in the tent of Har and Heva.	He meets Ijim who bears him on his shoulders.	Tiriel again, and this time with effect, curses his sons.	He curses daughter H who leads hi
AHANIA.	Urizon and Fuzon contend.			Fuzon is slain by the rock of the law.		

FIGURE 1 *Chart of the symbolic use of the triad in the structure of the poems*

	Loins.				Womb.	
Head.	Heart.	Loins.	Head.	Heart.	Loins.
Shadai is angry.	Pahad is terrified.	Jehovah is leprous.			
	Luvah is generated.			Albion is regenerated.	
The Tree of Mystery grows; Urizen tries to overcome Ore.	The Human Form is given to Ore, and the walls of Golgonooza are built. The Lamb of God is crucified.	Last Judgment.			
	America. England and America are at war—the Head with Loins.			Europe. The restrictive powers contend with Ore.	
Los binds Ore with a chain of days and years. The states become restrictive.	The Sons of Urizen are born. They are bound with a net—the spaces become restrictive.	The Sons know Mortality, Disease, and Law. They are men.			
Thel goes under the earth to see the secrets of the grave.					
Los fixes Urizen into the Sun, and gives a conscious Mind to the vegetative life.					
He comes to the caves of Zazel.	He comes again to the garden of Har and Heva and sleeps.				
	Fuzon is nailed to the Tree of Mystery.				

35. Erdman, *Illuminated Blake*, p. 99.
36. Dorfman, p. 211, notes that Ellis and Yeats used the phrase the "Four States of Humanity" and identified them as Blake does on this plate: Beulah, Alla, Al-Ulro, and Or-Ulro. But they ignored the fact that the latter three terms occur nowhere else in Blake's work and failed to recognise that elsewhere he names the states as Eden, Beulah, Generation, and Ulro. No doubt, Ellis and Yeats were taken with Blake's mention of the head, heart, loins triad and by a diagram at the bottom of the plate (the only one found in Blake's work) that resembles a number of their own, so much so, in fact, that they were certain they had found the key to Blake's system.
37. For the association of Tharmas with "loins" see "Tharmas" in Damon. Damon also identifies Tharmas as the "Parent Power" and associates him with the first person of the Trinity, the "ever-pitying father". Ellis and Yeats obviously gave this role to Luvah.
38. Yeats's poem "The Moods" (first published August, 1893) and a short essay with the same title (1895) both suggest that "moods" with their origins in the imagination are not evanescent but timeless and permanent. They are the sources of all art (an idea emphasised also in *Rosa Alchemica*, *VSR* 143, ll. 469–81); and in a specifically Blakean context, Yeats opposes them to "the restraints of reason" *E&I* 195, *VP* 142. See also the useful discussion of "The Moods" in Allen R. Grossman, *Poetic Knowledge in the Early Yeats* (Charlottesville: University Press of Virginia, 1969) pp. 67–75.
39. Dorfman, p. 212.
40. Dorfman, p. 210, notes that Ellis and Yeats saw Blake's system "as an ascending Jacob's ladder of emotional 'states' or moods forming 'spaces' around them which reached to God. This is the first articulation of Blakean (dialectic) progression found in nineteenth-century criticism. (Yeats adapted this motion into his image of the gyres.)"
41. This information was presented by Harper in his paper on Yeats's automatic script at the LeMoyne College Yeats Conference, October 1982. The paper anticipates a longer study Harper is now preparing which includes a presentation of the chart.
42. In a letter to the authors (15 April 1983) Harper reports that the first reference to the triad occurred on 22 November 1917 in an interrogation by Yeats of George's Control concerning the "head, heart, loins" scheme found in Blake.
43. See for example A. Norman Jeffares, *A Commentary on the Collected Poems of W. B. Yeats* (Stanford: Stanford University Press, 1968) pp. 43–6; also Frank Kermode, *Romantic Image* (New York: Vintage Books, 1964) pp. 96–100.
44. Other commentators point up the similarities between this plate and Blake's print "The Good and Evil Angels". See *The Marriage of Heaven and Hell*, Geoffrey Keynes (ed.) (London: Oxford University Press, 1975) commentary for plate 4.
45. Richard Ellmann, *The Identity of Yeats* (New York: Oxford University Press, 1964) p. 76.
46. Hartmann, p. 161.
47. Swedenborg, *Arcana Coelestia*, p. 50.
48. Yeats uses the mirror image in exactly the same sense in much later poems such as "Ribh Denounces Patrick" and "The Statues".
49. See for example Robert F. Gleckner's "Joyce's Blake: Paths of Influence" in *William Blake and the Moderns*. Gleckner refers to the edition as "monumentally careless and strange", pp. 135–6.

Note: The authors gratefully acknowledge the generous hospitality of Miss Anne Yeats and the archival work of Roger Nyle Parisions in the library of W. B. Yeats.

Portraits of W. B. Yeats: This Picture in the Mind's Eye

William H. O'Donnell

W. B. Yeats's keen interest in portraits of himself is unmistakably evident in the extraordinarily large number of those portraits. A preliminary checklist appended to this essay contains 138 portraits made during his lifetime, and of those he sat to at least 96. There are, in addition, at least 27 formal studio portrait photographs taken at 20 sittings.

Usually we would expect most of the portraits to have been from late in his life, as was true, for example, with Robert Browning, but Yeats's portraits were spread fairly evenly from the 1880s to 1938, with a particular concentration from 1895 to 1908. Yeats got off to an early start, of course, by being the son of a portrait painter. His father made at least 35 portraits of him from 1871 to 1907, not counting three extant drawings of Yeats as an infant and three caricature sketches in letters during the 1910s. Those portraits were enough to make Yeats familiar with the usually onerous task of being a model, but they do not in themselves account for the intensity or the persistence of his fascination with portraits of himself. Yeats assumed, for example, that among the first information his biographer would want to know was the location of his portraits, as Austin Clarke discovered with amused astonishment in his first discussion with Yeats about a biographical study that Clarke proposed to write in the 1920s. Clarke reports that Yeats announced, "as if by rote, 'There are portraits of me in the National Gallery [of Ireland] in Merrion Square, and also in the Dublin Municipal Art Gallery. There are others in the galleries of Liverpool, Birmingham, Bristol, Leicester and Edinburgh' ". Clarke, who found all of this "not very helpful", eventually abandoned the project.[1]

Yeats's interest in his portraits was founded on the power of a portrait to give enduring and vivid expression of personality. In the 1920s Yeats delighted in surrounding himself with portraits of his friends, as if the portraits were emblems of those people. And a decade later, he testified to the power of portraits to dominate memory. In *Dramatis Personae*,

Yeats said that when he tried to recall the physical appearance of Standish O'Grady, who had been dead for six years, his father's oil portrait in the Municipal Gallery of Modern Art, Dublin "blots out my memory" (*Au* 425).

The supremacy of an artistic likeness to the memory of direct physical reality resides in a portrait's special ability to reveal personality. A portrait first catches our attention by the abstract pleasure of skilful design and by our interest in recognising a likeness. Although modern taste plays down the importance of realistic delineation in a portrait, Yeats never ceased to value realism. He insisted on the sitter's importance in a portrait and in 1924 he applauded portraits by the Swedish artist Ernest Jungson for not allowing an interest in the personality of the sitter to be subordinate to such painterly matters as light, colour, and design. Yeats had no sympathy whatever for an artist who forgot the sitter and became "so preoccupied with the light that", as Yeats put it, "one feels he would have had equal pleasure in painting a bottle or an apple" (*Au* 552). That penchant for representational art was echoed in 1927 by a traditionalist but hardly reactionary art critic, Herbert E. A. Furst, who attacked James McNeill Whistler's portrait of Thomas Carlyle, "Arrangement in Grey and Black, No. 2", for paying more attention to artistic design than to the details of Carlyle's boots, hat, and the creases of his trousers, all of which are at least partially obscured in Whistler's painting: "The artist who treats the clothes of his sitters with levity is taking liberties with the personality of his sitter and deceiving the spectator." Instead, Furst strongly preferred a similar but more carefully detailed portrait of Carlyle by Walter Greaves, who was Whistler's studio assistance and pupil. Furst went so far as to announce, "One may learn more about Carlyle by looking at his trousers and boots as painted by Graves, the pupil, than by looking at his head as rendered by Whistler, the master."[2]

Yeats and Furst also would have agreed that a successful portrait must express the sitter's personality. Yeats's father said that a portrait drawing should give a "comment" and not be content with the "facts" that could be captured by a photograph. John Singer Sargent told Yeats, probably while drawing a portrait of him in 1908, that a sitter's true character was always easily visible to Sargent: "All people are exactly what they look. I have just painted a woman who thinks herself completely serious; here is her portrait, I show her as she looks and is, completely frivolous" (*Ex* 447). One of Yeats's unflattering judgements of George Moore as "a man carved out of a turnip" had its rhetorical basis, at least, in Manet's drawing of Moore.[3]

Moore himself subscribed to the widely held belief that portrait-painters have special abilities to discover evidence of character in a sitter's physical appearance. When Moore's reaction against the Boer

War produced changes that, at least according to his account in *Hail and Farewell!*, amounted to a 'new self ", he tells us:

> I wandered across the room to consult the looking-glass, curious to know if the great spiritual changes that were happening in me were recognizable upon my face; but the mirror does not give back characteristic expression, and to find out whether the expression of my face had changed I should have to consult my portrait-painters: Steer, Tonks, and Sickert would be able to tell me.

That same day, at Steer's house, Moore felt himself "to be unlike the portraits they had painted of me, every· one of which had been done before the war. The external appearance no doubt remained, but the acquisition of a moral conscience must have modified it". He cornered Henry Tonks, professor at the Slade School of Art and told him: "I can't believe that I present the same appearance. After all, it is the mind that makes the man. Tell me, hasn't the war put a new look on my face?" Tonks replied, "There's no doubt about it, you seem a different person." And rather than try to describe the tell-tale evidence, Tonks said, "I'll do a drawing of it, and then you'll see."[4]

Although not everyone accords that much power to portrait painters, nearly every sitter has some nervous uncertainty about how he or she will look in the finished portrait. And that nervousness is an acknowledgement that a portrait is a public, important, and permanent statement about the sitter. The acute self-consciousness that a sitter feels is fully merited, for the portraitist intensely examines the sitter's physical appearance for evidence of personality as well as for shapes and proportions that will establish the likeness. The sitter is posing – literally and figuratively – and his or her pleasure in the outcome is partly based upon how successfully the pose which the sitter has in mind – the picture in the mind's eye – matches the public image produced by the artist. Rodin, who greatly admired Puvis de Chavannes, made a portrait bust of him, only to be disappointed that Puvis did not like the bust even though critics gave it high praise.[5] Yeats scoffed at the wagon-loads of society ladies with purses large enough to buy flattery from their portrait painters,[6] but Yeats's interest in the outcome of the portraits for which he posed was no less careful than theirs.

Yeats knew what he wanted in these public expressions of a pose, and he regarded the portraits almost as an integral part of his career. The portraits were permanent records of his continuing insistence that a poet must look like a poet. Yeats, who paid careful heed to his appearance and clothing, even when he had little money for tailors, could skilfully portray aspects of himself in poems and, more directly, in autobiography. But because he lacked the skill to draw or paint a portrait of himself,[7] he was subject to the power of artists for that particular expression of his artistic personality.

An unpleasing portrait of a society lady is an affront that can produce some private disappointment or even outrage, but once she has discharged the artist – like any unsatisfactory employee – the portrait can be kept hidden, and the whole episode can be forgotten. But portraits of public figures – as Yeats increasingly became – are likely to find their way into public view even if the sitter considers the portrait to be unsatisfactory. And Yeats's concern here was not limited to simple vanity about his physical appearance. His elaborate analysis and categorisation of personalities in *A Vision* is clear testimony of his confidence that external evidence can reveal personality. The importance that Yeats assigned to portraits as particular sources of information about personality can be demonstrated by his insistence on trying to solve the puzzle of Bishop Berkeley's portraits, which according to Yeats, contradicted the other available information about that eighteenth-century philosopher: "I hate what I remember of his portrait in the Fellows' Room at Trinity College; it wears a mask kept by engravers and painters from the middle of the eighteenth century for certain admired men . . . the smooth gregarious mask of Goldsmith's *Good-Natur'd Man*, an abstraction that slipped away unexamined when Swift and Berkeley examined and mocked its kind" (*E&I* 397–8).

The portrait of himself that Yeats kept in his mind's eye – the criteria by which he judged his portraits – was what he thought a "Poet" should look like. His regard for that generalised "type" or "ideal" provided, I think, the philosophical basis for his quarrel with Augustus John's art. Yeats acknowledged John's talent, but disliked his modern fascination with idiosyncrasies of individual character, as for example in a John drawing, "Epithalamium", displayed at Coole Park. Rather than celebrating the ideal of marriage, this drawing shows, as Yeats tells us, "an ungainly, ill-grown boy" who is about to embrace "a tall woman with thin shoulders and a large stomach" (*Au* 501). Yeats preferred solidly traditional painters whose figures measure themselves against and aspire toward ideal forms. And although it is unfair to say that John was mainly interested in individual ugliness, he was, as Yeats said, in "revolt" from all that makes one man resemble another (*Au* 501). Yeats wanted art to celebrate and thus foster the ideals which inspire a society. He specifically associated "poetical" painters, such as Botticelli and Rossetti, with the pursuit of the ideal or "type" (*Au* 501) and with the traditional taste of Charles Ricketts and Charles Shannon. Those two artist friends of Yeats's proudly declared themselves to be twentieth-century reactionaries devoted to preserving the traditions of G. F. Watts and especially the techniques of Renaissance artists, notably Titian. Ricketts and Shannon ardently admired such poetical and romantic artists as Blake, Delacroix, Puvis de Chavannes, Moreau, and Rossetti.

In the other camp, Yeats placed the defiantly unidealised art of Augustus John, who, Yeats said, "has no quarrel with his time, its moon and his almost exactly coincide" (*Au* 294). Yeats, who did not fear to quarrel with changing modern values, maintained his loyalty to the old-fashioned and what he considered permanent ideal of "Poet".

That model was based, for the most part, on Shelley and Keats. Both were clean-shaven, unlike Tennyson and Browning. Yeats's father also wore a beard. But Yeats shaved off his youthful (and rather thin) beard at the start of the 1890s and remained clean-shaven except for one winter of convalescence in 1930, when he humorously announced that the beard's alteration of his appearance would require him to take up a different occupation (*L* 773). Yeats remained equally loyal to the other familiar, almost emblematic, ingredients in this poetic physical appearance. The absence of a beard allowed the long, thin lower part of his face to emphasise the etheral impression given by his tall (6 ft 1 in) and, until late middle-age, lanky body. To accentuate his long, artistic fingers, Yeats relished displaying, on the little finger of his left hand, a large ring designed for him by Edmund Dulac in 1917. A bald Yeats is nearly unimaginable, and although his "pretty plumage" changed from jet black to white, his hair was always thick and "beautifully untidy", in Edmund Dulac's apt phrase.[8] His informal, soft collar and an extravagant, loose tie which was an essential part of the uniform for poets and artists, proclaimed his exile from ordinary society. Yeats wore that large, flowing tie in most of his 1890s portraits and in all of the portraits made for his 1908 *Collected Works*. After about 1915 he took to wearing an ordinary bow tie, but in each of his studio portraits it is tied with a carefully casual looseness.

The carefully calculated result of all this was obviously a pose, but it was effective, both in his portraits and in life, as we know from nearly everyone who saw him. Katharine Tynan summarised his appearance in 1889: "In looks, Mr. Yeats is as picturesque as one could desire. . . . Nature has written the poet upon his face." Padraic Colum recalled that Yeats's "pose" challenged his viewers all the more by giving the impression that Yeats believed in it. The American professor Cornelius Weygandt recorded that during Yeats's first lecture tour of America, in 1903, "Yeats was very poet[ic] in appearance, and that appearance helped considerably to make the occasion memorable." Yeats was sure to have been pleased that on his 1911 tour another American, Jessie B. Rittenhouse, found him to be "the visible embodiment of the poet" and that her society counterpart in London, Mrs Beddington, could say, "It is not every poet that looks the part, but you could never mistake Yeats for anything else." Junzo Sato, the young Japanese who presented the now famous sword to Yeats, recalled that Yeats in 1920 was "gallantly attired and looked very much like the poet he was". And in 1935 Stephen Spender, a member of the brash young generation of poets who were distinctly unsympathetic to Yeats, amusingly acknowledged the seventy-year-old poet's "artistic" pose. Spender said that Yeats displayed "something of the appearance of an overgrown art student, with shaggy, hanging head and a dazed, gray, blind gaze".[9]

The success of the pose depended equally upon its extravagance and upon Yeats's unwavering dedication to it. Roy Pascal, in his perceptive study of autobiographical expression, points out that a "consistent misrepresentation of oneself is not easy.[10] And AE's observation in the late 1890s that Yeats had set about "to create or rather re-create W. B. Yeats in a style which would harmonise with the literary style"[11] soon found its fulfilment. Alvin Langdon Coburn, the artistic young photographer, judged that Yeats's manner in 1908 "would have been a pose in anyone else, but with him it was quite natural, for Yeats was a real poet".[12] This stiff-mannered poet and Senator admitted, in his 60s, to never having set foot in an Irish pub, and the witty conjectures, by some twentieth-century practitioners of Dublin's venerable tradition of acerbic wit, about the possibly therapeutic value for Yeats of a pint of stout only serve to reinforce the consistency of Yeats's pose.[13]

The importance to Yeats of that pose is also strikingly evident in his favourable attitude toward caricature drawings of him. Although he was annoyed by the prose satirical portraits of him by George Moore and by the outrageously vituperative Aleister Crowley,[14] there is no evidence of any displeasure at any of the numerous – and often quite funny – published caricatures and cartoons of him. I think this is because the caricatures invariably emphasised precisely the same emblematic details of physical appearance that Yeats so carefully laboured to bring to public attention: his lanky figure, loose tie, dark coat, dark hair falling across his brow, and long fingers. In 1923, when a visiting American asked the Dublin caricaturist "Mac" (S. M. "Isa" Macnie), who drew Yeats twice in that year, why Yeats held such an extreme pose, she replied, "It isn't a pose, it's the man." She added that Yeats believed in "pose" and told young poets to acquire it.[15] Another of Yeats's caricaturists, his artist-friend Edmund Dulac, whose two drawings of Yeats are clever caricatures, repeated that same defence of Yeats's posing: "There is a difference between acting a part for the benefit of an audience and living it for the sake of one's soul."[16]

The selection and handling of emblems also affected Yeats's opinion of serious portraits of him. His intense dislike of a four-inch diameter bronze relief portrait medallion made by Theodore Spicer-Simson in 1922 is based on the medallion's employment of two small shamrocks as decoration after the date and before the sculptor's name.[17] Yeats was unhappy about the shamrock's unsophisticated associations with common Irish "drink and jocularity" (*UP2* 487). He spoke of "the disgust that will always keep me from printing that portrait in any book of mine, or forgiving its creator". We might also note that the shamrock's

unwelcome connotations perhaps are visually reinforced in the medallion portrait by the highly uncharacteristic – because unintended –
carelessness of having his coat collar turned-up. Yeats presumably
disapproved of that unauthorised addition to his own, carefully managed artistic emblems of tousled hair and loose tie. I think those
emblematic considerations account for the violence of his dislike of this
portrait; the stiffness of the profile pose and the heavy fleshiness of neck
and cheek were not likely, by themselves, to have produced so strong a
reaction from him.

By comparison we can consider Yeats's very favourable judgement of
a highly emblematic portrait photograph taken by Chancellor of Dublin
in November 1902 (plate 6). Yeats delightedly announced that it was
"the first good photograph" of him and was "really very good".[18] The
Chancellor photograph, like each of the three or four other studio
portrait photographs of Yeats made between 1894 and 1902, prominently displays his loose tie and the lock of hair falling gracefully across
his left brow. The likeness is flattering enough, but no more so than an
1894 portrait photograph by Lafayette. The Chancellor photograph's
advantage probably is its elaborate use of emblems. Yeats sits with a
book open on his lap and gazes pensively off to his right. His left elbow
rests on a table and his left hand lightly supports the side of his head, in a
gesture which suggests thoughtfulness. The background, blessedly in
soft focus, is filled with the ornate Neoclassical portrait trappings of a
huge column and drapery. The impression given by this photographic
portrait is that Yeats is highly serious and "European". While the sitter
is shown to be literary and artistic, no one would confuse him with a
romantic, youthful Keats or with a shamrock-festooned Irishman.

Additional evidence about Yeats's opinions on portraiture can be
found in his extensive negotiations in 1907 and 1908 about the portraits
of himself to be published in his *Collected Works*. We have already seen
that Yeats assigned great importance to the use of emblems in a portrait
to establish and to convey meaning. He was also much concerned with
the artistic reputation of the portraitist, as is evident in his vehement refusal of a suggestion from his publisher, A. H. Bullen, to consider using a
reasonably flattering portrait photograph by Lafayette as a frontispiece
in the *Collected Works*. Yeats regarded all photographers, even those with
artistic ambitions, as inferior to artists and he therefore was reluctant to
use any photographs in the *Collected Works*, especially as the frontispiece
of the opening volume. He told Bullen, "I don't think it would do to put
even the finest photograph into what is supposed to be the place of
honour, and portraits by famous artists into what would seem by
contrast a sort of appendix" (*L* 504). Yeats was particularly upset about
a photograph by Lafayette, whose reputation was, in Yeats's phrase,
founded on "a great many glossy portraits of Royalties and Actresses".[19]
If a photographer were required, he wanted one whose reputation was in

the world of artists, not of "Royalties and Actresses". His example was the young Alvin Langdon Coburn, who, with help from the artist William Orpen, had recently persuaded Yeats to give him a sitting. Yeats had not yet seen the photographs from that session when he proposed them to the publisher. Bullen obligingly had a plate made from one of Coburn's artistically out-of-focus and not particularly successful photographs of Yeats. Finally, however, no photographic portraits were used in the *Collected Works* of 1908. Two years later Bullen published the Coburn photograph as the frontispiece to Yeats's *Poems: Second Series*, but when that book was re-issued in 1913 the Coburn photograph was replaced with J. B. Yeats's 1896 watercolour portrait of Yeats. And we should note that the Coburn photograph, which was published only once, in 1910, is the sole instance of a photograph among the thirty-one portraits of Yeats that were published in his books during his lifetime.[20] Although he might have preferred a world without photographs, he recognised the practical advantages of economy and speed that made photographs useful in journalism and in publicity for promoting his lectures, plays, and books, and he often gave autographed photographs to visitors and friends. Furthermore, his at least 20 sittings for studio portrait photographs suggest that he sought to have serious, interpretive photographic portraits available for use whenever a painting or drawing would have been impractical. But because the mechanistic character of photography necessarily limited a photographer's ability to interpret the personality of the sitter, paintings and drawings carried much more artistic authority and could make a more important contribution to his books. Yeats tried to exert some control over his portraits by presenting a consistent and heavily emblematical pose of the "Poet" to each of his portraitists. At the same time he openly acknowledged, and perhaps even welcomed, the inevitable multiplicity of expression that portraits by different artists would provide. The divergence of each resulting portrait from the self-image that he carried in his mind's eye was thus a validation of that portrait's artistic merit, but was at the same time a direct, and potentially even dangerous, challenge to Yeats's personal purposes in having the portrait made. Those personal purposes are never directly stated, perhaps because to do so would bring into uncomfortably sharp focus the potential conflict between his general aesthetic principles and his individual desires or vanity. Yeats mused about writing an essay to introduce and thus to control his readers' reactions to the several contrasting portraits of himself in the 1908 *Collected Works*, but he never wrote it (*L* 502).[21]

Beyond those general issues, his favourable and unfavourable opinions of the specific portraits used in the 1908 *Collected Works* are instructive. He was pleased with Sargent's much-admired drawing of him (plate 7), commissioned by John Quinn for Yeats's use in the *Collected Works*. The drawing met Yeats's requirements that a portrait use his requisite emblems, be of artistic value, and be at least reasonably flattering. The lock of hair that falls across his left brow is conspicuously highlighted, and the now familiar soft collar and large tie take prominent roles in the visual design. The artist's fame was unquestioned – although Yeats, who found Sargent to be "good company", was amused that Sargent looked "not so much like an artist as like some wise, wealthy businessman who had lived with artists" – the same aspect of Sargent's appearance that Yeats's friend Edmund Dulac so wittily parodied in a watercolour caricature.[22] Sargent, in all fairness, was equally amused by Yeats's appearance, and later told some luncheon guests: "When he sat for me he wore a velvet coat and a huge loose bow tie, and a long lock of hair fell across his brow. He told me that he did these things to remind himself of his own importance as an artist!" One of Sargent's luncheon guests interrupted quietly, "Why didn't he tie a string around his finger?"[23]

The Sargent drawing of Yeats is handsome in its striking contrast of light and shadow on the smooth lower face and in the finely drawn nose and lips that are balanced by the tousled dark hair, the obscurely shadowed small eyes, and the soft modelling of the coat and very large tie. Yeats called it a "fine" and "charming aerial sort of thing, very flattering as I think" (*L* 507, 509). It was given the pride of place as the frontispiece to the first volume of the 1908 *Collected Works*, and, when the photo-engraved plate was transferred to Macmillan in 1916, was used in four more of Yeats's books during his lifetime.[24] The publishers' admiration for the Sargent drawing was shared by Yeats's sisters, who kept a large, framed reproduction of it on the mantelpiece at the Cuala Industries office.[25] But Yeats's large personal collection of art, which includes some 400 originals and reproductions, has no reproduction of the Sargent drawing, except, of course, as frontispieces in his books. The absence of this best-known of his portraits might seem surprising, but is consistent with his collecting habits. For although Yeats invested many long hours sitting to portraits, and although he owned at least 49 portraits or reproductions of portraits (without counting any by J. B. Yeats), he kept very few portraits of himself. Only four are extant and there is evidence for no more than three others.[26]

The 1908 oil portrait by Charles Shannon, which was used in the *Collected Works*, more than adequately satisfied Yeats's requirements for emblems, for it incorporates not only the lock of hair over his left brow, the soft collar, large tie, and dark coat, but also an Arnold Dolmetsch psaltery and, on the table near Yeats's hands, a laurel wreath – the poetic bays – that perhaps few readers will regret has nearly disappeared into the increasingly age-darkened pigments with which Shannon experimented in imitation of Renaissance masters.[27] Even before the painting was begun, Yeats was confident that it would "probably be very fine",[28] but thought it would be somewhat too idealistic (*L* 502). His judgement of the painting to John Quinn, who was footing the bill,[29] politely concentrates on the opinions of Shannon and of Kathleen Bruce, who was at that time rumoured to be in love with Shannon: "The Shannon portrait is now finished and is, I believe, exceedingly fine. Shannon is himself delighted with it and Miss Bruce, a sculptor . . . told me to-day that she thinks it one of the finest he has ever done, and extraordinarily like" (*L* 509). But a few days earlier Yeats gave a franker and less enthusiastic report to Florence Farr: "His portrait, certainly not flattering, is one of his grave distinguished old masterish things" (*L* 507).

At the other extreme among the *Collected Works* portraits were ones which he decried, usually privately but sometimes publicly, because they showed a personality with which he did not wish to be associated. His unpainterly lack of regard for technique is apparent in his willingness, even if at one of the highest pitched moments in the arguments over the 1908 *Collected Works*, to praise Antonio Mancini's excitingly rapid but otherwise clumsy and quite unremarkable pastel portrait as "a master work of one of the greatest living painters" (*L* 504). The publisher, Bullen, who did not share Yeats's enthusiasm, had refused, a month earlier, to consider the drawing for use as a frontispiece.[30] Although the Mancini finally was used in the *Collected Works*, it, alone among the four portraits from the *Collected Works*, was never reused in any of his later books, even though he owned the portrait and even though a photo-engraved plate was available.[31]

The personality shown in that rather wild portrait was, in Yeats's estimation, useful to him, but only for counteracting the equally unwelcome interpretations by his other portraitists. Yeats announced, "Mancini, who was filled me with joy, has turned me into a sort of Italian bandit, or half bandit-half cafe king, certainly a joyous Latin, impudent, immoral, and reckless." Yeats thought that although none of those characteristics had the slightest connection with his personality, they might be useful for giving the lie to the "emaciated" figure in J. B. Yeats's November 1896 portrait of him, to the "tinker" in Augustus John's 1907 etching (plate 8), and to the "idealist" whom Yeats accurately forecast would be seen in Shannon's then-unstarted oil portrait. At the same time, of course, the Mancini portrait itself would be given the lie. In the absence of any one portrait that exactly expressed the image of himself that Yeats kept in his mind's eye, he would undercut the power of each portrait by providing contrasting ones.

During the protracted struggle to assemble appropriate portraits for the 1908 *Collected Works*, Yeats treated the Augustus John etching of him with a revealing combination of disgust, fear, and admiration. John's etching carried the authority of a well-known artist and therefore should have been a welcomed contribution to Yeats's campaign to mould a strongly artistic and poetic image of himself in the eyes of his readers.

Certainly John's deservedly praised talent as a draughtsman found plenty of concentrated exercise in the "numberless" (*L* 492) drawings (five heads are extant) and three oil studies made at Coole Park in September 1907 and then in five etched copper plates, the last of which was revised three times before reaching its final state. Yeats's intense dislike of the portrait was not based on the treatment of his favourite portrait emblems, for John dutifully included Yeats's loose tie, soft collar, dark coat, and tousled hair (the printing reversal of the etching makes his hair appear to fall across his right brow rather than his left). And although John's treatment of light and shadow strongly emphasises a crease running down Yeats's cheek, the etching is at least somewhat more flattering than Mancini's rapid, sketchy pastel. William Rothenstein, who thought the etching "admirable", recalled that Yeats "didn't think John's etching did justice to his looks".[32] Lady Gregory's judgement of it was resolutely uncomplicated. She wrote to John Synge, "John has done such a horrible etching of Yeats!" and then to John Quinn, "John has done a terrible etching of Yeats. . . . It is rather heartbreaking . . . for he did so many studies of him here, and took so much of his time. . . . But if they are not like Yeats, and are like a tinker in the dock, or a charwoman at a prayer meeting[,] they and the plate shall go into the fire."[33]

Yeats, while no less firm than Lady Gregory in disliking it as an "ugly gypsy" portrait of himself, did admit to its merits as a drawing, per se. He called the portrait "powerful", "very fine", "wonderful", and even "beautiful" (*L* 493, 502, 504). And he cautioned Bullen, who at one point had refused to consider either the Mancini pastel or the John etching as a suitable frontispiece,[34] to "remember that all fine artistic work is received with an outcry, with hatred even" and to "suspect all work that is not" (*L* 504). But, in Yeats's view, the John etching was "useless for my special purpose" and "fanciful as a portrait" because John had translated him into a "drunken, unpleasant and disreputable" tinker or "a melancholy English Bohemian" or "a gypsy, grown old in wickedness and hardship" (*L* 496, 502, 504) or a ruffian.[35] The key term here is "translated", for while Yeats greatly valued artistic individuality, the individual portraitist needed to have values with which Yeats could agree if Yeats were to be able to accept the work of art through which the artist gave expression to his or her values. Quite simply, John's values were so alien to those of Yeats that no matter how talented John might be, his works of art were disfigured, in Yeats's view, by the stamp of John's values. Yeats explained this to Bullen by saying, "I myself am not a Johnite. His work is an expression, as are Ibsen's plays, of the [modern, realistic] school opposed to everything I care for or try to accomplish myself."[36] Yeats found a willing listener in Bullen, who was decidedly not a "Johnite", but even when Yeats confronted Rothenstein and Quinn, who were "Johnites", Yeats did not back down on this basic aesthetic issue. Just after John had finished the preliminary sketches, Yeats explained to Quinn, "I feel rather a martyr going to him" because despite John's skill as a draughtsman, "he makes everybody perfectly hideous", which, of course, is "beautiful" according to John's "own standard".[37] In John's letters written during the visit to Coole when he drew Yeats, John reported that Yeats was "most delightful", and then, only partly in jest, that "nobody seems to know him but me". Yeats, he continued, "is now 44 and a robust, virile and humorous personality (while still the poet of course). I cannot see in him any definite resemblance to the youthful Shelley in a lace collar. To my mind he is far more interesting as he is, as maturity is more interesting than immaturity". But because Yeats, like his friends such as Lady Gregory, has a "natural and sentimental prejudice in favour of the W. B. Yeats he and other people have been accustomed to see and imagine for so many years. . . . My unprejudiced vision must seem brutal and unsympathetic to those in whom direct vision is supplanted by a vague and sentimental memory. Is it difficult also to assure people that my point of view is not that of a particularly ill-natured camera – but on the contrary that of a profoundly sympathetic and clairvoyant intelligence." John ended with an affirmation: "I never paint without admiring."[38] Those pronouncements might suggest that John would have portrayed Yeats sympathetically as a mature poet of the new century and no longer a wanderer in the Celtic twilight. But because Yeats's notion of the mature decorousness that would be appropriate to a poet whose *Collected Works* were about to be published in eight, quarter-vellum volumes differed so radically from John's standards, no portrait could meet Yeats's requirements and still please John.

The John etching was not used in the *Collected Works*, even though at the very last minute Yeats had told Bullen to print it (*L* 551). Yeats, however, probably knew that there was little chance that Bullen would print it because all four of the plates used were probably already in hand and, further, that Bullen disliked the John etching.

Two decades later, when Yeats next sat to John for a portrait, John found the poet "now a mellow, genial and silver haired old man" who regaled John "with anecdotes".[39] In the two portraits from those 1930 sittings, Yeats looks at us (and at the artist) with a spritely, sparkling gaze that suggests a lively sympathy between sitter and artist, particularly in the smaller, unfinished portrait.[40] The success of those 1930 portraits – Yeats thought the finished one (plate 9), "a fine portrait" and the unfinished one "amusing" –[41] and the comforting safety of his quarter-century of separation from the image in John's 1907 portraits probably led Yeats to publish, in the 1933 *Collected Poems* (Wade no. 171/172), the 1907 John oil portrait that was the least "tinker"-like of the preliminary studies for the 1907 etching. In 1932 he had suggested the 1930 John portrait for use in the never-published Macmillan *Edition de*

Luxe; the painting was used in *Dramatis Personae* (1936, Wade no. 186/187). Finally, in 1934, he felt confident enough to ask Macmillan to use the 1907 etching, in *A Vision* (1937, *Wade* no. 191/192).[42]

In 1908 Yeats regarded his father's portraits of him only slightly more favourably than those by John. Of the four portraits that were published in the 1908 *Collected Works*, the portrait by J. B. Yeats was consigned to last place, in volume 7. And in a March 1908 letter to the publisher, Yeats had objected to his father's portraits, "because he has always sentimentalized me" (*L* 505). But even if, as Yeats claimed, his father always viewed him "through a mist of domestic emotion" (*L* 502), his father managed to catch enough glimpses of him through that mist to be able to complete some 35 portrait drawings and paintings of him. But none of the 13 drawings, watercolours, and oils made between 1894 and 1904 has the vitality found in J. B. Yeats's more successful portraits of other sitters. The November 1896 watercolour portrait which Bullen had published two times prior to its use in the 1908 *Collected Works*, and which he also used in 1913, is far less successful than a 1900 oil that was not conveniently available for photo-engraving for the *Collected Works* because the portrait had been in John Quinn's collection in New York since 1902.[43]

Part of the weakness of J. B. Yeats's portraiture of his son, especially from the mid-1890s and onwards, results from the lack of attention paid to the sitter's eyes, which, admitted, were small and were partially obscured by his glasses. As a consequence, J. B. Yeats's portraits of his son lack the strong eye-contact that occurs when the sitter in a portrait looks straight out at the viewer. The resulting eye-contact creates an impression of immediacy – that the sitter is "here", almost in the same room as the viewer. A stunningly successful instance of this is J. B. Yeats's 1901 oil portrait of Lily Yeats, in which she looks directly at the viewer. Her calm, poised gaze is riveting.[44] If, on the other hand, th sitter looks off to the side or even slightly away from the viewer, the lack of direct eye-contact suggests that the sitter is more distant, abstracted, or aloof – that the sitter is "there" rather than "here". This difference, and its resulting loss of visual impact, can be seen in J. B. Yeats's best portraits of his son, for example, the 1900 oil in John Quinn's collection. Even though that portrait shows his son's eyes with strong highlights and much more clearly than any other of the J. B. Yeats paintings or drawings of him, and even though his left eye looks straight out at the viewer, the right eye is slightly out of coordination with the left eye and looks slightly off to the side. The result is that the portrait, even without considering the slight distraction of his pince-nez glasses, is powerless by comparison with J. B. Yeats's portrait of Lily Yeats.

Yeats's displeasure with his portraits by his father probably was also reinforced both by his father's preference for posing him with his head turned so that the lock of hair on his left brow was partially obscured and by the lack of prominence his father's portraits paid to the emblematic loose black tie, which often merges indistinctly with the black coat.

W. B. Yeats insisted that art must be founded upon the personal vision of an imaginative individual artist, and that, as he had announced in 1905, "the greater the art the more surprising the vision; all bad art is founded upon impersonal types and images, accepted by average men and women out of imaginative poverty and timidity" (*Ex* 94). But whenever a portrait artist's imaginative, individual vision was directed at W. B. Yeats, the resulting portrait was useful to the poet only if the portrait also happened to articulate W. B. Yeats's equally imaginative, individual vision of himself – in his public role as "Poet". That rigid criterion did not diminish his interest in portraiture, but when each of the completed portraits of him failed to meet that criterion, Yeats found little reason to admire the portraits and he kept very few of them with him. As we have noted, Yeats's personal art collection contained a large number of portraits of other people, but very few portraits of himself. Similarly, he showed perhaps less interest than we might otherwise expect in having portraits of himself published in his books. Only five of the eleven paintings or drawings of him used in his books were published more than once during his lifetime.[45] The seven or eight portraits of himself that were among the eighteen illustrations he proposed in 1938 for Scribner's never-published "Dublin" edition of his works included only two additions to the list of his portraits already published in his books, and neither of those drawings was recent: William Strang's 1903 drawing that Yeats had presented to the National Gallery of Ireland (no. 2729) in 1923 while a member of its Board of Governors and Guardians, and William Rothenstein's 1923 chalk drawing that the artist had just published in *Contemporaries: Portrait Drawings*, October 1937 (p. 110).

It is both amusing and instructive that the portrait which may well have given Yeats the most pleasure might have been Edmund Dulac's safely disguised portrait of Yeats as "Giraldus", in the extravagantly serio-comic front matter of *A Vision*. This ink drawing, commissioned by Yeats as an imitation of the style of a sixteenth-century woodcut, shows a bearded figure with an archly raised eyebrow that sweeps into the bridge of the nose in a manner very closely resembling Dulac's 1915 caricature of Yeats.[46] In the fictional letter appended to the "Stories of Michael Robartes" materials (written 1930, slightly revised 1936) in the front matter of the second edition of *A Vision*, "John Aherne" reports to "Mr. Yeats" that "John Duddon" has noticed "a resemblance between your face and that of Giraldus" in the "woodcut" (*AV[B]* 55). Here then was an amusing and arcanely "private" portrait that he could publish with none of the "public" risks that usually attended his portraiture. The possibility even exists that one of Yeats's reasons for retaining the elaborate Giraldus-Judwalis framing apparatus in the second edition of *A Vision* was a desire to reprint Dulac's portrait of Giraldus, complete with the newly added public hint about its "resemblance" to "Mr. Yeats".

NOTES

1. Austin Clarke, "Glimpses of W. B. Yeats", *Shenandoah*, 16, no. 4 (Summer 1965) 35–6. Clarke's memory of the statement is general rather than precise, for in 1920 only the two Irish galleries on his list owned portraits of Yeats.
2. Herbert E. A. Furst, *Portrait Painting: Its Nature and Function* (London: Lane, 1927) p. 68 and plate xx, which shows both Whistler's "Arrangement in Grey and Black, No. 2: Portrait of Thomas Carlyle", 1872–73, oil on canvas, 171 × 144 cm, City Art Gallery, Glasgow (purchased in 1891 for £1000) and Greaves's "Thomas Carlyle" (which fetched only 26 guineas at auction in 1924 and 34 guineas in 1932).
3. *Au* 404–5. Manet's pastel (1879, 55 × 34 cm, Metropolitan Museum of Art, New York; Jamot and Wildenstein, no. 365; Orienti, no. 278B) was aptly nicknamed "Le Noyé Repêché" (The man fished out of the water).
4. George Moore, *Hail and Farewell! Ave* (London: Heinemann, 1911) pp. 293–5.
5. 1891, bronze, height 50 cm, Musée Rodin, Paris. See John L. Tancock, *The Sculpture of Auguste Rodin* (Philadelphia Museum of Art, 1976) pp. 521–2 and illus. 90–3, p. 524.
6. "His Phoenix" (1916) *VP* 353 and the MS version quoted by A. N. Jeffares, *A Commentary on the Collected Poems of W. B. Yeats* (Stanford: Stanford University Press, 1968) p. 185.
7. The only extant self-portrait drawing is a very rough sketch intended as a Golden Dawn diagram rather than a portrait: "Self-portrait with planets (7) in proper places." (Coll. Senator Michael Yeats [microfilm at Yeats Archives, State University of New York, Stony Brook, no. 11.3.64].)
8. *VP* 444. "Without the Twilight", *The Arrow*, Summer 1939, p. 14; rpt. in *Scattering Branches*, ed. Stephen Gwynn (London: Macmillan, 1940) p. 138.
9. Katharine Tynan, "William Butler Yeats", *Magazine of Poetry*, 1 (October 1889) 454, rpt. in *W. B. Yeats Letters to Katharine Tynan*, Roger McHugh (ed.) (New York: McMullen, 1953) p. 174 note. Padraic Colum, [Thomas Davis lecture, Radio Éirèann] in *The Yeats We Knew*, Francis Macmanus (ed.) (Cork: Mercier Press, 1965) p. 15. Cornelius Weygandt, *On the Edge of Evening* (New York: Putnam's, 1946) p. 147. Jessie B. Rittenhouse, *My House of Life: an Autobiography* (Boston: Houghton Mifflin, 1934) p. 232. Mrs Claude Beddington [Frances Ethel Homan-Mulrock], *All that I have Met* (London: Cassell, 1929) p. 179, 178: Yeats "used to create a small sensation among the lovely ladies at my . . . parties, with whom he was something of a cult". Shotaro Oshima, ["An Interview with Mr. Junzo Sato,"] *W. B. Yeats and Japan* (Tokyo: Hokuseido Press, 1965) p. 121. Stephen Spender, *World within World* (New York: Harcourt Brace, 1951) p. 148.
10. Roy Pascal, *Design and Truth in Autobiography* (Cambridge, Mass.: Harvard University Press, 1960) p. 189.
11. AE ltr. to George Moore, quoted in John Eglinton [William M. Magee], *A Memoir of AE* (London: Macmillan, 1937) p. 110. Ronsley, p. 2.
12. Alvin Langdon Coburn, *Alvin Langdon Coburn: Photographer: an Autobiography*, Helmet and Alison Gernsheim (eds) (New York: Praeger, 1966) p. 70.
13. William R. Rodgers, "W. B. Yeats: A Dublin Portrait" (transcript of BBC broadcast, June 1949), rpt. in *In Excited Reverie*, A. N. Jeffares and K. G. W. Cross (eds) (New York: Macmillan, 1965) p. 3 has an amusing account of Yeats's single try, under the careful supervision of F. R. Higgins. Yeats remained only a moment or two!
14. George Moore, *Evelyn Innes* (1898), and *Hail and Farewell! Ave* (1911); for Yeats's contribution to a revised edition of *Evelyn Innes*, see *LTWBY* 44–5. Aleister Crowley, "At the Fork of the Road" (1909), *Moonchild: A Prologue* (1929), and *The Spirit of*

Solitude: An Autohagiography subsequently re-Antichristened The Confessions of Aleister Crowley (1929). In the last of those, Crowley spitefully and inaccurately described Yeats as "a lank dishevelled demonologist who might have taken more pains with his personal appearance without incurring the reproach of dandyism". (*The Confessions of Aleister Crowley: An Autohagiography*, John Symonds and Kenneth Grant (eds) [New York: Hill and Wang, 1970] p. 177.)

15. Harold Speakman, *Here's Ireland* (New York: Dodd, Mead, 1927) p. 306.
16. Edmund Dulac, "Without the Twilight", *The Arrow*, Summer 1939, p. 14; rpt. in *Scattering Branches*, ed. Gwynn, p. 138.
17. Illustrated: Theodore Spicer-Simson, *Men of Letters of the British Isles: Portrait Medallions from the Life* (New York: Rudge, 1924), facing p. 131; Oliver St. John Gogarty, *William Butler Yeats: A Memoir* (Dublin: Dolmen, 1963), frontispiece; Richard J. Finneran, *The Olympian & the Leprechaun: W. B. Yeats and James Stephens* (Dublin: Dolmen, 1978), frontispiece (and front cover).
18. *L* 382; see illustrations in *The Sphere*, 13, no. 176 (6 June 1903) 220 (accompanying a review of *Ideas of Good and Evil*); *The Bookman* (London) 27 (January 1905), front cover (cropped); *The American Monthly Review of Reviews* 46 (December 1912) 751 (cropped); Cornelius Weygandt, *On the Edge of Evening* (New York: Putnam's, 1946) facing p. 108.
19. *L* 503–5; Wade misread "Lafayette" as "Lytton" in the second letter. See also "Samhain: 1908," section IV (*Ex* 237). This 1894 photograph by Lafayette is illustrated in *L* facing 146; D. J. Gordon, *W. B. Yeats: Images of a Poet* (Manchester University Press, 1961), plate 1; and William M. Murphy, *Prodigal Father: The Life of John Butler Yeats (1839–1922)* (Ithaca: Cornell University Press, 1978) p. 176. The general competence of Lafayette's firm was not at issue here, for Lafayette in January 1924 was to take the photograph that Yeats sent to well-wishing friends on the occasion of his Nobel prize. (WBY ltr. to Mrs Beddington, 9 February 1924, quoted in Mrs Claude Beddington [Frances Ethel Homan-Mulrock], *All that I have Met* [London: Cassell, 1929] p. 178 and photograph facing p. 178; also illustrated in *Senate Speeches of W. B. Yeats*, Donald R. Pearce (ed.) [Bloomington: Indiana Univ. Press, 1960], facing p. 30; Hugh Hunt, *Abbey Theatre*, plate 1, facing p. 114; Peter Kavanagh, *The Story of the Abbey Theatre* [New York: Devin-Adair, 1950], between pp. 116 and 117.)
20. Portraits of Yeats were published in these books: *Wade* no. 1, 17/18/19/20, 24, 35/36/37/38, 75, 77, 81, 83, 99, 100, 128, 133, 139/140, 151/152/198, 153, 154, 165, 171/172, 173, 177/178, 186/187, 191/192, 198. In 1932 Yeats categorically excluded any consideration of using portrait photographs in the never-published Macmillan *Edition de Luxe* (Harold Macmillan unpublished ltr. to Yeats, 15 April 1932, coll. Senator Michael Yeats [microfilm at Yeats Archives, State University of New York, Stony Brook, no. 1.6.119]). No portrait photographs were used until 1953 in New York editions or until 1961 in London editions. I exclude a photograph of John Quinn and Yeats, taken by Arnold Genthe in 1914, which Quinn published as the frontispiece to a privately printed edition (*Wade* no. 109) of only 25 copies presented to guests at a farewell dinner given by Quinn, 1 April 1914, at the end of Yeats's American tour.
21. For the possible influence of Yeats's attitude to masks in relation to the 1908 *Collected Works* portraits, see Elizabeth W. Bergmann, "Yeats's Gallery", *Colby Library Quarterly*, 15 (1979) 130–1.
22. *L* 509. Dulac's caricature, c. 1919–20, present whereabouts unknown, is illustrated in Martin Birnbaum, *The Last Romantic* (New York: Twayne, 1960) p. 137.
23. Martin Birnbaum, *John Singer Sargent: January 12, 1856–April 15, 1925: A Conversation Piece* (New York: Rudge's, 1941) p. 26.
24. *Wade* no. 75, 128, 139/140, 165, 177/178.
25. Oshima, *Yeats and Japan*, p. 116 (in 1938); they acquired this half-size reproduction between 1908 and 1923; it is now in the collection of Miss Anne Yeats.
26. The four extant portraits of himself are by William Rothenstein (1898, lithograph and 1923 drawing [reproduction]); Antonio Mancini (1907, pastel); and Mary Klauder (Mrs Jones) (1936, bronze head). Yeats might have owned two chalk drawings (not

extant) by an unidentified Madame Tronsky (1903) and an Augustus John reproduction (not extant) (1907 or 1930). He apparently did not share my enjoyment of William
Rothenstein's striking 1898 lithographic drawing of him, for when Yeats saw it for the
first time in a shop window he wrote to Lady Gregory that it was a reasonably good
portrait, but was of a self whom he disliked and had long struggled with. (18 May
[1898], Berg Collection, New York Public Library.) Yeats framed and kept the
lithograph that Rothenstein gave him, but a deep stain under the cracked framing
glass suggests that this portrait was not hung during at least the latter portion of his
lifetime.

27. 114 × 109 cm, Houghton Library, Harvard University.
28. *L* 505; Yeats had made the same statement to John Quinn in the unpublished portion
of a letter of 7 January 1908 (Berg Collection, New York Public Library).
29. John Quinn, with the assistance of Robert Gregory, commissioned the painting for
£100, which was only one-third of Shannon's usual fee.
30. WBY unpublished ltr. to Quinn, 7 February [1908], Berg Collection, New York Public
Library.
31. Yeats did, however, prefer it to the Shannon portrait for use in the never-published
Macmillan *Edition de Luxe* in 1932, along with the Sargent and J. B. Yeats portraits
from the 1908 *Collected Works* (Harold Macmillan unpublished ltr. to Yeats, 15 April
1932, coll. Senator Michael Yeats [microfilm at Yeats Archives, State University of
New York, Stony Brook, no. 1.6.119].)
32. William Rothenstein, *Men and Memories*, II, 145.
33. Ltr. to Synge, [21 December 1907], in *Theatre Business*, Ann Saddlemyer (ed.)
(University Park: Pennsylvania State Univ. Press, 1982) p. 259; ltr. to Quinn, quoted
by Michael Holroyd, *Augustus John*, p. 261.
34. WBY unpublished ltr. to Quinn, 7 February [1908], Berg Collection, New York Public
Library.
35. Ibid.; see also L 493.
36. Frank C. Nelick, "Yeats, Bullen, and the Irish Drama," *Modern Drama*, 1, no. 3
(December 1958), 196–202; quoted in *Theatre Business*, p. 259.
37. 4 October 1907, Berg Collection, New York Public Library (excerpted L 496).
38. John ltrs. to Alick Schepeler, quoted by Michael Holroyd, *Augustus John*, pp. 263, 261.
39. Augustus John, "Fragment of an Autobiography – V," *Horizon*, 4 (1941) 291.
40. Oil, coll. Col. Eric Phillips, Toronto (in 1952), illus. Arland Ussher, *Three Great
Irishmen* (New York: Devin-Adair, 1953, 1952), facing p. 63. (The London: Gollancz,
1952 edition lacks illustrations.)
41. WBY unpublished ltr. to Lady Gregory, 30 July [1930], National Library of Ireland,
MS 18747.
42. Harold Macmillan unpublished ltrs to Yeats, 15 April 1932 and 12 September 1934,
coll. Senator Michael Yeats (microfilm at Yeats Archives, State University of New
York, Stony Brook, nos. 1.6.119 and 127).
43. *Wade* no. 24 (1897), 35/36/37/38 (1902), 81 (1908), W83 (2nd issue only, 1913); (1900,
oil, 77 × 64 cm, Hugh Lane Municipal Gallery of Modern Art, no. [299]/National
Gallery of Ireland, no. 872.) J. B. Yeats said, of the 1900 oil: "I am glad to say that at
last, after only three sittings, I have painted a good portrait of Willie" (*Letters from
Bedford Park: A Selection from the Correspondence [1890–1901] of John Butler Yeats*, William
M. Murphy (ed.) [Dublin: Cuala Press, 1972] p. 59).
44. 91 × 71 cm, National Gallery of Ireland, no. 1180; illus., James White, *J. B. Yeats and
the Irish Renaissance* (Dublin: Dolmen Press, 1972) plate 5.
45. *JBY*, 1886, ink (as a period piece) in *Wade* no. 151/152 (1926/1927), 198 (1938); *JBY*, 28
January 1899, pencil in *Wade* no. 17 (1899) and eight reissues; *JBY*, November 1896,
watercolour in *Wade* no. 24 (1899), 81 (1908), 83 (2nd issue only, 1913); Sargent, 1908,
charcoal in *Wade* no. 75 (1908), 128 (1921), 165 (1929), 139/140 (1923/1924), 165
(1929), 177/178 (1934/1935); Charles Shannon, 1908, oil in *Wade* no. 77 (1908), 133
(1922), 151/152 (1926/1927), 198 (1938).

46. "Portrait of Giraldus," 1923 (sketched 1918), ink, illustrated in *AV(A)* frontispiece, *Stories of Michael Robartes and his Friends (Wade* no. 167), facing p. 24; *AV(B)* 39. "W. B. Yeats and the Irish Theatre", 1915, watercolour and ink on board, National Gallery of Ireland (no. 2981), illustrated in Frank Tuohy, *Yeats* (London: Macmillan, 1971) p. facing p. 188.

PRELIMINARY CHECKLIST OF PORTRAITS OF W. B. YEATS

(Readers who have any additional information on these or other portraits of W. B. Yeats are invited to write 'to the author at 117 Burrowes Building, University Park, PA 16802, USA)

(Dimensions: height × width. Posthumous portraits excluded.)

Key to Abbreviations:
MGofMA: Hugh Lane Municipal Gallery of Modern Art, Dublin
NGI: National Gallery of Ireland, Dublin
NLI: National Library of Ireland, Dublin
NPG: National Portrait Gallery, London
Oxford: Ashmolean Museaum, Oxford
Sligo: County Library and Museum, Sligo
Tate: Tate Gallery, London
Texas: Humanities Research Center, University of Texas at Austin
Yeats: Senator Michael Yeats, Dalkey, Co. Dublin

BARKER, George, [date unknown], ink, coll. Texas, no. 66.99.

BEERBOHM, Max, 1899, ink, "Celtades Ambo", (caricature), coll. Robert H. Taylor, Princeton.

——, [1900], ink, [George Moore and WBY clutching a harp and perched on a steeple], (caricature), coll. W. A. Clark Library, UCLA.

——, [1899–1904], ink and wash, 31.8 × 19.9 cm, "Mr. W. B. Yeats Presenting Mr. George Moore to the Queen of the Fairies", (caricature), coll. MGofMA, no. 14468.

——, [?c.1900], ink and watercolour, 32 × 19 cm, "W. B. Yeats", (caricature), coll. MGofMA (ex-coll. NGI, no. 3773).

——, [1901], drawing, (caricature), not extant.

——, 1913, drawing, "Members of the Academic Committee of the Royal Society of Literature . . .", (caricature), coll. [J. C. Thomson].

——, 1916, drawing, "Won't it be rather like 'Rep'?" coll. [Sir Charles Forte].

——, 1924, ink, "Are you saved?" (caricature), coll. Oxford.

——, 1925, ink, "Some Persons of 'the Nineties' . . .", (caricature), coll. Oxford.

——, [1932–1933], drawing, "Shades of Rossetti, Ruskin, Swinburne, Pater and Whistler . . . this other later Romantic [WBY] . . .", (caricature), not extant.

BRUCE, Kathleen (later Mrs. Scott; Lady Kennet), [April] 1908, sculpture (plaster life-mask, bronzed), 17½ in. height, coll. NPG, no. 3644 and 3644a.

BRYDEN, Robert, [c.1899], woodcut (from a photograph).

CAVERS, J., [date unknown], oil, coll. Texas, no. 67.39.

CHUTE, Desmond, 1929, pencil, coll. Texas, no. 65.314.

DULAC, Edmund, 1915, watercolour and ink on board, 35.6 × 29.0 cm, "W. B. Yeats and the Irish Theatre", (caricature), coll. NGI, no. 2981.

——, 1918, drawing, "Portrait of Giraldus", (caricature), coll. Yeats.

——, 1923, ink, "Portrait of Giraldus", (caricature).

GREGORY, Robert, [?c.1900], drawing (sketch of hair and eye-brows only), (ex-coll. Lady Gregory).

GYLES, Althea, [c.1899], ink, coll. British Library.

HORTON, William T., [1898], ink, 15.6 × 10.0 cm, (caricature), coll.Emory Univ. Library (ex-coll. Lady Gregory).

——, [1899], ink, 12.7 × 10.2 cm, (caricature), coll. George Harper (ex-coll. the artist).

JOHN, Augustus, [1907], pencil,
24.8 × 21.6 cm, study (2 on one sheet),
coll. Tate Gallery, no. 5298.

——, [1907], chalk, study (2 on one sheet),
coll. Cummings Catherwood,
Philadelphia (in 1941).

——, [1907], pencil and wash, 13½ × 7½ in,
coll. NPG, no. 4105.

——, [1907], oil sketch (monochrome),
24 × 17½ in, coll. Lady Dunn, Canada
(after 1961) (ex-coll. Gogarty).

——, [1907], oil, 50.5 × 45.5 cm, coll.
Tate, no. 5218.

——, [1907], oil, coll. City Art Gallery,
Manchester (ex-coll. Lady Gregory).

——, [1907], etching, 17.8 × 12.5 cm.

——, [1907], etching, 15.1 × 10.1 cm.

——, [1907], etching, 17.8 × 12.8 cm.

——, [1907], etching, 17.6 × 12.8 cm.

——, [1907], etching and dry-point,
17.4 × 12.5 cm.

——, 1930, oil, 122 × 97 cm, coll. Glasgow
City Art Gallery (Kelvingrove),
no. 1817.

——, [1930], oil (unfinished), coll. Phillips,
Toronto (in 1952).

KAPP, Edmond, 1914, drawing, coll.
Barber Institute of Fine Arts,
Birmingham Univ.

KEATING, Sean, [c.1924], oil,
72 × 82 in., "Homage to Sir Hugh
Lane", coll. MGofMA (NGI trans.
1970).

KERNOFF, Harry, [?1934], pastel,
13¼ × 9¾ in., coll. Texas, no. 65.60.

——, [?1934], woodcut, 13.8 × 9.4 cm,
coll. Texas. (Same pose as Texas,
no. 65.60.)

——, 1934, pastel, 38.1 × 28 cm, coll.
Texas, no. 65.306.

——, [?1934], oil, 5¼ × 7½ in., coll.
Deighton Bell & Co., Cambridge (in
1965). (Same pose as 1934 pastel.)

——, 1934, [15 × 12 in. (?frame)], pastel.

KLAUDER, Mary (Mrs. Jones), 1936,
sculpture (bronze head), 24.5 cm
(height), coll. Anne Yeats.

LALOR, Tom, [?c.1907], ink, "Yeats
addressing the audience . . .",
(caricature), coll. NLI.

LE GALLIENNF,Gwen, [1938], pencil,
26.3 × 21.9 cm. coll. Texas, no. 65.178.

"M", [1916], ink, "Yeats, Mr. Ito and the
Hawk", (caricature).

"Mac" [MACNIE, S. M.], [c.1923], ink,
"Chin-Angles or – How the Poets
Passed", (caricature).

——, 1923, ink and wash, "The Elbow"
(3-frame cartoon), (caricature).

MANCINI, Antonio, 1907, coloured
pastel, 57.9 × 45.6 cm, coll, Anne Yeats.

"Matt" [UNKNOWN ARTIST], [March
1919–July 1921], ink, "Famous People as
'Matt' Sees Them – No. 53. W. B.
Yeats". (caricature), *Daily Dispatch*
[Manchester].

OAKLEY, Harold, [c.1905], ink.

OPFFER, Ivan, [December 1923],
lithograph, 31 × 24 cm. coll. Warwick
Gould.

——, 1932, charcoal, 46 × 30.7 cm, coll.
Texas, no. 69.139.

——,? 1932, chalk, 18½ × 12 in, coll. NPG,
no. 3965.

ORPEN, R. C., 1907, ink, "The Poet
addressed the Audience", (caricature).

ORPEN, William, 1907, ink, 8 × 5½ in,
"Lady Gregory, Hugh Lane, John M.
Synge, W. B. Yeats", (caricature), coll.
NPG, no. 4676.

O'SULLIVAN, Sean, 1933, crayon and
white, 47 × 34 cm, coll. NGI, no. 3537.

——, 1933, charcoal and chalk on grey
paper, 69 × 57 cm, coll. Sligo, no. 62.

——, 1934, oil, 127 × 102 cm, coll. Abbey
Theatre.

PAGET, Henry Marriott, 6 April 1899, oil,
coll. Ulster Museum, Belfast.

PATTERSON, James, 1906, pencil or
chalk.

PLUNKETT, Grace, [1907], [ink], "The
Rising of the Moon", (caricature).

POWER, Albert, 1917–18, sculpture
(bronze head on rough wooden base),
35.3 cm (height), coll. Texas, no. 65.302.

PURSER, Sarah, [?c.1898], coloured
pastel, 17 × 10 in, coll. MGofMA,
no. 14047 (NGI trans. 1970).

ROTHENSTEIN, William, 1897, pencil,
24.7 × 16.3 cm, coll. Texas, no. 65.177.

——, [1898], chalk (on lithographic
paper), coll. Lord Walston, UK.

——, 1898, lithograph, 29.8 × 18.8 cm.

[——, (attributed to)]. [?c.1900], ink and
crayon, 37.5 × 25.1 cm, coll. Texas,
no. 65.308 (ex-coll. Lady Gregory).

——, 1914, pencil, 9 × 4½ in, coll. Mrs J
Montgomery Sears, Boston (in 1926).

——, [1916], charcoal or soft pencil, 22 × 14 cm, coll. NGI, no. 3851.

——, [1916], pencil, 13½ × 10¼ in, coll. the artist (in 1926).

——, 1916, pencil, 7¼ × 4¼ in, coll. John Drinkwater, London (in 1926).

——, 1916, chalk or soft pencil, 23 × 19 cm, coll. MGofMA, no. 14423 (NGI trans. 1970).

——, 1916, pencil, 21 × 12 cm, coll. Leeds City Art Gallery.

——, [?1916], pencil, 30.8 × 22.2 cm, coll. Texas, no. 65.198.

——, 1923, chalk (sanguine and white), 10⅛ × 5⅜ in, coll. Laing Art Gallery, Newcastle-on-Tyne.

——, [late 1920s], pencil, coll. Mary Lago.

——, [c.1930s], sketch of WBY (perhaps with Dorothy Wellesley) at "Penns in the Rocks". not extant.

RUSSELL, George ("AE"). [?c.1885], pastel, 13 × 10 in, coll. Sligo, no. 61 (ex-coll. Lady Gregory).

[——], [?1897], pastel, 41 × 31 cm, coll. NGI, no. 2933 (ex-coll. Lady Gregory).

——, [?c.1900], ink on card (sketch), (ex-coll. Lady Gregory).

——, [?c.1900], drawing (unfinished sketch), ink on card, (ex-coll. Lady Gregory).

——, 1903, pastel, 45.1 × 31.6 cm, coll. NGI, no. 2988.

SARGENT, John Singer, 1908, charcoal, 62 × 47 cm, private collection, USA (in 1970) (ex-coll. John Quinn).

SHACKLETON, Kathleen, 1925, drawing, (photograph in Mary Evans Picture Library).

SHANNON, Charles H., 1908, drawing, not extant.

——, 1908, oil, 45 × 43½ in, coll. Houghton Library, Harvard Univ. (ex-coll. John Quinn).

SLOAN, John, 1913, ink (rough sketch in a letter), (caricature).

SMITH, Pamela Colman, 1901, ink (2 rough sketches in a letter), 2.8 × 4.5 cm (combined), (caricature), coll. Huntington Library, AP1677 (page 3).

——, [c.1903], drawing.

——, [c.1904], oil (perhaps taken from a drawing), coll. Ann Saddlemyer.

SPICER-SIMSON, Theodore, 1922, sculpture (medallion), coll. Anne Yeats; another copy NGI, no. 8215.

STRANG, William, 1903, drawing, 39 × 26 cm, coll. NGI, no. 2729.

——, [c.1903], chalk, coll. Fitzwilliam Museum, Cambridge.

TRONCEY (Madame), 1903, black chalk, not extant.

——, 1903, coloured [?chalk], not extant.

[UNKNOWN ARTIST: "German Symbolist in Paris"]. [1896–98], [?drawing], not extant.

WATTS-RUSSELL, Anthony (Tony) E., [?c.1900s] watercolour sketch on card, 29 × 22 cm, (ex-coll. Lady Gregory).

WOOLF, Samuel Johnson, 1932, charcoal and white chalk, coll. Texas, no. 70.62.

YEATS, Jack B., [1893–1909], [?stencil; "coloured lithograph"], not extant.

——, 1903, ink (rough sketch in a letter), (caricature), coll. William M. Murphy.

YEATS, J. B., [1866], drawing, 21 × 19 cm, [baby with cat], coll. Yeats.

——, [1866], pencil, 10 × 26 cm, [baby], coll. Yeats.

——, 1866, drawing, 10 × 7 cm, [baby seated on floor], coll. Yeats.

——, [c.1866], drawing, 25 × 18 cm, [baby seated in high chair], coll. Yeats.

——, [c.1870], drawing, 19.5 × 12 cm, [as a boy], coll. Yeats.

——, [c.1872], pencil, 24 × 17 cm, [as a boy], coll. Yeats.

——, [c.1874], pencil, [as a boy, hands in pockets], coll. Yeats.

——, [c.1875], pencil, [in chair, with a book], coll. Yeats.

——, [c.1875], pencil, (same sheet as Susan Pollexfen Yeats), coll. Yeats.

——, [?1883–1884], oil, 76.5 × 64.0 cm, [holding book with two hands], coll. MGofMA, no. 14299 (NGI trans. 1970).

——, [?c.1885], pencil, 10.7 × 13.5 cm, [moustache, no beard], coll. NLI.

——, [?c.1885–88], pencil, 20.9 × 12.2 cm (or perhaps 18.8 × 11.0 cm), coll. NLI.

——, [?c.1886–88], pencil, 18.8 × 11.0 cm (or perhaps 20.9 × 12.2 cm), [beard], coll. NLI.

——, [c.1886], "King Goll" (W. B. Yeats was the model) [?oil] painting, not extant.

——, January 1886, ink, 25.0 × 23.0 cm [head and shoulders], coll. Yeats.

——, [January] 1886, ink, 23.0 × 13.5 cm, [holds book in right hand], coll. Yeats.

——, [c.1888], pencil (2 sketches on one sheet), coll. Yeats.

——, [c.1888], pencil, 19 × 13.5 cm, coll. Yeats.

——, [c.1888–89], drawing, 12 × 19 cm, [in a lawn chair], coll. Yeats.

——, [c.1888–89], oil, 45 × 60 cm. [in a lawn chair], coll. Yeats.

——, [1889 or before], "The Cavalier's Wife" (perhaps W. B. Yeats was the model for the cavalier), probably chalk and charcoal or perhaps watercolour, not extant (ex-coll. W. B. Yeats).

——, June 1889, watercolour sketch, coll. Yeats.

——, [c.1894], pencil, ex-coll. Lennox Robinson.

——, March 1894, pencil, 8¾ × 12½ in, coll. Colby College.

——, [1896 or before], [illustration to "The Lake Isle of Innisfree"] (perhaps W. B. Yeats was the model), drawing, not extant.

——, November 1896, [?watercolour], not extant.

——, 8 December 1897, pencil, coll. Yeats. (Unconfirmed; perhaps identical with 8 Dec 1899, pencil.)

——, [?January] 1898, watercolour (or drawing with wash), coll. NGI, no. 2942. (ex-coll. Lady Gregory).

——, 28 January 1899, pencil, 23 × 19.5 cm, coll. Yeats.

——, 1899, pencil, coll. Yeats.

——, 1899, pencil, coll. City of Birmingham Museum and Art Gallery.

——, 8 December 1899, pencil, 17 × 12 cm, coll. Yeats. (Unconfirmed; perhaps identical with 8 Dec 1897, pencil.)

——, [c.1900], blue crayon, 10 × 7 in, Sotheby, Parke Bernet, London, sale 21 July 1983, lot 567 (ex-coll. Lady Gregory).

——, [January] 1900, oil, 77 × 64 cm, coll. MGofMA, no. [299]/NGI, no. 872 (ex-coll. John Quinn).

——, [c.1902], oil, 76 × 65 cm, coll. Sligo (permanent loan).

——, 3 June 1903, pencil, coll. Richard Londraville (ex-coll. John Quinn).

——, 20 March 1904, pencil, 19 × 13 cm, coll. Yeats.

——, 29 June 1904, pencil, coll. Yeats.

——, 1907, oil, 30 × 25 in, coll. William M. Murphy.

——, 13 April 1918, ink (rough sketch in a letter to W. B. Yeats).

——, 24 April 1918, ink (rough sketch in a letter to Lolly Yeats).

——, 1 June 1918, ink (rough sketch in a letter to Lolly Yeats).

YEATS, W. B., [mid-1890s], drawing (rough sketch diagram in a manuscript book), "Self-portrait with planets (7) in proper places".

STUDIO PORTRAIT PHOTOGRAPHS

[before Autumn 1889]. GLOVER, M. (Dublin).

[1890]. Frederick HOLLYER. (London), publ. 1893, 1901.

1894. LAFAYETTE. (Dublin).

[?1899 or perhaps 1903]. ELLIOTT & FRY. (Dublin), publ. 1903.

[?c.1900]. Frederick HOLLYER. (London).

[?c.1900s]. E. O. HOPPE. (London).

[c.1902]. RUSSELL & SONS. publ. 1905.

1902. CHANCELLOR. (Dublin), publ. 1903, 1905, 1912.

[c.1905]. G. C. BERESFORD. (London), coll. (print and negative) NPG. no. X6397 and X6623.

1904. Alice BOUGHTON. (USA), publ. 1904, 1905.

1908. Alvin Langdon COBURN. (Dublin), publ. (in a WBY book) 1910 (replaced 1913 ff.).

1908. ——, (Dublin).

1908. ——, (Dublin).

1911. Alice BOUGHTON. (USA), publ. 1911.

1914. Arnold GENTHE. (New York), publ. (in a WBY book, privately printed for Quinn) 1914.

1920. MELINDA. (USA), publ. 1920.

1920. UNDERWOOD & UNDERWOOD. (New York).

[?1920]. Sherril SCHNELL. (London).

1924. LAFAYETTE. (Dublin), publ. 1929.
1932. Pirie MACDONALD. (New York).
1932. ——, (New York).
1932. J. ROSS. (Dublin).
[1932–1933]. VOS, Martin. (New York).
1935. Howard COSTER. (London), coll.
(probably) NPG. no. AX3510.
X1961–65.
1935. ——.
1935. ——, (NPG probably has two additional negatives.)
[c.1935]. George A. FLEISCHMANN. (Dublin).

Yeats, Synge and the Georgians

Michael J. Sidnell

Much of the commentary on Yeats's poetry has been intensely concerned with the process of his development but there has been almost no attempt to correlate that process, in detail, with the poetic movements of the half-century or so that Yeats's career spanned. It is only the Yeats of the nineties who is seen in a clear relation to his contemporaries. Thereafter we have a split image of, on the one hand, the sustained coherence of Yeats's work and, on the other, of several revolutions each attempting to supplant, rather than to develop, the poetry of the previous régime. For such poetic continuity as there is in this period, Yeats's work is the prime evidence. Yeats, however, directed attention to the personal aspect of his poetic struggle and his poetry is so obviously the "flower" of a man, has such a richly satisfying autobiographical pattern, that we tend to lose sight of its general poetic context; and also of the fact that younger poets' work made a great impact on Yeats's poetic personality.

Indeed, the "anxiety of influence", in Yeats's case, seems to have had as much to do with poetic sons and brothers as with fathers; with Lionel Johnson, Synge, Joyce, D. H. Lawrence, Eliot, Pound and Auden. More basic even than Yeats's well-documented struggle for unity – and compounding its difficulty – were the battles, at various crises in his career, for poetic survival and, indeed, supremacy. His undiminishing capacity to adapt to momentous changes in literary and social sensibility and to incorporate new poetic tendencies into his work made him something of an intellectual nuisance in his later years. Middleton Murry's untimely assertion that *The Wild Swans at Coole* was "Mr. Yeats's 'swan song' ", that he was "empty, now", is a memorable example of the awkwardness of the fact of Yeats's capacity for poetic renewal.[1] T. S. Eliot tried to cope with Yeats's unseemly vitality, at this time, and keep him at a distance, by designating him "a foreign mind".[2] Michael Roberts' elegant solution to the problem of Yeats's continuing relevance, in 1936, was to invest him in an old mythology.[3] This met the demands of the age and also satisfied Yeats, who assumed with gusto the role of a mythical figure haunting the present.[4]

105

For the poets and critics of the thirties, the most awkward thing about Yeats was that, having been a predecessor and instigator of the modernist movement, he remained an active participant in it. His unflagging power suggested a continuous poetic development from the Victorians, through the Symbolist and Georgian movements right into the present; than which, nothing could have been more alien to the modernist perception of radical discontinuities in social and personal experience, and in poetry.

How Yeats survived into the second major phase of his career is what I am concerned with here; how he span out a poetic web that stretched from a symbolist to a realist poetic; how he prepared the way for the modernist revolution and ensured his own survival of it. This Yeatsian phase roughly corresponds in time and character to the so-called Georgian Movement and I have made use of the label, despite its limitations, in order to draw attention to the way in which Yeats was linked with a number of Georgian poets; linked chiefly by a common debt to John Synge.

John Masefield was one of the poets in whose work the influence of Synge was most strongly felt and, perhaps, transmitted. Masefield had become "Yeats's disciple" in 1900 and it was Yeats who, two years later, at one of his Mondays in Bloomsbury, introduced him to Synge.[5] As Masefield got to know Synge he discovered that he "felt curiously akin in mind to him".[6] He was impressed, above all, by the fact that Synge's "interest was in life, not in ideas."[7] And, as with the Georgians generally, it was on the attempt to make poetry a medium for observed and felt life that Masefield's realism, emulating Synge's, was based.

As to Yeats's direct relation with the Georgians, the reservations on both sides may be indicated by the fact that when Rupert Brooke suggested that the first volume of *Georgian Poetry* should be dedicated to Yeats, Edward Marsh, the compiler of those best-selling anthologies rejected the idea. He shrank, he said, from offering Yeats "a dedication from English poets. I somehow feel he would take it in the spirit of a lion receiving the homage of a dozen jackals."[8] Even after he decided that James Stephens should be included amongst the contributors Marsh insisted on the Englishness of the movement and thus helped to keep it out of Yeats's orbit. Years later Yeats observed in his Introduction to the *Oxford Book of English Verse* that "The *Shropshire Lad*", was "worthy of its fame, but a mile further and all had been marsh" [*OBMV* xiii]. A few miles beyond Housman nearly all *was* Marsh, so powerfully was English poetry and its reception affected by Marsh's promotion (which included the name "Georgian" itself) and patronage.

Yeats was on good terms with Marsh but he was not disposed to see the English civil servant as a latter-day Duke Ercole; nor to be listed on the historic roll of a poetic school named for the English King whom he invited the devil to take.[9] Nor, according to Ezra Pound, did he think much of the first volume of *Georgian Poetry*, which " '*no one*' could read with pleasure" and which he nevertheless kept in his rooms because "he 'ought to know something about these people' ".[10] Yet Yeats admitted to having once been in the same school as James Stephens, who managed to be a prominent Georgian and unequivocally Irish at the same time; to be, in effect, the undesignated Irish wing of the movement. [*OBMV* xli][11]

Stephens's role as an Irish poet fallen among Georgians was no more paradoxical than the fact that the movement itself was largely Irish in inspiration. It was above all the poetry, plays and manifestos of Synge enabled the Georgians to define their Englishness. Synge guided them in making a two-pronged attack on the ponderous, moralising, imperial sensibility of the high Victorians and on the aestheticism, neuroticism, urban cosmopolitanism, despair and metaphysical pretensions of the poets of the nineties; and it was Synge, preeminently, who directed the attention of the Georgians to regional subjects and to the poetry embodied in dialect speech. Thematically and linguistically some of them attempted to deal with Northumberland, Gloucestershire, Nottinghamshire or Cornwall as Synge had dealt with the Aran Islands and Wicklow. As Edward Thomas – who himself narrowly escaped the official "Georgian" brand – put it:

> the freedom and simplicity connected by them [the Georgians] with some forms of country life foster that cultivation of the instinctive and primitive which is the fine flower of a self-conscious civilization, turning in disgust upon itself.[12]

"Flower" is precisely *not* the word that Synge himself chose but it was the "cultivation of the instinctive and primitive" that he proposed as an alternative to *fin-de-siècle* attenuation on the one hand and linguistically pallid realism on the other. If literature was to recover a comprehensive sense of reality and a copious, energetic language, said Synge, it had to look to the lives and speech of rooted people: men and women whose lives and language were still shaped by forces of nature. It was in 1908 that he put up what soon became a familiar and compelling literary signpost:

> In these days poetry is usually the flower of evil or good, but it is the timber of poetry that wears most surely, and there is no timber that has not strong roots among the clay and worms . . . the strong things of life are needed in poetry . . . to show that what is exalted, or tender, is not made by feeble blood. It may be said that before verse can be human again it must learn to be brutal.[13]

Learning to be brutal had long been Synge's poetic discipline when he read "Danny" to Masefield in 1907.[14] In this poem the unsentimental realities of folk life displace the charm of folklore. Danny, the local bully and lecher, is ambushed by a gang "of Erris men" out for revenge. [*CWP* 56–7] Synge's description of the uneven battle in which Danny gives a good account of himself before he is beaten to death in the mud – his description of the nose-smashing, lip-splitting, biting, tripping, throttling, and destruction with the heels, is as full of gusto as it is devoid of any hint of poetic moralising or sympathy. Several years earlier Synge had begun to riddle myth with realism. In "Queens", for example, written in 1902, the lover cites "All the rare and royal names / Wormy sheepskin yet retains: / Etain, Helen, Maeve and Fand," etc. These "Queens who wasted the East by proxy, / Or drove the ass-cart, a tinker's doxy" were not only "eaten of fleas and vermin" in their lifetimes but now,

> are rotten – I ask their pardon –
> And we've the sun on rock and garden,
> These are rotten, so you're the Queen
> Of all are living, or have been (*CWP* 34)

There are only a few love poems in which physical corruption figures as prominently as in this one; and Synge's affirmation of such realities was in great contrast to Yeats's idealising treatment of love and mythological personages up to this time.

Yeats and others have given various reasons for the transformation in his verse that occurred shortly after the turn of the century. There was the general change in the literary climate of the new century; there were the premature deaths of a number of the poets of "the tragic generation". There was the non-occurrence of the expected Armageddon; and there was Yeats's acute disappointment over Maud Gonne. Whatever the part played by these factors, it is certain that the challenge to Yeats's poetic assumptions posed by Synge was by no means the least effective stimulus for Yeats as he re-shaped his poetic in that rather bleak period, as far as his lyric poetry was concerned, between the publication of *In the Seven Woods* in 1903 and that of *The Green Helmet and Other Poems* in 1910.

In England the direct influence of Synge was most strongly felt after his death. 1911 Masefield produced *The Everlasting Mercy*, the long poem that has been called "the seminal work of the new realistic school".[15] Seminal or not, it certainly sold; in such quantities as to reveal to Marsh and others an immense readership fairly gasping for poetry of some kind. "Here at last", as L. A. G. Strong remarked, "was a man who had followed Synge's precept and put into his poetry the life he knew."[16] The narrator of *The Everlasting Mercy*, it may be recalled, is Saul Kane, a tough, blasphemous, wenching, poaching, drink-sodden, rural sinner who in his unregenerate days runs naked through the town. On one occasion, he settles a quarrel with a fellow-poacher in an old-style boxing match. The episode displays that non-cerebral communion between men that Lawrence made one of his themes. They drove (a dodge that never fails)

> A pin beneath my finger nails.
> They poured what seemed a running beck
> Of cold spring water down my neck;
> Jim, with lancet quick as flies,
> Lowered the swellings round my eyes.
> They sluiced my legs and fanned my face
> Through all that blessed minute's grace
> They gave my calves a thorough kneading,
> They salved my cuts and stopped the bleeding
> A gulp of liquor dulled the pain . . .[17]

Since Kane repents, all the sin and sex is made morally palatable; and Masefield's treatment of violence was much too literary to cause offence.

Like other Georgian poets, and like Synge and Yeats before them, Masefield sought objectivity in playwriting. The dialogue of his *Tragedy of Nan* is in the Gloucestershire dialect. Its quaintness and the fact that the harshness of the action is unrelieved make the play seem something of an exercise in the depiction of the savagery of rural life. The monotony undermines the attempted realism, which might otherwise be intolerable. In Wilfred Gibson's series of short verse plays about "gangrels", or gypsies, we see an even stronger infusion from Synge. The struggle to lead the pack, ruthless sexual competition and the very naming of the characters – "Blackadder", "Red Rowan", "Weazel" – express the restoration of man to his place among the other animals, as in this sample from Gibson's dialogue:

> I'm master now
> As Nettle says; and I'll not let my doxy
> Be bossing me. By gox, I've stood enough
> From you and Weazel! He hooked it just in
> time
> To save his thrapple, the varmint: I'd have
> slit
> The weasands of the pair of you, I would,
> If I'd to swing for it. You give a squint
> At any other man; and I'll . . .[18]

In *Kestrel Edge*, a play about Northumberland Shepherds, Gibson attempted a new and English *Old Testament*. He portrayed a primitive society in which myth is still emerging from nature: the men fighting like rams over a favourite ewe; their pastoral occupation and stern tribality

all mixed up with their sex-drives in the earthiest way. Lascelles
Abercrombie, Gordon Bottomley and D. H. Lawrence were other
Georgian poet-playwrights in whose work the influence of Synge is
apparent.

Lawrence wrote to a friend in 1910 that he found Synge's "folk . . . too
bodiless, mere spirits" but, he added, "he is a great dramatist and I love
his work".[19] *Riders to the Sea* he thought "the genuinest bit of dramatic
tragedy, English, since Shakespeare".[20] And he excepted Synge from the
group of dramatists ("Shaw, Galsworthy and Barker and Irishy") that
his own plays were written in reaction against.[21] In *The Widowing of Mrs
Holroyd* of 1914 he attempted to capture the communal vitality and
linguistic vigour of the Nottinghamshire mining folk; and to convey the
emotion of the women whose menfolk who go down the pit, as Synge had
done in relation to the Aran Islanders and the sea. Lawrence's play is
concerned with sex in a way that has much more to do with theatrical
cliché than with Synge but in the scene between the young widow and
her mother-in-law, at the end of the play, we hear a clear echo of Synge.
The elder Mrs Holroyd laments the disasters that have befallen her sons:

> Eh, they'll bring 'im 'ome, I know they will, all smashed up and broke!
> An' one of me sons they've burned down pit till the flesh dropped off
> him, an' one was shot till 'is shoulder was all of a mosh, an' they
> brought 'em 'ome to me. An' now there's this . . .
> I'm sure I've had my share of bad luck, I have. I'm sure I've brought
> up five lads in the pit, through accidents and troubles, and now there's
> this. The Lord has treated me very hard, very hard . . .
> Haven't you put him by a pair o' white stockings nor a white shirt? . . .
> Then he'll have to have his father's . . .
> You don't want no other woman to touch him, to wash him and lay
> him out, do you?[22]

The theatrical situation here is parallel to that at the end of *Riders to the
Sea* where Maurya keens her sons and prepares the last of them for burial,
but that similarity would not be remarkable if Lawrence's rhetoric did
not pay Synge the tribute of what seems to be conscious imitation.

Lawrence was so far a Georgian that *The White Peacock* of 1911 remains
one of the best guides to the movement. When Cyril Beardsley returns to
his native place he finds that his perceptions are the keener for his recent
sojourn in an aesthetically sophisticated urban *milieu* but that his vital
powers have correspondingly diminished. He has become too desensual-
ised for the blood and the intellect to run together. The very snowdrops,
elaborately described, seem foreign to him, as though they belonged to
"some old, wild lost religion . . . to some strange-hearted Druid-folk"[23]
Annable offers to show Cyril the way back. Half-gentleman, half-animal,
once a curate married to a lady who refused to breed with him, Annable

is now a gamekeeper. He sets animal traps to catch poachers and he lives, in his den by the kennels, with a woman who produces an annual brat. His philosophy is as homely as his dialect:

> When a man's more than nature he's a devil. Be a good animal, says I, whether it's man or woman. You, Sir, a good natural male animal; the lady there – a female un – that's proper – as long as yer enjoy it. . . . Do as th'animals do. I watch my brats – I let 'em grow. They're beauties, they are – sound as a young ash pole, every one. They shan't learn to dirty themselves wi' smirking deviltry – not if I can help it. They can be like birds or weasels, or vipers, or squirrels, so long as they ain't human rot, that's what I say (*WP* 131).

Annable is the type of the Old Adam, who figures so prominently in the Georgian consciousness, steeped in sweat, sex and blood. He is also a precursor of Oliver Mellors in *Lady Chatterley's Lover*, a novel in which Yeats found a "noble" expression of an "ancient, humble and terrible" poetry [*L* 810]. Yeats's Old Man in *Purgatory* – the son of a fine lady and, to his shame, a gamekeeper – may have been informed by Lawrence's portrayal of the half-gentleman. Certainly Annable, Mellors and the Old Man are in the Georgian tradition of the Old Adam.

Lawrence was one of those who saw in the first, 1911–12, collection of *Georgian Poetry* the signs of a renaissance. In describing it he adopted several of Synge's key words:

> What are the Georgian poets, nearly all, but just bursting into a thick blaze of being? . . . The time to be impersonal has gone. We start from the joy we have in being ourselves, and everything must take colour from that joy. It is the return of the blood, that has been held back, as when the heart's action is arrested by fear. Now the warmth of the blood is in everything, quick, healthy passionate blood.[24]

Lawrence was not, in this quoted instance, an altogether impartial observer, since his own "The Snapdragon" was included in the volume he had under review.

One of his contributions to the next, 1913–15, collection was "Cruelty and Love", in which he indulged all his youthful and quintessentially Georgian feeling for the pulsatingly sexual and cruel natural world.[25] A woman waits for her lover and, as she waits, the vegetable and animal kingdoms disclose their omnisexuality. Leaves are like hands groping towards her bosom: and a moth is at dalliance with the woodbine, of which it is said:

> Then her bright breast she will uncover
> And yield her honey-drop to her lover. (*GP*2 156)

Meanwhile, the *woman's* lover, coming up through the farm, disturbs a "swallow's marriage bed", as he looks in at the pig-sty, and then traps a doe-rabbit:

> The rabbit presses back her ears,
> Turns back her liquid, anguished eyes
> And crouches low: then with wild spring
> Spurts from the terror of the oncoming
> To be choked back, the wire ring
> Her frantic efforts throttling:
> Piteous brown ball of quivering fears!
>
> Ah soon in his large, hard hands she dies,
> And swings all loose to the swing of his walk.
> Yet calm and kindly are his eyes . . . (*GP*2 157)

The climax of the poem comes when, having presented her with the rabbit, the man embraces the woman, for whom the poet now speaks:

> He raises my face to him
> And caresses my mouth with his fingers,
>   smelling
> Of the rabbit's fur! God, I am caught in a
>   snare
> I know not what fine wire is round my throat . . . (*GP*2 157–8)

and so on, to make a passionate association of sex and death in the animal – that is to say, human – kingdom.

For literary purposes, Lawrence set much store by the killing of a rabbit, whereby the inevitable human complicity of the brutality of life and death is established. And in many another Georgian work a cony's anguish is the modest figure for the suffering inherent in the natural order. "The Snare" by James Stephens, which appeared in the same volume with "Cruelty and Love", seems at first a too simple *crie de coeur*:

> I cannot tell from where
> He is calling out for aid!
> Crying in the frightened air,
> Making everything afraid!
>
> Making everything afraid!
> Wrinkling up his little face!
> As he cries again for aid;
> And I cannot find the place. (*GP*2 190)

When we realise that the place is not to be found because Stephens' rabbit is a being, like Yeats's Fisherman, that "does not exist", the sensibility evident in the poem becomes a little more complex. The mean actuality has invaded the imagination. As Synge observed, in 1908,

> what is highest in poetry is always reached where the dreamer is leaning out to reality, or where the man of real life is lifted out of it, and in all the poets the greatest have both these elements, that is they are supremely engrossed with life, and yet with the wildness of their fancy they are always passing out of what is simple and plain.[26]

*　　*　　*

There is a note in one of James Joyce's notebooks which reads: "WBY likes mice, rabbits, hares (rodents) . . .".[27] Joyce probably drew this mocking inference from Yeats's "Introductory Rhymes" to *The Shadowy Waters*. This poem, written at the turn of the century, refers to a very considerable assortment of woodland creatures: fox, badger, marten-cat, wild ducks, wild bees, squirrels, hares and mice, as well as the ubiquitous rabbit. In it, Yeats compares such creatures with the "immortal shadows" of mythology and asks a big question:

> How shall I name you, immortal, mild, proud shadows?
> I only know that all we know comes from you,
> And that you come from Eden on flying feet.
> Is Eden far away, or do you hide
> From human thought, as hares and mice and coneys
> That run before the reaping hook and lie
> In the last ridge of the barley? (*VP* 218)

The ludicrous incongruity between the "immortal shadows", as object, and the rodents, as image, arises from the strain of Yeats's attempt to straddle a transcendent world and the not-unpleasant reality of Lady Gregory's countryside. The question, "Is Eden out of time and out of place?" posits the possibility that it might not be. But Yeats was not inclined to re-light what he disparagingly called "the serviceable lamp of Emerson and Whitman", by which he had seen something of paradise on the Lake Isle of Innisfree. Nor could he find his way back to Eden by the imaginative nature-trail taken by Walter de la Mare in "All that's Past":

> Very old are we men;
> Our dreams are tales
> Told in dim Eden
> By Eve's nightingales . . .

Very old are the woods;
And the buds that break
Out of the briar's boughs,
When March winds wake
So old with their beauty are –
Oh no man knows
Through what wild centuries
Roves back the rose.[28]

Synge's Eden was a characteristically unambivalent, unmythical,
sexual and ephemeral "new wild paradise" found in the midst of natural
desolation:

                there I asked beneath a lonely cloud
Of strange delight, with one bird singing
                        loud,
What change you'd wrought in graveyard, rock
                        and sea,
This new wild paradise to wake for me . . .
Yet knew no more than knew these merry sins
Had built this stack of thigh-bones, jaws and
                        shins. (*CWP* 551)

The numinous realism of de la Mare – "the dreamer leaning out to
reality" – and that of Synge – "supremely engrossed with life" – may
serve, between them, to make more distinct the phase in Yeats's work
that opened with some of the poems included in *In the Seven Woods* in 1903
and, coincidentally with the efflorescence of the Georgian Movement,
developed through *The Green Helmet*, *Responsibilities* and *The Wild Swans at
Coole*.
Synge mocked "Cuchulanoid" heroes and ousted the gods and sidhe in
favour of present things:

Adieu, sweet Angus, Maeve and Fand,
Ye plumed yet skinny Shee,
That poets played with hand in hand
To learn their ecstasy.

We'll search in Red Dan Sally's ditch,
And drink in Tubber Fair,
Or poach with Red Dan Filly's bitch
The badger and the hare. (*CWP* 38)

De la Mare, by contrast, insituated into the natural world the
content of a brooding, idealising imagination. So he could entertain the

English fairies with a charming ingenuousness and ambivalence through a memory of a girl's story-telling:

> "Once . . . once upon a time . . ."
> Like a dream you dream in the night,
> Fairies and gnomes stole out
> In the leaf-green light."
>
> And her beauty far away
> Would fade, as her voice ran on,
> Till hazel and summer sun
> And all were gone.
>
> All foredone and forgot;
> And like clouds in the height of the sky,
> Our hearts stood still in the hush
> Of an age gone by. (*CP* 105)

Whether that "age gone by" belonged to the fairies or to childhood there is no saying.

Yeats would neither discard his myths, moods and magic nor retain them on such tenuous conditions as de la Mare accepted. In 1906, Yeats described his crisis as the general one:

> There are two ways before literature – upward into ever-growing subtlety . . . or downward, taking the soul with us until all is simplified and solidified again. That is the choice of choices – the way of the bird until the common eyes have lost us, or to the market carts. . . . If the carts have hit our fancy we must have the soul tight within our bodies, for it has grown so fond of a beauty accumulated by subtle generations that it will for a long time be impatient with our thirst for mere force, mere personality, for the tumult of the blood. (*E&I* 266–7)

Clearly Yeats did not make this choice of choices. He felt and continued to feel both the desire to soar like the falcon, out of earshot of the man on the ground, and the necessity of dragging the market cart. He chose both "pure imagination" and "tumult of blood"; and it was the opposition of these contraries that he found, ultimately, so productive.

A rather unsuccessful poem may best show how Yeats went to work. In "The Two Kings", the mortal King Eochaid comes into conflict with the mythical King Midhir.[29] Midhir has taken the form of a stag with which Eochaid fights from horseback before he is forced to dismount:

> Dropping his sword
> Eochaid seized both the horns in his strong hands
> And stared into the sea-green eyes, and so
> Hither and thither to and fro they trod
> Till all the place was beaten into mire.
> The strong thigh and the agile thigh were met –
> . . .
> Through bush they plunged and over ivied root
> And where the stone struck fire, while in the leaves
> A squirrel whinnied and a bird screamed out;
> But when at last he forced those sinewy flanks
> Against a beech bole he threw down the beast
> And knelt above it with drawn knife. On the instant
> It vanished . . .
> . . . .
> . . . all had seemed a shadow or a vision
> But for the trodden mire, the pool of blood,
> The disembowelled horse. (*VP* 278 v)

In locating the struggle of god against man in the natural context, Yeats was going further than the merely figurative relation of immortals and rodents earlier quoted. The poem defines a realm of brute force in which the god may even be defeated. The blood, the mire and the disembowelled horse remain as evidence of the supernatural visitation; the last, it appears, by way of compensation to the reader for the remoteness of an old story. The god Midhir, indeed, not only loses in the physical combat but is also rejected by the woman he is trying to reclaim. She chooses to stay with the mortal king whose wife she is in her present incarnation:

> "Never will I believe there is any change
> Can blot out of my memory this life
> Sweetened by death, but if I could believe,
> That were a double hunger in my lips
> For what is doubly brief." (*VP* 285)

The other narrative poem in *Responsibilities*, "The Grey Rock", earned Yeats some prize money that he diverted to Ezra Pound – a gesture appropriate to the poem's theme. Like "The Two Kings", "The Grey Rock" presents a conflict between human and divine personages; in this case between the goddess Aoife, of the Grey Rock, and Dubhlaing, the young warrior whom she loves. While Dubhlaing is fighting against Ireland's invaders in the great Battle of Clontarf, he repudiates the special protection that Aoife has afforded him. Military honour dictates that he share his king's vulnerability. Following this code, Dubhlaing earns his death and also the goddess's bitter reproaches. Yeats, as narrator, passionately sides with the goddess of the Grey Rock and contrasts his own conduct with that of the man who chose to preserve his human, military obligation rather than in his supernatural, amatory one. Yeats addresses Ernest Dowson, Lionel Johnson and other dead poet-friends of the Nineties, fellow members of the Rhymers' Club:

> *I have kept my faith, though faith was tried,*
> *To that rock-born, rock-wandering foot,*
> *And the world's altered since you died,*
> *And I am in no good repute*
> *With the loud host before the sea,*
> *That think sword-strokes were better meant*
> *Than lover's music – let that be,*
> *So that the wandering foot's content. (VP 276)*[30]

He extravagantly compares the meetings of the Rhymers' Club with a convivial assembly of the Irish gods and envisages the shades of his dead friends in their Valhalla. They "kept the Muse's sterner laws" and are now apotheosised in the permanent world they believed in, the world of "pure imagination". In Yeats's imagination, at least, they consort with the gods; and this relation of myth and recent history is the most notable feature of the poem.

Yeats had anticipated this technique in the two narrative poems of *In the Seven Woods*. In both "Baile and Aillinn", written in 1902, and, shortly afterwards, in "The Old Age of Queen Maeve", the telling of the old tale is spliced with the narrator's commentary on his own situation. In Synge's "Queens", the mythical beauties are rotten and the living one reigns supreme: in Yeats's "Baile and Aillinn", by contrast, living girls are overshadowed by dead beauties:

> *No common love is to our mind,*
> *And our poor Kate or Nan is less*
> *Than any whose unhappiness*
> *Awoke the harp-strings long ago. (VP 190)*

Nevertheless Yeats acknowledges that in reality we have Kate or Nan or nothing:

> *That all this life can give us is*
> *A child's laughter, a woman's kiss.*

In the narratives of *In the Seven Woods*, the juxtaposition of mythical subject and personal situation to disclose a harsh, even tragic, discrepancy between "pure imagination" and "tumult of the blood" was a distinctively Yeatsian departure. Eliot later described it the "mythical method, the method adumbrated by Mr. Yeats", and declared it to be the poetic equivalent of a great scientific discovery; one that was essential to the subsequent work of Joyce, as well as to his own.[31] I propose that this "method" came about as a result of Yeats's stubborn attachment to a romantic mythology and its values in the face of an enforced assent to a new realism; especially in recognition of the power of Synge's poetic confrontation of "harsh facts, for ugly suprising things, for all that defies our hope" [*E&I* 308]. The fact that this new "method" made its first appearance in the two long narratives, "Adam's Curse" and one or two other poems included in *In the Seven Woods* makes that book a very significant one in history of modern literature. From this point of view it is a pity that Yeats chose to dismember the collection by removing the narrative poems as well as the play from it.

The Georgian treatment of myth tended to unqualified realism and it lacked the Yeatsian juxtapositions of past and present, personal and traditional. The steamy sexuality and intrigue of Laurence Binyon's *Arthur* counteracts more ideal presentations of Camelot, and Masefield's version of *Tristan and Isolt* is an example of even more extreme realism. Masefield sets his play partly in a pig-pen, portrays King Marc as successful pig-farmer and allows that Tristan, a swineherd, must stink. "Dung of swine" (in the phrase from *A Full Moon in March*) authenticates, as it were, old romance. Yeats's *The Green Helmet*, with its barnyard atmosphere, is his nearest approach to this Georgian manner of treating myth. Even here, though, the artificiality of Yeats's treatment strongly qualifies "the smell of the cattle".

T. R. Henn remarked that the beggars in *Responsibilities*,

> seem to have become mouthpieces for fables; they have nothing of the individuality or richness that Synge has presented in his tramps and tinkers, and which Yeats, for all his proclaimed intentions, never succeeded in understanding to the marrow-bone.[32]

The contrast with Synge is well-founded but it is clear that Syngean realism was not at all what Yeats was attempting. In "The Three Beggars" the description of the fight is comparable with that in Masefield's *The Everlasting Mercy* in that the savagery of the action is heavily modified by the literariness of the treatment:

> They mauled and bit the whole night through;
> They mauled and bit till the day shone;
> They mauled and bit through all that day

And till another night had gone,
Or if they made a moment's stay
They sat upon their heels to rail,
And when old Guaire came and stood
Before the three to end this tale,
They were commingling lice and blood.[33] (*VP* 297)

The brutality is emblematically conceived and Yeats's rhetorical deliberation makes his kind of artificiality quite distinct from Masefield's. There is a savouring of energy, a delight in filth and blood but the poet remains detached from it; like the bird whose words frame the poem:

> *'Maybe I shall be lucky yet,*
> *Now they are silent,' said the crane.*
> *'Through to my feathers in the wet*
> *I've stood as I were made of stone*
> *And seen the rubbish run about,*
> *It's certain there are trout somewhere*
> *And maybe I shall take a trout*
> *If but I do not seem to care.' (VP* 297)

That trout mediates between nature and Irish myth; and the crane who waits so patiently for it is one of several figures of expectation in *Responsibilities*. Amongst these are the dissatisfied Magi, "waiting to find once more / The uncontrollable mystery on the bestial floor"; and the Sleeper in "The Hour Before Dawn" [*VP* 302].

The one-legged beggar in this poem, "A cursing rogue with a merry face, / A bundle of rags upon a crutch", is deeply attached to the world by his present misery and his hopes for the next season. The Sleeper, by contrast, seeks oblivion in a tub of beer, like any sensible Shropshire lad, as he waits for the end of the world. Cruachan, the site of Queen Maeve's court, where they meet, is now a heap of stones, and deserted save for "a pair of lapwings, one old sheep". The Sleeper's pessimism robs the Beggar of "every pleasant thought" and the Beggar beats up the Sleeper in revenge. In the personae of "The Hour Before Dawn" a dreamer such as Yeats saw himself as having been confronts a realist such as he had been forced to become. It is a bitterly ironical exchange. But in the early hours of the morning we are most vulnerable to despair, and the title of the poem intimates the arrival of dawn.

The trout, the crane, the beggars, the Sleeper, the dawn and the fisherman are characteristic symbols of Yeats's realist phase. First he placed myth in ironic juxtaposition with present reality, then the mythical figures tended to give way to more natural ones.

Intimations were the modest Georgian substitute for overt symbolism.

In de la Mare they frequently came through whispers, as also in this example from Edward Thomas:

> if I could sing
>
> . . .
>
> I should use, as the trees and the birds did,
> A language not to be betrayed;
> And what was hid should still be hid
> Excepting from those like me made
> Who answer when such whispers bid.[34]

Less positively Yeats, in *Responsibilities*, declares that the "reed-throated whisperer" still "comes at need, although not now as once / A clear articulation in the air, / But inwardly . . ." [*VP* 320]. In the absence of impersonal symbols the whispered inner promptings were articulated as an expression of personality.

In 1913, Yeats wrote to his father:

> Of recent years, instead of "vision", meaning by vision the intense realization of a state of ecstatic emotion symbolized in a definite imagined region, I have tried for more self protraiture. I have tried to make my work convincing with a speech so natural and dramatic that the hearer would feel the presence of a man thinking and feeling. (*L* 583)

Yeats's command of this new poetic was marvellously complete in *The Wild Swans At Coole*. Here, myth and symbol are validated by the need of the "bitter soul" that adopts them and are thus placed in context with history and the mere accidents of life. Fact and myth are put in a relation by which fact becomes a pattern of passionate human existence and myth is made credible. Characters as diverse in their origins as Cuchulain, King Lear, Jonathan Swift and Maud Gonne enjoy the same ontological status in the poet's phantasmagoria. So Yeats can say of the dead Synge and others that they have become "a portion of my mind and life" [*VP* 325].

From *The Wild Swans at Coole* the presentation of an integral and controlling self becomes ever more powerful in Yeats's poetry until it becomes strident. Where in the middle poems myth is carefully enclosed within subjectivity – the Magi are seen only in "the mind's eye" – in the later poems the subjectivity is superbly taken for granted. Poetic creation forces, rather than follows, revelation; it makes the natural rose a symbolic one [*VP* 419]. But in Yeats's final phase the struggle to assert personality seems, if only for rhetorical reasons, strained, in acknowledgement of what he saw as "a general surrender of the will" in the arts;

a surrender to a new mood in which all personality "revolts not morals alone but good taste" (*AV[A]* 210–12). Yeats's self-assertion is now an oppositional *bad* taste, his defiance pitched as high as raving: brute life making its last resistance to dissolution. During the "the Georgian revolt" Yeats had defended his poetic position through the dramatisation of personality. Against the modernism of Eliot personality was more offensively deployed.

Yeats astutely compared Eliot's poetry with Lionel Johnson's, saw in Pater a foreshadowing of Pound and in the poetry of the nineties a preparation for modernism (*OBMV* xxii, xxx). Eliot himself recorded his debts to John Davidson, Ernest Dowson and Arthur Symons, and Martin Greene has remarked that "the influence of the Nineties returned to Western Europe just after England seemed to have defeated it" to be re-imported as a major current by the avant-garde of the twenties.[35] Yeats saw well enough that Eliot was a revolutionary poet, but he also found something familiar in his work. Lionel Johnson had already sought the hard spiritual fact in the waste and incoherence of London; John Davidson had juxtaposed images of urban dinginess with those of a green Spenserian world in his *Fleet Street Eclogues*; Symons had made urban enervation a theme; Henley had done London in free verse. Having descended to the "tumult of the blood" after his symbolist phase, Yeats resisted the modernism he had helped to bring into being. Through imagery, language and personae celebrating filthy, vigorous carnal life, his "old foul tune" (*VP* 627); through the "complete coincidence between period and stanza" (*E&I* 522); and through the use of the full rhyme "felt by many moderns to be too arbitrary and too noisy for serious poetry" (*FBMV* 28), Yeats expressed his antagonism to the impersonality, rhetorical fragmentation and despondency of Eliot and his followers.

"The Spirit Medium" is an example of how Yeats countered the intellectual complexity and philosophical anxiety of his modernist contemporaries. The essential mediumship, it appears, is not that of art, not that of clairvoyance but the work and sex of a fallen Adam:

> Poetry and music I have banished,
> But the stupidity
> Of root, shoot, blossom or clay
> Makes no demand.
> *I bend my body to the spade*
> *Or grope with a dirty hand*. (*VP* 600)

Yeats did not deny the "two gross of broken statues" or the "heap of broken images" but refused to contemplate the collapse of civilization in an attitude of dejection:

... Those that Rocky Face holds dear,
Lovers of horses and of women, shall,
From marble of a broken sepulchre,
Or dark betwixt the polecat and the owl,
Or any rich, dark nothing disinter
The workman, noble and saint ... (*VP* 564–5)

As Yeats had once associated some poets of the nineties with the mythical Aoife of the Grey Rock, so at the end of his career the "lovers of horses and women", who have kept a different, earthlier, faith, are associated with a related symbol of permanence: a symbol created, like some Moore sculpture, in collaboration with a natural form.

NOTES

(I thank Warwick Gould and Ronald Schuchard for their helpful criticism and suggestions, A. Walton Litz for note 10 and Michael Groden for note 27.)

1. Reprinted in *The Permanence of Yeats*, James Hall and Martin Steinmann (eds) (New York: Collier Books, 1961) pp. 9–13.
2. "A Foreign Mind", *Athenaeum*, 4653 (4 July 1919) pp. 552–3 (a review of *The Cutting of an Agate*).
3. *The Faber Book of Modern Verse*, [hereafter *FBMV*] (London: Faber & Faber, 1936) p. 25.
4. I am thinking not only of Yeats's Prologue to *The Death of Cuchulain* [*VPl* 1051–2], but also of his Introduction to the *Oxford Book of Modern Verse* (Oxford: Clarendon Press, 1937), [hereafter *OBVM*] pp. v–xliii), of his broadcast on "Modern Poetry", *E&I* 491–508, and such late poems as "The Man and the Echo" (*VP* 623–3).
5. John Masefield, *Some Memories of W. B. Yeats* (New York: Macmillan, 1040) p. 10; *So Long to Learn* (London: Heinemann, 1952) p. 127; *Recent Prose* (London: Heinemann, 1924) p. 181.
6. *Letters of John Masefield to Florence Lamont*, Corliss Lamont and Lansing Lamont (eds) (London: Macmillan, 1979) p. 119.
7. *Recent Prose*, p. 183.
8. Christopher Hassall, *Edward Marsh: patron of the arts: a biography* (London: Longmans, 1959), [hereafter *Marsh*] pp. 196–7.
9. See *Marsh*, pp. 207, 211, 228. For Yeats's attitude to King George V see "Cracked Mary's Vision" of 1929, printed in Richard Ellmann's *The Identity of Yeats* (London: Faber & Faber, 1944) 101–2; and "Crazy Jane on the Mountain", [*VP* 628].
10. Letter from Ezra Pound to Dorothy Shakespear, 22 December 1912, [supplied by A. Walton Litz.]
11. Three poems by Stephens appeared in *Georgian Poetry, 1911–1912* (London: Poetry Bookshop, 1912), the first volume of the series. His suggestion that Seamus O'Sullivan also be invited to contribute was not taken [*Marsh* p. 197].
12. Edward Thomas, *The Country* (London: Batsford, 1913) p. 39.
13. J. M. Synge, *Collected Works, Vol. 1, Poems* Robin Skelton (ed.) (London: Oxford University Press, 1962) [hereafter *CWP*] xxxiv.
14. *Recent Prose*, p. 195.
15. Robert H. Ross, *The Georgian Revolt: Rise and Fall of a Poetic Ideal 1910–22* (London: Faber & Faber, 1967) p. 37.
16. *John Masefield* (London: Longmans, Green, 1952) p. 19.

17. John Masefield, *The Everlasting Mercy* (London: Sidgwick & Jackson, 1911) p. 9.
18. Wilfred W. Gibson, *Kestrel Edge and Other Plays* (London: Macmillan, 1924) pp. 91–2.
19. *The Letters of D. H. Lawrence*, vol. 1, James T. Boulton (ed.) (Cambridge: Cambridge University Press, 1979) p. 183.
20. Letter to Sallie Hopkin, 26 April 1911, *Boulton* pp. 260–1.
21. Letter to Edward Garnett, 1 February 1913, *Boulton* p. 509.
22. D. H. Lawrence, *Complete Plays* (London: Heinemann, 1965) pp. 50, 51, 57.
23. D. H. Lawrence, *The White Peacock* (London: Heinemann, 1955) p. 128.
24. Review of *Georgian Poetry, 1911–12*, repr. in *Phoenix: The Posthumous Papers of D. H. Lawrence, 1936* Edward D. MacDonald (ed.) (New York: Viking Press, 1968) 306.
25. *Georgian Poetry, 1913–1915* (London: Poetry Bookshop, 1915), [hereafter *GP2*] pp. 156–8.
26. J. M. Synge, *Collected Works, Vol. II, Prose* Alan Price (ed.) (London: Oxford University Press, 1966) p. 347.
27. James Joyce, *Finnegans Wake: a facsimile of Buffalo Notebooks VI.B9–VI.B12*, prefaced and arranged by David Hayman (New York: Garland, 1978) p. 101 [VI.B10–44].
28. Walter de la Mare, *Complete Poems* (London: Faber & Faber, 1969) [hereafter *CP*], p. 116.
29. The text of *Poetry* (Chicago), (October 1913) is quoted from *VP*.
30. The text from *Poetry* (Chicago), (April 1913) is quoted from *VP*.
31. "Ulysses, Order and Myth", *Dial*, LXXV, 5, (November 1923) 480–3.
32. *An Honoured Guest*, Denis Donoghue and J. R. Mulryne (eds) (London: Edward Arnold, 1965) p. 45.
33. The poem was first published in 1913. In *Later Poems* (1922), Yeats made this passage more artificial by the repetition of "mauled and bit", as in the text quoted here.
34. "I Never Saw that Land Before", Edward Thomas, *Collected Poems* (London: Faber & Faber, 1969) p. 100.
35. Martin Burgess Green, *Children of the Sun* (New York: Basic Books, 1976) p. 26.

Three Sketches by Jack B. Yeats of the Camden Street Theatre, 1902

Christopher Murray

The three theatrical sketches here reproduced have only recently come to light. They formed part of a sketch-book in the possession of Elizabeth Curran, who was secretary to the committee for a special Jack B. Yeats National Loan Exhibition at the National College of Art in Dublin in June 1945. In May 1982 the various sketches from the book appeared as part of a general exhibition of Irish art in the Tulfarris Gallery, county Wicklow, where I happened to see them. I thought the theatrical ones quite significant, since they provide evidence of the interior of the Camden Street Theatre.[1]

The three sketches are captioned as follows, in the order used in the Tulfarris exhibition, which is presumably the order they had in the original sketch-book:

(Plate 11b) XVIII: "John Quinn at rehearsal in Fays [sic] Little Theatre"
(Plate 11a) XIX: "Quinn and Russell at Fays Theatre Dublin"
(Plate 10) XXIV: "Rehearsing Willies Wise man/FAYS LITTLE THEATRE"

The purpose of the present article is to comment on the sketches as evidence in the theatrical history of the time, including in that history reference to the particular play being rehearsed in sketch XXIV.

To dispose first of the elementary matter of the personnel involved in the sketches. John Quinn (1870–1924), who appears in two of the three sketches, needs no introduction to Yeatsians. He made his first trip to Europe in 1902, met Jack Yeats in London and bought between eight and twelve of his paintings (accounts differ) on exhibition there. He then came on to Dublin and made contact for the first time with W. B. Yeats, Lady Gregory and other prominent members of the Irish literary movement. On 31 August he attended the Feis organised around Raftery's memorial at Killeenan, county Galway, and afterwards stayed

125

at Coole. "There seemed to be magic in the air," he wrote later, "enchantment in the woods and the beauty of the place, and the best talk and stories I ever found anywhere."[2] So impressed was Quinn that he immediately became a firm friend and supporter of Irish artists, beginning with his securing the American copyright on behalf of *Where There Is Nothing*. He arranged an exhibition for Jack B. Yeats in New York in March 1904, and a lecture tour for W. B. Yeats the following November. As time went on, Quinn was to prove invaluable to Synge and Joyce, and the Abbey Players were to find in him a stalwart defender during their first tour of the United States in 1911–12. First impressions were therefore all-important in introducing Quinn to the Irish literary movement, and the new direction about to be taken by the dramatic wing of that movement was something he was, apparently, sensitive enough to discern.

Yet it is rather odd that Quinn himself writes, in the piece already quoted from *Our Irish Theatre*, as if the first time he visited the Camden Street Theatre was in 1903, when he saw a rehearsal of Synge's *The Shadow of the Glen*, though not as odd, perhaps, as his biographers' giving October 1904 as the date when Quinn first saw the players.[3] It is quite clear from Yeats's *Letters* that Quinn saw Frank Fay in rehearsal at the Camden Street Theatre in 1902 (*L* 378). Jack Yeats's sketch (no. XVIII; Plate 11b) makes this point conclusive. It means that by the time he returned to New York, in September 1902, Quinn was acquainted not just with the literary but also the theatrical potential of the strengthening Irish renaissance. The point also has some significance in relation to the play's being rehearsed when he was first in Camden Street, to be discussed below.

The other personnel in the sketches hardly require much footnoting here. Russell, in sketch XIX, (Plate 11a) is of course George Russell (1867–1935), and the third figure in that sketch, arrowed as Fay, is the younger of the two brothers, William G. Fay (1872–1947). Jack Yeats calls the Camden Street hall "Fays [*sic*] Little Theatre" but it was actually the new home of the Irish National Theatre Society. The mistake is altogether understandable. In April 1902 the Irish plays which launched the movement on to its second and vital phase, *Kathleen ni Houlihan* and AE's *Deirdre*, were staged by W. G. Fay's Irish National Dramatic Company. It was not until August 1902 that the Irish National Theatre Society, the real forerunner of the Abbey, was formed, with Yeats as President, AE as one of the three vice-presidents, Willie Fay as stage manager, and Fred Ryan as secretary.[4] Because this change in title had only been a few weeks in operation Jack Yeats naturally continued to call the theatre after Willie Fay. Willie, although two years younger than Frank, was the more authoritative of the brothers. Padraic Colum describes him in terms which fit in well with Jack Yeats's sketch:

Willie was the centre of the Fays' Comedy Combination. He was much less nationalistic than Frank, and might have been content to go on playing comedy and farce [as the company did prior to April 1902]. Willie wore glasses, and the eyes behind them could give shrewd and reckoning glances; there was something in the face that suggested a man who had no bad opinion of himself; it was quick-tempered and controlled, and could be complacent when he reclined with a briar pipe in his mouth. Willie saw himself as a master-mind. . . . Nothing could go wrong if he made up his mind to keep it right.[5]

Unquestionably, the Fays were the dynamic force behind the development of the Irish theatre after 1902, and there is now a case for regarding the early Abbey as indeed "Fays' little theatre", in view of their contribution up to the time they resigned in 1908.

As to the theatre to which the Yeats sketches relate, it was a hall (long since demolished) rented for forty pounds per year in July or early August 1902. Frank Fay described it to Yeats on 12 August as follows:

> You have heard of the hall. It is not large and would perhaps seat 200; the Theatre Libre started in a hall that seated 300. Of course the comparison does not go much further. The hall is in Camden Street close to Harrington Street, and is No. 34. The trams pass the door, but it is so far from the street that there is no annoyance from tram bells. The stage is as deep as Clarendon Street [i.e., St. Teresa's Hall, 21 feet deep by 30 feet wide[6]] but not so wide and we will have to resort to the simplest of scenery so as to have room to dress and store props during the shows (*LTWBY*, ɪ 103).

Frank Fay's enthusiasm, visible in this letter, was short-lived, for the Camden Street hall was entirely unsuitable. The stage was a good deal shallower than he suggests and the lack of width presented an unsurmountable problem. As Willie Fay, who did most of the physical work in converting the hall for theatrical purposes, put it: "I could not make it any more than nine feet deep by sixteen feet wide from wall to wall, out of which, as there were no dressing-rooms, I had to leave room for the actors to make up – one side for the women and the other for the men."[7] It would appear from Jack Yeats's sketch (XXIV; Plate 10) that access to the stage was from the front only, on one side. Thus one can see what the critic meant who on opening night described the stage as so small "that one could not swing a cat on it".[8]

There were other problems also. The hall was somewhat inaccessible, being located behind the shops along a busy street. One of the actresses unflatteringly described the theatre as "the back shed of an egg and butter store, ingeniously and inconveniently hidden from its neighbours behind piles of provisions and other miscellaneous wares".[9] The diarist Joseph Holloway, future architect of the Abbey, while a little more appreciative of the place nevertheless conceded that (contrary to what Frank Fay said) "street-noises penetrate during the performances".[10] The seating in the theatre comprised hard, wooden benches only (school benches inexpensively obtained), which the American critic Cornelius Weygandt, who visited the hall in August 1902, considered "as rude as those in the bandstand of a backwoods country fair in the States".[11] Worst of all, perhaps, there was no heating in the hall, which was quite draughty. The audiences during the one and only time when the Irish National Theatre Society actually staged plays there (4–6 December 1902) had to exercise to keep warm.[12] Such conditions were regarded as placing too great a strain on the fidelity of even the most ardent supporters of the Society. Consequently, the company moved to Molesworth Hall for their next performances (March 1903), and retained the Camden Street premises for rehearsals only. This arrangement lasted until the opening of the Abbey Theatre at the end of December 1904.

Finally the question arises as to what play was being rehearsed when Quinn was present and when Jack Yeats made these sketches. Sketch no. XXIV (Plate 10) indicates that it was Yeats's *The Hour Glass*, which was originally entitled *The Fool and the Wise Man*.[13] Since that play was not staged until 14 March 1903 the question puts itself forward why it should have been rehearsed as early as August 1902. It is clear from Frank Fay's letter to Yeats, dated 12 August 1902, that it was the Society's intention to include *The Hour Glass* in the programme with which the Camden Street Theatre was to have opened at *Samhain*, the end of October. "The Hour Glass has been cast as you suggested. Would you tell me where I can get some of the folk-tales you mentioned in your last letter in which a fool similar to yours occurs. Can you give us or get us sketches of the dresses. They would want to be put in hands soon, as seven or eight will have to be made".[14] Yeats wanted Frank Fay to play the Fool (much to Fay's discomfort) and Dudley Digges (1879–1947) to play the Wise Man, which they eventually did. These are therefore the actors discernible in Sketch XXIV, (Plate 10).

On 7 September 1902 Yeats wrote to Frank Fay to say he was about to send costume sketches, and he included some words of advice for Digges: "Digges should not make up too old. The wise man is a man in the full vigour of life" (*L* 378). He obviously thought production was imminent at this point. He concluded this letter by referring to Quinn's reaction to the rehearsal of *The Hour Glass*: "I hear from Mr. Quinn that he [Digges] read the part very finely and you yourself I hear played very excellently. Quinn was very much struck." Since Quinn sailed back to New York only five days earlier, Yeats is here conveying Quinn's direct response to the rehearsal. First impressions, then, were favourable.

A hitch followed over the *Samhain* productions. They took place under the auspices of Cumann na nGaedheal at the Antient Concert Rooms and not, as expected, at the Camden Street hall. The programme was presented by Fay's Irish National Dramatic Company and not by the newly founded Irish National Theatre Society. Moreover, *The Hour Glass* was not included, for the repertory consisted of the following plays, staged between 28 October and 1 November. There were three plays which had already received a premiere performance, namely AE's *Deirdre*, Yeats's *Kathleen ni Houlihan*, and a play in Irish, *Eilis agus an Bhean Deirce*, by P. T. MacFionnlaoich (McGinley). There were in addition four new plays, *The Sleep of the King* and *The Racing Lug*, both by James H. Cousins, Yeats's *The Pot of Broth*, and *The Laying of the Foundations*, by Fred Ryan. In a curtain speech Yeats announced that his next appearance as a dramatist would be as "the author of an Irish miracle play, which will shortly be performed in a hall in Camden Street by Mr. Fay's Company".[15] But this did not happen. When the Camden Street theatre opened on Thursday 4 December 1902 with a three-day programme *The Hour Glass* was not included. Instead there were just three plays, culled from the *Samhain* collection. Thus although this was an historic occasion, a programme billed for the first time under the banner of the Irish National Theatre Society as their new home, it was something of a damp squib. On the opening night there were fewer than fifty people in the audience. It was obviously a mistake not to have opened with a new play. Frank Fay, however, put a brave face on it and wrote cheerily to Yeats on 11 December: "Financially speaking we have come out of our three nights exceedingly well. We had little expense and the profit is excellent. Our audiences were small but good."[16]

The most likely reason why *The Hour Glass* was not included in the December programme is that Yeats needed more time to work on the scene design. He first enlisted the aid of Robert Gregory (1881–1918), who did a sketch of the setting which Yeats then passed on to Sturge Moore for further refinement. In *The Noble Drama of W. B. Yeats* Liam Miller has given the details of Moore's assistance with the designing of *The Hour Glass*, and has reproduced Moore's superb drawing.[17] Interestingly, this drawing is scaled for a very small theatre, so the Camden Street hall was not at this time (November) being ruled out as the venue. Fay had to await Yeats's developing response to Moore's suggestions, though he himself favoured delay in the first place so as to have more time for rehearsal.[18] Another factor in the postponement, however, was the infighting among the players concerning two other plays, *Sold* by Cousins and *The Saxon Shillin'* by Colum, which had gone into rehearsal and then been abandoned. Writing to Yeats about February 1903 AE said that *The Hour Glass* would soon be produced and added: "I think the delay was caused by the rows" over the other two plays.[19]

To finish the story of *The Hour Glass*, it may be said that the premiere took place on Saturday 14 March 1903 at the Molesworth Hall. The play was very well received, but for all that Sturge Moore contributed to the scene design, the cast seems to have given the credit to Willie Fay. Maire Nic Shiubhlaigh, who played the Angel, described "Fay's setting" as "an outstanding example of that classic simplicity of decor which is so often sought on a stage but seldom achieved".[20] Frank Fay, writing to Yeats on 23 March, quoted a member of the audience (probably Joseph Holloway) who had much praise for *The Hour Glass* and who had said "that the decoration had exactly the effect we wanted – keeping the attention concentrated on the words" (*LTWBY*, I 121). That "we" is instructive. It is equally instructive to bear in mind that the big desk which Moore called for in the decor is there already in Jack Yeats's sketch made some three months earlier. What is implicit in such coincidence and such use of the first person plural is a very early example of the collaborative spirit which made the art of Synge possible in following years. The idea of a theatre being formulated was not exclusively a literary or a poetic one but something much newer, a combination of many arts at once. This idea is in fact inherent in Lady Gregory's report to Synge on the production: "The Hour Glass went off splendidly," she wrote about the premiere, "it is a very strong acting play, & was beautifully acted and staged."[21] It is appropriate that Joseph Holloway, after praising the acting of Fay as the Fool and Digges as the Wise Man, concluded his account of the premiere with the prophecy: "I think the evening was the turning point in the career of the Irish National Theatre Company, and has placed them on the wave of success."[22] The famous tour to London soon followed, in May 1903, with the result that Miss Horniman came to Dublin to support the company and, in time, to present it with the Abbey Theatre.

By that time, indeed by December 1903 when *The Hour Glass* was revived at the Molesworth Hall, Dudley Digges had left the company (in protest against Synge's *The Shadow of the Glen*). Frank Fay stepped into the role of the Wise Man and George Roberts (1873–1953) took the part of the Fool. Roberts continued in this role when the play was staged at the Abbey in June 1905, though he too left the company later that year in disagreement over policy. James W. Flannery reproduces a photograph of Frank Fay and Roberts in *The Hour Glass* in his *W. B. Yeats and the Idea of a Theatre* (Yale University Press, 1976) but he wrongly identifies the actors as the two Fays. His photograph is a reproduction of a picture postcard, one of the Irish National Theatre Series, on the back of which is an announcement for the production of *The Hour Glass* on 9–16 June 1905.[23] Holloway saw this production and confirms that Roberts played the Fool.[24] Later, certainly by 12 July 1906, Willie Fay did take over the role of the Fool.

These sketches are of interest because they throw a certain amount of light on details minor in themselves but significant enough in their implications. There must be a lot of this kind of material still unrecognized or as yet buried under more glamorous records. For example, there is a pencil drawing of Synge among the playbills at the National Library of Ireland. Who made it? It is unsigned. It may have been but a greenroom doodle, but it is fresh and vivid in style. Some Synge scholar may yet find it useful. In a similar way, the Jack Yeats sketches can modify the received picture of the Irish dramatic movement. The Camden Street Theatre was a white elephant as a theatre, but it marked a step forward just the same, and was to prove fruitful as rehearsal hall and social centre. Perhaps Jack Yeats sensed that great work was to stem from such humble origins. For Frank Fay it was now or never. "It was a matter of waiting until doomsday for a proper hall or taking the present one and I think we can do our work here small though the place be" (*LTWBY*, 1 104). As Maire Nic Shiubhlaigh was later to write, summing it all up for us, "Whatever its shortcomings, this little hall became the first Irish theatre. . . . Here, more than anywhere else, were the foundations of the theatre laid." [25]

NOTES

1. Most of the other sketches deal with the Feis at Killeenan, county Galway, on 31 August 1902. The sketchbook was originally dated September 1902 and had the place names Sligo and Killeenan on the cover. I am grateful to Dr Karl Mullen, owner of Tulfarris Gallery, for permission to reproduce the three sketches here. I also acknowledge the kindness of the editors of *Prompts*, Bulletin of the Irish Theatre Archive, for permission to make use here of material first published in *Prompts*.
2. See Lady Gregory, *Our Irish Theatre* (Gerrards Cross: Colin Smythe, 1972) Appendix VI, p. 249. For other details of the Killeenan Feis see also Lady Gregory, *Poets and Dreamers* (Gerrards Cross: Colin Smythe, 1974) pp. 248–50. The date is wrongly given as 1900 on p. 248, n. 1. See also Hilary Pyle, *Jack B. Yeats: A Biography* (London: Routledge & Kegan Paul, 1970) pp. 81–2.
3. *The Man from New York* (New York: Oxford University Press, 1968) pp. 16, 123.
4. The evolution of the Fays' early theatrical enterprises into the company which put the Irish National Theatre Society on stage in 1902 is well documented by Brenna Katz Clarke, *The Emergence of the Irish Peasant Play at the Abbey Theatre* (Ann Arbor: UMI Research Press, 1982) pp. 6–31, and Appendix C.
5. Padraic Colum, "Early Days of the Irish Theatre," *Dublin Magazine*, xxiv, No. 4 (October–December 1949) 17.
6. See Lennox Robinson, *Ireland's Abbey Theatre: A History 1899–1951* (London: Sidgwick & Jackson, 1951) p. 27.
7. W. G. Fay and Catherine Carswell, *The Fays of the Abbey Theatre* (London: Rich and Cowan, 1935) p. 124.
8. R. M., "The 'Irish Theatre': The Camden Street Playhouse", *The Evening Mail*, 5 December 1902, p. 2. See also Maire Nic Shiubhlaigh, *The Splendid Years* (Dublin: James Duffy, 1955) p. 194.
9. Maire Nic Shiubhlaigh, *The Splendid Years*, p. 23.
10. Ibid., p. 193.
11. *Irish Plays and Playwrights* (London: Constable; New York & Boston: Houghton Mifflin, 1913) p. 20.
12. Maire Nic Shiubhlaigh, *The Splendid Years*, p. 32.

13. A. Norman Jeffares and A. S. Knowland, *A Commentary on the Collected Plays of W. B. Yeats* (London: Macmillan, 1975) p. 124.

14. *LTWBY*, I 104. Fay had acknowledged receipt of the script of *The Hour Glass* on 25 July 1902.

15. Clipping, undated, in W. A. Henderson, "The Irish Literary Theatre and up to the Opening of the Abbey Theatre", vol. 2, p. 233, MS. 1729, National Library of Ireland.

16. Quoted by Robert Hogan and James Kilroy, *Laying the Foundations 1902–1904*, The Modern Irish Drama: A Documentary History, II (Dublin: Dolmen Press, 1976) p. 41.

17. (Dublin: Dolmen Press, 1977) p. 81.

18. Robert Hogan and James Kilroy, p. 31.

19. *LTWBY*, I 119. Cf. Fay to Yeats, 30 January 1903, pp. 117–18.

20. *The Splendid Years*, p. 33, p. 34.

21. Ann Saddlemyer, ed., *Theatre Business: the Correspondence of the First Abbey Directors*: William Butler Yeats, Lady Gregory and J. M. Synge (Gerrards Cross: Colin Smythe, 1982) p. 43.

22. *Joseph Holloway's Abbey Theatre*, ed. Robert Hogan and Michael J. O'Neill (Carbondale and Edwardsville: Southern Illinois University Press, 1967) pp. 23–4.

23. National Library of Ireland, MS. 19 844, "Irish Theatre", vol. 2.

24. National Library of Ireland, MS. 1803 (January–June 1905) pp. 320ff. The Abbey Theatre programme for 16 June 1905 lists Roberts as the Fool.

25. *The Splendid Years*, p. 25.

"The Pilgrimage Along the Drogheda Road": W. B. Yeats, George Barker, and the Idea of Ireland

Robert Fraser

W. B. Yeats spent the month of September 1935 quietly at Riversdale, his Dublin home, working on the compilation of *The Oxford Book of Modern Verse*. On the evening of the 8 September he wrote to Lady Dorothy Wellesley enclosing a draft of the Introduction he had written for the selection of her poetry she was preparing. He then added a postscript describing his day's activities:

> I am tired, I have spent the day reading Ezra Pound for the Anthology – a single strained attitude instead of passion, the sexless American professor for all his violence.
>
> I delight in a young poet called George Barker (Faber & Faber) a lovely subtle mind and a rhythmical invention comparable to Gerard Hopkins . . . (*LDW* 23)

That summer Faber had issued two volumes which had caught Yeats's eye. The first was Pound's *A Draft of Cantos XXXI–XLI* which on its appearance was reviewed for *The Criterion* by a twenty two year old poet called George Barker.[1] The second was Barker's own *Poems*[2] refreshingly free from the dogmatic opinions and suspect erudition Yeats found so objectionable in the new Cantos.

When *The Oxford Book* appeared the following year it confined itself to an early Canto, the seventeenth, whose undulating grace of movement brought it close to the limpid lyricism of the early volumes.[3] Meanwhile Yeats had succumbed to his partiality for Barker, to whom he had sent a copy of a cyclostyled letter headed by the blue insignia of The Oxford University Press requesting the permission of those poets destined for inclusion in *The Oxford Book* to reprint their work. When forwarded from Faber's offices in Bloomsbury to Barker's cottage in Piddletrenthide, Dorset, this turned out to contain a request to reproduce four poems on

133

an "attached sheet", together with a terse but flattering postscript in
Yeats's own hand: "I have taken much from your work. I like you better
than I like anybody else in the new generation."

That Yeats should have seen Barker's work as a signal of the turning of
the poetic tide is scarcely surprising. When *Poems* (1935) had appeared,
its light blue dust jacket carried a commendatory blurb in the editorial
style of T. S. Eliot:

> Those who look for new poets will remember a few poems in *The
> Criterion*, *The Listener*, *New Verse*, and one or two other periodicals,
> which could not be classified as paraphrases or imitations of the living
> poets now generally admired. Some of these poems have been over the
> signature of George Barker. There are many people who have wanted
> to see more of George Barker's work so that they might make up their
> minds about him. This volume gives them the opportunity of
> committing themselves to an opinion of a poet younger than those
> whom they have recently been discussing.

Prominent among those motivated to "look for new poets" in 1935 was
Yeats in his capacity as editor of the Oxford anthology. When published
in 1936 this carried an Introduction which went some way to explaining
the nature of its editor's preferences. The concluding pages of the book
were devoted to a short but representative selection from the work of
"the living poets now generally admired", namely the young men whose
astringent verses had featured in Michael Roberts's influential anthology *New Signatures* of 1932. Yeats's introductory remarks, however, left his
readers in little doubt as to his opinion of some of those writers "whom
they have recently been discussing".

> Spender has said that the poetry of belief must supersede that of
> personality, and it is perhaps a belief shared that has created their
> intensity, their resemblance; but this belief is not political. If I
> understand aright this difficult art the contemplation of suffering has
> compelled them to seek beyond the flux something unchanging,
> inviolate, that country where no ghost haunts, no beloved lures
> because it has neither past nor future.

> This lunar beauty
> Has no history
> Is complete and early;
> If beauty later
> Bear any feature
> It had a lover
> And is another.[4]

It is the quotation from Auden's *Poems* (1930), offered up as typical of the school, which sets the seal of Yeats's lack of enthusiasm. For him the poets of the early 1930s were demolitionists who had sought to clear the terrain of history in order to erect a streamlined palace of glass and steel, a sort of Bauhaus haven. It was the reassuring touch of a human hand, and the fleeting glimpse of ghostly presences that he missed in much contemporary verse, and it was in Barker's four short pieces, with which he ends the book, that he apparently found them.

His selection is strongly biased towards one particular kind of Barker poem. Overlooking the convoluted and slightly Audenesque "Daedalus", which had first attracted Eliot's attention, he makes straight for a group of poems remarkable for their wistful fancy: for "The Wraith-friend" and "He Comes Among" (Poems 375 and 378) with their suggestions of a shadowy other self intermittently perceived; for the whimsical soufflé "The Leaping Laughers" (376) and for "The Crystal" (377) with its enshrining of a luminous Blakean moment. Grounds for his partiality are not hard to find. Yeats had himself edited Blake, towards whose mystical strain he was, for obvious reasons, attracted; he had himself a marked proclivity towards light, song-like structures. It is the choice of "The Wraith-Friend", imperfect as it is, however, which is the most revealing. Beginning with an echo of Eliot's "Prufrock", this proceeds to blend others from Nashe, Lionel Johnson and Yeats himself.[5]

> Following forbidden streets
> Towards unreal retreats,
> Returning, lost again,
> Encircling in vain:
> No lunar eye, no star
> Beckoning from the far
> Wastes the trackless feet
> Leading their beaten beat
> Back onto the broad
> And multitudinous road.
> In what unearthly land
> I fugitively stand,
> Between what frenzied seas
> Gaze, with my burning miseries
> Miming the stars?
> O angel in me hidden
> Rise from the laden
> Sorrow of this dark hand!
> Companion and wraith-friend
> From the rib's narrow prison

Step, in miraculous person!
Touch into these exhausted limbs
The alacrity of the birds
Which over the greatest ranges
Widely and eagerly range!

Though to wings those dark limbs
Spread, and that deep breast climbs
Eagerly the heights of the skies, or
Of the earliest lark's soar,
Until brushing against cold heaven
Like bluebirds in storms, even
Then that known flesh must fall.
Soon, within this prison's wider wall
Lie with those giant arms, that form,
For there is no upward egress from
This earthly, this unearthly land
Upon whose dust may stand
None, though heavenly high can fly,
But in whose dust all brighter dust must lie.[6]

One interesting facet of this piece is the comparative closeness of its
opening to the mood of the Auden poem which Yeats cites in his
Introduction. Both are set amid trackless wastes in which the mind
roams in search of familiar landmarks. For Auden, however, the
landscape's lack of "any feature" is an occasion for pride, since it offers
an escape from the visible pressure of history. Barker's isolation, on the
other hand, is hopefully relieved by the emergence of an *alter persona* swift
with "the alacrity of birds". To some readers it might have seemed that
this gesture of reassurance marked a retreat in the face of social reality.
For Yeats, however, it was evidence of a fresh development in English
poetry which would bring it closer to a style of writing which he
recognised. It thus displayed a shift in sensibility at once radical and
conservative.

It is this complementary forward and backward movement which is
the theme of the tantalisingly short comment on Barker in his
Introduction.

I would, if I could, have dealt at some length with George Barker, who
like MacNeice, Auden, Day Lewis, handled the traditional metres
with a new freedom – *vers libre* lost much of its vogue some five years
ago – but has not their social passion, their sense of suffering.[7]

The formal point is both appropriate and misleading. Like Auden and his followers Barker had, as Yeats's comments to Lady Wellesley imply, learned much from Hopkins's technique of Sprung Rhythm: "The Wraith-friend", for instance, employs an elastic three stress line. He also possessed, however, an alertness to quantitative procedures which marked him out as unusual. "He Comes Among", for instance, cultivates assonance in a manner quite unlike anything in Auden. It is this slight conservatism in Barker which seems to appeal to Yeats more than the "freedom" of his accentual practice, providing as it does a sense of continuity which he missed in so much contemporary verse. By "social passion" he evidently means to imply the ideological fervour which brought the Auden school too close for comfort to that "intellectual hatred" whose destructive effect he had witnessed in Ireland.[8] The lack of it in Barker prompts no criticism – there is more than enough *personal* suffering in his verse – but appears rather as proof of an absence of cant to which the Irishman could not but respond.

There were sound biographical reasons for the freedom in Barker's work from display of cosmetic commitment. Put simply, he was far too near to the real proletariat to feel free to adopt a revolutionary stance lightly. In the backstreet Chelsea tenement where he spent much of his childhood were two palpable symbols of his family's disadvantaged origins. The first was the loaded pistol which his father, a Lincolnshire farmer's son and former junior army officer, kept under the pillow in his bedroom as a token of pride in the post-war years when he trudged the streets of the capital in search of a job. The second was a framed certificate which proved that Barker's mother, Marion Taaffe, was descended from the licensed Pilot of the port of Drogheda. It was Marion Taaffe, later immortalized by her son in a famous sonnet as she sat in war-time London, "gin and chicken helpless in her Irish hand",[9] who had transmitted to her children a dogged Catholic faith transplanted from her homeland along with memories of a childhood spent close to the Irish Sea. It was she too who had put George in the way of the only formal literary instruction he was ever to have, as, half a century later, he recalled:

> When I was still at school my mother used to receive visits from a Jesuit attached to the Brompton Oratory by the name of Father O'Roberts. When I was thirteen she told him that I had been writing verses which she then showed to him. He was very taken by all this nonsense, so he arranged for me to go along for two hours on Tuesday and Thursday evening. This went on for about four years, from the time I was thirteen to the time when I was about seventeen, and that was where I was really educated. They told me everything to read, but didn't badger me, simply asked me questions. I remember them

asking me what I thought about a passage in Newman about the human race being implicated in "some huge aboriginal calamity" and Father O'Roberts saying, "Can you take this as a serious remark?" [10]

That passage of Newman's,[11] with its built-in imperatives and Augustinian sense of Original Sin might well be said to be the foundation of much of Barker's subsequent thinking, and much of his work to be an answer to it. The inherited chemistry of Catholic guilt, however, took some years to work itself through his blood-stream, and, meanwhile, Ireland, which he had not as yet visited, remained for him a source of mystery wrapped in an enticing theological mist.

Though the Barker children had not set foot in Ireland, the two halves of the family corresponded. It was an open verse letter to his cousin Margaret Taaffe, printed in the *Listener* on 7 July 1937, under the heading "By the Boyne" which eventually became the "Poem on Ireland" collected in *Lament and Triumph* (1940).[12] This is a piece which evokes that peculiar sense of exile experienced only by those who have never visited their mother land. In it there is no groping after historical fact or political aspiration, but instead a strongly expressed need to establish a personal past upon which to build the greater abstractions. Barker's imagined Ireland has been fed exclusively by report and gossip; what he now needs is a tactile reality with which to flesh these out:

My mother reminds me that my birth line,
Accompanying undersea cables, carries
From London back to a Drogheda origin.
Being born in England, like miscarriages
In tubes and taxis, means nothing, for my home
Is there by the Boyne, where never I
Have bathed with my cousins in summertime,
Rowed in my grandfather's coracle, or ever
Slept with my head on the afternoon arm
Of Mourne. Not, not once have I made
The pilgrimage along the Drogheda Road
Where, crossed with stone, stands the martyrdom
Of James O'Hanlon, who died at the hand
Of the Black and Sin, the Blood and Tan.[13]

James O'Hanlon is a local rather than a national hero; he is a creature of the poet's mother's memory. The "coracle" belongs to the same pilot of Drogheda whose Certificate hung on the kitchen wall during the poet's childhood: like O'Hanlon, it is part of a private world promoted by hungry phantasy. For, as much as Ireland, Barker here is seeking to explain himself. He is a member of a generation for whom provincial, and preferably Celtic, roots are important; as he wrote in the contemporary "Epistle to Dylan Thomas": "like the pearl I came from hurt".[14] This sense of exclusion, of a deprivation based on ancestry, is important to him as something which demands concrete realisation. Myths as such are of little use, since they serve to set an already remote island at one further remove.

Thus, though the name of Yeats is never mentioned, throughout this poem the implied contrast is with that great fellow poet who, born and bred in Ireland, was impelled by the forces of public history to supplement the immediacy of sight and sound with abstractions and presences drawn from a moribund past. For Barker, by contrast, born in England and tired of mental compensation, legends are a luxury he can ill afford:

> From Ireland exiled in the womb, still,
> Like the birthmark of the mother's wild
> Craving at labour, that stamps the child,
> I wore the shape of Ireland on my mind.
> I can brush Lake Sligo when I take
> The tear from my eye, or when I talk
> Hear the foiled tongues of the streams
> That cannot convert rocks to their water
> Near Mornington. Not mythological dreams
> I am haunted by, Ireland as my daughter;
> But by the wild obscurity of Leinster, by
> The giant shore of the West, greater than heroes:
> By the tongue of the Boyne in my ear, and by
> My cousin's letters, more than myths and stories.[15]

Deprived of an Irish childhood, Barker has been obliged to create one from scraps: from his mother's conversation and from family correspondence. In the absence of visual sensations, it is on the ear that he relies to supply a continuity with a verbal tradition which he wishes to claim for his own. He becomes Irish by listening to himself: to be Irish, in his terms, is to be a poet. But to retain some vestige of authenticity, his voice must speak of things handled and felt, or at least of an imaginative life which fastens on the actual. To court myth, on the other hand, is to risk a charge of intellectualising in an empty void.

Thus though in this poem the procession of national heroes is seen on parade, the poet-in-exile himself is "prohibited sentimental pleasure" and "like the sadist" must "revert to the real".[16] Bruised by a national history in which he has taken no part, he must also beware the easy solace of idealisation, must see Ireland as she really is, "Europe's sore that will not heal", rather than as her more indulgent sons and daughters often like to think of her. Hence where Yeats saw a land populated by ghosts and emblematic grandees, "the spectres of Collins, / Swift and

Connolly, Mac Swiney Mayor of Cork", Barker is obliged to discover poverty, degredation, dirt, and a rural populace much as they were before the Liberation, "Weeping among the seed potatoes".[17]

It is precisely this starkly felt quality of Irish life which Barker seems to have been straining to catch when in the Spring of the following year he was requested by Desmond McCarthy, editor of *Life and Letters Today*, to review for the journal one of the last plays which Yeats was to write, *The Herne's Egg*, which had just been published by Macmillan.[18] Barker's piece begins by identifying in the play three qualities between which he wishes to distinguish: Yeats's "love of Gaelic mythology, his passion for the human passions, and his magnificent manipulation of words." It is the first of these elements, "the rather cumbersome and crepitating machinery of a not too good mythology" that strikes him as the weak link in a drama otherwise characterised by firm realisation, bold human outlines and exacting dramatic language. His "Not too good" here is an equivocal phrase susceptible to many interpretations: defective because vague, incoherent or merely inconsistent. It is, however, none of these possible defects which worries Barker, who seems troubled instead by the very aspect of Yeats's mythological thinking which he implicitly condemns in the "Poem on Ireland": its remoteness from the textures of daily living, its abstractness.

So concerned in fact is the reviewer to set this facet of the play, and the Great Herne as the embodiment of it, apart from the rest of its achievement that he arguably overlooks an important strand in Yeats's plot: the insisted-upon kinship of Attracta, the bird's votaress, to Leda and hence of the bird himself to the divine swan, "brute blood of the air", whose knowledge permeates her. The sonnet "Leda and the Swan" of fifteen years earlier had closed on a question and so, some readers might think, does this play. There are thus further subtleties of meaning throughout which Barker, in his impatience to explore the palpitating centre of "the human passions" appears to miss. For instance, The Herne, as he comments, is never observed but "sits just above the wings and guffaws down at the King of Connaught and his rapscallion soldiers". This invisibility is attributed in Barker's review to Yeats's failure to infuse an abstract emblem with imaginative power, but may just as feasibly be viewed as an accurate reflection of the mental attitudes of Congal and his men, determined as they are to eradicate an alien ideal and restraint regarded by them as unacceptable:

> Women thrown into despair
> By the winter of their virginity
> Take its abominable snow,
> As boys take common snow, and make
> An image of god or bird or beast
> To feed their sensuality:

Ovid had a literal mind,
And though he sang it neither knew
What lonely lust dragged down the gold
That crept on Danae's lap, nor knew
What rose against the moony feathers
When Leda lay upon the grass. (*VPI* 1016)

Again, so intent is Barker to shift the Herne from the centre of the play that he assumes that the usurpation of the bird's matrimonial rights of which Cognal and his companions boast after the banqueting scene takes place, where Yeats himself had left the matter open. The rationale behind Barker's reading is clear: the Herne represents in his eyes an unearthly loftiness of which he is as suspicious as were Congal's soldiers, who thus come to represent for him a conquest of the real over the speculative which he is keen to vindicate:

> The scene in which they violate Attracta to violate the Herne is conspicuously fine: personally I like this most because I understand the soldiers and the priestess – they become actual creations and creatures – whereas the Great Herne, who merely sits and broods and governs, loses his look of immortal authority when he leaves the bogs and shadows of his native place.

This preference for the earthy and human over the rarified and supernatural also affects Barker's view of Yeats's dramatic verse. The Herne's failure to speak becomes proof positive of its impotence. The poetry which Barker quotes with approval, on the other hand, is that contained in the sinewy, assertive lines given to the defiant Congal in the majesty of his final self-impalement. The whole play thus emerges less as a cohesive work than as a thing of shreds and patches, and the vigour of Congal's concluding statements as a sleight-of-hand whereby Yeats, insufficiently convinced of his own allegorical logic, contrives to undermine the Herne's power and set Congal, the flesh and blood mortal, up in his place. It is a view of the play which reinforces the reviewer's distrust of the stitched mythological costume of Yeats, who is thus confirmed in his admiring but sceptical eyes as "a grand if erratic poet".

The grandeur was something which Barker had experienced himself on the one occasion on which the two poets met, in the bar of Henekey's in the Strand with T. S. Eliot, who, throughout the somewhat stiff conversation, eased his own disquiet by chasing single with double gins. However warmly the older man felt about Barker's poetry, he was clearly too reserved to give his feelings conversational expression, and, on his part, Barker came away with a feeling of magnificence tinged with arrogance.[19]

The feeling of remoteness, the sense of thwarted affection, is something which recurs in much of Barker's later writing on Yeats. When, the year after the publication of *The Herne's Egg*, the patriarch of Irish letters passed away, Barker was moved to express the complexity of his reactions in a poem entitled "The Death of Yeats", one of a procession of elegies which he wrote in the late 'thirties when he was especially interested by the form. Here, as in much of his writing about Yeats, Barker shows an inclination to begin where the master left off. Thus the very first stanza leads in with the closing line of "Byzantium", adapted to the needs of formal portraiture:

> That dolphin-torn, that gong-tormented face
> With the trumpets of Andromeda rose and spoke,
> Blaring the pitiful blast and airing hope
> So hope and pity flourished. Now the place
> Cold is where he was, and the gold face
> Shimmers only through the echoes of a poem.[20]

Viewed with the respect of a mourner, Yeats's death-mask here fuses with the "golden handiwork"[21] of his living vision. Ordained to articulate the mythological needs of a nation, the mask has itself now grown or dwindled into a myth, and thus achieved both perfection and inscrutability. Yeats's physical mortality, then, appears as a final seal set on a deliberately willed process, since the absorption of the artist's identity in the wider personality of the Nation is not something which the late Senator would have been tempted to disown. Exempt himself from this kind of ideological pressure, and suspicious of the elaborations of national mythology, Barker then allows a note of personal criticism to intrude. Though Yeats's life and work were imbued with purpose, the renaissance of Irish culture which he sought to orchestrate features as a shadow play, even a gesture of hopelessness:

> The swan mourns on the long abandoned lake,
> And on the verge gather the great Irish ghosts
> Whom only he could from their myth awaken
> And make a kingdom. The luckless and the lost
> Got glory from the shake of his hand as he passed,
> The lunar emperor whom Time could not break.[22]

To speak of myth as a state of suspension from which frozen presences may be roused is to betray a scepticism about the continuity of inherited memory profoundly detrimental to the conception of cultural nationalism which Yeats, amongst others, advanced. The political efficacy of the Irish movement has then to be credited less to its pertinacity and relevance than to the unique magnetism of the man largely instrumental in its inception. The "Irish ghosts" in Barker's elegy are therefore seen to be "great" principally by virtue of their obedience to the summoning inspiration of the one artist capable of enlivening them. Yeats himself thus comes to be viewed, less as the mouthpiece of his time than as the supreme *magister* around whom the flood of history swirled in a vain attempt to engulf him. He is a magician whose spells last just as long as his readers find themselves held by his words. With his personal disappearance, history reverts to its usual pattern, leaving only his poetry to speak for him:

> But now the cloud only shall hear: the ant,
> The winter bulb under the ground, and the hidden
> Stream be made dumb by his murmur in death,
> Lying between the rock and the jealous plant.
> No matter how close to the ground I bend, his breath
> Is not for me, and all divisions widen.[23]

"Under Ben Bulben", Yeats's own anticipatory self-elegy, had appeared in *The Irish Times* on 4 February that year and been re-printed in *Last Poems* the same June.[24] This stanza in Barker's elegy may be read as a response to it; certainly the self-supporting stoicism which Yeats advocated in the epitaph to his poem seems to extend here into a veiled indifference towards the deceased himself. "His breath / is not for me" is ambivalent, implying either personal unworthiness or a disposition to reject. The "divisions" which yawn as communication is frustrated are partly the political wounds which Yeats later tried to heal, and partly the diverging perspectives of Barker and the deceased, whose strenuous metaphysics and mythological enthusiasms he is finally inclined to disown. Ultimately, the poem conveys reverence, but it is an awe bred of incomprehension, and of a recognition that respect is sometimes best expressed by a resolve to admire and then do otherwise.

The parting of the ways which "The Death of Yeats" appears to signal had roots in the political circumstances of the time. In the mid-1930s, when the autonomy and independence of the smaller countries was a matter of public concern, Barker was inclined to a conception of Irishness which could accommodate ethnicity as its binding element. In his contributor's note to the issue of *Life and Letters* in which his review of *The Herne's Egg* appeared, he announced himself as "of mixed Irish and English parentage", one of the few occasions on which he does so.[25] With the onset of the international crisis, however, and the death-knell of nationalism which it appeared to herald, ethnic considerations had a tendency to give way before questions of a wider moral import. Certainly by 1940, when Barker had escaped from England to a Professorship in Japan, his writing was increasingly turning on a theological axis. In Japan, squatting like a "one man Europe" on an island with which he

had no personal connection, it is of the metropolis that he thought with
regret, so that the *Pacific Sonnets* of that year speak of a nostalgia for
recognizably English pleasures. And, as, finding in this alien land
nothing which he can recognize or to which he wishes to lay claim, he
reaches out for a symbol of the incomprehensible, it is of Yeats that he
thinks, and Yeats's yearning for a fabulous Japan:

> By the now westward China, and, to the east
> The spoiling, coiling, the blue beast toiling sea . . .[26]

Now that Barker inhabits the Asia of Yeatsian myth, he finds there
nothing but an "island colonized by ideograms / Of poverty and
moongazing, hate and gardens, / Where the soul is shallower than a bowl
of tea / And negative as water". Puzzled by this contradiction, he is
deserted not merely by Yeats himself but by the very sustaining idea of
Ireland. Hounded by intimations of sexual and political guilt, for him
henceforth to be Irish is to be Catholic, and to be Catholic to be largely
human. From now on Barker's Irishness will be observed only in the
twists and turns of his thought, his love of aphorism, the passionate
waywardness of his logic, and a partiality for lost causes. Meanwhile,
Yeats the master has drifted over the horizon, never to return.

And yet there is a certain descent to be observed even in the later verse.
Speaking in 1982 of his conception of form in poetry, Barker had this to
say about the practical usefulness of Yeats's example:

> Of all modern poets Yeats constructed his work most beautifully. He
> started by writing it out as prose; then he picked out the words which
> were going to rhyme, setting those on the right hand side of the page.
> He then proceeded with the aid of a little toy drum which he beat while
> he said the words. By this means he'd work out what the rhythm was,
> and set that down. Then he'd work out the whole poem until finally it
> went click like a Chinese Box.[27]

The analogy to the Chinese Box occurs in the first paragraph of the very
letter to Lady Wellesley in which Yeats commended Barker to her
attention, where, returning his draft Introduction, he remarks "The
correction of prose, because it has no fixed laws, is endless, a poem comes
right with a click like a closing box" (*LDW* 22).

It is easy to see why this remark should now prove so attractive to
Barker. The growing concern with traditional poetic decorum has
involved an increased fascination with the "fixed laws" of prosody which
the reigning aesthetic of the inter-war years tended to exclude. The fixity
of such laws is, in the eyes of both Barker and Yeats, less a matter of iron
discipline than of a careful attention to the textures of perceived sound.
The ground of Yeats's and Barker's agreement on the question of form,

then, would seem to lie in their shared belief that each poem has within it a distinct shape which will eventually emerge provided the artist is prepared to wait and respond.

This process of ingestion and applied skill is evidenced clearly in the composition of Barker's most recent poetry. His long religious poem *Anno Domini*, (1983) for example, takes the form of a half-jocular act of supplication addressed to the marooned God of history.[28] Its deployment on the page is unusual consisting as it does of a series of couplets, the second line of each of which is heavily indented. This physical arrangement only occurred to Barker after a period of two months in which he dictated the lines into a tape recorder in the hope of discovering the shape which he knew to be latent within them. Describing the moment when he happened upon the eventual structure, he returns to Yeats's analogy:

> At first I had no idea what I was doing technically, which is why it was so difficult to work out. Sometimes I wondered whether there was any system to it. I was convinced that I had written a poem: at least I thought that I had. And when I eventually came upon it, it was like examining a Chinese Box which suddenly goes snap.[29]

Sometimes this process may take years. An idea will occur in one form, then settle briefly before setting off a new phase of experimentation which may lead to a final crystallization along quite different lines. In the late 1960s, for example, Barker, then Arts Fellow at the University of York, was interested in composing a set of lucid little quatrains which he eventually strung together into *The Golden Chains* (1968), lyric 67 of which reads:

Ben Bulben Hill his white head under
  Old man, old man, lie still
rolls in the sunset and the thunder
  old man, old man, lie still.

His old bones in the roaring grave
  old man, old man, lie still
cry to his old bones as they rave
  old man, old man, lie still.[30]

It was another fifteen years before this tiny seed blossomed into the fully-fledged elegy which stands at the foot of this essay.[31] In it, nearly half a century after Yeats placed Barker at the end of *The Oxford Book* as the new hope of English poetry, the custodian of his wishes, now three years younger than the Yeats who looked forward to laying down his bones in Drumcliff Churchyard, can turn back and see a certain kinship which, despite the changes and chances of the twentieth century, still survives. For Barker now, deepened in his sense of human culpability, both by a continuing sense of Pascalian dread and by the frightening drift towards international chaos, the beast which slouched towards Bethlehem has at last entered the stable. And in the myth of Armageddon lies a communion of vision at which Yeats and Barker, the passionate mystical humanitarian and the Catholic renegade, may once again drink at the same table, and, fifty years after Henekeys in the Strand, keep Eliot not unworthy company.

NOTES

1. Ezra Pound, *A Draft of Cantos XXXI–XLI* (London: Faber, 1935). Reviewed by George Barker in *The Criterion*, xiv, July, 1935, pp. 649–51.
2. George Barker, *Poems* (London: Faber, 1935).
3. Ezra Pound, *A Draft of XXX Cantos* (London: Faber, 1933) Canto XVII, pp. 80–3. Repr. in *The Oxford Book of Modern Verse, 1892–1935* W. B. Yeats (ed.) (Oxford: The Clarendon Press, 1936) pp. 243–7. Subsequent references to *The Oxford Book*.
4. *The Oxford Book*, p. xxxviii.
5. Cf. *The Complete Poems and Plays of T. S. Eliot* (London: Faber, 1969) p. 13.
   For the echo of Lionel Johnson in the second stanza, see "The Dark Angel" in *The Oxford Book*, pp. 105–7, especially the lines

   > Dark Angel, with thine aching lust
   > To rid the world of penitence:
   > Malicious Angel, who still dost
   > My soul such subtile violence.

   > Because of thee, no thought, no thing
   > Abides for me undesecrate:
   > Dark Angel, ever on the wing,
   > Who never reachest me too late!

   Line thirty may allude to the title of Yeats's "The Cold Heaven" from *Responsibilities* (1914) in *VP* 316.
   Lastly, the very end of the poem may have reminded Yeats of Nashe's lines

   > Brightness falls from the air,
   > Queens have died young and fair,
   > Dust hath closed Helen's eye.

   which are quoted *E&I* 7, and which also supplied the title for the essay "Dust Hath Closed Helen's Eye" in *Myth* 22–30.
6. *The Oxford Book*, pp. 435–6.
7. *The Oxford Book*, p. xli.
8. Cf. "A Prayer for my Daughter", *VP* 403–6.
9. "To My Mother", George Barker, *Collected Poems, 1930–1955*, p. 151. Subsequently referred to as *Collected Poems*.
10. "A Conversation between Robert Fraser and George Barker" in *P. N. Review* 31(9, no. 5) p. 44.
11. John Henry Newman, *Apologia pro Vita Sua* (London: Longman, 1900) p. 242.

12. "By the Boyne", *The Listener*, 7 July, 1937, p. 20. Repr. in George Barker, *Lament and Triumph* (London: Faber, 1941) pp. 66–8. Repr. in *Collected Poems* pp. 96–8.

13. *Collected Poems*, pp. 96–7.

14. "Epistle to D. T.", *New Verse*, no. 25, May 1937, pp. 2–3. Repr. as "Epistle I" in *Lament and Triumph*, pp. 43–5. Repr. in *Collected Poems*, pp. 84–6.

15. *Collected Poems*, p. 97.

16. *Collected Poems*, p. 98.

17. *Collected Poems*, p. 98.

18. W. B. Yeats *The Herne's Egg* (London: Macmillan, 1938). Repr., *VPl* 1012–40. Reviewed by Barker in *Life and Letters Today*, 18, no. 11 (Spring, 1938) p. 173.

19. Conversations with George Barker at his house in Itteringham, Norfolk, October 1981.

20. "The Death of Yeats" in *Poetry London*, 1 no. 1 (August, 1939) p. 1 Repr. in *Lament and Triumph*, pp. 23–4. Repr. in *Collected Poems*, p. 73.

21. Cf. "Byzantium", *VP* 497.

22. Barker, *Collected Poems*, p. 73.

23. *Collected Poems*, p. 74.

24. "Under Ben Bulben", dated 4 September 1938, first appeared in *The Irish Times* and *The Irish Independent*, 3 February 1939. Repr. in W. B. Yeats, *Last Poems and Two Plays* (Dublin: The Cuala Press, 1939). Repr. in *VP* 636–40.

25. *Life and Letters Today*, xviii:2 (Spring 1938) 173.

26. "Pacific Sonnets", iv in *Collected Poems*, p. 108.

27. Remarks from a recorded conversation between the author and George Barker, October 1982, basis of the published interview, lodged with the National Sound Archive under catalogue no. NSA 6537 WR.

28. George Barker, *Anno Domini* (London: Faber, 1983).

29. *P.N. Review*, Interview, p. 47.

30. George Barker, *The Golden Chains* (London: Faber, 1968) p. 42.

31. First published in *P.N. Review*, 32 (9, no. 6) p. 39.

Ben Bulben Revisited

George Barker

Lie still, old man, lie still,
Nothing's here to disturb you.
The ghosts are gone, the heroes
Lie snoring under the hill.
And the sea-bedded hoydens
That used so to perturb you,
Yes, you and your monkey gland,
Now sleep and never feel
The hallowing in your hand.
But now the beast is real
Slouching from Nazareth
With death under its elbow
And filthy on its breath
The ordure of Armageddon.

Old man, old man of the mountain
Only us silly sheep
Wander over the mountain
To populate your sleep.
The statesmen they may rave
And the soldiers roar
And old Adam behave
As foolishly as before –
Now that we take our leave
Of every thing we have,
There is nothing to save
Old man, any more,
Only, only the ground and the grave
And the angel at the door.

Old man, old dreaming man
Dream us also asleep
And then perhaps we can
Somehow manage to keep

The dream with which we began:
That vision of walking through
The common or garden wood
Until we came home to
The knowledge of evil and good
Wherein, like a holy house
We sat down at last
And found ourselves free to choose
An agape, or feast
With the black mystical beast.

Was it no more than a dream
This holy house of knowledge
In which we seemed to seem
At liberty to encourage
Either evil or good? Time
And the triumphant fiend
Have blown the house down
Bombed and blasted and blown
The homely house down
And now nothing remains
For all our many pains
Save us and a few ruins.
Neither evil nor good,
Only wrack and the wreckage,
And where old Adam stood
Only the brute and its carnage.

Sleep on, old man, among
The ruins and the echoes,
The small lies and the great rimes,
The stones and the rocky poems,
For they at least belong
By the Ben Bulben of dreams.

SIGNIFICANT RESEARCH COLLECTIONS

The Lady Gregory–Yeats Collection at Emory University

Ronald Schuchard

When the general editor of Yeats's letters, John Kelly, visited the young collection of books, manuscripts, and letters by W. B. Yeats in the Robert W. Woodruff Library for Advanced Studies at Emory University in 1981, he remarked with astonishment that "If anyone had told me in 1979 that they were starting out to build a major Yeats collection, I would have said it was impossible." Yet in that year the library vigorously began the mission by acquiring the personal collection of Richard Ellmann (who is now Woodruff Professor of English at Emory) and much of Lady Gregory's personal collection of books and manuscripts presented to her by Yeats.[1] The subsequent acquisition of scores of first and variant editions, manuscripts, letters, photographs, and other research documents has made the new collection a unique complement to collections at the National Library of Ireland, Stony Brook, the Berg, Texas, Kansas, Indiana and elsewhere. As the late F. S. L. Lyons, Yeats's biographer, wrote after his examination of the collection in February 1983, "It seems to me to be beyond question that recent gifts and purchases have brought the collections in this library into the front rank of major American sources for the study of Anglo-Irish literature, and this is true equally of quantity and of quality."

The growing collection of Anglo-Irish literature at Emory is greatly strengthened by its holdings of Lady Gregory's literary papers, including early diaries (1880–82), the unpublished manuscript of "An Emigrant's Notebook" (1884), manuscripts and typescripts of plays and stories, corrected page proofs of most of her books (some with Yeats's corrections, as in the proofs for *The Unicorn from the Stars*, 1908, where he makes over seventy alterations), the revised typescript of *Coole* (1931), privately printed editions of her plays, and numerous other documents relating to the Abbey Theatre, the Hugh Lane pictures, and the Irish political situation, such as the typescript for "What Was Their Utopia?", an unpublished meditation on the Easter Rising. There is also a substantial number of books from her library, including presentation copies with title-page sketches presented to her by AE, and her

153

bookplate copies of works by other authors, notably W. T. Horton's *A Book of Images* (1898), which contains a pen and ink drawing pasted in, entitled "Aspiratus" and inscribed "to W. B. Yeats in affection and deep gratitude. 23/7/01" (see plate 12a) and Lionel Johnson's *Ireland with Other Poems* (1897), containing pencil drawings by John Butler Yeats of W. B. Yeats, Douglas Hyde (dated September 1903), and Lady Gregory. Her correspondence includes unpublished letters from AE, W. S. Blunt, Padraic Colum, William G. Fay, Kuno Meyer, Lennox Robinson, John Butler Yeats, Eamon de Valera and others from 1882–1932. Two of the ten letters from AE contain pen and ink caricatures of Yeats. On 3 September 1898, admonishing Lady Gregory to keep Yeats away from

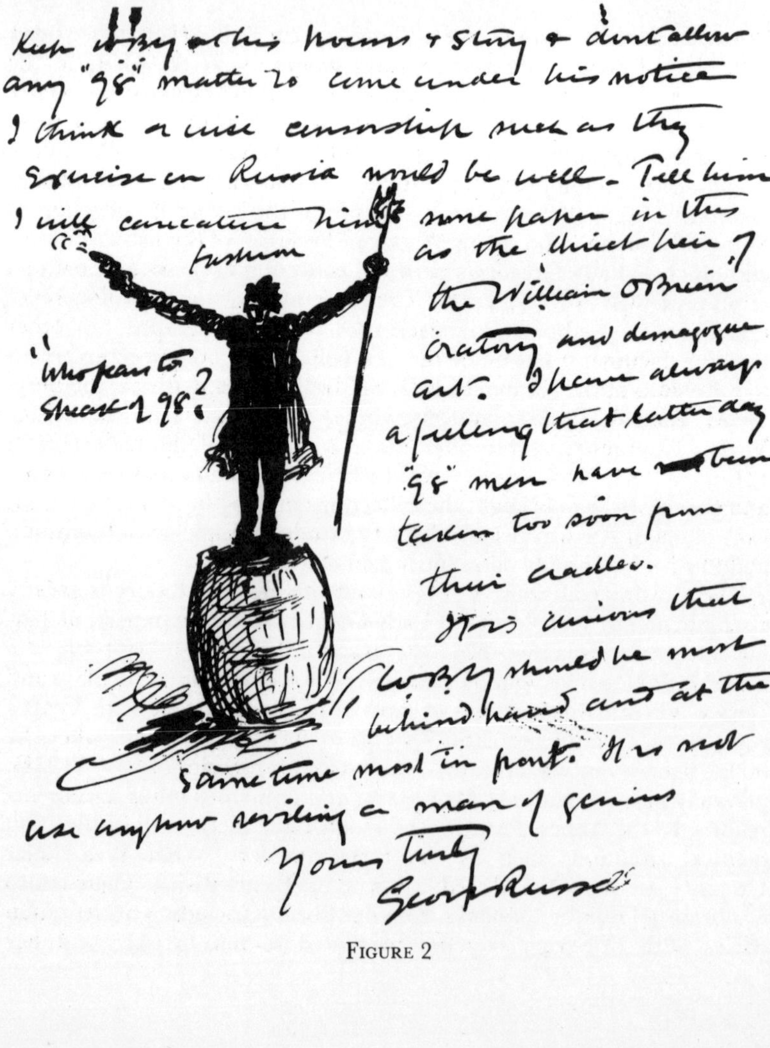

FIGURE 2

1898 activities, AE jokingly threatened to portray him in the newspapers
"as the direct heir of the William OBrien oratory and demagogue art"
and sketched him on a barrel with pistol and lance in outstretched arms,
captioned "Who fears to speak of 98?"

In an undated letter of June 1898, well after Yeats had published
"The Valley of the Black Pig", he mocked Yeats's inordinate love of the
Black Pig with both caricature and doggerel:

> You know that this uncanny creature is more to W.B.Y. at present
> than god or love or country. He fondles it in his heart as a lover the
> sweetest glance of his girl. I believe in dreams he tucks this weird
> animal under his arm and roams through the Vast.

FIGURE 3

I foresee Yeats and his Black Pig in many a ballad and tale of
future Ireland and many a wild vision:–

> "Who is he that rides upon the storm?
> Who carrieth a black porker
> And sheds shadowy terror and laughter.
> It is William MacYeats:
> Bard of the Gael!

Another considerable archive is the Gregory Family Papers, comprising historical documents of Sir William Gregory – his letters to Lady
Gregory, Sir Austen Henry Layard and others, his scrapbook[2] when he
was governor of Ceylon, with a rich collection of photographs, cartoons,
press cuttings, invitations, and drawings dating from 1873 – legal
documents concerning Coole, and Lady Gregory's correspondence with
her son, Robert Gregory, concerning whom there are also three

notebooks: one titled "In Memoriam" contains memories of Robert
from infancy to April 1917 by Lady Gregory's sister, Arabella Waith-
man, and two contain short descriptions of Robert from boyhood to
1898, typed and pasted in chronologically. In Lyons's view, "All of this
material would be absolutely indispensable to a properly documented
biography of Lady Gregory, and it must rank the collection as second
only to that in the Berg, as a Gregory archive."

The overall strength of the Yeats material as a working collection for
scholars lies in printed books, but, as will be seen, what makes the
collection unique, in addition to books containing notes and annotations
by Professor Ellmann, is the extensive collection of books given to Lady
Gregory by Yeats. As a quantitative measure, however, Emory presently
holds approximately 75 per cent of Wade's 211 entries for books and
separate editions, 65 per cent of the 345 total entries for books, books and
periodicals edited, prefaces and introductions, and contributions to
books. Most texts and editions essential to sustained research are
present, including the Ellis–Yeats edition of *The Works of William Blake*
(1893), Bullen's edition of the *Collected Works* (1908), the limited and
signed edition of *A Vision* (1925), and an extensive run of Dun Emer and
Cuala Press books (lacking nos 3, 15, 17, 34), several from Yeats's own
library. The percentage of Yeats's contributions to periodicals is more
difficult to measure, but the library has a strong collection of the late
nineteenth- and early twentieth-century periodicals in which Yeats
published poems, essays, stories, and reviews, including the *Dublin
University Review*, 1885–87 (broken); *The Irish Monthly*, 1886; *The Irish
Fireside*, January–June 1887; *The Girl's Own Paper*, 1889; *The Leisure Hour*
(broken); *The Old Country*, Dec. 1893; *The Bookman*; *The Pageant*, 1896–97;
The Yellow Book; *The Savoy*; *The Dome*; *The Irish Homestead*, 1897–1900,
1910–17 (230 issues, broken), plus *The Celtic Christmas*, 1902–5. There are
mostly complete runs of *Beltaine* (Yeats's presentation copy to Lady
Gregory), *Samhain*, *The Arrow*, *The Shanachie*, *The Dublin Review*, and *The
Irish Statesman* (180 issues, broken).[3] To facilitate research in Special
Collections, the library has duplicated there most of its extensive
holdings of secondary critical works on Yeats.

Yeats's presentation copies to Lady Gregory provide a wealth of
information, from specific dates to publication history, from alterations
not recorded in the variorum editions to attitudes toward the volumes
themselves. The most important copies contain original manuscripts,
described below, but others, briefly and characteristically inscribed "To
Lady Gregory from her friend W B Yeats", are revealingly dated. From
the beginning of their friendship Yeats slowly recovered copies of his
early publications for her, presenting *The Old Country, Christmas Annual
1893* (containing his story, "Michael Clancy, the Great Dhoul and
Death") on 19 October 1897, but not giving her a copy of *Poems and
Ballads of Young Ireland* (1888) until 5 December 1910 – probably from his

own library, as it contains his holograph notes, corrections, and an unrecorded transposition in the fourth line of "Love Song" (My love, I and you, we will hear, we will hear"). In May 1899, during the inaugural performances of the Irish Literary Theatre, he presented a copy of *The Countess Cathleen*, originally published in 1892; but in this instance he gave her in vellum a rare and unrecorded copy of a limited edition issued for the first performance of the play on 8 May.[4] Yeats gave her vellum copies of his works whenever possible, sometimes ordered from the publisher, and Lady Gregory apparently sent others off to Venice to be rebound in vellum, such as her vellum presentation copy of *The Land of Heart's Desire (Wade* 10). Yeats frequently quoted stanzas from his poems above the dedication, and in her vellum copy of *The Tables of the Law* (1897) he inscribed three lines from "Red Hanrahan's Song about Ireland", very close to the printing that year in *The Secret Rose*: "Like tufted reeds our courage droops in a black wind & dies: / But we have hidden in our hearts the flame out of the eyes / Of Kathleen the Daughter of Hoolihan." In December 1901 he inscribed her vellum copy of *John Sherman and Dhoya* (1891) with amusement: "I dont think any of my Sligo relations – except possibly George Pollexfen – has ever read this Sligo story. One apologised to me every summer for not reading it, for several years. She used to say 'I had a copy once but somebody borrowed it' I am sure that copy was given her. She would never have spent a 1/- on such a purpose." But other inscriptions reveal his dismay over public taste and the reception of his serious work, as in *A Selection from the Love Poetry* (1913): "In this book of my love poetry I notice that only those poems that I dislike are popular W B Yeats June 1922." In her copy of *Four Years* (1921) he wrote: "This little book was the first of my memoirs, for which in their completed form people were ready to praise me so much more & pay me so much better than for my poems. I tried to write first only for publication after my death but found after writing some hundred of pages that one does not write well for so remote an audience." Later, pulling off the shelf her copy of *Reveries Over Childhood and Youth* (1916), he wrote of public inattention to his autobiographical writing: "I wrote this to clear up my own mind as I speak of myself & not of the notable people that come at 'Four Years' but few have read it. It is for my friends & my children." Lady Gregory's copy of *The Death of Synge* was signed and dated by Yeats on 15 June 1928.

It becomes clear that Yeats and Lady Gregory both freely used her collection as a veritable storehouse for bits of information and reflective commentary about editions and texts, and Yeats frequently used her copies for revising texts for reprinting, much as he revised his "Introduction" to Horton's *A Book of Images*, inscribed to her on 28 July 1899, as "Symbolism in Painting" for *Ideas of Good and Evil* (1903). In 1902 John Quinn helped Yeats in his battle with George Moore over the authorship of *Where There Is Nothing* by privately printing a limited edition for copyright purposes. Quinn wrote in 1908 that fifteen copies were printed, but in the dedication copy to Lady Gregory, who with Douglas Hyde helped Yeats draft the play during a fortnight at Coole, Yeats not only offered it to her as "a book which is in part your own" but made clear that there were "only ten copies printed of this first edition, which was printed to secure American rights".[5] In copies of other works the contexts of specific poems are clarified, as in *Poems* (1901), which Yeats took off the shelf on 25 August 1907 to write on a free end paper the first untitled draft of "On a Recent Government Appointment in Ireland" (later "An Appointment"), with unrecorded variants. Above the manuscript Lady Gregory wrote: "On the appointment of Count Plunkett to curatorship of Dublin Museum by T. W. Russell & Birrell, Hugh Lane being a candidate." And in *Responsibilities* (1914) Yeats wrote above his poem, "To a Friend whose Work has Come to Nothing," a similar explanation: "This poem is to Lady Gregory though she thought it was for Hugh Lane." Further, on a preliminary blank leaf of this same volume he wrote in 1922: "This seemingly final version of The Hour Glass had to be revised again. I have just published a version in which there are passages in medieval Latin, to avoid the boredom of the same words coming too often during stage representation."

Another important copy of *Responsibilities* at Emory is from Yeats's library. It includes substantive autograph revisions of *The Hour-Glass* and is characteristic of his practice of using one edition to make insertions and changes for a succeeding edition, in this instance for *Responsibilities and Other Poems* (1916). His copy of *Two Plays for Dancers* (1919) contains several punctuation changes and alterations in *The Only Jealousy of Emer* for inclusion in *Four Plays for Dancers* (1921). He apparently decided to give the revised copy away, as it is inscribed "An aimless joy is a pure joy" (from "Tom O'Roughley", 1919) and dated September 1927.[6] But of even greater interest to textual scholars is Yeats's bookplate copy of *A Packet for Ezra Pound* (1928), which was used to set the corresponding section of *A Vision* (1937). The text contains copious notes and emendations by Yeats, as well as notations by other editorial hands – those of the compositor, J. Manson, and Yeats's editor at Macmillan, Thomas Mark. Finally, in his copy of *Last Poems and Two Plays* (1939), the manuscript page on which Yeats numbered and wrote out the contents for the volume is tipped in opposite the contents page. The autograph table contains errors in the titles, a parenthetical request after "The Statutes" ("would like another copy if George takes this to Dublin"), and probable slips ("Cuchulain's Death" for "The Death of Cuchulain").

The heart of the Emory collection lies in some extraordinarily rich presentation copies which contain manuscripts and drafts of poems written in by Yeats or tipped in by Lady Gregory, who made her vellum copy of *Poems* (1895) virtually a repository for manuscript material.

Pasted in at appropriate places in the text are drafts of "Hanrahan the Red Upon His Wanderings" (later "Maid Quiet"), "The Valley of the Black Pig", "To His Heart Bidding It Have No Fear", "The Rose in My Heart" (later "The Lover Tells of the Rose in His Heart"), a revised and unrecorded draft version of the second stanza of "The Sorrow of Love", and two untitled drafts of "He Tells of the Perfect Beauty", with some unrecorded readings. During this process of accretion Yeats drafted in "O Do Not Love Too Long", the third stanza of which is an unrecorded variant:

> In a moment she was changed
> Because I had loved too long;
> I had grown to be out of fashion
> Like an old song.

The draft is signed and dated 12 March 1903, with a further note that the poem was "written July 8th and 9th". Lady Gregory's beautiful vellum copy of Yeats's next volume of poetry, *The Wind Among the Reeds* (1899), with Althea Gyles' cover design stamped in gold, was inscribed on 14 April 1899 below an unpublished quatrain on friendship:

> The loud years come the loud years go,
> A friend is the best thing here below;
> Shall we a better marvel find
> When the loud years have fallen behind?

But on 25 March 1903 he took the volume down and wrote on the end papers a draft of "A Rider from the North" (later "The Happy Townland"),[7] with unrecorded variants. Earlier he had corrected the misprints, "breast" and "by" for "head" and "on", in the penultimate line of "Aedh Hears the Cry of the Sedge".

The most striking book to open is *Poems* (1899), inscribed to Lady Gregory on 10 May 1899, for on a preliminary leaf is the autograph draft of a major unpublished poem, "On a Child's Death" (see Plate 16), dated 5 September 1893 and evidently written on the death of the first son of Maud Gonne, Georges. (The poem is discussed further in a note in this volume, see p. 190). On the facing page is the autograph manuscript of yet another unpublished poem, "The Song of Heffernan the Blind: a translation", evidently first translated into prose for him after late 1888 by Douglas Hyde from a Gaelic quatrain quoted by John Daly in his study of Heffernan in *Reliques of Irish Jacobite Poetry* (1844):

> I often am in Shrone hill, in Conroy is my bed
> I grind an old quern, I grind it for my bread,
> And Teig and Nora with me, no other souls than these;
> I grind an old quern & them I do not please.

Lady Gregory's copy of *Poems* (1901) not only contains the manuscript of "An Appointment", described above, but also that of the three musicians' songs from *Deirdre* (1907), though Yeats may have written the songs when he began work on the play at Coole in the summer of 1904, as "Queen Edain" was published in *McClure's Magazine* in 1905, and the three songs appeared as the songs of two women under the title "The Entrance of Deirdre" in *Poems, 1899–1905* (1906). Her vellum copy of *Poems* (1904), inscribed on 21 July 1904, has tipped in still another, yet late, draft of the second stanza of "The Sorrow of Love", originally published in *The Rose* (1893). It is marked in pencil by Lady Gregory, "altered in 1924," clearly for publication in *Early Poems and Stories* (1925), where Yeats notes that he has altered this and another "till they are altogether new poems. Whatever changes I have made are but an attempt to express better what I thought and felt when I was a very young man" (p. 528). Here, however, the stanza-in-progress exhibits two unrecorded readings, "swept by" and "hurricane driven":

A girl swept by with her red mournful lips,
And seemed the greatness of the world in tears,
Doomed like Odysseus' hurricane driven ships,
And proud as Priam murdered with his peers.[8]

At the close of an unpublished letter of 15 September 1908 to Gordon Craig, Yeats wrote out a draft of an untitled poem ("All Things Can Tempt Me"), said to have been written that morning. At about the same time he inscribed a draft of the poem, with revisions, into Lady Gregory's copy of volume one of his *The Poetical Works* (1906), together with an untitled draft of "At Galway Races", both dated September 1908 and subsequently published together in *The English Review* for February 1909 as "Distraction" and "Galway Races". Yeats's habit from 1897 of drafting new poems into old volumes continued through the 1920s, as in Lady Gregory's copy of *Seven Poems and a Fragment* (1922), which Yeats inscribed in June 1922: "I wrote 'All Souls' Night' some months ago at Oxford. H . . . is Horton a very dear friend who died three years ago, & I have accurately described the chief emotion of his life." At that time Yeats made a minor correction in the sixth stanza of the poem, changing "plunged" to "plunge", but in the following month he wrote in the volume an early, three-stanza draft of "The Stare's Nest" (later "The Stare's Nest by My Window"), dated 14 July 1922. A fourth stanza was added before the poem was published in *The Dial* and *The London Mercury* the following year. Finally, in a presentation copy of his *Selected Poems* (1929), initially inscribed to Lady Gregory in September 1929, he wrote opposite the contents page in September 1930 a draft of "Yellow Hair / For Anne Gregory". Less than two years later Lady Gregory was dead, and the great living library was still.

The thirteen separate manuscripts of Yeats's work at Emory range from about 1892 to 1925 and include drafts and revisions for nine poems and three early plays, including thirteen lines of verse from the end of the second scene of *The Countess Kathleen* (1892). The draft begins with the speech of Kathleen (here spelled "Cathleen") to the Steward ("Keeping this house alone sell all I have"), contains ten lines and stage directions that were revised or discarded before the play was printed, and ends with her saying "He may come in. He brings good news perhaps." There are also reworked drafts of the Old Woman's two songs in *Cathleen Ni Houlihan* (two drafts of "Do not make a great keening" and one of "They shall be remembered forever"). The drafts are undated, but Yeats began writing the play in the fall of 1901, before Maud Gonne chanted the songs in the first production of the play in April 1902. In preparing *The Pot of Broth* for inclusion in *Plays in Prose and Verse* (1922), Yeats wrote in April of that year a three-page revision, noting that his text for the revisions begins on page 76 of Bullen's edition of *The Hour-Glass, Cathleen Ni Houlihan, The Pot of Broth* (1904): " . . . used to be singing / Philomel, I've listened oft / To thy lay . . .". It should be noted that the Emory copy of *The Hour-Glass*, as printed in *The North American Review* for September 1903, is signed by Yeats and has pasted in the typescript of the new ending printed in Bullen's 1904 edition (*Wade* 53).

A separate (and probably the first) draft of "O Do Not Love Too Long" (another draft of which is described above in Lady Gregory's copy of *Poems*, 1895), is comprised of three four-line stanzas with revisions, deletions and unrecorded variants. Written too late for inclusion in *In the Seven Woods*, the poem was first published as "Do not love too long" in *The Acorn* for October 1905 and added to *In the Seven Woods* in the *Collected Works* (1908). In December 1903, when Yeats was on his first American tour, he wrote "Old Memory", alluding to Maud Gonne, who had married earlier in the year: " 'Your strength that is so lofty & fierce & kind / That might call up a new age calling to mind / The Queens that were imagined long ago / Is but half yours . . .". The signed draft at Emory precedes the printing in *Wayfarer's Love* (1904), edited by the Duchess of Sutherland, and as it contains unrecorded alterations it probably precedes the fair copy that he sent to her about 20 December. The manuscript of "The Ragged Wood" is also probably the first draft, as almost every line is reworked, and the version contains several unrecorded variants.[9] It is closest to the text published in *Stories of Red Hanrahan* (1904), where it first appeared before being considerably revised when included in later collections of *In the Seven Woods*. Among these early poems are untitled drafts of "Brown Penny", first published as "The Young Man's Song" in *The Green Helmet and Other Poems* (1910), and "Friends", where Yeats was as yet undecided between the unrecorded "In labouring ecstasy" and the final "Labouring in ecstasy", dated 21 January 1911 and published in the enlarged 1912 edition of the same volume (*Wade* 101).

On 8 August 1912 Yeats wrote to Lady Gregory from Maud Gonne's villa in France that he had completed a poem "on a child dancing" and that he thought the lyric "one of the best I have written".[10] The undated draft of this poem, "To a Child Dancing on the Shore", was apparently copied out sometime later on Coole Park stationery. It corresponds closely to the title and text of the poem when first published as "To a Child Dancing upon the Shore" (later "To a Child Dancing in the Wind") in *Poetry* (Chicago) for December 1912. But the proof sheet for "While I, from that reed-throated whisperer" does not match the text of the poem in *Responsibilities* (1914). Annotated by both Yeats and Ezra Pound, the proof sheet is an interesting document in the evolution of the text, which was first published in *The New Statesman* for 7 February 1914. For insertion in the proof Yeats wrote a new manuscript of four and one-half lines on the back of stationery engraved "President's House/ Amherst Massachusetts", which he visited from 13–16 March on his third American tour. Yeats may have read proof there and returned it to Pound, for some of Yeats's suggested and unrecorded emendations to other lines were discarded before publication, possibly by Pound, whose recommendations stood: he advised against the name "Kyle-na-Ino", as originally printed in the *New Statesman*, and argued that "its got to be *No* or *Kno* to scan. He pronounced it Kyle-na-No".[11] On reading the last two lines of the poem ("Notorious, till all my priceless things / Are but a post the passing dogs defile"), Pound reportedly remarked, to Yeats's great pleasure, that he had at last become a modern poet. As Richard Ellmann put it, "An image of urination had finally brought Pound to his knees" (*Eminent Domain*, 1970, p. 67).

The present manuscript collection at Emory is rounded out by the typescripts and partial drafts of two of Yeats's most important poems – "In Memory of Major Robert Gregory" and "The Tower". The four-page typescript of the former poem, here titled "In Memory of Robert Gregory", comprises eleven eight-line stanzas with Yeats's autograph revisions, together with the inserted eighth stanza (here "7a"), beginning "When with the Galway foxhounds he would ride", written entirely in Yeats's hand on a separate slip of paper. The poem first appeared in *The English Review* for August 1918, following Major Gregory's death on 23 January, but the typescript contains two deletions and a discarded substitute reading for lines 75–7, all unrecorded: "And blossoming garden path, or understood / How to paint emblems upon wood / Or draw out letters to be carved on stone". Lastly, Emory has what appears to be the first autograph draft of the final section of "The Tower", beginning "It is time that I wrote my will" and continuing for twenty-five lines, with unrecorded variations and with all but the first and the last of the concluding nine lines crossed out.

Or that of the Fabulous horn
Or the bursting fruit or the falling shower
of the swan that sees
The first appro[a]ch of the hour
When he must fix his eyes
Upon a fading gleam
And plung[e] into that long,
Broad still glittering stream
And then sing his last song.

The poem first appeared in T. S. Eliot's *The Criterion* for June 1927, but Yeats dated it 1925 in *October Blast* (1927).

There are presently eighteen unpublished letters by Yeats in the collection, the earliest to Stephen Gwynn in late 1887 regarding the contents and publication of *The Wanderings of Oisin* (1889), the latest one of the twelve letters to Lady Gregory that date from 4 November 1904 to 25 May 1930. In the earliest of these he expresses delight over some new pictures of Charles Ricketts, and in a letter of 19 February 1913 he describes discussions with Sir Hugh Lane, Lady Gregory's nephew, over a site for the Municipal Gallery, a letter that looks forward ten years to four letters in January 1923 that concern the difficulties of returning the Lane pictures to Dublin, followed by a letter of 21 June 1925 expressing outrage at the Commission's latest report on the pictures. The last letter to Lady Gregory described his reaction to being passed over for the poet laureateship in May 1930:

> . . . I am more relieved than anything else for I have no quality that could have moved the great mass of English readers, & I would have had to postpone the new edition of "A Vision" (the great wheel I shall probably call it) not to hurt their feelings.

In other letters of general interest Yeats writes to Rosamund G. Langbridge on 11 February 1907 about the recent riots at the Abbey Theatre, and in September of that year he and Lady Gregory jointly sign the carbon of a petition, organised by C. H. Norman and addressed to Sir Edward Grey, Secretary of State for Foreign Affairs, concerning "the advisability of an immediate release of the persons concerned in an assault on certain British officers near the village of Denshawai [Egypt], on Wednesday, 13th June 1906". On 16 May 1918 Lady Gregory, Yeats, James Stephens, AE and Douglas Hyde sign a letter to the editor of *The Nation* in protest of conscription in Ireland. In a letter of 9 April [1919] Yeats indignantly asks Eric Gorman to bring the present letter concerning Lennox Robinson's casting of *The Player Queen* before the Board of the Abbey Theatre, and on 24 May [1926] he writes to Henry Mead Bland of the State Teachers College in San Jose, California, regretting not having met his friend, Miss Virginia Sanderson, and remembering that he spoke in San Jose twenty-two years past "in some Catholic school with a court-yard full of palm trees". Yeats's recollection of the distant event was accurate; he lectured at Santa Clara College on the evening of 29 January 1904 on "The Intellectual Revival in Ireland". Ironically, Professor Bland was present on the speaker's platform. Yeats spent the night in San Jose, and the next day he wrote to Lady Gregory that he had lectured "among palm trees and there was an orange tree by the hotel where I slept" (*L* 429).

An assortment of photographs collected by Richard Ellmann gives a final dimension to the Yeats papers at Emory. Though the photographs of Maud Gonne have been published elsewhere, as have most of the photographs of portraits of Yeats by John Butler Yeats, Sarah Purser and Charles Shannon, there remains a unique group of photographs of Yeats with family and friends. The family pictures include a photograph of George Yeats taken by Elizabeth Corbet Yeats and inscribed "George at our house at Gurteen Dhas, Dundrum when we knew her first. 1917." There are snapshots of Yeats with his daugher, Anne, at the age of three weeks in 1919, one of Yeats and George by the "flowering pomegranates" at Mission Concepcion in San Antonio, Texas, in 1920, another of Yeats with Michael and Anne in 1926, and a family portrait made by Graphic Studios, Dublin, about 1928. There are earlier snaps of Yeats with brother Jack, Jack's wife, Cottie, and Sarah Allgood, dated 20 July 1911. The trip to Rapallo in 1929 is recorded in eight photographs, some of Yeats sitting alone, some of Yeats with George and Ezra Pound at the Cafe Aurum. Among other literary friends, Yeats is snapped with Barrett Wendell in Boston in 1903, with Lytton Strachey, probably at Garsington about 1930, with Dorothy Wellesley at Penns-in-the-Rocks, Sussex, in 1937, and with Edith Shackleton Heald and Mrs Edmund Dulac at the Chantry House, Steyning, in his last years.

The miscellaneous items related to Yeats, Lady Gregory, and their literary-theatrical activities are too numerous to catalogue, but notable for critics and historians and indicative of the range are Lady Gregory's address book, prospectuses of the Dun Emer Press, illuminated poems of the Cuala Press, and several Abbey Theatre programmes – from the opening on 27 December 1904 to the twenty-first anniversary performance on 27 December 1925. In addition to the parodic pamphlet by Page L. Dickinson, Joseph Hone, and Frank Sparrow, *The Abbey Row: not edited by W. B. Yeats* (1907), there is the rare *Paragraphs from Samhain, 1909*, issued by Yeats and Lady Gregory as a "Statement of Affairs" of the Abbey Theatre. Several of the rarer limited editions of Yeats's works are present, including Frederic Prokosch's private printings of *The Singing Head and the Lady* (*Wade* 180), no. III of twenty copies, signed by Yeats on 6 November 1935, and *Leda and the Swan* (*Wade* 185), one of twenty-two copies. Emory's copy of the privately printed edition of *Mosada* (*Wade*

206), number thirty of fifty, is signed by George Yeats. Among numerous anthologies are H. Halliday Sparling's *Irish Minstrelsy* (1888) and Edward Martyn's bookplate copy of Yeats's *A Book of Irish Verse* (1895). Martyn's presentation copy to Lady Gregory of *Literary Ideals in Ireland* (1899) contains Yeats's corrections to his contribution, "John Eglinton and Spiritual Art", with a three-page draft typescript of the essay tipped in. A recent addition to the material is a copy of "The Way of Wisdom", as printed in *The Speaker* for 14 April 1900, with Yeats's autograph revisions for reprinting the essay as "The Pathway" in volume eight of the *Collected Works*.

A vigilant staff at the Robert W. Woodruff Library daily keep an eye on catalogues and auction announcements for *desiderata*, which include some early *Wade* numbers (1, 3, 5, 7, 9, 12–14, 23, 29, 32, 34, 36–9, with fewer gaps thereafter), and selective additions, measured primarily by research value, to all areas described above. While the library continues to build to the strength of the Lady Gregory–Yeats collection, it hopes to make further significant additions to its holdings of AE, Synge, Joyce and other authors of the Irish Renaissance. The library may not be so fortunate to match the extraordinary acquisitions of the past five years, but by the end of the decade it may well be established as one of the primary research centres for the study of Anglo-Irish literature and history. In the meantime, concludes Lyons, "it is clear that there now exists in Emory a major collection with many facets and much exciting material which will undoubtedly attract an increasing number of scholars in years to come".[12]

NOTES

1. Many of the items described in this essay were purchased at auction and are described in detail in Sotheby's *Catalogue of Valuable Autograph Letters, Literary Manuscripts and Historical Documents* for 23–4 July 1979 (lots 341–9, 352–69, 379, 383–92, 403, 406, 410, 415, 420, 424) and for 17 December 1979 (lots 218–23, 243–6, 248–57, 260–1, 263–5, 267, 270, 272–3, 279, 285–6, 295).
2. This valuable scrapbook was presented to the library by the Gregory family in memory of Major Richard Graham Gregory (1909–81).
3. More recently, at the Sotheby auction of modern English literature on 22 July 1983, Emory acquired a private collection of 250 periodicals, most of them with contributions by or about Yeats, including runs of *The London Mercury*, *The Dublin Magazine*, *The Bell* and *Envoy*.
4. See Colin Smythe's note on this edition of *The Countess Cathleen* on page 193 of the present volume.
5. Quinn later corrected the number in his Sale Catalogue (1924), but Wade, who took the correction as "an error of memory", continued to give the number of copies as fifteen. Though Quinn knew the whereabouts of eight copies in 1908, there are presently five known copies: two in the Library of Congress, one in the Lilly Library, Indiana, one in private hands, and Yeats's presentation copy to Lady Gregory at Emory. I am grateful to Colin Smythe for this and other bibliographical information.

6. Yeats wrote this same inscription in his presentation copy to Lady Gregory of *October Blast* in August (1927). This copy, lot 425 in the Sotheby *Catalogue* of 23–4 July 1979, did not go to Emory.

7. The poem first appeared as "The Happy Townland" in the *Weekly Critical Review* (Paris) for 4 June 1903, as "The Rider from the North" in *In the Seven Woods*, and thereafter as "The Happy Townland". When in 1908 Wade asked Yeats why he had made the back and forth changes, "he said that he had completely forgotten doing so" (See *Wade* 49).

8. The draft of the second stanza tipped into Lady Gregory's copy of *Poems* (1895), discussed above, is similarly marked in pencil "Altered at Coole – Autumn 1924". It differs from this version only in the third line, "Doomed like Odysseus & his scattered ships", except that there are two cancelled lines after the second line: "Mourning Odysseus & his scattered ships / Or mourning Priam dead among his peers."

9. The back of one page is numbered "4" and contains what appear to be the continuation of notes for a lecture on symbolism, concluding: "Symbols not mere channels of will but powerful in themselves."

10. Unpublished letter in the Robert W. Woodruff Library. I am grateful to the Yeats estate for permission to quote unpublished material in this essay.

11. Yeats wrote "Kno" in the manuscript insertion, but "Kyle-na-no" was printed. In 1917 he published "To a Squirrel at Kyle-No-gno", altered it to "Kyle-Na-Gno" in *The Wild Swans at Coole*, and finally returned to "Kyle-na-no" in *The Collected Poems of W. B. Yeats* (1933).

12. Lyons's typed report is on file in Special Collections, where the collection is available from Monday to Saturday, 9 a.m. to 6 p.m. Copies of policies on use and information for out-of-town visitors may be obtained by writing to the Special Collections Department, Robert W. Woodruff Library, Emory University, Atlanta, Georgia 30322.

ADDENDA

The three songs from *Deirdre* discussed *supra*, p. 160, were probably inscribed into Lady Gregory's copy of *Poems* (1901) on or about September 28, 1904, when Yeats wrote to John Quinn that he had just finished those songs.

Since the above was written, Emory has acquired the holograph manuscript of Yeats's "Preface" to *At the Hawk's Well*, dated October 24, 1916, though the text was misdated "December 1916" when first printed as "A Note" to the play in the Cuala edition of *The Wild Swans at Coole* (1917). Emory has also acquired the four volumes of Lady Gregory's press cutting books (1897–1913) and the extremely rare ("about four copies") 1938 edition of *On the Boiler* (Wade 201).

R. S.

The University of Reading Collections[1]

Elizabeth Ingli James

The University of Reading emerged as a centre of Yeats studies in the 1950s with a photographic exhibition organised by the late Professor D. J. Gordon and colleagues in the English department. This, together with the accompanying descriptive guide attracted so much attention that a larger and more elaborate exhibition was put together on the basis of the first, and was shown in Manchester and Dublin in the summer of 1961. The published catalogue *W. B. Yeats: Images of a Poet* (Manchester 1961), a standard work, has recently been reprinted by the Greenwood Press (Westport, Conn., 1979).

The acquisitions in Reading relating to Yeats and his associates have in the main resulted, directly or indirectly, from work initiated in connection with these exhibitions, and its continuance, particularly by Emeritus Professor Ian Fletcher (who has kindly provided me with helpful suggestions and information) in editions, discoveries, publications.

The photographic collection assembled by D. J. Gordon currently remains in the keeping of the English department, with supplementary material in the same categories. *Images of a Poet* nonetheless provides, especially in the section on symbolic art, an introduction to some of the library's own archives.

Among early influences and counter-influences upon Yeats was of course the impress of his father, with the ideas and personalities encountered in his milieu. The library possesses a substantial archive of the papers of John Todhunter. From the large number of letters here may be derived an impression of Todhunter's elevation upon the cultural ladder: able to dispense a degree of patronage to J. B. Yeats, J. T. Nettleship and George Wilson (his painting confrères), and lesser fry, he in turn collects polite commendations for his books and plays from Browning, William Watson, J. A. Symonds, Jane Harrison. W. M. Rossetti was a friend: Shelley is discussed, a propos of Todhunter's monograph (1880); and there are letters from, for example, Edward Dowden, Lionel Johnson, Ellen Terry, and from both Arnold Dolmetsch and his aggrieved ex-wife – the range itself is valuable. Of particular note here however is the series of letters, 1868–71, from J. B. Yeats, animatedly detailing the progress of the "brotherhood" – "I think you are greatly in error calling us a clique" (25 November 1869) – and exhorting Todhunter to come to London. A letter of 1885 describes the poetical progress of "Willie", and his enthusiasm for Todhunter's poetical dramas. In turn, the poet encouraged Todhunter, once they had become neighbours in Bedford Park, towards the *success d'estime* of *A Sicilian Idyll* in May 1890, with important repercussions on Yeats's own thinking about plays. For Todhunter himself though, "every book was a new planting, and not a new bud on an old bough" (*Au* 117), or so Yeats judged in 1922, to the indignation of A. P. Graves, in one of his letters here to Todhunter's widow. Graves deplores also in the "Memories" Yeats's "record of self-glorification as regards the Irish Literary Society for which Willie Rolleston and I worked hardest . . ." (31 July 1922). A letter from Lily B. Yeats (10 July 1939) accompanies a sketch by her father of Todhunter at a Calumet meeting: "a talking club" in Bedford Park.

The collection also includes copies of Todhunter's letters to Herbert Horne (from a private collection), literary manuscripts including that of *A Comedy of Sighs*, and four lectures on Blake from Todhunter's Alexandra College days which Ian Fletcher has edited, *Blake Newsletter* 29–30 (1974) 4–14. (J. B. Yeats in an 1871 letter here, makes much of the responsibility of Todhunter's post among the female students, given the peculiar influence that Irish women have over their men, exhorting him to teach them that Blake's is the highest morality. Todhunter at any rate emphasises the difficult, necessary submission of "poor little Mrs. Blake".)

The library also holds a collection of the early "Blake drawings" by Nettleship, who liked to insist that even his Landseerish animal pictures were "symbols" (*Au* 157): Yeats responded with "On Mr. Nettleship's Picture at the Royal Hibernian Academy" (1886) and with his first attempt at art criticism. Though the poem was never reprinted the symbolism it commemorated found its way to, for instance, "What Magic Drum?" in *A Full Moon in March*. Nettleship's work like Blake's helped to provide Yeats with the visual symbols which enforced his conclusion that "it may be our lot to worship in terror" (*E&I*). Morton Paley gives an account of the artist, a checklist of Reading's Nettleship collection and illustrations in *Blake Quarterly* 14 (1981) 185–94.

Some assiduous detective work by Ian Fletcher resulted in the acquisition by the library of what remains of the "Ellis–Yeats–Blake manuscript cluster", his own account of which, with a checklist, is indispensable: *The Book Collector*, 21 (1972) 72–94. The essay expounds the context of this project, important for both authors, and refers also to the other archives mentioned here. Different stages of draft survive, from injudicious first attempts: "Tatham was a bigotted Irvingite . . ." (in Yeats's hand), to final – though not always fair – copy for printers.

"Much of the revision was done in the same room at the same time. . . . The Yeats–Ellis commentary was collaboration in the deepest sense." (*Book Collector*, 1972, 94.)

From the same source, as well as books including Ellis's copies of Yeats's, and of the *Blake*, with marginalia, came mss. of literary works by Ellis (including poems, a dialogue: "Occultist & Materialist", an "Essay on the Unconscious") and letters from Yeats. Two are of the period of the book – Yeats presents an early scheme of work, and rehearses anxieties about the vulnerability of their interpretative divergences, which we might guess lay behind the emphasis in the preface on Blake's multiplicity of meaning. Three further letters (c.1910, 1913) contain news of Maud Gonne, Florence Farr, the Abbey, emotional tributes to Lady Gregory, and vatic utterances: "I am becoming mythical even to myelf." There are four of his letters to Ellis's widow in 1922.

Copies of related material from collections elsewhere have been placed with these papers, and there are also two letters from Yeats to Geoffrey Keynes, in 1913, concerning a Blake query.

From the family of Althea Gyles the library acquired her literary remains, including poems, two incomplete novels, and drafts of a play. Ian Fletcher has used this material in "Poet and Designer: W. B. Yeats and Althea Gyles", *Yeats Studies: an international journal*, no. 1, Bealtane, (1971) 42–79.

The library contains a very large collection (approximately 900 items) of W. T. Horton's graphic work including drawings, pen and ink, pen and wash work and watercolours in a range of styles: direct caricature, exercises in the grotesque dominated by his admiration for Beardsley (who said that he had "a sort of a kind of talent") and an idealising mode related to the mystical impulses which issued in *The Way of the Soul*, Horton's celebration of his platonic marriage with Audrey Locke, published 1910. At least two drawings in the collection employ Yeats as model (see Plates 12b and 13b) as does the illustration on page 119 of the book. There is also an illustration of a line from "The Ballad of Moll Magee" among the "visionary" drawings (see Plate 13a). Yeats was first struck by Horton's visionary propensities, but soon began urging him to the exercise of will and intellect, advising him to draw bathed in imaginary sunlight, to nurture a more healthy art. The library possesses transcripts made by the poet "John Gawsworth" (Terence Ian Fytton Armstrong) of over eighty letters from Yeats to Horton, now in the Humanities Research Institute, Texas; these are summarised in George Mills Harper *W. B. Yeats and W. T. Horton: the Record of an Occult Friendship* (1980) with Horton's side of the correspondence in the collection of

Michael B. Yeats, published in full. Gawsworth also transcribed Rider Haggard's letters to Horton.

Horton's own copy of *The Way of the Soul* is in the library, signed on the flyleaf, with a holograph poem written after Audrey Locke's death.

"There was more in him than his art ever did justice to" wrote T. Sturge Moore, of Horton, in 1937, to his friend John Gawsworth. The library has Moore's letters to Gawsworth, which contain observations and comments upon young poets and the dead, giving a picture of him at a later period than that of the published correspondence with Yeats, and complementing the large Sturge Moore archive in the Sterling Library, University of London.

The principal item among unpublished Yeats papers here is a typescript of four of the lyrics "Upon a Dying Lady". Simply headed " 'Poems' by W. B. Yeats", the sequence contains an untitled draft of "Her Courtesy", of "We bring her dolls and drawings" [sic], "She turns the dolls' faces to the Wall" and (also untitled) "Her Courage". The copy was sent to Mabel Beardsley at "The Nook", a nursing home in Holford Road, Hampstead, and she – or someone on her behalf – pencilling it "André with Mabel's love", gave it in turn to Andre Raffalovich. Accompanying the typescript is a letter to Raffalovich from Lady Gregory, written on 10 October 1928. She thanks him for some memoirs (he had published memoirs in *Blackfriars* that year), and anticipating Yeats's interest in these reminders of his "salad days".

Some of these earlier readings offer slight but interesting variations upon the versions published: the second poem ends more tamely, "What have we left but toys?"; the third lacks the exotic "domino" – here, "silken vest". The fourth (sixth as published) varies most extensively:

When she has found – long hence! long hence! her dancing place
  (I have no speech but symbol, the pagan speech I made
Amid the dreams of youth), let her come face to face
  While wondering still to be a shade, with Grania's shade,
All but the perils of the woodland flight forgot,
  And all the rest forgiven, and some old Cardinal
Pacing with half-closed eyelids in a sunny spot
  Who had murmured of Giorgione at his latest breath –
Aye and Achilles, Timor, Babar, Barhaim, all
  Who lived in shameless joy, and laughed into the face of Death.

As for other personal letters of Yeats's: there is a note from Stockholm in 1923; and a compilation of correspondence between Yeats and Frank Fay, mainly of the period 1901–4, transcribed from several sources, including unpublished letters; and the Elkin Mathews collection contains six letters from Yeats. Four of these are published, edited by Ian Fletcher, in *Yeats Studies: an international journal*, no. 1 (1971) 204–8. There are also many notes and letters to Mathews from Jack B. Yeats (discussed by Patricia Hutchins in "Jack Yeats and his Publisher", *Yeats Studies: an international journal*, no. 2, 1972, 121–6 where some of the illustrated examples are reproduced), a letter from John B. Yeats of 23 August 1918, and one from Elizabeth C. Yeats.

The Elkin Mathews papers were acquired by the library in 1964, to complement its increasing holdings of 1890s material. A collection of Beardsley papers has been accumulated, for example, including letters, photographs and cuttings; John Gray is represented by his translation of Theodore de Banville's *Le Baiser* and articles from *Le Revue Blanche* in 1896; among other names appearing in the accessions list are Lionel Johnson, Victor Plarr, Le Gallienne, Robert Bridges, R. H. Sherard, Machen, Symons.

The large correspondence to Elkin Mathews (not, however, including publisher's letterbooks) contains letters from Lane concerning the establishment of the Bodley Head, while the split in their partnership is documented in letters – from Ernest and Dollie Radford, G. A. Greene, Dowson, Le Gallienne – and in a statement by Mathews himself. Among many other letters of interest, one from Rolleston recommends the art of J. B. Yeats for the *Yellow Book* and offers Mathews a copy of the Ellis and Yeats *Blake*, "*cheap* – it is in first rate preservation" (13 September 1894). Other correspondents include Todhunter, Nettleship, Masefield, Gordon Bottomley, Joyce and Pound. An attempted autobiographical sketch by Mathews is here, as well as his commonplace book. There are items of publishing ephemera including catalogues. Mathews's collection of press cuttings provides a guide to the critical reception of minor poetry in the 1890s of great interest to students of the period. There is a fine chalk drawing of Mathews by John B. Yeats (Plate 14). The Elkin Mathews collection is available on microfilm as part of Chadwyck-Healey's series "Archives of British Publishers".

This library has established an archive of British publishing, and holds material from George Bell, Longman's (including a file of Thomas Moore papers), Routledge and Kegan Paul, and Macmillan's. In the last of these are letters from Beerbohm, Blunt, Dunsany, Sturge Moore, AE and from Yeats – mainly copyright requests in connection with the *Oxford Book of Modern Verse*.

Reading University Library offers the student of Yeats research material in several interconnected areas; principally (to date) his father's circle, the Blake study, and some of the contemporary artists and writers whose works – and whose lives – gave him potent images.

NOTE

1. Reading University Library, Whiteknights, Reading, Berks., UK (tel. Reading 874331). The Archivist is Dr J. A. Edwards. I am most grateful to him, and to his assistant, Mr Michael Bott, for their helpfulness.

SHORTER NOTES

Yeats's Birthplace

A. Norman Jeffares

The Women Writers' Club decided in 1940 to produce a small book about the various authors who were born in Dublin. It was to be written by Kate O'Brien, Lilian Davidson was to sketch the houses involved, and Sybil Le Brocquy was to do the research work. She quickly found out that there were some surprising gaps in knowledge – for instance, no one knew the house in which Synge was born. She did, subsequently, find a map in the Pembroke Estate Office on which "Mr Synge's house" was marked, now 2 Newtown Villas, Churchtown. Then, in conversation with George Yeats, she realised that Yeats's birthplace was at the time unknown also. All George Yeats could tell her was that W. B. had once returned from a walk (probably when the Yeatses were living in Merrion Square) and intoned "I have seen the house in which I was born and it is a mean house" (see Plate 15b). From Jack Yeats came the information that the family used to make jokes about Willie's being born on a lane, at which, Sybil told me, Lennox Robinson whinnied "Does it matter where a great man is born?" I was myself told by Lily Yeats – the story is also in Joseph Hone's *W. B. Yeats 1865–1939* (1942) p. 9 – that Robert Corbet used to tease John Butler Yeats by addressing letters to him at "The Quarry Hole", remembering that the house had been built on the site of a quarry.

Sybil began work. W. B.'s birth certificate, easily obtained at the Custom House, Dublin, was no help. It stated that he was born in 1, George Villa, Sandymount Strand. But there never was a George Villa or Ville in Sandymount Strand, and when she discussed this with an official in the Custom House he remarked – in characteristic Dublin fashion – "If you knew the state some fathers are in when they register the births you'd not be surprised *what* they'd put down!" She realised that all the papers of the Pembroke Township (in which Sandymount was situated) had been destroyed in protest when that township was forcibly taken over by Dublin Corporation, but some official suggested that she *might* be able to examine the rate-collectors' books which were in Ely Place. She followed this hint up and in a small notebook in which the entries were made in pencil she discovered that in October 1864 "John Yeats" was tenant of 3 Sandymount Avenue, the landlord being a Mr Robertson. (*Thom's Directory*, incidentally, lists "Robertson & Co., General Drapers and tea agents and post office receivers" at No. 1, Sandymount Square. At a later date "and money

175

order office" was added. Did this firm own the houses in Sandymount Avenue?) On the Sandymount map of 1864, 3 Sandymount Avenue was a new house, so W. B. was the first child born in it.

This house, 3 Sandymount Avenue, was later renumbered 1 George's Ville. Sybil Le Brocquy found that the capstone (see Plate 15a) of one of the gateposts had 1 George's Ville cut on the face which had been reversed when the road was *again* re-numbered and the house became 5 Sandymount Avenue. However, this capstone now faces Sandymount Avenue and reads "George's Ville No. 1".

The house was simply called "Georgeville" by Joseph Hone (op. cit., p. 9); possibly his information came from Lily Yeats as did mine in *W. B. Yeats: man and poet* (1949; 1962) p. 1, and *A Commentary on the Collected Poems of W. B. Yeats* (1968), p. xiii, which describe it as Georgeville, Sandymount Avenue. The mistake has continued in other books on Yeats. Edward Malins, *A Preface to Yeats* (1974) p. 161, calls the house "Georgeville, No. 2 Sandymount Avenue, Dublin" saying that it is still there, "though now No. 5 with its name inscribed on the stone wall", which is misleading. Frank Tuohy, *Yeats* (1976) pp. 22–3, merely describes John Butler Yeats and his wife as setting up house "at Sandymount near Dublin" where they were "not far distant from . . . Sandymount Castle". William M. Murphy in his excellent biography *Prodigal Father: the Life of John Butler Yeats (1839–1922)* (1978) p. 43, calls the house "Georgeville" but does give "5 Sandymount Avenue" correctly as the (current) address of the birthplace. He gives the source of his information as the late Dr Oliver Edwards, saying that Edwards cited the Registry of Birth, Marriages and Death, Custom House, Dublin for this fact, adding that the father was listed as a law student. Was Oliver Edwards's account of the entry in the Registry correct? Or Sybil Le Brocquy's? The actual entry does give as the birthplace 1, George Villa, Sandymount Strand, so presumably Oliver Edwards got his information from some other source.

Curiously enough, John Butler Yeats's name does not appear in *Thom's Directory* (the only Yeats listed in 1865 is John Yeats, hosier, 66 William Street, South; and *Thom's Directory* lists a Mrs Butler as occupying 1 George Villas in 1907). The *Directory* first mentions "George Villas" in 1870, as numbers 1 and 2 Sandymount Avenue. By 1885 five houses are listed (a block of three larger houses was built next to the two semi-detached houses numbers 1 and 2) under George Villas; they are last listed as George Villas in 1909). Sybil, however, discovered from her examination of the rate collectors' books (she was fortunate in getting access to them and to the valuation books, as they are normally "not available" to members of the public) that John Butler Yeats was the tenant of 18 Madeley Terrace, Sandymount Road in 1863. Is that where he and his wife first lived after their marriage? Or is it more likely that this is the house that his father occupied after he retired (at about the age of fifty) from his rectory at Tullyish? It was "a small house in Sandymount next to the large 'Castle', from which it was separated by a high wall and a wicket gate" (William M. Murphy, op. cit., p. 29). It is possible John Butler Yeats appeared officially as the tenant after his father, the Rev. William Butler Yeats (b.1806), died on 26 November 1862.

John Butler Yeats was married to Susan Pollexfen the following year, on 10 September in 1863.

The young couple bought most of their furniture at auctions, "purchasing new only the drawing-room carpet, the bedsteads and the bedding" (William M. Murphy, op. cit., p. 43). The house they were to occupy, described by Hone (op. cit., p. 9) as "a recently built six roomed semi-detached house" has its hall door at the upper level (which is built of warm coloured red brick) in a manner typical of many Dublin houses of the period. There is a small garden in front, another at the rear; the front room has two windows, that at the side a bay window slightly cantilevered out over the path and the small strip of garden which runs down the side of the house, enclosed by a wall of Dublin granite about seven feet high, which continues at a right angle to form the end wall of the back garden. The front garden is enclosed by an iron railing about five feet high set in a low wall made of cut granite slabs.

This house in Sandymount Avenue was obviously a most convenient place for John Butler Yeats to live. It was near the railway station at Sandymount Halt – the Dublin and Kingstown Railway, later to become the Dublin and South Eastern Railway, had been opened as early as 13 May 1837 (see W. Ernest Shepherd, *The Dublin and South Eastern Railway* (1974) pp. 12–14) – not far from the terminus of the line at Westland Row, itself adjacent to the backgate of Trinity College, where John Butler Yeats continued to meet the friends he had made as an undergraduate, among them the Dowden brothers and John Todhunter. And Sandymount Avenue is not in any case a long walk from the centre of Dublin, while from George's Ville No. 1 it was only about half a mile at most to Sandymount Castle, the eighteenth century house (now demolished) owned by John Butler Yeats's uncle Robert Corbet, who lived a comfortable, sociable and elegant life there. It was a way of living that appealed to John Butler Yeats, who called Sandymount Castle the "Capua" of his youth. He had known it before he entered Trinity College in late 1857, and as an undergraduate he spent much time there. S. B. Bushrui and J. M. Monro, *Images and Memories. A Pictorial Record of the Life and Work of W. B. Yeats* (1970) p. 2, describe him as continuing his studies in the tower of the castle after his marriage. In effect the castle continued to provide a gracious extension to his own Sandymount home as it had to his father's.

Having discovered the birthplace Sybil made an effort to have it acquired (it was then in flats), suggesting that both of the semi-detached houses, George's Ville Nos 1 and 2, should be made into a Yeats Centre with a small theatre in the united gardens, where plays could be staged. Michael Scott, the distinguished Dublin architect, became interested in the idea. Above the theatre, she suggested, there could be small apartments perhaps owned by universities, probably American, where numerous graduate students could be housed while they were working on the MSS which George Yeats promised to lodge there. Jack Yeats promised to donate some of his pictures, and Sybil privately hoped that a good flat could have been given to George Yeats as the Honorary guardian of the Centre.

All was going well when an American suggested a memorial to W. B. Yeats should be erected in St. Stephen's Green. Sybil Le Brocquy was subsequently invited to a luncheon at the Arts Club in Dublin where the Trustees begged her to desist from her plan until the monument was safely erected – she thought that the American had given £300 on condition that this was matched by the Arts Council. Fifteen years later the Henry Moore figure was finally in place in St. Stephen's Green. Sybil Le Brocquy wrote to me in November 1970 to say that the Yeats birthplace was still in peril, as it occupied extremely valuable building ground; she added wryly that, though the city engineer, John Bourke, had many years before told her that he had made a note that the house was "not to be demolished without permission from Mrs Le Brocquy", that joke would not hold much water in today's "progressive times".

This acquisition of information about Yeats's birthplace typifies Sybil Le Brocquy's persistent and rewarding curiosity, as students of Swift will well recognise. She played a quiet but an influential role in Dublin's intellectual life and she cared deeply about the preservation of the city's architectural heritage – a fact suitably recognised in the tribute paid to her memory in the restoration of the fountain in Merrion Square – her vision was not always matched by a corresponding imaginative response on the part of her fellow citizens, as this brief mention of her plans for a Yeats Centre in Dublin based on the poet's birthplace may show.

The house, George's Ville No. 1, 5 Sandymount Avenue, now bears a plaque to the right of the entrance:

BIRTHPLACE

OF

WILLIAM BUTLER YEATS

POET

DRAMATIST AUTHOR

JUNE 13 1865

"Song of Spanish Insurgents": a Newly Discovered Poem by Yeats

John S. Kelly

"Song of Spanish Insurgents", an hitherto unnoticed poem by Yeats, appeared on page 5 of the Dublin weekly *North & South* on 5 March 1887, wedged incongruously between an article about the balance sheets of three Irish drapery companies and another on the salaries of law officers. *North & South*, which offered its readers not only financial news and poetry but also political and social comment, started at the beginning of 1887 but had foundered before the end of the same year. It was often badly proof-read and seems to have had a small circulation since the file in the Library of Trinity College, Dublin, is the only complete one that I have been able to discover. The editor evidently knew and respected the poet's father, J. B. Yeats, and on 29 January, in announcing his election as an Associate of the Royal Hibernian Academy, remarked that the honour would "strike most people as a very tardy recognition of striking and original power". Admiration for the father's painting apparently extended to the son's poetry, for "Ephemera" appeared in the magazine on 26 February, although this first printing is not recorded in Wade's *Bibliography*, and his Spanish poem was published the following week.

"Song of Spanish Insurgents", which may have been a chorus in an early unpublished play variously entitled *The Equator of Wild Olives*, *The Blindness* and *The Epic of the Forest*, is clearly a youthful work but it turns upon a familiar Yeatsian and indeed Romantic theme whereby men of contemplation are obliged to become reluctant men of action. Yet, as often in Yeats, even in his early verse, matters are not quite so straightforward as they may seem. The simple pastoral-military dichotomy is troubled by the description of the falcons, a species of hawk that will make a more awesome appearance in a famous later poem. If sheep may safely graze on their hill, field-mice had better be more careful when they drink, for nature here is red in tooth and claw. And when it comes to human drinking, the scenes at the winepress pass beyond the pastoral or even bucolic into an apparent ritual of communal ecstasy.

Although at the time of the poem's publication Yeats had become a disciple of John O'Leary and through him a temporary admirer of Thomas Davis and the Young Irelanders, the patriotic element in the poem is strangely muted and the

179

enemy curiously unidentified. The history of Spain could have provided Yeats with many examples of revolutions and uprisings but these insurgents are, one imagines, part of the popular revolt of 1808 against French occupation and the collaboration in it of the *afrancesados* in the Spanish establishment. If so, the parallels with English rule and Ascendancy anglicisation in Ireland would have been, one might have supposed, irresistible to a young nationalist poet. Yet, unlike many of the poems in *The Spirit of the Nation*, the goal of war is not seen as some immediate and palpable improvement of social, political and economic life. These insurgents are interested in conservation not reformation, knowing that, whether going forth to the battle or a little later, man's fate is inevitably to fall. The days of humanity's measureless toil are set against the labourless coiling of everlasting rivers. The final line expands gracefully from the vibration of the pulse to a corresponding cosmic rhythm, but the interstellar spaces are filled with light ironic laughter as eternity mocks the evanescent struggles of time. The Hill of Falcons is an Iberian version of the Lake Isle, but its dream-laden stillness is periodically broken not by the linnet's wings but by a falcon's strike and the intoxicated shout at the wine vat, its passivity challenged by the ambiguity of "the ache and hunger of battle" in the heart, and the certain knowledge that peace does not necessarily come "dropping slow" but must be won at sword point.

After his move to England in the spring of 1887 Yeats contributed no more to *North & South*. Of the two poems he published there, "Ephemera" found a place in *The Wanderings of Oisin* but "Song of Spanish Insurgents" was omitted. Perhaps he was discontented with its interesting but not always successful rhythms, or the uncertainty of some of its rhymes. Moreover, as he made his final selection he became more adamant that "the Irish poems must all be kept, making the personality of the book" and may have felt that Spain was too far from Sligo for this poem to be included.

SONG OF SPANISH INSURGENTS.

Oh! would on the hill of the falcons we tended our flocks –
  The rams and the ewes and the young lambs that follow them bleating –
Away and away 'mong the dewberries over the rocks,
  With the sun on their wool and the width of their wide foreheads beating.
Oh, would that we were with our flocks on the face of the mountain
  A-counting the falcons above us, on wide wings a-hover,
  As they watch tor [*sic*] the trembling field-mice, who steal from the clover
To drink of the dew of the spray-dabbled rim of the fountain.
  We have girded our swords, we have girded our swords for our flocks,
  For the quiet and stillness and peace of the dew-covered rocks.

Rejoicing we gather, rejoicing from tending the vine
  And startling with laughter the heart of the dream-ridden day:

Wine-stainèd and shouting we trampled the press of the wine.
  In our hearts is the ache and the hunger of battle; away
  In the vineyards are brooding the merle and the throstle and jay.

We have girded our swords that the land may have silence and peace
  And we may have stillness for days of a measureless toil
  On the fiery plains of the valley where labourless coil
The rivers whose labourless voices will never more cease;
  But will laugh by our graves as they laugh where our forefathers are,
  With a laughter as light as the pulse and the beat of a star.

W. B. Yeats.

Yeatsian Magic and Rational Magic: an Uncollected Review of W. B. Yeats

John S. Kelly

Even without further corroboration, the unsigned review of Charles Leland's *Gypsy Sorcery and Fortune Telling*, which appeared in the *National Observer* on 18 April 1891, might confidently be ascribed to Yeats. Through his friendship with W. E. Henley, the editor, he was a regular contributor to the magazine and since Henley knew that folklore and magic held a particular fascination for him, he would have been the natural choice to review a book of this kind. Moreover, the references to, among others, "the Rosicrucian Fratres of Germany," and "the great shoemaker" of Altseidenberg pick up Yeats's recent association with the Golden Dawn and the study of Boehme he had just undertaken in connection with his work on William Blake. The anti-rationalist and anti-modernist slant of the argument, as well as certain turns of phrase, would also argue strongly for his authorship.

In fact the matter is put beyond doubt by an unpublished letter to James Nicol Dunn, who shared the editorial duties on the *National Observer* with Henley, in which Yeats thanks him for sending the book and promises to set to work on the review "as soon as I can get through a couple of articles that cry out for accomplishment." The letter is undated but must have been written in mid-February 1891 as he goes on to apologise for the delay in delivering his article on Hyde's *Beside the Fire*, which was to appear on 28 February, explaining that he has been deep in Blake and mysticism. Work on Blake continued throughout the spring and his collaboration with Edwin Ellis became yet more difficult when Mrs Ellis banned him from the house because she supposed that he was putting a magic spell on her. These complications, as well as other journalism and attempts to find a publisher for *John Sherman*, delayed the review for two months. It is not clear why the notice was unsigned when it did appear since Yeats was averse to anonymity. Possible Henley felt that his name had been appearing too frequently in the magazine of late.

It was not merely his professional duty towards Henley, nor even the more pressing need of the reviewer's fee, that led Yeats to persevere with the book at so busy a time. *Gypsy Sorcery*, although in the main a compilation of gipsy charms, shamanism, superstitions and witchcraft drawn from many sources, touched upon religious and psychological questions that were of urgent concern to him as he began his initiation into the ritual magic of the Golden Dawn and formulated his occult reading of William Blake. Yet, before reading the book, Yeats would have known Leland, as the review indicates, as the humorous writer of the "Hans Breitmann" ballads, rather than as a folklorist. Born in 1824, the son of a wealthy merchant from Philadelphia, Leland had finished his education at Heidelberg and Munich and was to put his knowledge of the German language and his sympathy with the people to good use when he found himself editor of *Graham's Magazine* for a few months in 1857. Needing to fill odd corners in the periodical, he composed a series of ballads around the German–American Hans Breitmann, "one of the battered types of the men of '48", as he described him, "one whose Lutheranism does not go beyond *Wein, Weib und Gesang*". But beneath Breitmann's hedonism lay, as Leland also noted, a "natural shrewdness, an excellent early education, and certain principles of honesty and good fellow-ship".[1] The *Breitmann Ballads*, with their skilfull Anglo-German macaronics, gained enormous popularity on both sides of the Atlantic, so that when Leland settled in England in 1869 he was already something of a celebrity.

It was while staying at Brighton in the early 1870s that he first became acquainted with gipsies and learned Romany. His interest in them was aroused by George Borrow's books and he never lost an initial romantic attitude towards them. A convinced diffusionist, he believed that they had originated in India, home of magic and divination and he delighted in their customs and esoteric language which seemed to offer a key to myths and lore that were fast disappearing. He hastened to record what was left and his *The English Gypsies* was published in 1873, to be followed by *The Gypsies* in 1882.

By then he had returned to Philadelphia where from 1879 to 1884 he tried to popularise industrial arts in education as part of an ambitious scheme to encourage children to exploit the full potential of their memories. On his return to Europe he again took up the study of gipsies and in May 1888 agreed to become president of the recently formed Gypsy Lore Society with David Mac Ritchie (who insisted that "gypsy" should always be spelled thus to show its derivation from "Egyptian") and Francis Groome as its secretaries. Although the membership of the Society was not large, it was not undistinguished for it included Archduke Josef of Austria and it managed to support a *Journal* which enjoyed a brief but honourable existence, printing articles on gipsy vocabulary and languages (Leland claimed to have discovered an entirely new one, "Shelta", indigenous to British gipsies and based on the Celtic languages) and collecting gipsy lore from many different countries. The *Journal* and the Society ceased their independent existence in the spring of 1892 when both were merged into the Folk Lore Society. By this time Leland had already moved to Florence, where he was to remain until his death in 1903 and where he devoted himself to a study of Tuscan witchcraft. His concern for gipsy lore never disappeared and in 1898 he wrote the Coronation speech for the King of the Gipsies on his crowning at Yetholm.

To understand why a man like Leland should have been so fascinated by the gipsies is to enter into the intellectual history of the post-Darwinian nineteenth century – into those currents and cross-currents of thought that were to be so influential in Yeats's early intellectual development. As a young man Leland, like Yeats, seems to have lost the simple faith of his childhood but there was in his nature, as in Yeats's, a leaning towards mysticism which found its focus in folklore. Unlike Yeats, however, he attempted to acquire an alternative and positive creed grounded in humanism and science. The reader of *Gypsy Sorcery* is quickly made aware that a spontaneous delight in the magical and mysterious is at odds with a continual need to rationalize and explain everything in terms of scientific truth. Just as Leland had picked up the prevailing humanist orthodoxies in religious thought, a loose amalgam of the ideas of Feuerbach, Comte and Mill, so he subscribed to the prevailing evolutionary optimism in sociology and anthropology. He believed that the gipsies were important because they were "the colporteurs of the old faith"; an oriental race that had existed on the roads of Asia since prehistoric times, their folklore cast "a great deal of light on the early history of mankind, and the gradual unfolding or evolution of religion and mind." [2] That there was evolution and not degeneration he never doubted and looked forward to the time when "science by absorbing man's love of the marvellous in stupendous discoveries shall so put to shame the old thaumaturgy, or wonder-working, that the latter will seem poor and childish." [3]

In Chapter XI Leland makes a determined effort to explain just how science is to absorb and transcend magic. This chapter, which was obviously the one that most interested Yeats since he quotes extensively from it, is entitled "Gypsy Witchcraft" and in it Leland offers a psychological account of fortune-telling and other wonders. Making use of contemporary investigations into the physiology of the brain and the operation of memory, he postulates that there are two separate personalities in every human consciousness – the waking will and a dreaming alter-ego, "a more mysterious Me, in some respects a more gifted Self". This dream-self comes into play when the will sleeps and seems to have the key to the total but mostly subliminal memory that all men possess. It

> throws open brain or memory-cells, which waking Common Sense has forgotten; in their chaotic or fantastic searches and mingling they produce poetry; they may chance on prophecy, for if our waking self had at command the immense latent knowledge . . . it would detect sequences and know to what many things would lead, now unto us all unknown. [4]

Fortune-telling and prophecy are thus a function of the memory not of magic: the dream-self is able to recall and recombine images so as to perceive patterns that project into the future and have a direct predictive value. To learn to utilise more effectively this vast and at present subconscious memory would confer upon mankind a "power beyond all our present dreams of greatness" [5] and Leland suggests that education should be designed to develop the powers of perception and recall.

Leland is no less a millenialist than Yeats but his apocalypse will usher in a golden dawn of science. Yet his belief in science is an act of faith: throughout the book science remains more of a potential than an achieved panacea and his arguments, gesturing as they so often do to a future but ill-defined perfection of knowledge, lack persuasion. In speaking of the soul he is confident that "Physiology is probably on the high road to explain it all", but then adds lamely "as yet it is not explained".[6] When physiology did grapple more closely with problems of the mind and the subconscious it found them a good deal more complex than the simplistic equations offered by Leland and his mentor, David Kay.

The study of folklore brought both Leland and Yeats up against similar problems; the issue between them is the facility with which the former provides scientific solutions. As far as Leland is concerned questions about the imagination that were to preoccupy Yeats for the whole of his life either had been, or were on the point of being, answered rationally. For Yeats the question of whether visions and symbols emanated from an internal or external source, whether they are " 'the eternal realities' of which we are the reflection 'in the vegetable glass of Nature,' or a momentary dream", remained open, "the only controversy in which it is greatly worth taking sides" but yet "the only controversy which may never be decided."[7] Leland was, however, confident that he had supplied a satisfactory psychological account of such phenomena. Yeats would hardly have found Leland's concept of memory which, no matter how extensive in the subconscious remains individual and isolated, adequate to account for his own imaginative processes and went on to postulate instead the *anima mundi*, the "memory of Nature herself"[8] of which all individual memories are part and which can be evoked by symbols. Nor will Leland's theory of the "dream-personality", although close to his own thinking on the alter-ego, satisfy Yeats. While Leland's dreamer has little in common with the waking will (if they belonged to the same club they would not, he alleges, speak to each other) it is capricious and lacks the deliberate tensions and complex oppositions generated by Yeats's concept of mask and daemon.

For young Yeats as for young Shelley mysterious things are dear, and yet dearer for their mystery. It is Leland's too facile attempt to de-mystify the world to which Yeats particularly objects since in this he is wilfully turning his back on much that he obviously finds strange and strangely beautiful. The chief glory of folklore for Yeats was that it affirmed "the ancient supremacy of the imagina-tion". Folklore, as he was to write in a later review on another "scientific" collector, "is at once the Bible, the Thirty-nine articles, and the Book of Common Prayer, and well-nigh all the great poets have lived by its light".[9] It is not merely that Leland is trying to secularise the sacred books but that he supposes that in so doing he is improving and expanding them. That he has found in folklore a golden world which he wishes to deliver to us as stainless steel, saddens Yeats; that he should then pass this impoverishment off as enrichment enrages him.

Leland kept a scrap-book of press cuttings relating to gipsy lore, including reviews of his own books on the subject. It is now in the British Library

(1855 b. 18). He obviously collected favourable reviews of his work: unsurprisingly, perhaps, Yeats's review is not preserved by him.

GYPSY SORCERY

Gypsy Sorcery. By C. G. LELAND London: Unwin

When young Hartley Coleridge, aged four, was asked why he was named Hartley, he replied: "Which Hartley? there's a deal of Hartleys. There's Picture Hartley and Shadow Hartley and there's Looking-glass Hartley and Echo Hartley", and then, catching his arm with his hand, "there is Catch-me-fast Hartley".[10] Mr. Leland in his *Gypsy Sorcery* has adopted this theory without acknowledgement, and decided there is a Dream Mr. Leland and also a Waking Mr. Leland who is perpetually aghast at the amount of things that Dream Mr. Leland must know, and the quantity of sweetness and light he must possess. Magic, it appears, is the power of getting this knowledge out of the all-remembering dreamer into the soon-forgetting Philistine of common life. "We visit a sick man, and the dream spirit out of the inexhaustible hoards of memory, aided by association, which results in subtle, occult *reasoning*, perceives that the patient will die in a certain time, and this result is served up in a dramatic dream."[11] Mr. Leland is so delighted with his theory that he insults every witch, warlock, and fairy doctor in creation. He should not do so, because though a good folk-lorist he is a very bad occultist, and remains a trophy to the enemy when he writes such sentences as: "In the whole range of occult literature, from *Hermes Trismegistus* down to Mme. Blavatsky, there is not a shade of a suspicion that all the absolutely authentic marvels of magic began and ended with man himself." This statement must have been made by Waking Mr. Leland, because the other who knows all things would have known better. Then, again, when he asserts that "outside of us was always somebody else to be invoked, conciliated, met in vision or trance, united to in spiritual union or syncope,"[12] he forgets the salutation of the Rosicrucian Fratres of Germany: "Man is God and son of God, and there is no God but man."[13] Nor is the notion of a dream personality from which come visions, omens, and such strange gear a discovery, as Mr. Leland imagines, of "Murriker" and science, but it has been perfectly familiar to all students of magic worth their salt from the days when the great shoemaker of Altsedenberg [sic] saw the sun glitter on a tin pot hung on his wall, and fell into a three days' walking trance in which, in his own phrase, "truth fell upon him like a bursting shower."[14] It does not belong to Mr. Leland, even though he has given in proof of it a quite new story told him by a lady "of excellent family."[15] No: nor is it made any more his by knowledge of a system of education founded upon it which can make any child "exceptionally clever in *all* studies" (italics his own).[16]

It is really a pity that "Hans Breitmann"[17] wrote this book when he was awake, for it is full of interesting material: of such pleasant sayings as that the

bones of wizards turn into black hens and chickens;[18] such charming and
temperate incantations as this against the toothache:

My mouth is not thy house:
I love thee not at all:
Stay thou away from me.
When this straw is in the brook
Go away into the water.[19]

But no sooner has the mind set forth voyaging on the seas of faëry lands forlorn
than the ship goes to pieces on some irrelevant truism, flattery of our time, or
discussion worthy a school debating society or a Secularist lecturer as to the
merits of the Church of Rome. How gladly one would welcome, too, his tales of
Nivasis and Pchuvuse, spirits of wind and flood,[20] if he were not so fond of telling
us that all this old magic, whose ideal was after all spiritual power and spiritual
insight, was, even if true, wholly less beautiful than a telephone with a
stockbroker thoroughly awake at each end. Let us think if we must that space is
empty of spiritual beings, or even put the word "spirit"itself in inverted commas
like Mr. Leland, or go if needs be as far as the learned German scientist who
considers the soul of man "a volatile liquid capable of solution in glycerine";[21]
but let us be honest with ourselves, and by no means pretend that this new creed
is beautiful and ourselves are happy to live in its day. Let us frankly admit that
the body and pressure of time has brought us the last degradation and mingled us
with the dust. Because we hurry over the ground at sixty miles an hour, and may
some day do so at a hundred and sixty, with a penny comic paper in our hands
and our nerves awry from the crush at the ticket-office, we are not proved, in spite
of Mr. Leland, wholly to over-top Merlin, or to be wise as Faustus or the Centaur
Chiron or he that met his image walking in a garden.[22] We are made great not by
the things we do or have done to us but by the thing we are in ourselves.

NOTES

1. *The Breitmann Ballads*, by C. G. Leland (London, 1871).
2. *Gypsy Sorcery and Fortune Telling Illustrated by Numerous Incantations, Specimens of Medical Magic, Anecdotes and Tales* by Charles Godfrey Leland, President of the Gypsy-Lore Society, Copiously Illustrated by the Author; Fisher Unwin, 1891, p. 8.
3. Ibid., p. 7.
4. Ibid., p. 167.
5. Ibid., p. 171.
6. Ibid., p. 166.
7. *E&I* 152.
8. *E&I* 28.
9. *UPI* 284.
10. This anecdote was related by Samuel Taylor Coleridge on 8 August 1811 at Charles Lamb's house and is recounted in Henry Crabb Robinson's Diary. See *Diary, Reminiscences, and Correspondence of Henry Crabb Robinson*, edited by Thomas Sadler

(London, 1872), vol 1, 177–8. Robinson recalls that Hazlitt had painted a portrait of Hartley Coleridge.

11. Like most of the quotations in the review this is taken from Chapter XI "Gypsy Witchcraft" and occurs in the last of Leland's five propositions about the Dream alter-ego. He argues here that "Magic is the production of that which is not measured by the capacity of the conscious working will. The dream spirit . . . can, if it pleases, by instantaneous reasoning or intuition, perceive what waking common sense does not." He adds after the passage quoted by Yeats that "The amount of miracles, mysteries, apparitions, omens, and theurgia which the action of these latent faculties cause, or seem to cause, is simply illimitable, for no man knows how much he knows." (pp. 169–70.)

12. This and the previous quotation occur on pages 170–1 where Leland argues that each man has within him the latent potential to be a magician if he can learn to tap the full resources of memory:

> It is awful, it is mysterious, it is terrible to learn this tremendous truth that we are indeed within ourselves magicians gifted with infinite intellectual power – which means the ability to know and do all things. In the past men surmised the existence of this infinite memory, this power of subtle research and combination, but between them and the truth in every land and time interposed the idea of objective spiritual or *supernatural* existences whose aid or medium was necessary to attain to wisdom. Outside of us always Somebody Else to be invoked, conciliated, met in visions or trance, united to in spiritual unity or syncope. Sometimes they hit upon some form of hypnotism or mesmerism, opiates or forced swoons and convulsions, and so extorted from the nerves and dream-power some of their secrets which were all duly attributed to the the "spirits". But in the whole range of occult literature from HERMES TRISMEGISTUS down to Madame BLAVATSKY there is not a shade of a suspicion that all the absolutely authentic marvels of magic began and ended with man himself.

Both of Leland's examples would have stuck a chord with Yeats for he had been a member of a Hermetic Society in Dublin in the mid-1880s and had only recently resigned from the Esoteric Section of H. P. Blavatsky's Theosophical Lodge.

13. Yeats had joined the Order of the Golden Dawn on 7 March 1890 and believed that its rituals were derived from German Rosicrucianism.

14. Jacob Boehme (1575–1624) was born in Altseidenberg but settled in Görlitz in the mid 1590s where he became a shoemaker and where, in 1600, sunlight reflected from a dish filled him with the illumination of God and opened the universe to him.

15. In discussing fortune-telling, Leland points out that many predictions are ambiguous and that people tend to remember the prophecies that come true and forget all those that do not. He illustrates this argument with the story of an "English lady of excellent family" who "meeting a gypsy, was told by the latter that in six months the most important event of her life would come to pass. At the end of the time she died. On her death-bed she said, 'I thought the gypsy meant a marriage, but I feel that something far more important is coming, for death is the great end of life'." p. 191.

16. Having argued that the memory is a far more potent force than the waking mind recognises, Leland turns (p. 171) to ways of exploiting its resources by developing powers of recall. He suggests that children should be taught to learn things by heart and to train their quickness of perception. He is especially concerned that they should study design and the minor arts, or expand their constructive faculties, since his experience in the school he established in Philadelphia, dedicated to education in industrial art, has convinced him that "by doing this alone a pupil becomes exceptionally clever in *all* studies".

17. Leland's major claim to fame was the Breitmann Ballads (see above).

18. In Chapter 11, on charms and conjurations to cure the disorders of grown people,

Leland remarks that "the *black* hen occurs frequently in mediaeval witch-lore and legend as a demon-symbol. . . . Thus the bones of sorcerors turn into black hens and chickens, and it is well if your black hen dies, for if she had not you would have perished in her place." p. 21.

19. These lines, not entirely accurate in Yeats's transcription, occur on p. 31 and are recited by Transylvanian gipsies as they "wind a barley-staw round a stone, which is thrown into a running stream."

20. On p. 46 Leland recounts that:

> there is among the Hungarian gypsies a class of female magicians who stand far above their sisters of the hidden spell in power. These are the *lace romni*, or "good women", who draw their power directly from the *Nivasi* or *Pchuvusi*, the spirits of water and earth, or of flood and fell. For the Hungarian gypsies have a beautiful mythology of their own which at first sight would seem to be a composition of the Rosicrucian as set forth by Paracelsus and the Comte de GABALIS, with the exquisite Indo-Teutonic fairy tales of the Middle Ages.

21. Perhaps Karl Vogt, a German chemist and materialist, who argued that the brain secreted thought like bile.

22. The centaur Chiron, son of Philyra and Saturn, was famous for his knowledge of music, medicine and shooting and was tutor to the greatest heroes in the Greece of his time. The Mage Zoroaster met his own image and Yeats is thinking of lines 191–4 in Act 1 of Shelley's *Prometheus Unbound*:

> Ere Babylon was dust,
> The Mage Zoroaster, my dead child,
> Met his own image walking in the garden,
> That apparition, sole of men, he saw.

These lines had been quoted by Leland himself in "How they met themselves" *Folklore* (1890) 403–4.

Yeats's "On a Child's Death": a Critical Note

Ronald Schuchard

Yeats's "On a Child's Death" (see Plate 16) is transcribed into Lady Gregory's copy of *Poems* (1899), now in the Robert W. Woodruff Library for Advanced Studies at Emory University (see p. 153 of this volume). That edition (*Wade* 17) was published in early May, and Yeats inscribed his copy to Lady Gregory in Dublin on 10 May 1899, during the opening performances of the Irish Literary Theatre. Why the poem bears the date 5 September 1893, and when it was transcribed into the volume are not known, but these questions raise further queries about Yeats's knowledge of Maud Gonne's child and about the circumstances that led him to unearth the poem at least six years later for private preservation. Some probable answers emerge from a chronological review of Yeats's unrequited relationship with Maud Gonne in the 1890s.

Early in 1890, following her affair with Lucien Millevoye, the French political journalist, Maud Gonne gave birth to a son, Georges ("Georgette").[1] We know from Yeats's *Memoirs* that in July 1891 she rejected his first proposal of marriage, saying that "there were reasons" why she could not and would never marry (*Mem* 46). They continued to see each other day after day, and when she was suddenly called to her sick child in Paris she left Yeats to believe that she was in the political service of a secret society. Sometime at the end of summer the child died of meningitis. Yeats then received "a letter of wild sorrow", telling him of the death of a child that she had adopted "some three years" before:

> Mixed into her incoherent grief were accounts of the death bird that had pecked at the nursery window the day when it was taken ill, and how at sight of the bird she had brought doctor after doctor. (*Mem* 47)

In October, in great grief, she returned to Ireland. Yeats, deeply sympathetic, comforted her with his continual presence and spiritual philosophy. Disturbed and preoccupied, Maud Gonne described at length the details of the child's death. "We spoke often of the state of death," he wrote, "and it was plain that she was thinking of the soul of her 'Georgette' " (*Mem* 48). In November, still in deep mourning, she accompanied Yeats to London, where she was initiated into the Order of the Golden Dawn.

Two years later, in a state of continued frustration over Maud Gonne, whose increased political activities in France and Ireland kept them separated, Yeats commemorated the death of her child. Indeed, the precise dating may indicate that 5 September was possibly the date of the child's death. In this biographically remarkable poem, which alludes to Maud Gonne in her most affected public guise – with "her squirrel and her birds" – Yeats initiates a recurring theme, the need of the absent love of "some fair thing" to counterbalance the single-minded, blinding love of country that leads her into "foolish blame and praise". But while the poet is sympathetic to the great "need" of the mother, he implicitly questions in the armies of the dead, who have amongst them the "purple kings" of the poets, their lack of sympathy toward him, who will continue to be shut out from a tranquil love by the unbalanced tumult of her life. Without the "sweet human words" and affection of the child, and implicitly of the poet, the love that she can know is "but a woodland flame", merely a rapidly consumed passion. The sentiment of the poem, however, lies in the poet's tender lament for the loss of a child he never knew. Yeats possibly believed, as he became even more dejected in his suit, that the "adopted" child, had it lived, could have been his child, that it could have been the object of their unification and mutual tranquillity. "If the boy had not died," he wrote in reflection, "she would have broken with Millevoye altogether and lived in Ireland. As it was, after its death she had thought of breaking with him, and had engaged herself for a week to someone else – I though, I may have had that poor betrothal for my reward – but had broken it off" (*Mem* 133). For obvious personal reasons, the poem was omitted from *Poems* (1895). Meanwhile, Maud Gonne returned to Millevoye. Out of her bizarre desire to reincarnate her dead child's soul, she led him to the child's vault and therein conceived her second child by him, Iseult Gonne, born unbeknownst to Yeats on 6 August 1894.[2] Maud Gonne did not finally break off from Millevoye until 1900, primarily over a conflict of political ideals.

Maud Gonne's eventual disclosure to Yeats of the details of her secret life was painful for both of them: "Then bit by bit came out the story of her life, things I had heard all twisted awry by scandal, and disbelieved" (*Mem* 132). Unpublished letters to Lady Gregory reveal the exact date of her initial disclosure to him, in Dublin, on 7 and 8 December 1898. Subsequent letters to Lady Gregory during the rest of the winter and his sojourn in Paris with Maud Gonne reveal that he relied heavily upon Lady Gregory for counsel. It is also clear that the details of Maud Gonne's affair with Millevoye, her two children, and her reasons for not feeling free to marry Yeats were not then communicated to Lady Gregory. After receiving distraught letters from him in Venice in February 1899, she told him "not to leave Maud Gonne till I had her promise of marriage, but I said, 'No, I am too exhausted; I can do no more' " (*Mem* 134).

In the spring of 1899, as he recovered from the emotional wrenching of the previous months, he possibly confided to Lady Gregory their emotional histories, reaching back into his unpublished manuscripts to retrieve for her eyes one of the earliest poetic records of his long and exhausting anguish. If he kept silence, he may have written it out as a way of indicating to her what could not be spoken of, as an expression of gratitude for her support and advice during the crisis. But sometime near the date of his original inscription, he must have taken the volume from the shelf at Coole, as was his practice, and transcribed the poem with the still agonising knowledge and partial disbelief that his loss of Maud Gonne had been sealed years before the loss of her child.

NOTES

1. The birth date of Georges Millevoye, mistakenly identified as a girl in some accounts, remains uncertain. Of those biographers and critics who date the birth 1890, Conrad A. Balliett states that George Gonne [*sic*] was born on 11 January 1890 and died on 31 August 1891. He bases these dates upon "documents in the possession of Thora Forrester", ("The Lives – and Lies – of Maud Gonne", *Eire-Ireland*: Fall, 1979, pp. 27–8).
2. Balliett precisely dates Iseult's birth as 6 August 1894 (ibid., p. 29).

The Countess Cathleen: a Note

Colin Smythe

On Monday 8 May 1899, W. B. Yeats's play *The Countess Cathleen* was presented by the Irish Literary Theatre with a corps of professional actors at the Antient Concert Rooms in Brunswick Street, Dublin.[1] It was directed by Florence Farr, assisted by the playwright. This play and Edward Martyn's *The Heather Field* were the first fruits of that 1897 discussion between Yeats and Lady Gregory "in Mr Quin's office" at the Comte de Basterot's home in Co. Galway.[2]

Earlier in 1899, when rehearsals were about to be started for the play, Yeats found he was without copies for the actors. The first edition of his *Poems* (1895) was out of print, and the second edition was not going to be ready until April at the earliest, so something had to be done to obtain texts. On Monday 20 February, Yeats therefore spoke to his publisher, asking whether he would provide him with a quantity of proofs of the play extracted from the new edition and on being asked how many copies would be required, replied

> 18 Woburn Buildings
> Euston Road.
> Thursday.

My dear Mr. Unwin: I enclose the remaining poems, corrected for the new edition of my book. I have nothing more to send except the preface, the introductory poem, & four or five pages of notes.

I am assured that 20 copies of the special proofs (for theatrical purposes) of the 'Countess Cathleen' are all that will be wanted. They however are wanted as soon as possible & it would be convenient if you could get them bound in some kind of paper cover.

> Yr sny
> W B Yeats[3]

The preface when published was dated 24 February 1899. The copies of the "special proofs" were supplied, and in a later letter dated "Sunday", Yeats wrote, in part,

Could you let me have half a dozen more of those brown paper covered copies of 'The Countess Cathleen'?

When will the book be out & may I see a proof of the cover? I can go to the binders & see it there if that would save time.

Apart from the copies for the actors, Yeats was very worried that the new edition of *Poems* would not be ready in time to catch sales prior to the first performance of *The Countess Cathleen*. He wrote to his publisher on 15 April

Dear Mr. Unwin: I return the proof of preface etc. I corrected a proof of these nearly three weeks ago – I suppose the printer lost it . . .

It is most important that this book should be out as soon as possible . . . the chief sales would be <u>before</u> the performance while people are curious and expectant. This Theatre has made a very great stir in Dublin & Edward Martyns play, which is far less known of than mine, is having a very large sale in Dublin. Could you not get this book out within a couple of weeks or less? Elkin Mathews has had my book of lyrics[4] bound & issued to the press little more than a week after the arrival of the sheets.

I have received the proofs of cover & will send you the one I chose in a day or two. The design[5] is a very great success. It is one of the finest I ever saw.

It is probable that he succeeded in his plea, and got Unwin to publish them at least a week before the performance, for the first reviews appeared in the papers on 6 May.[6]

Alan Wade in his *Bibliography of the Writings of W. B. Yeats* (1951, 1958, 1968) stated that P. S. O'Hegarty owned a copy of *The Countess Cathleen* and described it in a note to *Wade* 17, but did not dignify it with a separate entry and number. This copy, now in the Kenneth Spencer Research Library, University of Kansas, probably belonged to Florence Farr.[7] Wade does not mention any other copies, but John Quinn owned one, for it appeared in the great auction of his library in New York in 1924, as lot 11590, and it sold for $26.00. I do not know where this copy is now. Lady Gregory also posessed a copy, inscribed by Yeats to her, and frustratingly only dated "May 1899". Yeats kept a copy in his library and it is now in the possession of his daughter Anne. I know of one other copy, that in the Beinecke Rare Book and Manuscript Library at Yale University. It was acquired from Dobell on 7 October 1942, but nothing more is known of its provenance.

Lady Gregory's copy, now in the Robert W. Woodruff Library of Emory University, was rebound in full vellum for Lady Gregory to go with her other vellum-bound copies of Yeats's works, and the edges were trimmed. It is therefore smaller than the other three copies available for study – $6 \frac{13}{16} \times 4 \frac{7}{16}$ in. as opposed to $7 \frac{1}{8} \times 4 \frac{7}{8}$ in. – but it is different in a much more fundamental way to the other three. Whereas in the latter three the first four pages are p. [1] title, p. [2] quotation, p. [3] dedication to Maud Gonne, p. [4] blank, in Lady Gregory's copy the dedication leaf does not exist, and two blank pages appear before the title leaf – pp. [1–2] blank, p. [3] title, p. [4] quotation. The rest of the book remains the same in all four copies. It is reasonable to assume that Lady Gregory's copy belongs to one printing and the three to the other, but it would be a mistake to think that Lady Gregory's copy is of the small second printing and the others of the first, however odd this may seem.

It is normal bibliographical practice, in the absence of stronger evidence to the contrary, to consider that the offprint that most closely matches the published edition is the one that was printed most closely in time to the main print run, and in this case the three are the closest match. Why Yeats and Florence Farr had copies of the small second printing is not recorded, but there is no doubting the fact that they would have taken more care of their copies than would the professional actors, to whom they would be just one more play script, unlikely to be kept after the production.

As to disposal of copies, apart from Florence Farr there were thirteen actors in the play, Lady Gregory and Yeats each had a copy, the prompter must have had one, possibly Edward Martyn, certainly Fr Barry and Fr Finlay, the priests Yeats got to approve the plays for Martyn's peace of mind, each had one, a total of twenty. If Yeats had given all his spares away for publicity purposes prior to Martyn's crisis of conscience, then he must have given his and Florence Farr's copies to the priests, who most urgently needed them, rather than take them from the actors who had to learn their lines, and this would account for their having copies of the second printing. Lady Gregory's copy was almost certainly safely with her binder – she usually used a Venetian – and therefore not reachable.

The question of the date of each printing can only be guessed with the little evidence there is to hand, but here is what I have made of it. All the "special proofs" have a correction in Yeats's hand on p. 28. The words

SHEMUS
We go.

have been crossed through. They do not appear in the second edition of *Poems*, proving that both printings of *The Countess Cathleen* were printed before the pages of the book itself. Also, a further stage direction has been added to the page in *Poems*, which is not in either "special proof".

Lady Gregory's diary for 1899 records that W. B. Yeats returned to London from Paris on 17 February, coming to dine that night. After his depressing time with Maud Gonne in Paris, he set about the preparations for rehearsals in London of *The Countess Cathleen*, worked on revisions for *Poems*, and completed the main part of the Preface for that volume, dating it 24 February 1899, which was a Friday. In the first letter quoted above he writes that he has yet to send the preface, so that it is reasonable to deduce that the letter, dated "Thursday" can only have been written the day before, *if* the date that Yeats put to the Preface was an accurate indicator of the date he finished it.

Judging from the speed with which publishers at that time were able to work – *vide* Elkin Mathews's work with *The Wind Among the Reeds* mentioned in the letter of 15 April – I would expect that the copies would have been ready in about a fortnight, maybe slightly sooner, but it is evident that there were no copies around by 6 March (a Monday) for Lady Gregory records in her diary:

> I went off to Argyll Road . . . to get Yeats's Poems from Sir F. Burton,[8] as a copy can't be had, & one is wanted to show to possible actors – He I was grieved to find is in bed with pleurisy – & one dreads any illness at his age – not up to seeing me but I got the book & carried it off.[9]

According to Yeats's letter of 15 April, the original set of proofs he was then sent replacements for had been sent "nearly three weeks ago", presumably in the last week of March. The letter dated "Sunday" asking for six more copies would doubtless have been written soon after the first printing was used up and he was without one, after sending his and Florence Farr's to the priests on 24 March (*L* 316–17). This would have been 26 March. It could not have been a later one, for the Sunday after that he was in Dublin, and the next, 9 April, is also not possible, for in his letter he only mentions one friend telling him of the Dublin sales potential, hardly likely after he had been there himself for a week. His letter of 15 April shows he had got the same report from a number of friends in Dublin. In writing on 26 March he may also have hoped to take copies with him to Dublin for publicity purposes.

It is possible that on both occasions more than the numbers requested were produced by the printers, but variations would have been very slight. In the absence of Unwin's archives that is pure speculation, and one can only go by the numbers ordered, until further evidence appears – perhaps a cache of copies hoarded in some attic in Dublin by someone who looked after the copies once the production was over?

NOTES

1. Today the visitor looking for the Antient Concert Rooms would have to go to the Academy Cinema in Pearse Street, though that too is closed – as a cinema, at least.
2. Holograph diary, vol xiv, p. 20. How Lady Gregory got the date wrong by a year in *Our Irish Theatre* (G. P. Putnam's Sons, New York 1913, and London 1914) it is difficult to say, for she possessed the documentary evidence in her own diary and in the manuscript of the announcement about the Celtic Theatre, which was in Yeats's handwriting and dated by him "Summer of 97".
3. This letter and the extracts from the other two by W. B. Yeats are published by permission of and © 1984 by Michael B. Yeats and Anne Yeats.
4. *The Wind Among the Reeds*, to which this comment refers, had no reviews until 29 April, when one appeared in *Literature*, p. 439. Although Wade gives the publication date as April 1899, Lady Gregory notes in her diary entry of 2 March that Yeats has told her that "his poems are to be out in a week".
5. Dissatisfied with H. Granville Fell's design for the first edition, Yeats got Fisher Unwin to ask Althea Gyles to produce the design for the second.
6. Arthur Symons's review of it and *The Wind Among the Reeds* appeared in *Saturday Review* on 6 May 1899 (pp. 553–4) and Francis Thompson's review of it appeared in *Academy* (pp. 501–2) on the same day.

7. The cover of P. S. O'Hegarty's copy has on the front cover "the name Aleel, written in ink, but this has been struck through and another name, possibly Maire, written in pencil" (*A Bibliography of the Writings of W. B. Yeats, Wade* 17 in every edition). However, "Maire" is more likely to be "Music". Florence Farr not only played Aleel, but also dealt with the music.
8. Sir Frederic Burton (1816–1900) lived at 43 Argyll Road, London W8. He had been Director of the National Gallery, London, 1874–94.
9. This quotation from Lady Gregory's diary (vol. XIII, p. 141) is printed by permission of and © 1984 by the Berg Collection, New York Public Library, Astor, Lenox and Tilden Foundations.

Two Omissions from *The Secret Rose*, *Stories by W. B. Yeats: a Variorum Edition*

Warwick Gould

Upon p. 234 of the above work, the following should be inserted after "who" in l. 11:

[day who 1905 re-issue of 1904T]

Upon the same page, after l. 16 (end of item 5), the following should be inserted:

5a. [Note 1908, Vol. viii].
   Mr. Bullen has just shown me the fifth volume of this edition of my writings, and I discover that a note to the stories of *Red Hanrahan* has been forgotten by the printer. That note should have said that I owe thanks to Lady Gregory, who helped me to rewrite the stories of *Red Hanrahan* in the beautiful country speech of Kiltartan, and nearer to the tradition of the people among whom he, or some likeness of him, drifted and is remembered. – *April* 14, 1908.

I am grateful to Richard Finneran for pointing out to me the second of these omissions. The first, a punctuational change in a note on the verso of the title page of 1905 reissue of 1904T, came to light too late for the Cornell University Press to include an *errata* slip in the published volume.

How Ferencz Renyi Spoke Up, Part Two

Warwick Gould

Readers of Ferenc Molnár's "The Legend of Ferencz Renyi, a Hungarian Hero of Freedom, in English, Finnish, Irish and Polish Literature" (*Acta Litteraria Academiae Scientiarum Hungaricæ*, [XXI: 1979], 143–160), will have noted that Molnár draws attention to "A Question of Memory" the 1893 play by "Michael Field" (i.e. Katherine Bradley and Edith Cooper), which is based upon the same source cited by Molnár for Yeats's poem about Ferencz Renyi, and Edith Nesbit's "The Ballad of Splendid Silence".

A clipping of "A Hungarian Hero of '48" from the *Pall Mall Gazette* of 17 September 1886 (p. 12) is pasted in to the MS of the two women's journal *Works and Days*, now in the British Library, (Add. MS 46781 f. 71V). The article, which is reprinted here for convenience, was probably – as Yeats himself told Lajos Kropf – going "all around the English Press" (Molnár, op. cit., p. 145) at the time. Certainly it was reprinted without change in *The Pall Mall Budget* on 23 September 1886 (p. 27), which is where Molnár found it.

A HUNGARIAN HERO OF '48.

Hungarian papers announce the death of old Ferencz Rényi, a hero of one of the most terrible episodes of the Hungarian War of Independence in 1848. For thirty-six years Rényi has been a lunatic in a Buda-Pesth asylum, and the history of his sufferings is recorded after his death by the *Petit Parisien*. Ferencz Rényi was a young schoolmaster of twenty-seven years at the beginning of the war, proud, handsome, and full of buoyant life. His pupils adored him, and he was always welcome among the villagers, whether he came with his violin to play to their dances or whether his voice was heard among the patriots chanting the praise of their country. He lived with his mother and sister, and was engaged to a bright young Hungarian girl, when the Government, after proclaiming the independence of the country, called all good patriots to arms. Ferencz left his school and enlisted in the ranks. One day, after having fought valiantly at the head of a detachment of soldiers, he was taken prisoner by the Austrians. Brought before General Haynau, Rényi refused to indicate the place where the rest of his regiment lay hidden. On learning that his home was in a neighbouring village the general sent for the mother and sister, and brought them into the room where the prisoner was kept. "Now give me the information I require, if the lives of these two women are dear to you," said General Haynau to him. Rényi trembled, his eyes filled with tears, but he remained silent. "Do not speak, my son," cried the old mother, "do your duty, and think not of me, for at the best I have only a few days to live." "If you betray your country," added his sister, "our name will be covered with shame, and what is life without honour? Do not speak, Ferencz. Be calm; I shall know how to die." Rényi remained silent, and a few minutes later the two women were dead. Another trial was to come. General Haynau sent for Rényi's future wife, who was weaker than his mother and sister. With wild cries the girl flung herself at her lover's feet, pleading: "Speak, speak, Ferencz. See, I am young, I love you; do not let me be killed. You will save yourself and me if you speak out. When you are free we will go far away and be happy. Speak, my Ferencz, and save your future wife." She took his hands, clinging to him as a drowning man clings to his last support. The young Hungarian was choked with tears, but suddenly he pushed the girl aside and turned away. Once more she cried to him, but he did not heed her. Then the soldiers seized her. "Be cursed," she shrieked; "be cursed, you who let me die; you who kill me; who are my assassin." Rényi remained silent. The girl was shot, and the prisoner was taken back into his cell, but his reason had fled, and he was dismissed. Some friends found him and gave him a shelter; till after Hungary was once more suppressed and peace established, they obtained a place for him in the asylum in which he has recently died.

Molnár also draws attention to an hitherto unrecorded reprinting of Yeats's poem in *The United Irishman*, 24 December 1904 (p. 2). The poem, of course, had been reprinted before, in "A Celtic Christmas", the Christmas Number of Russell's *The Irish Homestead*, 1900. On that occasion forty five lines contained some variant or other, usually of punctuation, from the version in *The Wanderings of Oisin* (1889, 1892). Yeats disliked Russell's habit of reviving early poems for such issues, especially in that Russell failed to mention that they were early (*L* 390). He therefore probably did not authorise Russell's reprint.

The *United Irishman* reprint four years later may well be a different matter. Griffith published the poem in the course of an article entitled "The Splendid Silence", signed by "Cuguan". Much of the issue is taken up with articles on Hungarian themes, which seems to have been Griffith's unsubtle way of puffing his *The Resurrection of Hungary: a Parallel for Ireland* (Dublin: James Duffy & Co., M. H. Gill & Son, Sealy Bryers and Walker, 1904) which was running into its second edition, having been originally published as a series of articles in *The United Irishman* during the first six months of 1904. The second edition is heavily advertised in the Christmas number of his paper, which also carries a Hungarian folk-tale entitled "The Two Lovers" and "Petofi, Poet and Patriot", on Sándor

Pétofi, the Thomas Davis of Hungary, 1848, signed by "Carganac". This piece epitomises the various connections between Ireland and Hungary which Griffith had taken as the starting point for his book.

So lived and died the patriot poet Alexander Petofi – to-day the best-beloved name in Hungary's history. So, too, lived Thomas Davis; so might he have died. So, too, may ye live, O Poets of Ireland! So may ye die when Eire calls us to unsheath the sword, and sigh away your last breath with the song of freedom ringing in your years [*sic*] as the hosts of Eire sweep on to victory! Then shall future generations of freemen bless your names, and keep fresh the laurels of your fame with tears of reverence and love –
For by the magyar's God we swear –
The tyrant's yoke no more we'll bear!

It was natural that for such a purpose, Griffith would want to use Yeats's poem, especially in the version which had first appeared in *The Wanderings of Oisin*. The parallel between Hungary and Ireland is stressed in the added headnote, which pours out "Libations from the Hungary of the West" for the "nation of the bleeding breast". Griffith's book opens with a headnote, stressing that

Sixty years ago Ireland was Hungary's exemplar. Ireland's heroic and long-enduring resistance to the destruction of her independent nationality were [*sic*] themes the writers of Young Hungary dwelt upon to enkindle and make resolute the Magyar people. The poet-precursors of Free Hungary – Bacsanyi and Vorosmarty – drank in Celtic inspiration. . . . Times have changed, and Hungary is now Ireland's exemplar (p. 27).

Later, Griffith describes the bloody executions carried out by "Francis Josef's butcher", General Haynau, in 1849, (as "Cuguan", correcting Yeats also informs us). In doing so, he draws comparison with the heroic deaths of Irish patriots, such as Wolfe Tone.

THE SPLENDID SILENCE.

It was in Hungary – the year 1849 – Haynau sat in his tent; before him, bound, a village schoolmaster, Francis Renyi. "Speak," said the Austrian butcher; "say where the rebel leaders hide, and go free – free with gold in your pockets. Speak or die." There was silence. Haynau signalled to a soldier, and in a few minutes the mother and sister of Renyi were brought in. "Speak, or they die," sad Haynau. "Silence, Francis," said the mother. "Silence, my brother," said the sister. Haynau raised his hand. The women were led out, a volley and they lay dead. Francis Renyi stood silent. Haynau signalled again – Renyi's sweetheart was led in. "Speak," said Haynau. "Oh speak, oh, speak!" the girl cried. The schoolmaster trembled, but his lips did not move. His

sweetheart knelt at his feet, and clasped his bound hands. Renyi's face grew
grey; with a sudden jerk he pushed the girl from him. Haynau signalled again,
and in a moment she, too, was dead. With a superhuman effort, Francis Renyi
burst through his bonds and rushed toward Haynau. Suddenly he halted, his
lips opened – his splendid silence was broken by the awful laugh of a maniac.

   Mr. Yeats has written a poem on this tragic and glorious episode in
Hungary's fight for freedom, which is not to be found in any collected edition
of his works. He prefaces it with this stanza:

> We, too, have seen our bravest and our best
> To prison go, and mossy ruin rest
> Where homes once whitened vale and mountain crest,
> Therefore, O nation of the bleeding breast,
> Libations from the Hungary of the West!

   Here follows the Irish poet's story of "How Ferencz Renyi Kept Silence" –
Ferencz, it may be necessary to say, is the Hungarian form of Francis.

   It will be seen that the headnote, or first five lines, which contains variants as
listed below, is unitalicised, and that the poem has been retitled: it is not clear
who is responsible for this. A full list of variants from the copy-text in *VP* 709–15
follows, including, of course those variants which the UI text has in common
with the previous printing in *The Celtic Christmas* and, exceptionally in one case,
with that in *The Boston Pilot*.

Title   ... Silence. (Place and date missing, but article does give them – see
        above and note new date, 1849). UI.
1–5   [Unitalicised] CC, UI.
2   ... prison ... CC, UI.
3   ... crest, UI.
5   Libations from ... West! CC, UI.
7   ... shine, UI.
8   ... Haynau, he in ... UI.
10   ... well-guarded, with ... hands, UI.
12   ... Accurst! UI.
13   ... is–?
                    'Renyi,'
                            'Of–?'
                                    'This village,'
                                            'Good! UI.
14   ... wood, CC, UI.
15   On yonder mountain, where ... free, UI.
16   Silence – thou ... ! UI.
                            Now, suddenly ЄC, UI.
19   ... flickering, with ever undulant wing, CC, UI.
20   ... dovecot ... UI.

21	. . . form . . . CC, UI.
22	. . . farmhouse . . . , UI.
23	[lacking] CC, UI.
25	. . . currant-bushes . . . CC, UI.
27	. . . loved, fixed . . . , CC, UI.
28	. . . he hath bent . . . UI; . . . bough, all . . . CC, UI.
32	. . . – Why . . . ; CC, UI.
33	. . . good; CC, UI.
37	. . . striving
	If . . . UI.
38	. . . here he . . . CC, UI.
39	. . . one – this one!
	Now . . . UI.
43	. . . wine, UI.
46	. . . A boy goes . . . CC, UI.
	[between 48 and 49 no break] CC, UI.
49	. . . soldier, in . . . CC, UI.
50	Half-hid . . . , UI.
51	. . . one, and . . . UI.
53	. . . age
	'His . . . UI.
54	. . . thus; and . . . CC, UI; . . . 'Peasant speak, UI.
56	The ancient . . . cries; "speak . . . son, UI
58	. . . betide UI.
60	. . . country and . . . CC, UI.
	[between 61 and 62 a break] UI
62	. . . system lifts . . . UI.
63	. . . and, where . . . UI.
64	. . . spot UI
65	. . . off, 'neath . . . CC, UI.
	[between 65 and 66 no break] CC, UI.
66	. . . kin or . . . ?' CC, UI.
68	. . . girl, afraid . . . , CC, UI.
	[between 69 and 70 no break] CC, UI.
70	. . . flakéd . . . UI.
71	. . . walls, UI.
74	. . . said UI.
76	. . . red' UI.
77	. . . a falling crumb; UI.
78	. . . close; he . . . UI
81	. . . peasant, pale . . . CC, UI; . . . eyes with fear UI.
82	. . . moths a-tremble
	'Renyi, say UI.
85	. . . speechless. And . . . UI.
86	. . . me, CC, UI.

92   . . . thee and . . . CC, UI.
94   . . . prayerbook . . . UI.
96   . . . die; CC, UI.
100   . . . hand . . . P, UI.
102   . . . hands and . . . CC, UI.
105   . . . and then floats . . . cry, UI.
106   'Assassin – my . . . Thou . . . die UI.
109   . . . dewy plot. CC, UI.
110   . . . blot, UI.
113   . . . higher, gold, . . . UI; . . . light, CC, UI.
115   . . . soft one . . . CC, UI.
116   . . . struggling,
                      Now . . . UI.
        [between 116 and 117 no break] VI.
117   Haynau! . . . come – thy . . . UI.
121   . . . calf. UI.
122   . . . lips, a . . . laugh UI.

In these 71 altered lines there are 101 variants, of which two thirds are to be found only in the *United Irishman* text. Of these, some forty five are alterations in punctuation and necessary capitalisation, ten are substantive – all minor, and seven are matters of printing convention and layout. There are four possible new errors and three further probable errors have been repeated from the copy text for this printing, the *Celtic Christmas* text. The new errors – e.g. those of punctuation in the last two lines may well be due to the robust inaccuracy of Griffith's printers on Christmas Eve. But it would seem that there are too many sensible changes for even the most cheerful of compositors to have inspired, and close inspection of them would seem to suggest that someone might have revised a (to Yeats) not terribly loved poem for this special "Hungarian" issue.

Such improvements as are secured by the overall tightening of punctuation result in a more dramatic, a more orally directed style, and it is notable that it is the narrative sections of the poem, rather than those in direct speech, which have been more heavily worked over. Future editors of Yeats's poems will need to decide whether any of the variants in this version could have been approved by Yeats. (See Michael Sidnell's discussion of the *Variorum Edition*, below, p. 226).

There remains the problem of the new title. Here the possibility of error is considerable. "Silence" would seem to echo the title of the article, "The Splendid Silence", which itself gestures to the title of Edith Nesbit's poem about Rényi, "The Ballad of Splendid Silence".

Not content with reprinting a retitled, repunctuated poem, "Cuguan" rounded off his article by rounding on Yeats himself

A small thing is any sacrifice the artist can make for his country when it is set beside the sacrifice of Francis Renyi. Will Ireland fifty years hence cherish Yeats in her heart as Hungary cherishes Petofi? It is for him to decide. The fashion of London's anæmic critics or the Petofi of the Hungary of the West?

Yeats himself seems to have concluded that this sort of provincial and ungracious criticism was one of those occasions upon which a poet should "be silent". But the comment cannot have pleased him, and a month later he began his formidable series of letters to Griffith's paper on Synge's behalf over *The United Irishman's* attitude to *The Shadow of the Glen* (*UP2* 331 *et seq.*). By the time of *Dramatis Personae*, Griffith had become the "slanderer of Lane and Synge" (*A* 416), but prior to January 1905 *The United Irishman* had been the sympathetic vehicle for Yeats's own replies to criticism of Synge's work (*UP2* 306).

"MASTERING WHAT IS MOST ABSTRACT": A FORUM ON *A VISION*

"The Red and the Black": Understanding "The Historical Cones"

James Lovic Allen

The complexities of the historical gyres or cones in *A Vision* constitute problems with which most scholars or students of Yeats have wrestled, often in vain. In many instances, Yeats and his "instructors" have compounded the confusion through their manner of presenting the materials. A major case in point is the large double cone with dates and "phases" placed at the beginning of "Dove or Swan" in both versions of the book (1925 and 1937, hereafter referred to as *VA* and *VB* respectively).

Proper understanding of this major diagram is virtually impossible in *VA* because nowhere in the text does Yeats explain the reason for half the diagram's being in red. Without such clarification, the figure suggests that *no* cone or gyre has its point or beginning at the year zero near the birth of Christ.[1] That year appears to be identified instead with the widest expansion of both the interlocked gyres, while the year AD 1050 is evidently related to the narrowest points of both. Thus, there simply is no basis for meaningful association between the diagram and a text that speaks of the *primary* gyre beginning to expand from the birth of Christ. Examples of such implications in the text are, ". . . at His birth . . . the Solar [*primary*] gyre . . . passed from broad to narrow" (p. 168) and ". . . the irrational force . . . with the cry 'The Babe, the Babe, is born' . . . still but creates a *negligible* sect" (pp. 188–9; my italics). A further – though minor – textual inconsistency derives, of course, from Yeats's allusion to "the historical diagram facing page 180" (two references, p. 167), when the figure actually appears on an unnumbered page facing [178].

Adequate clarification of this obviously important graphic illustration entitled "The Historical Cones" came in the first printings of *VB*. The elucidative text occurs not in "Dove or Swan," as one might expect in light of the figure's placement at the head of that book or chapter, but rather in the preceding book, "The Great Year of the Ancients". First of all, we are told that this "system of cones [is] not used elsewhere in this exposition". Enlightenment then comes with the next two sentences: "If one ignores the black numbers it is simple enough. It shows the gyre of religion [*primary* in *tincture*, black in colour] expanding as that of

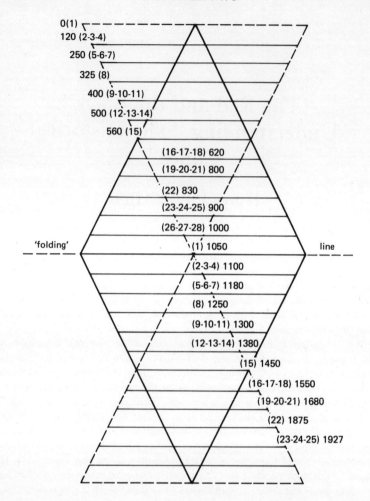

0(1)
120 (2-3-4)
250 (5-6-7)
325 (8)
400 (9-10-11)
500 (12-13-14)
560 (15)
(16-17-18) 620
(19-20-21) 800
(22) 830
(23-24-25) 900
(26-27-28) 1000
'folding'   (1) 1050   line
(2-3-4) 1100
(5-6-7) 1180
(8) 1250
(9-10-11) 1300
(12-13-14) 1380
(15) 1450
(16-17-18) 1550
(19-20-21) 1680
(22) 1875
(23-24-25) 1927

NOTE: The publisher regrets that cost prevents the printing of part of this diagram in red. Dotted lines therefore represent the red cone: originally also numbered and dated in red. The dates and phase numbers originally printed in black have been omitted from this diagram. Will it again be possible to have "The Historical Cones" in two colours in the forthcoming *Collected Edition*?

[Ed.

FIGURE 4   *The historical cones* (unfolded)

secular life [*antithetical* in *tincture*, red in colour] contracts, until at the eleventh century the movements are reversed" (p. 256). This makes sense as long as one remembers to disregard the black numbers and to apply only the *red* numbers to both the red cone *and* the black cone. (Yeats explains later on the page why his instructors included the black numbers.) Things are made even more intelligible when one later learns – though again not in "Dove or Swan" – that in the diagram "The [Solar or *primary*] cone shaped like an ace of diamonds . . . is folded upon itself" (p. 262). If the reader "unfolds" the black cone in the diagram – though applying only the red numbers, which takes a bit of imaginative juggling – he will discover a *primary* gyre that begins with the year zero, expands to its widest point at AD 1050, and then *contracts* again to a vertex at some unspecified time not long after 1927, which is the latest date given in the diagram. This diamond-shaped *primary* figure represents the history of Christianity, in contrast to the expositions of those exegetes (perhaps their confusions may be partially forgiven) who, early and late, have indicated that the gyre of that religious dispensation is to reach its widest *expansion* at or about the year 2000.[2]

Unfortunately, the intended benefits of depicting one cone and set of numbers in red have been lost in later reproductions of *VB*, where publishers have printed the diagram entirely in black, presumably to minimise costs. This bit of false economy makes Yeats's comments on page 256 about a red cone and red numbers meaningless, thus throwing everything back into something close to the original state of puzzlement for scores of scholars and students not fortunate enough to have access to the dual-coloured figure. Probably there should have been a note about this entire state of affairs in the recent critical edition of *VA*, and certainly there ought to be an explanatory note for page 266 (where the diagram appears) in the forthcoming critical edition of *VB*, especially if it is not to have one cone and set of numbers printed with red ink.

Extensive recent research on relationships between "The Second Coming" and *A Vision* has discovered not one commentator who so much as mentions the significance of red in "The Historical Cones". Even the specialists have missed the point. For example, in neither of his otherwise helpful articles dealing specifically with differences between various editions of *VB* does Richard J. Finneran note the change to all-black ink for the illustration in the 1956 American and 1961 London editions (not to mention numerous all-black copies in subsequent printings on both sides of the Atlantic).[3] Surely, under the circumstances, such absence of comment can only be construed as oversight of a significant textual variation, since the colour or colours of ink in the diagram relate directly to comprehension of an important aspect of the texts' theses. George Mills Harper and Walter Kelly Hood, editors of the critical edition of *VA*, do mention in their preface the absence of "red ink for the upper cone and its annotations in the diagram of the historical cones (p. 177) [sic]" (p. vii). However, they supply no elucidative note for page 178, where the all-black figure actually appears in their edition. Even though they failed to cite the clarifying comments on red print in *VB*, they might well have mentioned editorially that nothing in the text of *VA* explains the reason for two colours in the original diagram.

Instead, Harper and Hood have unfortunately created bibliographical problems of another sort in connection with "The Historical Cones". Their preface further states, ". . . no changes of any kind have been made in Yeats's text, which retains its original pagination" (p. vii). This is not wholly correct information. Examination of the privately printed *VA* reveals that the diagram is on an unnumbered, United Service bond, buff, singleton, inserted between pages [178] and 179. But Harper and Hood – or their publishers – have placed it on the previously blank [178] without comment, thereby changing the "original pagination" at one point. No matter what factors underlay this arrangement, production costs or some other, an editorial note should have been provided to indicate the variation.

When properly coloured and "unfolded", as seen above, the diagram of "The Historical Cones" (Figure 4) clearly seems to reflect Yeats's dominant interest in cycles or units of two thousand years' duration, just as do his famous poems "Leda and the Swan" and "The Second Coming". However, the parenthetically numbered phases on the figure apply instead to the two one-thousand-year "wheels" or cones within the larger period, as does much – though not all – of the text of "Dove or Swan" itself. These facts, once recognized, raise some questions about the self-consistency of the diagram, about the complete consistency of Yeats's placing it at the head of Book V in *VB*, and about the appropriateness of his giving that chapter the title that he did.

NOTES

1. Regardless of technicalities about whether there should be a year between 1 BC and AD 1, Yeats's diagram uses the year zero.
2. A. Norman Jeffares states, "In Yeats's mind the era of Christianity began with the point of the cone, and the gyre then begun had almost reached its fullest expansion [in the twentieth century]" (*W. B. Yeats: Man and Poet*, 2nd edn [London: Routledge and Kegan Paul, 1962], pp. 203–4). Similarly, Richard Ellmann says, "This poem ["The Second Coming"] could not have been written with such prophetic authority without the *Vision*, and the 'widening gyre' is obviously the gyre of objectivity [*primary tincture*] there discussed" (*Yeats: The Man and the Masks* [New York: Macmillan, 1948], p. 233). See also Morton Irving Seiden, *William Butler Yeats: The Poet as a Mythmaker, 1865–1939* (East Lansing: Michigan State University Press, 1962) p. 234, and Robert O'Driscoll, " 'The Second Coming' and Yeats's Vision of History" in *A Festschrift for Edgar Ronald Seary: Essays in English Language and Literature Presented by Colleagues and Former Students* (St. Johns: Memorial University of Newfoundland, 1975) pp. 173 and 176.
3. The 1962 and 1969 reprintings of the 1962 London edition preserved the use of two colours, but the 1974 reprinting inaugurated the use of black ink for both parts of the diagram, a practice continued in subsequent re-issues of this edition. Finneran's articles are "A Preliminary Note on the Text of *A Vision* (1937)" in *Yeats and the Occult*, ed. George Mills Harper (Toronto: Macmillan of Canada, 1975), pp. 317–20, and "On Editing Yeats: the Text of *A Vision* (1937)", *Texas Studies in Literature and Language*, 19 (1977) pp. 119–34. The latter article supersedes the former.

A Vision: Some Notes and Queries

Graham Hough

We know the literary kind to which *A Vision* belongs. It is an apocalypse, a revelation, of which there are numerous examples in our culture and in neighbouring ones. Revelations come in various ways: they are brought by angels; the heavens open and visions are seen; dictation is received from unseen powers. In Yeats's case the revelation came through the mediumship of his wife. This is a more domestic and familiar line of communication, without the transcendental authority of many of the classic revelations of the past. The "communicators", as Yeats generally called them, are unknown and unidentified. They are imperious but not infallible. They do not claim to be speaking with divine authorisation. Yeats can question their status and at times argue with their conclusions.

He is quite clear about this. "Much that has happened, much that has been said, suggests that the communicators are the personalities of a dream shared by my wife, by myself, occasionally by others" (*VB* 22). The others include sometimes the dead. Yeats affirms categorically his belief in the communion of the living and the dead, and those who want to quarrel with his premises can begin here. But he goes on to say that the dead are fantastic and deceitful, and quotes an Orphic warning – "The Gates of Pluto must not be unlocked, within is a people of dreams" (*VB* 23). Yeats opens himself freely to his vision, but there is always an element of scepticism and reserve.

Asked whether he believed in the actual existence of his "circuits of the sun and moon", i.e. his psychological and historical symbolism of phases, circles, cones and gyres, he replied "if, sometimes, overwhelmed by miracle as all must be when in the midst of it, I have taken such periods literally, my reason has soon recovered: and now that the system stands out clearly in my imagination I regard them as stylistic arrangements of experience" (*VB* 25).

To those who are repelled by the arbitrary and baffling nature of his symbolism (and that must include most readers of *A Vision*) his answer is simply that this is the way such things come; and he appeals to widespread precedents, citing some of the classic examples of obscure and fantastic imagery used as the vehicle of cosmic insights. "One remembers the six wings of Daniel's angels, the

213

Pythagorean numbers, a venerated book of the Cabala where the beard of God winds in and out among the stars, its hairs all numbered, those complicated mathematical tables that Kelly saw in Dr Dee's black scrying-stone" (*VB* 23). Thus Yeats claims the kinship of his vision with the visionary and prophetic literature of the past.

When he offered to spend the rest of his life in developing the philosophy of the unknown *communicatores* they forbade it, saying "we come to give you metaphors for poetry" (*VB* 8). This throws out a life-line to hard-pressed commentators, and could have been used as an escape-route by Yeats himself: metaphors for poetry, valid for the nonce, within the framework of the poem, with no status outside it. But he does not take this course. His metaphors are formed into a system, if not into a chain of reasoning; and though we may refuse the vehicle we are generally required to accept the tenor. He has a great deal of the Keatsian Negative Capability – "when a man is capable of being in uncertainties, mysteries, doubts, without any irritable reaching after fact and reason"; but this always rests on a substratum of strong and positive conviction.

It is therefore possible to come bustling up with a straight question and demand a straight answer – as is done by Harold Bloom, in a mood of unwonted positivism. "What precisely is Yeats trying to say about human life, and has he found an adequate image for his insight, if it is one?"[1] But if this question could be answered in the terms in which it is put it would not have been necessary to write *A Vision* at all.

It had been an article of Yeats's belief from his earliest days that the Great Memory, "the mind of Nature herself", the Anima Mundi could be evoked by symbols. Symbols meant something quite positive and definite – verbal formulae, and ceremonial, but also coloured shapes, talismans and hieroglyphs, and sometimes natural objects. It is axiomatic that their effect is not a function of meaning or intellectual content. They work by other agencies. Yeats found nothing repugnant in the "barbarous words" of evocation that he read about in Iamblichus, and takes satisfaction in symbols so old that their meaning has been forgotten. No doubt he often made the most of this way of thinking, *pour épater*; but there is no doubt either that he had a perfectly serious and, as he thought, well-founded conviction of the power of non-discursive symbolism, of imagery that cannot be translated into intellectual terms, or only partially and imperfectly. *A Vision* is a complex assembly of such images, and the central portion of it relies largely on a non-verbal symbol for its effect. So the answer to Bloom's question is that there is no answer, in terms that would satisfy him. If we are to put this work to the question it must be in another way.

It should be said at once that much of the symbolism of *A Vision* is extremely disconcerting. Untranslateable non-discursive symbolism derives much of its efficacy from neighbourhood – from kinship and assimilation to one of the great fountains of public imagery, such as the *Apocalypse* of St. John, the classical pantheon, the movements of the starry heavens – still relatively familiar even to-day. Over large tracts of *A Vision* Yeats denies himself this source of strength and intelligibility. Whether his alien apparatus was devised by himself or received ready-made from his mentors has never been clear. But what I believe is clear is that some of it works and some does not.

What does work, fortunately, is the largest and most crucial part of the system – the Great Wheel and the long detailed description of the phases (*VB* Book I); the analysis of the historical cycles in "Dove or Swan" (*VB* Book v); and the description of the after-life in "The Soul in Judgment" (*VB* Book III). We return to these in a moment; but first to filter out the dross. The detailed psychology – the four faculties and the relation between them (*VB* 80–92, 96–9) is important to the scheme, is ingeniously devised, and has some flashes of brilliance; but in general it brings less illumination than it should. The ancillary elaborations of this (*VB* 92–5, 100–4) – the four principles, perfections, automatisms, etc – are hopelessly fussy and superfluous, but easily dispensible as they are quite unintegrated with the main structure. The worst confusion, a source of endless exasperation and dismay, is unhappily in one of the best-known places, since its vocabulary penetrates into some of the famous later poetry. It is the machinery of the two interpenetrating cone-shaped gyres by which Yeats tries to illustrate the enantiodromia at the heart of his system. (*VB* 187–215; 67–80) Happily, the Great Wheel itself provides a far more lucid alternative illustration of the same phenomena. Finally, it is wise to pass lightly and selectively over the section on the Great Year of the Ancients (*VB* 243–63) and go straight on to its more lucid historical entailments in "Dove or Swan".

These dismissals are fairly extensive (about 80 pages), possibly mistaken, and quite likely impertinent. I risk them because I feel strongly that if the more cluttered and ill-arranged apartments are simply shut off the chances of a satisfactory progress through the rest of the edifice are greatly increased.

Then there is the question of the two versions. But that need not detain us long. Yeats expressly repudiates the first, 1925, version (*VA*), except for the parts he repeats in the second version of 1937 (*VB*). "The first version of this book, *A Vision*, except the section on the twenty-eight phases, and that called 'Dove or Swan' which I repeat without change, fills me with shame. I had misinterpreted the geometry and in my ignorance of philosophy failed to understand distinctions on which the coherence of the whole depended" (*VB* 19).

The two sections repeated, the 28 phases and "Dove or Swan" are substantial and of central importance. In fact Yeats repeats rather more than he says; the two poems "The Phases of the Moon" and "All Souls' Night" are also reproduced, and the Table of the Faculties. In all, 130 pages out of the 250 pages of Vision *A* reappear unaltered in Vision *B*, and the 30 page section "The Gates of Pluto" from *A* is more or less paraphrased and rearranged as "The Soul in Judgment" in *B*. The prefatory and fictional material of *A* is abandoned and replaced by new prefaces and fictions; but these are not integral to the system. What Yeats was dissatisfied with and amends considerably in *B* is the geometrical material of cones and gyres, and that connected with the Great Year. Whether the *B* version improves matters much remains doubtful. There are definitions and isolated apercus in *A* that we should be unwilling to lose; but the general upshot is that everything of substance in *A* is either reproduced

identically in *B* or is present in an amended form. And since *B* has also the
unfictionalised Introduction (*VB* 8–25) recounting the circumstances of composition, there can be no doubt that it should be accepted as the definitive text,
though it may be supplemented with passages from *A* when they are helpful.

The principal symbol is the Great Wheel. It is the key to all the rest, but I think
there is a tendency to expect too much of it. Because it vaguely recalls the spheres
and circles in Platonic myth, because it suggests dim analogies with Ptolemaic
astronomy, which Yeats actually makes use of in Book II, and because Yeats in
the past had always been so ready with astrological imagery it is easy to think of
the Wheel as the outline of a cosmology. But it is not. It has nothing to do with the
starry heavens. The phases of the moon are only a convenience of notation, and
the half-hearted attempt to introduce a solar symbolism as well (dark of the
moon = full sun) never comes to anything (see *VB* 82, 196) and is virtually
abandoned.

The Wheel is primarily a classification of psychological types, but it is always
more than that, for it is immediately fused with the doctrine (found in Theosophy
and in certain Gnostic sects) that it is the destiny of man to pass through all these
possibilities of experience in successive incarnations. The wheel symbol is
traditional and widespread among reincarnationists, found alike among the
Pythagoreans and in Indian thought – though it should be noted that Yeats uses
it in a different and more elaborate way.

The Wheel with its twenty-eight phases represents the twenty-eight incarnations which fulfil the whole possible range of human experience; and this pattern
is so fundamental that it appears, on a larger or smaller scale, in every aspect of
human life. Man passes through the same phases in a single incarnation, in a
single judgement or act of thought – though many of these movements must be
imperceptible. Since the Wheel is "every completed movement of thought or
life" it also realises itself in collective life, in the progression of cultures; it is the
rhythm of history. But comprehensive as this pattern is, it is confined to human
experience. There is no transition to the macrocosm, as in the more grandiose
occultist schemes, or indeed in Dante, where moral experience becomes the
pattern for the structure of the universe. Yeats may have been willing to make
this claim, but he does not do so in *A Vision*.

The driving principle of Yeats's thought is the interaction of opposites. In his
youth he found it in Blake – "without contraries is no progression"; and it is
prominent in *Per Amica*, the work that immediately preceded *A Vision* and
already contains the embryo of its central ideas.

The lunar symbolism is a happy equivalent for this, with its arresting contrast
between the dark, when the moon is "hid in her vacant interlunar cave", and the
brilliant effulgence of the moon at the full. And in between are twenty-six phases,
waxing and waning, familiar, beautiful, visible every month if we care to look.
But there are no astrological claims – that the phases of the moon cause or dictate
the development of man's nature; it is an appropriate metaphor, no more. And it
is not primarily a verbal metaphor; indeed the attempt to describe it in words
soon becomes clumsy, while the diagram on p. 81 of *VB* is simple and lucid.

The use of the phases of the moon as a notation means of course a quite arbitrary division of the psychological types into twenty-eight. If Yeats or his teachers had chosen a clock-face as a pattern, they would have been twelve. This might have been better. One often feels in reading the descriptions of the twenty-eight types that the divisions have been cut too fine and the distinctions are consequently not clear, even though the general progress and direction is not in doubt.

The two poles of Yeats's antithesis are not like anything in Christian philosophy. They are given no moral evaluation, they are not good and evil. The light and the dark, the full moon and the moon occulted, are like the Yang and the Yin of Chinese philosophy, though without the sexual connotation. Yeats has various terms for describing this opposition, and they are evaluatively quite neutral. The dark of the moon (phase 1) is *primary*, and the full moon (phase 15) is *antithetical*. These are further clarified as *objective* and *subjective*. It soon becomes apparent that Yeats's sympathies lie with the antithetical/subjective, and that he sees the primary/objective as inferior. But this is his artist's preference. As parts of the system they are co-ordinate and equal powers.

Further elucidations of this fundamental polarity come scattered throughout *A Vision*. The antithetical is that which creates, the primary that which serves. In antithetical phases man struggles with himself, in primary phases he struggles with the world. As the antithetical phases approach their climax at phase 15 there is a continual growth in beauty; as the primary phases return towards phase 1 they grow progressively more deformed.

This is one of the cases where Yeats's concepts are not adequately defined by the labels he gives them, and do not coincide exactly with any that we are familiar with in other places; but in reading *A Vision* and the later work generally we find ourselves becoming accustomed to them, we recognise their nature without any necessary recourse to a formal definition.

The phases are numbered and a particular phase is classified from the position of Will, this being the dominant and identifying faculty. But it is only one of four which go to make up the human psyche – Will, Mask, Creative Mind and Body of Fate. I follow Vendler here[2] in preferring the definitions given in *VA* (14, 15) because they are clearer; but even so I partly resort to paraphrase.

> *Will* is the "bias by which the soul is classified and its phase fixed"; it is the soul's intrinsic tone of feeling, prior to all desire, aspiration or action.
> *Mask* is correlative to Will; it is "the image of what we wish to become", the object of aspiration and desire.
> *Creative Mind* means "intellect, as intellect was understood before the close of the seventeenth century – all the mind that is consciously constructive."
> *Body of Fate* is "the physical and mental environment", which stands opposite to the creative intellect.

The reader's initial response is I think to refuse this strange classification, and try to assimilate it to a more familiar quaternity: the Jungian one, perhaps –

Thought, Feeling, Intuition and Sensation. But they do not fit; nor do any of the other quaternities that bedeck occultist thought – the elements, the compass-points, the Evangelists or Ezekiel's fourfold cherubim. The Blakean, Shelleyan and Freudian parallels suggested by Bloom[3] are ridiculous. Again we find that Yeats's concepts do not exactly correspond to any that we recognise; but again, on increased familiarity they become more distinct. Mask as the object of aspiration and desire is always at opposite phase to Will. Body of Fate, as the brute fact which intellect has to contend with, is always at opposite phase to Creative Mind. The relation between these two pairs is less clear.

Up to now it has been possible to regard Yeats's symbolism as being in the service of his psychology. Whether or not we are willing to see them as successive incarnations, the twenty-eight phases and their return journey between the objective and subjective poles make up an intelligible diagram of human potentialities, a taxonomy of psychological types, which in some measure we can match with our experience, as we are invited to do by the biographical examples. The four faculties divided into two pairs, will and its object, thought and its object, with their complementary interactions, also make an intelligible diagram of the internal dynamics of the psyche. On this basis we could give a sort of answer to Bloom's question "What is Yeats trying to say about human life?" Yeats is trying to say that the nature of any individual life depends upon its direction (is it moving towards self-realisation at Phase 15, or towards submission to the Other at Phase 1?); and upon how far it has travelled between these two poles. Its internal state at any given time depends on the ever-changing tension between will and its object, thought and its object. When the circle is complete it begins again; when the tension between the Faculties reaches its climax the movement reverses itself and begins to go the other way. It is a psychology of dynamism, of opposing tensions, offering no state of rest. That is to say something about human life; and the symbolism, though difficult to grasp at first, is not more difficult than the ideas behind it, and has the extra, supererogatory imaginative power that a symbol must have if it is not to be a mere useless riddle.

But beyond this stage (I mean this stage of the argument; we cannot pinpoint it exactly in the text, for there is much repetition and ellipsis) we encounter two difficulties of a much more serious kind. The first is a good deal of muddle and faulty exposition. The second is an uneasy sense that the symbolism is taking over, acquiring a life of its own, no longer in any intelligible relation to the human realities it is supposed to elucidate.

The muddles have mostly been mentioned already. First come the superfluous and dangling categories which are not afterwards made use of – perfections, automatisms, discords, contrasts etc. These, as we have suggested, can easily be dispensed with. Then there is the daunting solid geometry, cones and gyres. This can be left to those whose imagination can compass it. (Mine cannot). Nothing essential is lost without it. A gnomic but expressive passage on p. 73 says most of what matters:

[T]he *Faculties* can be represented by two opposing cones so drawn that the *Will* of the one is the *Mask* of the other, the *Creative Mind* of the one the *Body of Fate* of the other. Everything that wills can be desired, resisted or accepted, every creative act can be seen as fact, every *Faculty* is alternately shield and sword.

The growing independence, waywardness and complication of the symbolism is more formidable. (This section will be intolerable to all except aficionados.)

The Table of the Four Faculties (*VB* 96–9) is essential but confusing. It sets out in tabular form the title or short description of each Faculty as it arises in every phase. Mask and Creative Mind have true and false forms, e.g. Phase 3. *Will*: Beginning of ambition. *Mask*: True, Simplification through intensity; False, Dispersal. *Creative Mind*: True, Supersensual Receptivity: False, Pride. *Body of Fate*: Enforced love of another.

This is confusing because it does *not* represent the psychic condition of a man whose Will is at Phase 3. For that we have to turn to Phase 3 in the detailed description of the twenty-eight incarnations. Here we find that when Will is at Phase 3 Mask is at its opposite, Phase 17; Creative Mind is somewhere else again, actually Phase 27; and Body of Fate at its opposite, Phase 13.

And so with all the other phases. The oppositions are easily seen by consulting the diagram, the positions of the Faculties by consulting the detailed descriptions of the Incarnations.

So-called rules are given (*VB* 91–2) for finding true and false Masks, true and false Creative Mind and Body of Fate. But they are not rules, and they are quite unintelligible.

However, there *are* rules, given the position of Will, that enable us to find Mask, Creative Mind and Body of Fate, though Yeats does not give them. They are as follows:

Will moves counter-clockwise round the Wheel, starting from Phase 1.
Mask moves counter-clockwise, starting from Phase 15.
Creative Mind moves clockwise, starting from Phase 1.
Body of Fate moves clockwise, starting from Phase 15.

By applying these rules the state of the Faculties for any Phase can be found; and it will be found to agree both with what is given in the description of the twenty-eight Incarnations and in the Table of the Faculties.

e.g. *Will* at Phase 7 (6 places counter-clockwise from 1)
Mask at its opposite (6 places counter-clockwise from 15) Phase 21
Creative Mind (6 places clockwise from 1) Phase 23.
Body of Fate at its opposite (6 places clockwise from 15) Phase 9

It is all quite systematic, but since these rules are nowhere clearly given in the text (though obscurely mentioned at *VB* 74 and 80) the system is not easy to perceive, and I confess it was years before I saw what was going on. Others have doubtless been more acute; but I give the rules here for the benefit of those as imperceptive as myself.

What we have here is an elaborate ballet of the Faculties, one pair moving in one direction, the other in the opposite direction; and the individual members of each pair starting from opposite points.

This has a symmetry of motion that I suppose gives a certain aesthetic satisfaction. But can anyone believe for a moment that this elaborate schematism has anything to do with the constitution of the human mind? The twenty-eight phases are a possible description of the types of human motivation, the four faculties a possible description of the forces at work within the psyche; and they seem to have been devised with some reference to experience. But the dance of the four faculties and the rules for their mutual relation is schematism for its own sake; it has no reference whatever to anything encountered in life or deducible from it. From the way this part of the doctrine is presented – dogmatic, unargued, unpersuasive – we might surmise that most of it came from the unknown instructors, and that Yeats simply took it as it came.

But we do not know about this; and we do not know because those who are in a position to know – i.e. those who have been allowed to inspect the original documents – conspicuously refrain from telling us. Yeats's own comments however reveal that there was certainly much working up of the original material. The point to note here is a teasing discrepancy between what looks like descriptive psychology and what looks like *a priori* system-building. Any formula for the dynamics of the psyche – Freud's Id, Ego and Super-ego, Jung's four faculties, the Platonic threefold classification – must be more or less mythological; but most of them fulfil some evident analytical or moral purpose. Part of the Yeatsian scheme does so too; the subjective/objective antithesis, the one diminishing as the other increases, seems rationally satisfying and makes some sort of empirical sense. But the rest of the scheme – the sustained and rigorous opposition between Will and Mask, Creative Mind and Body of Fate, the counter-clockwise movement of the first pair, the clockwise movement of the second – seems to fulfil only the demands of a geometrical pattern. And since the mysterious affinity of geometry with the motions of the human soul is no longer part of our intellectual experience, it runs the risk of looking ingenious but meaningless.

Nevertheless, two reminders seem to be in order. The first is that arithmetical and geometrical patterning of this kind, and the application of it to the dynamics of the soul, to morality and religion, is a very ancient human activity. It goes back to Pythagoras, and passes from him to Plato. Bertrand Russell remarks[4] on the profound influence of geometry and mathematics on philosophy and theology, and goes so far as to say that theology in its exact scholastic form takes its style from Euclid. Yeats is following in the same tradition, and indeed is aware of it, as he shows by citing among the precursors of *A Vision* the numbers of Pythagoras, Dr Dee's mathematical tables and the diagrams in Law's *Boehme*. A passage in *On the Boiler* commends "those Greek proportions which carry into plastic art the Pythagorean numbers, those faces which are divine because all there is empty and measured" (*Ex* 451). And the late poem "The Statues" revolves around the same theme. I have to confess for myself that I can make little of this way of thinking, but it is quite clear that it has been found significant by men of subtle mind at various times in the past.

The second point we need to remember is Yeats's long-standing attitude to "symbols". Symbols, it will be recalled, need not be verbal or discursive. They can be visual, geometric, numerical. And they can have an intrinsic power. A talismanic image can have a meaning, though a meaning that has never been put into words; and it can affect the mind, though its meaning has never reached the level of conscious awareness.

The Wheel and its internal movements is such a talisman, and a very rich one. The principles of its movement are quite simple, but the resultant pattern (the twenty-eight phases and their mutual relations) is intricate. And Yeats feels this as a powerful symbolic design. How many of his readers to-day are capable of doing so is another question. One answer I think is that everyone finds brilliant flashes, occasional tantalising glimpses from inside the Wheel to a fragment of the outer world. The description of Phase 24 with its examples, Queen Victoria, Galsworthy and Lady Gregory, is a case in point. But some of the other phases remain quite opaque, or lead to mere bewilderment. So we ought probably to understand that the efficacy of the Wheel as a symbol is not really to be judged in this way. If it is "empty and measured" rather than obviously related to outer experience, that for Yeats is part of its virtue. Or – a more reassuring way of looking at it – we can see it as something like an orrery or planetarium; a working model, illustrating in a small-scale, more or less graspable form, much larger actions not visible to the untutored eye, yet of fundamental importance to the life that it seems to pass by.

NOTES

1. Harold Bloom, *Yeats*, (New York: Oxford University Press, 1970) p. 217.
2. Helen Vendler, *Yeats's Vision and the Later Plays*, (Cambridge Mass.: Harvard University Press, 1963) p. 9.
3. Bloom, op. cit., p. 213.
4. Bertrand Russell, *History of Western Philosophy*, 1979, p. 55.

Note: This paper was first given as one of the Lord Northcliffe Lectures at University College, London, 1983. A version of it forms part of *The Mystery Religion of W. B. Yeats* (Brighton: Harvester, 1984).

REVIEWS

Richard Finneran, *Editing Yeats's Poems* (London: Macmillan Press,
1983) pp. x + 144.
Richard J. Finneran (ed.), W. B. Yeats, *The Poems: a New Edition* (New
York: Macmillan, 1983; London: Macmillan, 1984) pp. xxv + 747.
A. Norman Jeffares, *A New Commentary on the Poems of W. B. Yeats*
(London: Macmillan Press; Stanford: Stanford University Press, 1984)
pp. xxv + 543.

Michael J. Sidnell

The collecting, arranging, editing and publication of Yeats's work had become a
very complicated affair by the early thirties, when the poet himself was making
his final attempt to set it all in order in a scrupulously revised, handsomely
produced, collected edition. In this effort Yeats was assisted chiefly by Thomas
Mark, who was the editor responsible for his work at Macmillan, and by Mrs
Yeats. The preparations for an *Edition de Luxe* (hereafter *EdL*) were thwarted by
the economic conditions of the times, interrupted by Yeats's death and
terminated by the outbreak of the Second World War; but the editorial work did
not altogether go to waste. One of its products was the *Collected Poems* of 1933
(hereafter *CP33* and meaning always the English edition), which was conceived
as a kind of stop-gap substitute for the first volume of the postponed, and
ultimately abandoned, *EdL*. Another was the two-volume edition of *Poems*
published in 1949 (hereafter designated *P49*), which became known as the
"Definitive Edition", chiefly because it was based on the proofs that Yeats had
corrected for the aborted *EdL* in 1932.

Though there has been sharp criticism of *P49* and the editions derived from it,
close scrutiny of these texts has been unsystematic and slow. This is partly
because much of the relevant evidence was gathered with a view to satisfying the
long-standing interest in the process in itself of revision, as distinct from its
bearing on Yeats's "final" texts. In this respect, the publication in 1957 of the
Variorum Edition of the Poems of W. B. Yeats, edited by Allt and Alspach, was a great
boon for the study of Yeats, but it has not been an altogether unmixed blessing.

So obvious is the value of *VP* as a compendium of printed versions that its users

225

have tended to turn a blind eye to the fact that it makes almost no attempt to discriminate Yeats's revisions from his editors' and printers' changes and errors. As Alspach freely acknowledged, *VP* perpetuated such errors as "the rather plentiful misprints and seeming misprints" in the American *Collected Poems* of 1933 [*VP* xxix]. On rare occasions *VP* does discriminate between variants, indicating misprints known to have been corrected in errata slips and those corrected in reprintings of an edition, but its general principle is uncritical recording.

The labour that would be involved in a textual criticism of Yeats's poems at *each* printed stage beggars imagination and would probably do the same for the life of any editor who undertook the task. It is, moreover, doubtful that the results of such an investigation could be reliable or significant enough to be of value *if* we assume that punctuational changes are just as important as verbal ones and that the two kinds are inextricable from each other. This is the assumption on which *VP* is based. Yet, though nobody in his right mind would use *VP* to trace changes in Yeats's habits of punctuation, the edition has been used, effectively, to trace the processes of his revision in terms of verbal changes. Users of *VP* have, in fact, adopted a triple standard, taking the verbal variants as Yeats's, taking the punctuation that goes with them sceptically or on trust and, usually, ignoring the solely punctuational variants. Had *VP* clearly distinguished between punctuational and other variants in its typography or layout it would have given readers a much clearer indication of the part of the process of Yeats's revision – the verbal changes – that can be more readily authenticated and analysed, and which has been of more literary interest. But had it done this, and had the solely punctuational variants not been considered inextricable from the verbal ones, the textual neutrality (and rather aggressive title) of *VP* would surely have been less readily tolerated, especially with respect to its uncritical adoption of the *P49* text as basic.

One of the salient points of this criticism of *VP* is that since Yeats is known to have delegated, to some extent, the authority for punctuation and to have accepted punctuational changes passively, his precise intentions in this respect are largely unknowable. Another is that this fact is not a sufficient reason for not attempting to determine the authority of all verbal elements, at least, of Yeats's texts. A third conclusion is that for scientific reasons (as well as for the sake of clarity and practicality) an editor of Yeats's texts should distinguish, in some way, variants and emendations involving verbal changes from those having to do with punctuation only. Not to do so may be to misrepresent the scale and effect of Yeats's or others – including the editor's – changes.

It is a pity that the kind of work that has gone into the making of Richard Finneran's *The Poems: a New Edition* (hereafter *PNE*) and that he has given an account of in *Editing Yeats's Poems* (hereafter *EYP*) did not precede – and so provide a basic text for – some such edition as *VP*. On the other hand, of course, Finneran has doubtless found *VP* as valuable a tool as he generously says, even though he must have had to confirm (and sometimes correct) its record of variant printings.

Just how far back into the printed and manuscript versions of Yeats's earlier texts Finneran has delved, and how far he has relied on *VP*, he does not say. But though *VP* has helped in the making of *PNE* and has influenced the scope and style of the new edition, the immediately relevant comparisons are with *P49* and, by extension, the current *Collected Poems*, for which *PNE* is conceived as a replacement.

This being the case it is most suprising that the differences between the current texts and this new edition are not specified. *PNE* is advertised in the blurb as having "remedied the flaws" of *P49* but Finneran's textual notes in *PNE* indicate only the "flaws" in his copy texts, of which *P49* is not one. He does, it should be said, give *examples* in *EYP* of variations between his texts and those of *P49* but it is symptomatic of the confusions of purpose that characterise *PNE* that readers should be left in the dark about the precise relation of its text to one it offers to correct and replace. The suppression of this information is a considerable obstacle to any assessment of the importance of *PNE* as an emended text, and of the justness of the claims made for it. I hope a full collation will soon be published. Sometimes, of course, Finneran's emendations of his copy texts bring *PNE* into conformity with *P49* (and thus tend to confirm late emendations made by Mrs Yeats, Thomas Mark and, perhaps, Yeats himself) and it would be as interesting to know where this has occurred as to know where the differences lie.

The editor is not entirely responsible for the blurb on the dustjacket but its misrepresentations do arise from his misplaced ambitions when it says,

> He has provided accurate texts for all of the poems that Yeats published or approved for publication during his lifetime, including those omitted from earlier collections by Yeats's widow and his original editor. Finneran has added more than 120 new poems, taken primarily from Yeats's plays and essays, that are not included in any of the earlier standard editions.

This (I am sorry to mention it) is doublethink, in which mode it could equally well be said that Mrs Yeats omitted from *P49* most of the writings that Yeats "approved for publication": nearly all his plays, all his essays, all his stories, *Autobiographies* etc. It is embarrassing to have to remind Finneran and his publishers that *P49*, whatever its textual deficiencies, was conceived as a "collected poems" not as a catch-all. Prudently, perhaps, Finneran does not use the word "collected" in his title. Instead we have the title magisterial, *The Poems of W. B. Yeats*, followed by the sub-title modest, *A New Edition*. But exactly what kind of new edition is this meant to be? Scholarly? Popular? Inclusive? Corrected And Re-Punctuated? For Foreign Students? The first volume of the so-long-delayed *Collected Works*?

It would be easier to decide what kind of edition *PNE* is if we knew whether the editor supposes that the question of what Yeats did or did not approve for publication in this, or any, form is a relevant one; and, if he does, why he includes many poems that Yeats did not so approve. *PNE* offers no answer to this question. The editor is facing both ways but the blurbist might truthfully have said something like this:

> This edition includes all the poems that Yeats published or approved for publication, a great many poems that he did not approve for publication and still more poems wrenched from their contexts in plays and stories – poems that Yeats, in an earlier marketing era, undoubtedly meant to be published in *those* contexts and deliberately omitted from his collected poems. By ignoring Yeats's views in a way that the poet's widow and his first editor were unwilling to do, the present editor and publisher have managed to give purchasers a BONUS of MORE THAN A HUNDRED EXTRA poems for little more than a REGULAR-SIZED edition would have cost.

Was *PNE* conceived, perhaps, as THE SUPERMARKET EDITION?

VP is partly the model for the inclusion in *PNE* of "Additional Poems", but *VP* having more reason to include poems that Yeats did not consider part of a collected poems, sensibly excluded "poems . . . that are an integral part of the context in which they appear and that were never published apart from that context" [*VP* 641]. Moreover, the additional poems of *VP* are not individually listed in the contents of the volume and are in other ways subordinated. In *PNE* they are very prominently presented as "Part Two: Additional Poems". Finneran's reason for this feature of *PNE* is that it "completes the record, bringing together works from a wide variety of sources . . . [*PNE* xxiii]. But what on earth *is* the record that it completes? The record of Yeats as a lyric poet? Hardly, since there are all those earlier versions missing from this record while speeches assigned to characters in plays are included in it. The fact that no rationale is given means, probably, that none can be given. Moreover, if the editor has been guided by his *feelings* for the work then a comparison of the procedures used in *PNE* with the attitude expressed in *EYP* makes it clear that his feelings are desperately confused.

In *EYP*, Finneran discusses the alternatives of a chronological arrangement of Yeats's longer poems and an arrangement that gathers them at the end of the collection in a "Narrative and Dramatic" section. These alternatives, he says, are

> not merely two different "arrangements", but two different incarnations of the archetypal "Sacred Book" of the poems, thus two different experiences of reading Yeats and of attempting to come to terms with his massive achievement [*EYP* 15].

Let us leave aside, for the moment, the arguments for and against a "Narrative and Dramatic" section and the Yeatsian idea of the sacredness of a book. How will the "experiences of reading Yeats" in the present *Collected Poems* and *PNE* differ? Will it make any difference that the reader of *PNE* will be confronted by the rejected poems and deracinated verse of Part Two? I think it will and that

Finneran himself must be burdened by some sense of having violated Yeats's intentions by adding about a third as many poems again as Yeats (by Finneran's own account) would have included in the most expansive collected poems; and, adding injury to injury, using gobbets of Yeats's plays etc. in order to obliterate the Yeatsian and establish the Finneranian canon. "Canon" is his own word, used [*EYP* 111] to include songs from the plays etc.

Mrs Yeats may have made some weak editorial decisions but she could never, never, ever have dealt with her husband's work with this kind of insensitivity and insincerity; nor, be it added, could the Macmillan editors of her day. It would be impossible, of course, to persuade the public at large that more poems is, in this case, less Yeats; that the present *Collected Poems*, though slimmer than *PNE*, gives a much better sense of Yeats the poet. "Marketingwise", it appeared, I suppose, that there was nothing to lose and a good deal to gain from *PNE*'s inclusiveness: the more shame to the editor for not making a stand against such commerce.

Whoever protests that the segregation of the "Additional Poems" in Part Two of *PNE* makes a clear distinction between Yeats's intentions and the editor's should be forced to read the "Explanatory Notes"; to study the implications therein for the intended readership of the volume. These notes, amounting to nearly a hundred pages, can leave no possible doubt that this edition is intended to represent the canon of Yeats's poems for a new generation of readers. And they reveal an attitude to those readers that is extraordinarily inconsiderate and depressing.

Many of the "Explanatory Notes" record the previous publication of "additional poems" and are not explanatory at all. Others are dead mice in the bread. Witness:

144.34   Mayo, a county in Ireland.
152.18   Walter Savage Landor (1775–1864), John Donne (1571 or
         1572–1631), English authors.
181.22   Jesus Christ, son [*sic*] of God in the Christian religion.
181.52   John Keats (1795–1821), English poet.

In extenuation of such seemingly "superfluous" notes, Finneran reminds his readers – his *other* readers, should one say? – that "this edition will be distributed throughout the world" [*PNE* 614]. But if they are not "superfluous" does it not follow that notes like these are hopelessly inadequate? As to that pair of "English authors", if there is no room here for explanation or quotation, why not direct the student to Yeats's other writings or to Jeffares' *Commentary* for relevant passages on Landor and Donne? And, come to that, why not *save* room by putting the glosses on proper names (i.e. most of the "specific allusions" to which, as Finneran says, his notes are confined) in a glossary, instead of so senselessly repeating rudimentary information at each occurrence? It may not be obvious "throughout the world" *why* Yeats thought Keats "unsatisfied" but the rules of this game forbid any explanation. The student would find more help by looking up "Keats" or "Christ" in the *Collins Dictionary*. It is true that *Collins* does not find it necessary to mention that Christ has a role "in the Christian religion", nor would the student discover from it why Yeats supposes, in line 22 of poem 181 of *PNE* ("Ego Dominus Tuus"), that the image of Christ's face is well known; but *Collins* would tell him that Christ is the Second Person of the Trinity, which might help with allusions to Him – him? – in other poems. Given that Islam and other large markets outside Christendom – to say nothing of some school boards inside it – have acute religious sensitivities and rigid censors, the utility of the recurrent tag "in the Christian religion" for members of the Holy Family is obvious; but the sharp-eyed agnostic, Buddhist or Jew will surely notice the arrogance of leaving the saints and their shrines untagged.

Since these notes are restricted to "specific allusions", the reader gets not one scrap of assistance with "What Magic Drum" or any of the intrinsically difficult passages in Yeats. But suppose that, reading "The Tower", he wants to know something about Hanrahan. In the "Explanatory Notes" he is directed to Yeats's notes in Appendix A. Thence, he is directed to the editor's notes on Yeats's notes. The editor's note tells him that Hanrahan is from *Stories of Red Hanrahan* – which is what Yeats's note has just told him – and provides the information that Hanrahan is an "invented character" (which is partly true), that Yeats is referring to the first story in the collection (which is largely true) and that the first edition of the book of stories was published by Dun Emer in 1904 (which is wholly true but not very useful). Now in all parts of the world the Dun Emer edition is much harder to come by than *Mythologies* (which is not mentioned) and in some parts of it, the reader might even have access to a recent scholarly edition (also unmentioned) of the stories in question. To whom, then, is this note addressed? And what kind of help does the editor think he is giving? What I find is a strange mixture of pedantic ritual – which may impress, but scarcely inform, the ignorant – and the assumption that *PNE* will be read on "the day after". There are, of course, some shiny things amongst the annotational corpses. I was particularly interested in the (conjectural) identification of the Tulka ostensibly quoted by Yeats in the epigraph to the "The Wanderings of Oisin".

Finneran's "Explanatory Notes" incorporate many of the notes that Yeats published in various editions, but not those that Yeats used in *CP33*. These latter are given separately in an appendix placed immediately after "Part Two: Additional Poems". Then come the editor's notes (which have the running title "Explanatory Notes") on Yeats's notes. Then comes Appendix B, containing "Music from New Poems, 1938". This appendix is followed by a page of notes and these are followed by the "Explanatory Notes". The two separate sets of running titles, "Explanatory Notes", may be the result of a copy editor's thoughtlessness but the confusion to which they contribute is inherent in the machinery. The notes to *CP33* are presumably printed separately out of some residual attachment to Yeats's idea of a "collected poems" but the effect of this, in the context of the editorial excrescences, is that they are very deeply buried.

I turn to Part One of this edition, which is intended to be, "in effect, a hypothetical reconstruction of the contents and order of an expanded 'Collected

Poems,' had Yeats authorized such an edition as of 28 January 1939" [*PNE* xxiii]. (The Deathbed Edition?) Looking down the list of contents of *PNE* the most striking feature of this "reconstruction" (i.e. *construction*) is its division into "Lyric" and "Narrative and Dramatic". One of the editor's remarks on this division is quoted above. I cannot agree with his assumption that Yeats must have had one view or the other about which arrangement was *in general* to be preferred; nor that Yeats's enthusiastic acceptance of the division, when it was proposed for *CP33*, must have been motivated either by principle or the desire for financial gain [*EYP* 15]. There are reasons to suppose that Yeats thought that different kinds of editions called for different arrangements of his poems and that he might well have retained the roughly chronological ordering proposed for the *EdL* had that edition come into being. (What he would have thought appropriate for an American edition is yet another question – one of the same order as whether the English and earlier title, *Autobiographies*, or the American and later one, *The Autobiography*, should be adopted for a new Anglo-American edition of that work.)

In considering the overall arrangement of his poems, the most important factor for Yeats was whether or not "The Wanderings of Oisin" should be the first, and possibly too daunting or dominant, poem in the book. In 1931 he recalled that in the 1899 *Poems* he had moved it, "in a rage", to the end of the collection in order to get more attention for the other poems [*L* 786]. In later editions he placed his longest poem in context with the early work but did not put it first. In *Early Poems and Stories*, part of a uniform edition, significantly, "The Wanderings of Oisin" again came first. Yeats was very conscious of the particular character of each edition and this would lead us to suppose that there is no single answer to the matter of arrangement. It is one of the choices that will define the character of the particular edition for which it is made.

I have observed that overall *PNE* is anything but respectful of Yeats's ideas about sacred books or even about his collected poems; so Finneran's choice of arrangement in *PNE* seems a matter indifferent. Personally, I believe that the roughly chronological arrangement of *P49* is to be preferred, especially since the only reason given for the alternative one (to prevent "Oisin" from dominating the attention of reviewers or browsers) is now irrelevant. "Oisin" certainly does not overshadow the rest of Yeats's poetry nor do readers come to Yeats as casual browsers. They might, however, overlook the importance of the poem in which Yeats layed up a rich store of imagery on which he continued to draw throughout his career. The separation of "The Old Age of Queen Maeve" and "Baile and Aillinn" from their original contexts makes it much more difficult to discern the emergence of Yeats's revolutionary "mythical method", and the displacement of "The Two Kings" (for the sake of filling out the "Narrative and Dramatic" section?) obscures a key moment in Yeats's development of that "method". And what did the "dramatic" designation do but overcome an awkwardness – no longer likely to arise – about the inclusion amongst both the poems and the plays of different versions of *The Shadowy Waters*?

The contents pages of *PNE* also reveal some changes in the titles of the sections of the collection. The smallest of these is one for which there appears to be no basis. *The Green Helmet and Other Poems* was one of the two books of poetry by Yeats that used the name of a play for its title. So the poems from the volume were headed, logically enough, "from The Green Helmet . . ." when they were reprinted in *Responsibilities and Other Poems* (1916) and *Later Poems* (1922). In *CP33* the "from" was omitted, as it is in *PNE*. Finneran is apparently prepared to accept the authority of *CP33* for a section title made nonsensical by the omission of a word.

In three other titles of sections Finneran makes radical changes. He does not know – any more, probably, than anybody else – how "from A Full Moon in March" came to be a section title in *P49* and he adopts instead, "Parnell's Funeral and Other Poems". This is the half-title that separates the poems from the play in the volume *A Full Moon in March*. The title adopted in *PNE* is made consistent with the others by the addition of the date of the volume. Finneran then signals the doubtful status of the whole title he has assigned by placing it in square brackets. Since there is a note on the origin of the title, the brackets seem to me rather in the nature of pedantic graffiti. The section title "New Poems (1938)" is not bracketed, though it too is a title first used here in the context of a collected poems. "New Poems" in *PNE* comprises what was formerly the larger part of "Last Poems"; while "Last Poems" survives (bracketed) as the reluctantly adopted title for the remaining part. This sensible change (first suggested by Curtis Bradford) is accompanied by a reordering of the poems and other textual changes that, in general, will cause Yeatsians no great surprise, though Finneran's detailed account of the textual history and its consequences will be of great interest to them.

Other differences from *P49* discernible in *PNE*'s list of contents occur in "The Tower" section. In *PNE*, the shorter version of one poem replaces the longer, and another poem is removed to a different place in the sequence. The reasons given for both changes are convincing.

In the process of preparing *CP33*, Yeats cut from "The Hero, the Girl and the Fool" the portions of the dialogue assigned to "the Girl" and "the Hero", reducing the poem to "The Fool by the Roadside". He also added the poem "Fragments" (the two parts of which had been published separately elsewhere). Inserting "Fragments" where "Wisdom" had stood, Yeats apparently moved "Wisdom" to the position immediately preceding "The Fool by the Roadside". Only one part of this revision – or "massive change", as Finneran (*EYP* 27) calls it – was carried into "The Tower" section of *P49*. In that edition, "Fragments" was included but the whole of "The Hero, the Girl and the Fool" appeared, instead of the portion of it surviving as "The Fool by the Roadside", and "Wisdom" was left in its old place. There is little doubt that Finneran is right about this matter but he makes heavy weather of describing it. Editors "still create strange monsters, and then quell them, to make their art seem something".

In *PNE* the titles of a few poems appear in forms different from those used in *P49*. "Pardon, Old Fathers" of *P49* is listed as "Introductory Rhymes" in the contents pages of *PNE* and is untitled in its text. "While I from that reed-throated whisperer" of the earlier edition is similarly listed as "Closing Rhyme". In each case *PNE* follows *CP33*. The American *Collected Poems* of 1933 was more consistent, using ". . . Rhyme" (singular) for both titles. I do not know how these titles appeared in the 1932 proofs. It would be interesting to know whether Yeats there used ". . . Rhyme" or ". . . Rhymes" consistently or otherwise – and so emphasised the structure of the original volume – or whether he used the first lines for titles as *P49* does. It could be argued that the latter would be more appropriate for a final collected edition.

The title "Easter 1916" first appeared thus in the second printing of the poem in *The Dial*. In the first, and all others before *P49*, there was a comma between the festival and its year. The excision of the comma is more in keeping with present usage in identifying what became more an occasion than a date, and Yeats may have wanted this. On the other hand *CP33* may have correctly retained the slightly anachronistic comma that *PNE* also preserves. The comma in "September 1913" had long since gone and *CP33* did not restore that. Neither does *PNE*.

Taking *CP33* as his copy text for nearly two hundred and fifty poems, Finneran makes seven emendations to it. Of these, one involves the introduction of a stanza break; another involves punctuation; a third the addition of a note on pronunciation; two more are changes in spellings; and two are verbal changes. In all seven instances *PNE* brings the text into conformity with *P49*. With respect to this large group of poems *PNE* pays *CP33* high tribute.

As I have said, the textual consequences of his dislodgement of *P49* are not specified by Finneran in *PNE*, though he does give examples of them in *EYP* 39–42. I take up some of the given examples and others. The hyphen in "road-metal" [*VP* 260] was introduced in *P49*. So was that in "beech-tree" [*VP* 286] and those in "O chestnut-tree, great-rooted blossomer" [*VP* 446]. These hyphens almost indubitably reflect a punctuational idiosyncracy of Thomas Mark and are rightly removed in *PNE*.

In the line "And pierce it through with a gimlet, and stare" [*VP* 330] the comma is unique to *P49* and threatens to break up the line. We are surely better off without it, as in *PNE*.

The case for adopting the spelling "Pallas Athena", as *PNE* does, is less secure. At different times and in different poems, Yeats specifically corrected the spelling both from "Athena" to "Athene" and from "Athene" to "Athena". The second of these corrections occurred in the final page proofs to *New Poems* but it was not carried through into the Cuala edition of 1938, for which they were made, nor marked for correction in the copy that Finneran takes as the basis for "Beautiful Lofty Things" [*VP* 577]. He amends on the authority of the proofs as represented Yeats's "last known wish" [*EYP* 32]. In this instance, Finneran is perhaps swayed by his opinion that "Athena" is "the standard spelling", and he adopts it elsewhere, too [*EYP* 32].

With "Athena" Finneran inclines to orthographic uniformity (as did Mark, Mrs Yeats and Yeats himself – who were concerned with the overall effect of a collected works, not solely that of a collected poem); so does he with the spelling of "Niamh" [*EYP* 48]. In dealing with "Aed" and "Aedh", on the other hand, he allows the difference to live on in the two spellings that survived Yeats's revisions. A uniform spelling of proper names in the text, with the variants noted in a glossary, would be preferable in my opinion. And there is a good deal to be said for a consistent policy in this respect for future editions – especially for the collected edition, if its day should ever come – of Yeats's works.

Rather different from the above examples of emendation is the unequal treatment of two readings unique to *CP33*. One of these occurs in "The Wanderings of Oisin" [*VP* 59], where *P49* reads "And because I went by them so huge and so speedy with eyes so bright, / Came after the hard gaze of youth . . .". In *CP33* the word "before" is substituted for "because". Finneran, thank heavens, rejects the nonsensical reading in his copy text. On the other hand he accepts, and describes as a revision [*EYP* 40], the substitution of "dancing" for "their dances" in this passage from "The Withering of the Boughs":

> I know where a dim moon drifts, where the Danaan kind
> Wind and unwind their dances when the light grows cool
> On the island lawns, their feet where the pale foam gleams. [*VP* 203]

Finneran's case for accepting "dancing" is based on his scrutiny of the physical appearance of the setting, in *CP33*, of the line in question. He sees the compositor trying to make the substitution without disturbing the indentation – which the shortening of the line had made unnecessary – of the last word. But the compositor's manipulations may well have do with how the printed text he was following was set, and I doubt that further inquiry into the habits of compositors A, B, C and D, employees of R & R Clark, Ltd., Edinburgh, will help Yeatsian editors much; except perhaps in asserting the dignity of their mystery *vis-à-vis* that of their Shakespearean colleagues. And scansion and grammar, though by no means hard evidence, are no softer than attempts to penetrate the dark mind of a compositor. Here, they are relevant and given that there is no evidence of an authorial revision, I would urge owners of *PNE* to strike out "dancing" at the bottom of page 79 and write in the original reading. *PNE*'s "dancing", it ought to be added, goes unremarked in the "Textual Notes" (since it is not a departure from the copy text). Surely some explanation of this most dubious reading was called for somewhere in the edition.

In using *CP33* Finneran has been very much concerned with the details in which it differs from the 1932 page proofs but he does not discuss its remoter antecedents – the printings and revisions traced back to their manuscript origins. It is unlikely that these mines will yield much textual ore but it would be interesting to know if Yeats can be seen correcting the plural "linnets' wings" of the first (periodical) publication of "The Lake Isle of Innisfree" [*VP* 117] to the singular that was adopted thereafter: to know which changes are certainly the result of active authorial revision and which may have arisen either from the poet's passive acceptance or his oversight.

An important element of the complex history of the aborted *EdL* is that it was not abandoned until after Yeats's death. Production of proof copy for it continued long after *CP33* appeared. It is not clear what, in 1939, the textual basis for the first two volumes – containing the poems – of the *EdL* (or the Coole Edition, as Mrs Yeats proposed to call it) would have been. But it appears, from Finneran's account, that there was some attempt to keep the copy for *EdL* up to date. This may have some bearing on the text of *P49*.

In his discussion of the text of "Crazy Jane and Jack the Journeyman" [*EYP* 19–22], Finneran's purpose is to demonstrate the superiority of *CP33*, the proofs of *The Winding Stair and other Poems* and the published text of that edition over the 1932 proofs for *EdL*. But with "Crazy Jane and Jack the Journeyman" we have a case (not untypical of Yeats) of a bifurcated stemma of revised texts. This double process of revision results in alternative readings [*VP* 511] for the last line of the poem. *CP33* and the page proofs for *The Winding Stair* read, "Mine would walk being dead." *P49* reads, "Mine must walk when dead."

Finneran offers a critical demonstration of the superiority of the *CP33* reading. It is more in keeping with the complexity of the poem, he says, in being "both literal and metaphorical". The literal interpretation – to which the *P49* text is restricted – is that Jane's ghost will walk after her death if, while living, she lies "alone / In an empty bed," and so fails to exhaust her passion before death. As I understand it, Finneran's metaphorical interpretation, as allowed by the *CP33* reading, is that Jane's spirit would die before her physical death and "walk" if she were to inhibit her passion [*EYP* 19–22]. The demonstration by interpretation does not convince me. Yeats apparently tried both lines more than once in different versions of the stanza. I would suggest that he was struggling with the use of the subjunctive mood of the sentence rather than a metaphorical meaning of "ghost". Be that as it may, the fascinating bibliographical fact is that, after considerable changes on various proofs, the *rest* of the stanza was brought into conformity verbally, in four states of the text: on the proofs of *The Winding Stair*; in the published text of that volume; in *CP33*; and in what Finneran calls "another revision of the 1932 page proofs". This last item excites curiosity. For what purpose and when was this stage of revision of the 1932 proofs made? It gives us the version of the lines that appeared in *CP33* and *P49* as:

The skein so bound us ghost to ghost
When he turned his head

In the 4 October 1932 proofs, these lines had read:

The skein so bound my ghost and his
When he turned his head about

Though I think Finneran is right, on present evidence, not to take his text from the revised proofs, the case is far from being a closed one.

Though Yeats saw the proofs for *CP33* (which are not extant) after those for

The Winding Stair and Other Poems Finneran takes the latter as his copy text in the belief that the discrepancies between them and *CP33* are "not the result of Yeats's last-minute revisions on the proofs for the later volume but of the publisher's failure properly to collate the two editions" [*EYP* 27]. This is largely borne out by his comparison of the two, but when he observes that "there is *never* an instance where *CP* is clearly superior" to *The Winding Stair* he must be forgetting what he himself was the first to point out. Yeats had two misprints in *The Winding Stair* corrected by errata slips and both these corrections were carried through into *CP33*. One of them was "yellow canvas" for "swelling canvas" in "Old Tom Again" [*VP* 530/*EYP* 18]; the other was in the notes and looks rather more like an authorial revision than a correction. Apart from these instances, in which *CP33* is clearly superior, Finneran lists the eighteen variants in punctuation which persuade him of the superiority of the *Winding Stair* volume and its proofs. In seventeen of these instances I would entirely agree. It would appear that more care was taken with the verbal part of the text than with the punctuation of *CP33* as far as this group of poems is concerned.

Moving on from the *Winding Stair* section we move also beyond the range of Yeats's own conception of a collected edition and into denser textual thickets. From this point, Finneran's overall activity is to re-assemble and scrutinise the texts of poems published after *CP33*; that is, those that appeared in *The King of the Great Clock Tower, Commentaries and Poems* (1934), *A Full Moon in March* (1935), *New Poems* (1938), the posthumous *Last Poems and Two Plays* (1939) and *Last Poems and Plays* (1940), as well as in more ephemeral printings.

For the first group of poems Finneran takes *A Full Moon in March* as his copy text. Most of these poems had already appeared in *The King of the Great Clock Tower* and the relationship between the two volumes presents no serious problems. Finneran's rejection of "From *A Full Moon in March*" as a section title has already been mentioned. Another major change is his exclusion from this section of "Three Songs to the Same Tune". His reason for doing so is "that Yeats intended the revised version to *replace*" (his emphasis) the one found in *A Full Moon* [*EYP* 45]. In support of his argument he notes that "Yeats took his own copy of *A Full Moon in March* and began the process of revision (in ink) directly on the text of the poem." This would seem to be an argument for printing the revised version *in this section*. But Finneran chooses to exclude "Three Songs . . ." from it and to place the revised version, "Three Marching Songs", in the "Last Poems" section of *PNE* (which partly corresponds to the original *Last Poems* volumes in which the revised version appeared). What Yeats himself would have done there is no knowing. Here Finneran begins to confront the problem inherent in "a hypothetical reconstruction" and I begin to question the propriety of such an ambition.

In *Last Poems* Yeats included a revision that he could scarcely hope to get into print – unless in the *EdL* – in a new edition of *A Full Moon in March*. The resulting editorial problem has no entirely obvious solution. Mrs Yeats's was to preserve the integrity of the *Full Moon in March* collection (and, therefore, the thematic connection between "Three Songs . . ." and "Parnell's Funeral") by printing both the unrevised and (in the "Last Poems" section of *P49*) revised version, accompanied by a note. It was an inelegant but not hypothetical solution. There was – and remains – a good case for following Yeats's usual practice, which would be to print the revised version in the original context. Finneran, however, chooses to preserve the doubtful structure of "Last Poems" at the expense of the *Full Moon in March* section. It seems quite thoughtless to rename that section "Parnell's Funeral and other Poems" and then seriously undermine its theme by the excision of "Three Songs . . .". Finneran observes that *P49* "improperly retains the earlier work" in the *Full Moon in March* section. The next editor of the poem may well conclude that Finneran's impropriety in excising "Three Songs . . ." from this section is even less defensible.

For the second group of later poems, Finneran takes a corrected copy of the Cuala *New Poems*, (1938), as his copy text. The result, with respect to the current texts, is the emendation (first proposed by Jon Stallworthy) of "dance attention" to "dance attendance", and many changes in punctuation. What, precisely, these are would require more time to discover than I have available at the moment. Presumably, they comprise first those corrections, if any, that were made on Finneran's copy text but not carried out in *Last Poems and Plays* and *P49*, and secondly Finneran's emendations of punctuation for which Mrs Yeats and Thomas Mark could be held responsible. Given some of the instances cited in *EYP* the inspection of a complete listing of the variants between *PNE* and *P49* would be worth the labour. I cite an example from "The Municipal Gallery Revisited" (or "Re-visited") [*VP* 601–4]. It involves the continuity between stanzas, as expressed by the punctuation. In *PNE* we have:

No fox can foul the lair the badger swept.
VI
(An image out of Spenser and the common tongue)
John Synge, I and Augusta Gregory, thought

Grammatically, the full stop after "swept" and the absence of punctuation after "tongue)" makes the human trio rather than the animal pair the Spenserian image, which is, of course, foolish. When John Sparrow, as Finneran records, alerted Yeats to the problem and suggested that "swept" should be followed by a dash, "tongue" by a full stop, Yeats thanked him for the "correction" and said he would "remember it" when he next corrected proofs. Apparently, Yeats then filed Sparrow's letter in his corrected copy of *New Poems* [*EYP* 59]. He did not enter the correction on his copy of *New Poems*, which agreed neither with Yeats's typescript (in which the Spenser line was set off by dashes) nor the first printing of the poem (in which there was a colon after "swept"). Finneran boldly eschews what he calls the "rules of prose" in opting for the senseless punctuation he gives. He overrules the typescript, the first printing, the correction that Sparrow thought that Yeats had accepted and the judgement of both Mrs Yeats (who asserted that the full stop after "swept" was wrong) and Thomas Mark. Here, as elsewhere, Finneran's case rests heavily on his theory, inherited from Bradford, that Yeats used "rhetorical as opposed to grammatical punctuation" [*EYP* 74]. Bradford may not have intended his remark to mean that Yeats ever deliberately used a "rhetorical" punctuation that *contradicted* grammatical meaning but if he did I would say he was wrong. Certainly I believe Finneran to be mistaken in supposing that grammatical nonsense was Yeats's intention; and so, in this instance, not to give Yeats (and good sense) the benefit of the murky textual evidence.

That Finneran is not very sincere about this crude theory of "rhetorical punctuation" is shown in the other example from the same poem, where he works the other, grammatical, side of the street. The most refined *grammatical* interpretation is adduced in support of the full stop in these lines from the first and second stanzas of the poem:

A revolutionary soldier kneeling to be blessed.
II
An Abbot or Archbishop with an upraised hand
Blessing the Tricolour. . . . [*PNE* 319–20]

In front of me I have *The Voice of Ireland* open at the frontispiece, which is Lavery's "Blessing of the Colours". The painting was done especially for reproduction in this volume and later went to the Municipal Gallery. It depicts a soldier, dressed in a green uniform, wearing a Sam Browne belt from which hangs, very prominently, a large holster containing, presumably, a pistol. He wears brown riding boots. I believe that he is a commissioned officer of the Irish Free State Army, but there is no identifiable insignia on his uniform. He kneels on one knee, holding the standard of the Tricolour. Before him stands a mitred figure, grasping a crook in his left hand and raising his right hand in a blessing. The vestments worn by this figure are rather eclectically chosen by the artist and there is no sign of a ring on his hands. To his left an acolyte holds a red, leather bound book, probably a missal. To the right of these figures there are other, shadowy ones, who seem to be in a procession of some sort. They might be monks. This is not a documentary painting or if it is then certain details have been deliberately blurred.

"Now Yeats," says Finneran, "was not so ignorant of church regalia as to mistake the mitred figure . . . for an 'Abbot'!" [*EYP* 61]. Now, "in modern ecclesiastical law an abbot with jurisdiction . . . enjoys the use of episcopal insignia", *Chambers Encyclopaedia* (1950) tells me, under the heading "Abbot". *OED* also explains "mitred abbot" very satisfactorily; so I do not see the need to defend Yeats from the charge of ignorance. This would arise, according to Finneran, if we were to suppose that Yeats were describing Lavery's picture in some simple-minded, undeconstructive way. What Yeats is actually doing, he says, is to make "two pictures out of one". Like the reference to "Abbot or Archbishop", the full stop after "blessed" is designed to effect this division. (Finneran does not tell us whether the next sentence of the poem refers to the soldier picture or the abbot/archbishop picture.) Lurking here is a "subtle irony", previously undetected, that Finneran has flushed out: "That is, within the poem the blessing is given only to the emblem of the state and not to the person who symbolises those who created it; the Church, in other words, looks the other way when confronted with the fact of violence but condones and accepts the results of that violence" [*EYP* 61]. Such nonsense deeply undermines my confidence in Finneran as a *reader* and so, of course, as an editor.

In placing the full stop after "blessed", Finneran is following his copy text. It is relevant to the quality of that text to mention an instance in which he emends it. In *New Poems* and in the previous printings of "Are You Content" [*VP* 605] the line, "The smuggler Middleton, Butlers' far back", appeared. Yeats did not delete the apostrophe in the corrected copy that serves Finneran for a copy text, though he added a comma after "back". Happily, Finneran finds support for the elimination of the apostrophe in its absence from a corrected typescript. But that absence would be slight evidence of Yeats's intentions if we had not sense to guide us. As it happens, somebody else had spotted the error before *Last Poems and Plays* (a text for which Finneran has little use) was printed and the apostrophe was eliminated in that and subsequent editions. So Finneran's "emendation" brings us back to where we were and we are not required to solve a syntactical riddle from which Middleton would emerge as a "far back" (a Cornish idiom for a long-time neighbour?) of the Butlers.

The ordering of Yeats's "Last Poems" as they appear in *P49* was first disputed by Bradford, since when it has been a notorious issue. The three main documents in the case are a list of contents for an untitled – significantly so, perhaps – collection that Yeats made in the last days of his life; the Cuala *Last Poems and Two Plays*, which conforms with that list; and the Macmillan *Last Poems and Plays*, which gathered the poems in *New Poems* and *Last Poems and Two Plays* and radically changed the ordering of the latter group.

The chief defects of *Last Poems and Plays*, in Finneran's opinion [*EYP* 65–6] are: its ordering of the poems; its inclusion of three poems – absent from the above-mentioned list – from *On the Boiler*; its incorporation of *New Poems*; and its title. The first of these objections is well-founded. The others are mere opinion.

The edition was planned posthumously. Finneran thinks that Yeats himself he would have called his last collection *Under Ben Bulben* [*EYP* 67]. However, Finneran does "not believe that he was indeed convinced that the poems listed on the table of contents were his 'Last Poems' " [*EYP* 66]. Would not the title "Under Ben Bulben" have implied such a conviction? Do not the epitaph and the retrospective reference to his own burial imply that Yeats thought he must be near the end? Such speculations are a rather silly way to go about hitting on a title for what were, *in fact*, Yeats's last poems. And, in the absence of a Yeatsian title, "Last Poems" was an appropriate one; one that indicated the impressive fact that Yeats was writing poems to the end, that his death was not perfectly tidy, and that, in its discourtesy, death did not permit him to make a final arrangement of his collected poems.

There was surely nothing untoward in the gathering of the contents of the two previous Cuala collections in the trade edition published by Macmillan, though the omission of "New" as a section title for the earlier group of poems was, perhaps, an insensitive decision. One can see how, at the time, "New" might have appeared to be a merely neutral and temporary designation but, in retrospect, it appears to be a deliberate and moving one (and one that is enhanced by "Last"). I think Finneran is right to restore it. The sequence of the poems in *New Poems* was not changed in later editions but that of *Last Poems and Two Plays* (and of Yeats's draft table of contents) was. Again I think Finneran has done well to restore this order, or, rather, would have done well to restore it as far as possible.

The qualification arises because of the three poems from *On the Boiler*, which the Macmillan *Last Poems* and *P49* included but which are relegated to the "Additional Poems" in *PNE*. The meaning of this is that Finneran (following Bradford) believes that Yeats would not have included these three – "Why should not Old Men be Mad", "Crazy Jane on the Mountain" and "A Statesman's Holiday" – in a collected poems. This is incomprehensible in the light of the only evidence he cites that bears on the matter. After Yeats had submitted final copy for *On the Boiler* he went back to his typescripts to correct these poems, which does indeed suggest that "he might have planned to include them in his next collection of verse" [*EYP* 116n.21]. The excellent reason for excluding these poems from *Last Poems and Two Plays* (and from the draft list of contents probably made for it) was that they would then have appeared in two Cuala publications almost simultaneously: excessive repetition, given that *Purgatory* was, in fact, placed in both. There was no reason not to include them in *Last Poems and Plays* and they were duly included, as they were in *P49* and later editions. Finneran has, I think, been mesmerised by that table of contents (which includes "Cuchulain's Death" – i.e. *The Death of Cuchulain* – and "Purgatory", incidentally). It was not made for a collected poems. In any case, Finneran's rejection of the three poems from *On the Boiler* saves him from having to find a place to put them in his "hypothetical reconstruction".

In arriving at texts for the "Last Poems" section of *PNE*, Finneran has examined a mass of evidence, including typescripts in various states and, of course, the periodical publications. Other than to say that there has never been such a thorough examination of the evidence bearing on the texts of these poems, it is possible neither to generalise about his choice of a copy text in each case, nor about his particular decisions to emend.

I will quote Finneran on one problematic example to indicate the impossibility of assessing this part of his work without having access to the physical materials. Finneran is discussing "Three Songs to One Burden", III, line 16 [*VP* 608]:

With a single line, Yeats crossed out "An admired, a" and indicated in the margin "A famous/———". I take it that Yeats intended "A famous" to be followed by what was not cancelled. As the cancellation line does not go through the comma, the proper reading would therefore be "A famous, brilliant figure" rather than "A famous, a brilliant figure", as in all published texts. [*EYP* 76]

It is hard to imagine just how, with a single (?) stroke, Yeats retained that comma while deleting the indefinite article, but the actual document may make this clear.

As an example of the emendations to the currently received text resulting from Finneran's choice of, and emendation of, his copy text for his "Last Poems" section, I take the conveniently short "A Stick of Incense" [*VP* 619]. Finneran's copy text is a carbon typescript. Compared with *P49* it gives a comma instead of a question mark at the end of the first line, and "like", instead of "liked" in the last line. Finneran emends "like" to "liked" on the authority of another typescript (which brings us back to the present reading) and (departing from the present reading) retains the comma. The question mark had first appeared in the printed text of *Last Poems and Two Plays*, which was published some five months after Yeats's death. It had not appeared on the proofs to that volume and on whose instructions it was inserted will probably be forever uncertain. I would say that the poem is better, rhetorically and grammatically, with it than without.

The last chapter of *EYP* is modestly called "Towards the Next Edition" and a good many people will be stimulated and provoked by *PNE* into thinking about a successor to it of some kind. That the next edition should profit immensely from Finneran's labours goes without saying. He has identified and examined a tremendous volume of textual material, proposed many punctuational changes and clearly identified textual cruces. So the editing of Yeats has undoubtedly advanced with the appearance of *PNE*. But I am of the opinion that the resulting edition is not, overall, an advance over earlier ones. I have mentioned objections to such major features as the "Explanatory Notes", the arrangement of the poems, the assortment of "Additional Poems", the placement of the "Three Songs . . ." in the wrong (to my mind) section and the relegation of the three poems from *On the Boiler*. When it comes to particular textual readings, Finneran's *critical* readings in *EYP* undermine my confidence in his judgement. Given Yeats's difficult handwriting, the fact of many typescripts not produced by the poet himself, the evidence of poor copy-editing of punctuation in many instances and of Yeats's clear oversights in this matter, and given Yeats's reliance on, and confidence in, Thomas Mark, I am not prepared to accept Finneran's text as a wholesale replacement of the one edited by Mrs Yeats and Thomas Mark. Too often, I believe, *PNE* merely substitutes Finneran's "feeling" for the text for that of his predecessors. His choice of "Rewarding" over "Rewording" in "The Happy Shepherd" [*VP* 66, l. 39] is an example of his choice of a verbal reading, where choice is possible; the examples of punctuational "choices" in the poems appearing after *CP33* are legion and examples have been given. As he truly says, "the editing of Yeats's poems will always remain as much an art as a science" [*EYP* 120]. This being so, the anthologists of the nineteen nineties will be able to justify the use of earlier texts than *PNE* on better grounds than mere evasion of royalties. And for the time being I would advise students to hang onto, or even to buy while they can, copies of *Collected Poems*.

Professor Jeffares' *A Commentary on the Poems of W. B. Yeats* was first published in 1968 and was subsequently reprinted, with additions and corrections, four times. I have used my copy of the first printing more or less continuously since it was published, chiefly for cross-references in Yeats's work, for biographical data and for dates of composition. Its strength is the appositeness and amplitude of the quotations from Yeats's prose. It is not so strong on extra-Yeatsian allusions and it is weak on textual matters.

The most obvious difference between the first *Commentary* and its latest successor is the bulk of the latter. The new book is fatter and wider by a centimetre each way and two centimetres taller than the old. Since it turns out to have fewer pages, this appearance is partly deceptive, but the mean margins of the new volume allow for more words to the page and the word-count overall must be a good deal higher.

Physically, the new book is much worse-produced than its predecessor and this may cause owners some chagrin, librarians extra expense. My old *Commentary* is in excellent condition after years of use and book-shaking removals across continents and campuses, but a signature of the new one (pp. 481–96) detached itself from the binding at first opening. The paper is of poor quality, too, being too transparent for good legibility, especially given the small type. And compounding the physical defects of the book is the plurality of the numeration employed by its quthor.

The contents pages deploy three sets of numbers: page references to *Collected Poems* (or other editions); the new poem numbers assigned by Finneran in his *PNE* and the book's own pagination. These sets of numbers – to which, in the body of the text line numbers are, of course, added – may express, in some inchoate way, the aspirations of a numeromaniac culture in which poems will at last become machine-readable. Anyway, the new layout looks more than ever like a computer program and soon caused me a problem when I tried to "run" it in the old way.

Perhaps it was thoughtless of me to suppose that a note to "Why Should Not Old Men Be Mad?" was intended to refer the reader to *PNE* itself. The note reads: "For Dante see note on 'Ego Dominus Tuus' (*PNE* 181)" [516]. Going to *PNE* I decided that cross-reference between volumes could not after all be intended and that "(*PNE* 181)" referred the reader to the relevant note in the *New Commentary* itself. But why not use the book's own pagination for internal reference? Is it merely to identify disbound pages?

As it happens, Jeffares' note to "Ego Dominus Tuus" is no more helpful than Finneran's as a note to "Why Should Not Old Men Be Mad?" The poem speaks of "all Dante": the notes are about *Vita Nuova*. My first assumption that the reference was to *PNE* rather than Jeffares' deployment of Finneran's numeric code may be further excused by the evident efforts that have gone into making a match between *A New Commentary* and *PNE*. That the marriage may be premature is indicated by the fact that Jeffares clings to the *CP* reference system as well as adopting Finneran's. If this is insurance it may well prove prudential.

Most of the new material in *A New Commentary* comes about as a result of the "Additional Poems" in *PNE*. Since many of these are integral parts of plays and other works, their contexts have to be described by Jeffares. For this Mutt and Jeff act between Finneran's editorial, and Jeffares' commentarial, procedures there may be sound economic motives but insofar as it is likely to undermine such confidence in scholarly activity as readers, publishers and taxpayers may have retained, we may pay dearly for it in the end.

Making a random comparison of entries in the commentaries new and old I find, in the glosses on "September 1913", that Emmet's "execution" is now more graphically recorded as a public hanging in Dublin and that the putative suicide of Wolfe Tone is made a sure thing [111]. Since I do not have available the later printings of *A Commentary on the Collected Poems* I cannot say whether these revisions appear now for the first time, but the salient point is that there is no radical change between the first and the latest set of notes to this poem.

Turning – selectively now – to a poem weirdly glossed and re-punctuated by Finneran (as I have indicated above) I go to Jeffares' note on lines 8–10 of "The Municipal Gallery Revisited" [399]. Jeffares quotes these lines and notes the allusion to Lavery's "Blessing of the Colours" precisely as he had in the first commentary. It appears that Jeffares accepts neither Finneran's gloss nor, more significantly, Finneran's text. It appears, indeed, that the textual basis of *A New Commentary* is not *PNE* – though Jeffares' adoption of the ordering and most – *but not all* – of the titles of *PNE* might suggest otherwise. Jeffares' silence on this matter evades the most important issue confronting the first comprehensive commentary to be published after *PNE*: the question of what text it is a commentary on. In this instance I agree with Jeffares' choice of text but I regret his diplomatic reticence.

As to the ordering of the poems in *PNE*, Jeffares himself regrets that, and he spends the greater part of his Preface arguing, effectively, against it. The alliance between *The Poems: a New Edition* and *A New Commentary on the Poems of W. B. Yeats* is clearly a rather cobbled-up affair, one which all the parties to it may now, at their leisure, repent.

Toronto, February, 1984

Phillip L. Marcus (ed.), *"The Death of Cuchulain": Manuscript Materials Including the Author's Final Text*, The Cornell Yeats (Cornell University Press, 1982) pp. x + 182.

Richard Allen Cave

This, the first play to appear in The Cornell Yeats, is a splendid achievement. Setting out, as the series intends to do, to illuminate Yeats's creative process, Phillip L. Marcus offers photographs of all the extant manuscripts of the play with, on facing pages, careful transcriptions (no easy task given the difficulty of Yeats's handwriting, aggravated here by age, illness and a feverish haste to complete the composition); following these are photographs and transcriptions of the typescript now identified as NLI MS 8772#6 which bears the bulk of the holograph revisions; finally a transcription of this revised typescript is used as a basic text against which to record variant readings to be found, firstly in a further typescript on which Mrs Yeats wrote out the revisions made by Yeats to NLI MS 8772#6 together with others possibly dictated by her husband before his death – it is annotated by her "corrected Jan 22 1939" which gives the variants some authority – and, secondly, in the printed versions in the Cuala's *Last Poems and Two Plays by W. B. Yeats* and Macmillan's *Collected Plays*. A series of notes on textual problems points out places where revisions by Yeats, carefully copied by Mrs Yeats into her clean text for printing, have been changed back to earlier readings from the manuscripts in the Cuala text which are then copied in subsequent printed versions. (The most significant of these are both in the episode between the dying Cuchulain and Aoife. When she binds her veil about the hero and the pillar stone, Yeats revised her initial prosaic remark, "And fasten you to it", to the more precise, "And fasten down your hands", thereby more clearly defining her intention which is to prevent his attacking her as she proceeds to slay him, should he manage to summon up one last effort of strength. Later the equally flat enquiry, "But how did my son fight?", was revised to read more idiomatically as "Our son – how did he fight?", which succinctly establishes the link between them – the begetting of a child in a mysterious moment when the antipathies of love and loathing were relaxed and resolved, a shared felicity in the past which comes to preoccupy their thoughts in the present so as once again to extinguish the vehement hatred in Aoife's thought that has brought her to the scene of Cuchulain's death. In both instances, the Cuala adopted the earlier reading for no clear reason and to the detriment of the dramatic intensity.)

244

It is disappointing that so little of the prose draft of the play survives and no scenario. The extant material certainly justifies Professor Marcus's claim that "even at the very end of his life the creative act was for [Yeats] still an act of exploration"; but one would have liked more conclusive information about why Yeats came to treat the subject of Cuchulain's death in this particular way. It appears to have been consciously his *last* drama, since it was somehow "*necessary* to wind up my plays on that theme"; the choice of subject is no surprise but the manner of treating it is. Yeats had long admired Lady Gregory's account of the legend in *Cuchulain of Muirthemne*; but Professor Marcus's summary of the incident with all its intricate magical trickery and deceptions, the complex claims and counterclaims of foes and friends that the hero should or should not go out to fight alone to prove his valour, leaves one astonished at the bold simplicity of Yeats's version of the event, pared down to essentials that give the appropriate tone to the circumstance and a nicely judged degree of confusion against which to measure Cuchulain's assured decision and his absoluteness for death. But how quickly did Yeats arrive at this shape for his plot-line and at the decision to ignore legendary accounts and make the companions of Cuchulain's dying Aoife and the Blind Man from *On Baile's Strand*? The relative smoothness of composition of the middle section of the play would indicate the working through of a substantially devised scheme: the many rephrasings suggest a concern to clarify the tone, define more pointedly the psychological tensions of the scenes and achieve levels of pathos and irony within the texture of the speeches: it is the putting of style and finish on a planned sequence rather than an experimenting with form that chanced to prove right. Certain memorably vivid features are *there* right from the start and are left virtually untouched by revision as if they were the formative inspirations shaping the episodes in the subliminal reaches of the poet's mind: the sickening, reiterated sighs of the Blind Man, for example, that characterise his coarse, sadistic self; the visual horror of his hands feeling over Cuchulain's body culminating in the grim matter-of-factness of "Your shoulder is there. / This is your neck" as he aims the death-blow.

What continued to give Yeats difficulties throughout all the stages of composition was the framework of the play. Initially Yeats appears to have wanted a sung lyric not only at the close but also at the start of the play (in the manner of his earlier dance dramas) in addition to the prologue; while the role of the Old Man was to extend beyond the function of Presenter making him more obviously a Stage Manager and Director of the piece controlling and thereby distancing the action throughout in a manner interestingly akin to Brecht's theories of alienation. He was to return masked as the Morrigu and then read in the lines as the attendant soldier in the opening scene with Eithne; in his own person, not masked, he was to appear before Emer's dance carrying in the symbolic representations of the severed heads and commenting in his laconic style on the consequences of Cuchulain's death. Further, in a development of the chilling dramatic climax of *Purgatory* where the father croons a nursery rhyme over the body of his murdered son, the Old Man here while fetching and arranging the heads was to be heard singing "Sing a Song of Sixpence" (later revised to "Bo Peep"). As Yeats's sense of Cuchulain's attitude to death which defines his heroic status became stronger in the writing of the play so the Old Man's role became more and more curtailed; the denigrating, anti-heroic voice of the Blind Man came to carry sufficient weight to be the kind of challenge against which Yeats could test and prove the worth of his hero's calm in the face of death; to follow this scene with a return to the off-hand scoffing of the Presenter was to sustain a negative, critical tone when clearly a change of mood was called for after Cuchulain's ecstatic vision of his after-life. Surprisingly few revisions were necessary to achieve the curt, oracular voice of the Morrigu as the figure of destiny, a voice totally without human emotion aptly evoking a mind conscious only of the patterning of life against life to shape events to a just and balanced conclusion. The change here necessitated a change with the Morrigu's first appearance and quickly the Old Man's function became confined to the Prologue.

One interesting consequence of this change of plan was the development of a new conception for performing the play that would maintain a sense of distancing the action through a conscious theatricality. Yeats first thought of opening Eithne's scene on a bare stage but he scored through that direction and wrote "when light goes up Eithne Inguba is alone on the stage". By the typescript-stage when the Old Man's role is finally decided on, Yeats began to reconsider his original idea and slowly the direction emerges that "the curtain rises . . . on a bare stage" in silence while Eithne's entrance is delayed for "half a minute". In holograph on the typescript Yeats then devised a similar start to the second episode with the lights going up on an "empty stage" before "Cuchulain enters wounded". The deliberate fragmenting of the action into separate, disconnected episodes becomes a structural pattern which beautifully substantiates Professor Marcus's suggestion that the play has marked affinities with a letter of 1938 (*L* 916–17) in which Yeats defines his philosophy concerning death as "a series of 'critical moments' in which various 'sensuous images' from [the] past are analyzed and . . . dissolved". Each scene in the play noticeably ends with the action arrested in a tableau as the stage "grows dark". What we watch in the theatre are not the facts of Cuchulain's death but the *process* of that death and the states of mind in which he confronts it, ending as it does on a note of vision, wonder ("And is not that a strange shape for the soul / Of a great fighting man?") and assured acceptance ("I say it is about to sing.").

The visual patterning in the late stages of composition has a counterpart in verbal patterning within the dialogue. Only in the typescripts does Yeats begin to perceive the dramatic possibilities of reiterating the phrase "about to die" in contexts which subtly differentiate between the companions who witness Cuchulain's end: for Eithne the phrase expresses horror and despair; for the aged Aoife, a sense of natural justice; for the Blind Man, a gloating satisfaction. Generally the revisions are directed at achieving an austere style of verse that avoids expansiveness and epithet: the emotional colour of the exchanges is brought ever more sharply into focus and *poetic* writing eschewed. This is notably the case with the sequence of memories through which Aoife and Cuchulain explore their shared past – its hatreds, its felicities and its tragedy in the slaying of their son. There are no bitter accusations, no railing against fate, only a quiet acceptance of the facts through which we are left to gauge the wealth of complex feeling now being resolved. The sequence through its revisions comes to *render* the emotion, does not seek to *describe* it. A good example of this occurs in the way the transition from Aoife to the Blind Man is accomplished. In the earliest versions Aoife suspected an intruder – "I hear a stick strike upon clay & rock" – and chose to hide among the rocks till she could resume their talk in peace since "no other ears / Must know the things I ask the things you say". The moving of the Blind Man's stick in search of the standing stone and his grunt of pleasure on locating it elicit from Cuchulain the bluntly obvious "I think that you are blind". Subsequent versions elaborate Aoife's account identifying the intruder immediately as "a blind old man" who "stands still – now he moves on again / There is something he is looking for"; on arrival the Blind Man touches Cuchulain, sighs and asks the hero to identify himself and Cuchulain in replying addresses him as "Blind Man". On the typescript Yeats first extends the description even further ("I hear a stick strike among the black thorn trees"), which is now so different in tenor from the rest of the verse as to be glaringly incongruous, before in holograph he re-writes the whole passage paring it down to the terse "Somebody comes" and the quick supposition "Some countryman" who will rapidly depart when he finds himself alone and unprotected in Cuchulain's presence. As Aoife hides, the now unidentified character appears to be recognised immediately by the audience; when he touches Cuchulain's body and sighs, the hero quietly affirms "I think you are a blind old man": he has recognised in an instant the appropriateness of this particular intruder on his dying and accepts the inevitability of it all and the cruel irony. Revision has heightened the dramatic excitement of the moment and sharpened our appreciation of Cuchulain's psychological temper. Repeatedly through revision a greater terseness and simplicity of expression makes for an increase in dramatic tension by more subtly intimating complexities of characterisation. Only the great death-cry in its splendid defiance comes as a result of amplifying Cuchulain's moment of metaphysical awareness.

One late revision of sufficient moment to deserve comment concerns the scenario for Emer's dance. This and the closing lyric for long eluded satisfactory definition. Interestingly the final shape of the dance was achieved by transposing a passage in the lyric into pure movement. At one stage the singer exploring the question, "Are those things men adore and loathe / Their sole reality?" mused on the significance of the dance: "now that [he] is dead, now that hes unreal she can give him unmixed love. Perhaps / that is right, perhaps she can hear his soul / Sing in its eternal joy". It is only with the typescript that an extended direction for the dance is offered and in holograph Yeats reworked the passage to indicate meticulously how the dancer should convey the significance of the moment as it is explained by the lyric: that through the dance Emer begins to identify imaginatively with her husband and appreciate the transcendence he found at his death; and with that knowledge she too finds stillness. Given a truly expressive dancer with a gift for improvisation like Ninette de Valois (the draft material confirms that it was she Yeats had in mind in the prologue and not Isadora Duncan as some scholars have attempted to prove), the moment can convey all, rendering the commentary in the lyric redundant; hence in the final version of the song the idea of the creative power of imaginative identification with the hero is substantiated by the one example of Pearse and Connolly during the Easter Rising.

This is a deft and scrupulous work of scholarship as one would expect of Professor Marcus, setting the highest of standards for the volumes that follow. Not the least of its many virtues is that in his commentaries on the various stages of composition Professor Marcus intimates rather than exhaustively enumerates the insights the drafts give one into Yeats's artistry. Reading the variant texts as he presents them here becomes truly an act of creative exploration.

Ann Saddlemyer (ed.), *Theatre Business: the Correspondence of the First Abbey Theatre Directors: William Butler Yeats, Lady Gregory and J. M. Synge* (Gerrards Cross: Colin Smythe; University Park, Penn: Pennsylvania State University Press, 1982) pp. 330.

Richard Allen Cave

"It is such a break in our very very small group of understanding friends – which indeed has been little more than a triangle", wrote Lady Gregory to Yeats on the occasion of Synge's death. Where the Abbey was concerned, it was, as she wrote elsewhere, a matter of "we three always". Though the story of the founding and sustaining of a theatre movement in Ireland has been told many times (often from suspiciously subjective viewpoints) it has not been explored before in terms of the day-to-day existences of the triumvirate who made the running of the Abbey their life's work, pursuing it with a dedication and fervour that created between them a powerful bond of respect and friendship, which survived and was strengthened by a series of crises that might as easily have stretched their loyalty to each other to breaking point. They did take sides inevitably – one pair against the third – but there was always the shared ambition for the Abbey and a deep trust in each other as artists that helped to heal the divisions. They could be malicious about their opponents – Lady Gregory telling Synge of a letter Yeats received from AE accusing him of "sneering at *Deirdre* and saying it was a bad & popular play" adds the aside: "I am sure he never said it was popular!" – but were never spiteful or harboured grudges among themselves; they knew how to give in gracefully; and victory meant survival of the Abbey, not personal vindication. (If Lady Gregory once confessed to Synge: "I am rather tired of acting as drag on his [Yeats's] impetuosity, but am comforted by the thought that it means vigorous health", she quickly restored the balance: "When you impetuously wanted to rush into offering Darley a yet unbuilt room I was glad to know that you also were in vigorous health!"). The safety-valve was the fact that they considered themselves *writers* principally and theatre-managers only for want of someone better to undertake the task; none of them enjoyed the power of management; all at times resented the responsibilities and were glad of the sharing the "triangle" permitted.

Allowing the joint correspondence of the three directors from 1897 to 1909 to stand as an account of the early years of the theatre-movement was a brilliant idea of Professor Saddlemyer: she makes it seem so much the obvious way of approaching the subject that one is astonished no one has thought of it before. But this volume would not be the comprehensive, meticulously objective history that it is, if it were not for Professor Saddlemyer's prodigious feats of scholarship as editor, for every letter is scrupulously annotated so that one is informed of the whole career and involvement with the Abbey of the actors, theatre-staff, dramatists and critics referred to within the letters; salient extracts from replies received to decisions of the directors are quoted and newspaper reactions to matters of policy; Miss Horniman who provoked so much heart-searching discussion about the kind of theatre the Abbey should be – its performance-style, manner of rehearsal, the composition of the company – is generously allowed her say to balance the deliberations of the "triangle". What is impressive is the sheer range of the cross-reference not only to contemporary material but to subsequent books of criticism, biography, literary and theatrical history (often quietly pointing out the errors of earlier scholars in this field). There is an apt sense of timing too about the annotations: it is fitting that, when the relationship between the directors and Miss Horniman became strained, we should be reminded that this coincided with Miss Horniman's increasing her subsidy by some £200 and then, to put the figures in a proper perspective, that "privately to Yeats she noted that she had spent £1070 in six months on the company, 'which is very nearly half my income for a whole year' ". Further perspective on the matter is offered two letters later when Synge writes informing Lady Gregory of his meeting with Karel Musek of the National Theatre in Prague, for, though the letter is couched in general terms, he cannot resist one specific detail: "They have £12,000 a year *and* all scenery and light from the government so they can afford to do things well". Statistics, such as the number of performances given a week at particular periods of the theatre's development or the composition of programmes for given seasons, are included where they add appreciably to one's grasp of the issues under discussion and the varying pressures being brought on the directorate. This admirable work is supplemented by a selective bibliography, cleverly incorporated within, firstly, a chronology of significant events for the years 1878–98, and then a detailed list of public announcements and productions from 1899 to 1904. Finally as an appendix Professor Saddlemyer reprints the text of the Illustrated Programme designed for the summer tour in Scotland and the North of England in 1906, which is a statement of current principles and an assessment of the company's achievement to date. A lifetime's scholarship is here most sensitively deployed; one cannot imagine a fuller account of these years being possible.

What *Theatre Business* reveals is that it was not the public crises like the *Playboy* riots that taxed the resources and stamina of the directors but internal issues like the exodus of many of the leading players, including Mary Walker, over the question of how nationalist the organisation should be (which led to the founding in 1906 of the rival Theatre of Ireland); Miss Horniman's interference in matters of policy, acting strength and future objectives; and the secession of the Fays, all of which threatened the stability of the company and the future of the enterprise. All three crises posed challenges to the directors' sense of the principles that led them to work for the theatre in the first place and that they fervently believed would make that theatre unique. They were not committed to Nationalism to the extent of being propagandist or accepting plays on the basis of their message rather than their artistry. It is attention to the *quality* of a performance that lies at the root of so much of the thinking and reasoning in these letters, the refusal to accept the second best because it was politically expedient or reflected the values of their patron. This last was the really difficult matter for all three were conscious of a profound debt to Miss Horniman and sincerely wished to make her proud of the theatre but refused to compromise with their own standards to accommodate her enthusiasms. They at least showed willing and tried out several of her schemes to prove their shortcomings, having no wish to abuse her involvement or authority. They accepted Miss Darragh into the company till she proved unequal to the task of playing Yeats's Deirdre and Dectora and showed that a *finished* actress on the London model ('finished' being Miss Horniman's preferred epithet), even one of Irish extraction, was not right if work as original as Yeats's was to be seen to advantage. They appreciated that a stage-manager/producer like Ben Iden Payne would relieve Willie Fay of the onus of running the company and directing all the plays to allow him time to perfect his art as an actor, but again Miss Horniman's protégé seemed capable only of imposing on the productions a manner which the directors found outdated and stagy. But what the conflicts with Miss Horniman threw into sharp relief was a disagreement over subsidy which threatened to jeopardise the harmonious relationship of the "triangle", the resolving of which in the long term changed the course of Yeats's development as a dramatist.

Subsidy all three knew was a necessity even to the point of financing the right kind of stage-manager who was sympathetic to their principles – that alone would give them freedom to pursue their own work as dramatists. (The letters constantly voice regret at delays in composition because of time spent on affairs of management or the revision of other playwrights' offerings to make them adequately stageworthy). There was also a pressing need for the company to experiment to find a proper style for the performing of verse plays, which Yeats felt would be possible only if the Abbey could attempt good revivals of the classical repertoire: the Greeks, Racine, early Ibsen. This Miss Horniman wished to promote because it was Yeats's ambition and furthering his ambitions was her motive for getting involved in the whole enterprise. The Fays were sympathetic to this scheme too wanting the chance to prove themselves against demanding material and seeking variety for the repertoire. If Lady Gregory and Synge had reservations, it was *not* because they did not wish to see Yeats's work advanced at the expense of their own (Lady Gregory took care to inform Synge honestly that "I think his work more important than any other (you must not be offended at this) and I think it our chief distinction"; and she was genuinely distressed for Yeats when Miss Darragh failed to live up to his expectations). Their concern was that such an extended repertory was beyond the capabilities of the present company who would not play it well; a fall in standard would lose them audiences who would become suspicious of verse plays which would be to lose the ground gained in performing Yeats's own plays to date. If they were to seek subsidy from a source other than Miss Horniman, it would have to be an Irish one and there would be more chance of success if their work had a national rather than an international stamp on it. Both sides of the argument were sound and Synge was right to aver that they wished to stake their claim to excellence on being a writer's theatre not, as the new scheme would risk their becoming, a director's theatre. Time was what was wanted – the time to experiment in rehearsal without the pressure of constant performance to make an income necessary for survival; but this would necessitate either a larger company or a studio theatre whose work, frankly exploratory, would appeal to a select few. Either development would demand an increased subsidy; and as that was not foreseeable, caution won the day. Yeats in the grip of an enthusiasm, as the correspondence frequently demonstrates, could be impetuous; and it is doubtful whether the Abbey could have survived had it immediately implemented his scheme for an expanded repertoire; there would have been little to distinguish it from any other provincial repertory theatre, overworked, shoddy, lacking in originality of drive or vision. What Lady Gregory sought to preserve was what over a remarkably short time the Abbey had made its exclusive excellence; she was defending a proven *quality* of performance, thereby remaining true to their fundamental principles. That Miss Horniman chose to question Lady Gregory and Synge's motives as selfish is a judgement against her rather than against them. Sudden changes in the Abbey's circumstances were to prove Lady Gregory's view wise: Miss Horniman retired to found her own company in Manchester leaving the Abbey to fare by its own endeavours; the loss of the Fays and then Synge's failing health and death were to increase the burden of managerial responsibilities for Yeats and Lady Gregory. There was now no subsidy and the directing of plays as well as theatre business took precious time from writing (though Sara Allgood and W. A. Henderson offered sterling support); wide-ranging experiment in modes of presentation was quite beyond their means. But Yeats's vision was not without value, only patience was wanting: in time the Dublin Drama League did allow Abbey actors to extend their range undoubtedly to the benefit of their standard work and it educated the public taste so that there was an audience ready for the Gate Theatre at its inception though, in confirmation of Synge's view, that theatre with Edwards and MacLiammoir was resolutely a director's and actor's theatre. In time, too, with the Peacock, Yeats founded his studio theatre and in Ninette de Valois, with her experience of working with her cousin Terence Gray at his Festival Theatre in Cambridge behind her, discovered an artist who was truly sensitive to the demands of his work, while in F. J. McCormick the Abbey boasted an actor of unrivalled range and technique in heroic verse drama that made *Oedipus* and *King Lear* possible at last. But at the time of Synge's death, consolidation of achievements was essential; defiance and daring would have risked exhausting the company's already depleted reserves of stamina and invention.

What emerges most powerfully from the correspondence viewed in relation to subsequent theatre history is the solid worth of Lady Gregory's tactical skills; she was always the best judge of which of the three directors should handle a difficult incident and when it was advisable to caution Yeats to use "more of the harp string in your voice". When the Theatre of Ireland was founded she sensed instinctively that their best policy was to wait, not provoke ugly situations that the newspapers could aggravate into scandals: "let them act what they will, and show their weakness, and fizzle themselves out". The opposition was best left to destroy itself through their lack of artistic merit (which they quickly did in fact) but they should on no account be given any opportunity that would allow them to appear to die like martyrs: mediocrity should reap its proper reward. (Her letter to Colum at this time asking him to allow the Abbey to continue performing *The Land* is a model of the art of persuasion that is yet quite without guile – she appeals to his integrity as an artist and his trust as a friend.) More interesting still is her solacing Yeats after the demise of his scheme for developing the poetic side of the theatre's work with the suggestion that in future he consider writing an acting version of his plays in prose "and put it into verse afterwards", which would make effecting alterations easier if there were no longer the worry of continually re-writing the verse. This too would obviate the need for certain kinds of experiment in staging his work. Given the agonies of composition over *The Shadowy Waters*, this was sound advice; only *The King of the Great Clock Tower* exists in two such versions, but prose scenarios and drafts became increasingly a part of Yeats's method of playwriting. However, it seems curious that Lady Gregory should be attempting to create a division between the theatrical and literary qualities of his drama. There is unfortunately no comment from Yeats to clarify the matter or define his response.

If one has a regret about this correspondence it is that the pressure of theatre business prevented them from exploring aesthetic issues together. Insights into the directors' views of each other as writers tend to come indirectly in such moments as Yeats's fear expressed to Synge that the Fays will make their quarrel with the directorate over *The Canavans* and so will win the public and the actors over by an easy advantage since "I do not like the Canavans myself and I have not met anyone who does, except you". Or again Synge holidaying in the Blasket Islands carefully intimating that the revised *White Cockade* could merit more strokes of the blue pencil since he found the language at times "too figurative" for his taste while "once or twice I felt doubtful if there was quite current enough in a scene, but I cannot be sure that it was not the fault of the gannets and choughs that were distracting my attention". It is the marked scarcity of such comments that make Synge's suddenly detailed accounts of his progress with *Deirdre of the Sorrows* so telling, as if subliminally he anticipated his rapid decline and death and wished his fellow artists to understand his intentions with the play so that it might, if necessary, be completed by them; yet Yeats and Lady Gregory both scrupled against posing a question that would clarify his motives as indelicate. Tact and generosity prevailed between them all to the end. When Lady Gregory wrote to Yeats on hearing from him of Synge's death, she both sought and offered consolation in the fact of "we three always", of three lives united by a common purpose that elicited the best from each of them: ". . . you gave him his means of expression – You have given me mine". Within the "triangle" each found a distinct identity.

James Lovic Allen, *Yeats's Epitaph: a Key to Symbolic Unity in his Life and Work* (Washington: University Press of America, 1982) pp. 270.

Karen Dorn

From the roadside tombs of the ancient world to the elaborate Victorian graveyards, tombstones and their epitaphs have a long European tradition drawing upon the artistic and religious forms of the community. Professor Allen is a prolific commentator on the religious and symbolic aspects of W. B. Yeats's work, and his first book-length study, *Yeats's Epitaph: a Key to Symbolic Unity in his Life and Work*, is a most interesting account of the way Yeats drew upon and modified the traditional epitaph for his own use: "Cast a cold eye / On life, on death. / Horseman, pass by". Unlike the shepherds in Poussin's painting, "Et in Arcadia ego", however, who have a quiet and uncluttered view of the tombstone, Professor Allen's readers will need to pull back the ivy and bramble to understand clearly the argument of the book; there are many skirmishes with critics in the undergrowth that may distract from what should remain the central issues: who is the speaker of the epitaph, who is the horseman and what view of death are we invited to consider.

Professor Allen deals initially with the circumstances of composition. Yeats worked on the prose and verse drafts during the final year of his life, from June to September 1939. Using Curtis Bradford's recent dating of the last manuscripts, Allen refutes the widely held view that Yeats wrote the epitaph in angry reaction to an essay on Rilke's notion of death, a view stemming from Yeats himself who wrote to Dorothy Wellesley that the essay on Rilke had "annoyed" him and caused him to write upon the margin a draft of his epitaph (*LDW* 184). Yeats in fact used the occasion as a chance to contrast his epitaph, already in draft form, with Rilke's belief that death is an end and consummation of life.

Yeats had placed these two views of death in dramatic opposition a few years earlier in his play, *Words Upon the Window-Pane*, where the tormented ghost of Jonathan Swift disturbs a Dublin seance to belie the sentiment of Swift's own epitaph composed for St. Patrick's Cathedral: in Yeats's English version, "Swift has sailed into his rest; / Savage indignation there / Cannot lacerate his breast". Professor Allen cites Hugh Kenner's remark that Swift's epitaph belongs to the tradition of the "formula of . . . decline" of which Wordsworth was perhaps the most typical representative. Allen would find further support for his discussion of the conventional in the art of tombstones in Nicholas Penny's *Church Monuments in*

Romantic England (1977) which traces the change from the neo-classical tombs that appeal to family pride through to the late Victorian Gothic monuments that appeal to personal sentiment. In contrast with that Victorian appeal to emotion, Yeats's own epitaph was dispassionate (Cast a cold eye . . .) and his view of death was a refutation of the formula of decline. Yeats's interests were directed towards the images and legends of reincarnation, and Professor Allen's study is informed throughout by a sympathetic perception of this metaphysical dimension in Yeats's work. He offers as a prose version of the epitaph Yeats's own remark in *A Vision*: "Neither between death and birth nor between birth and death can the soul find more than momentary happiness; its object is to *pass rapidly* round its circle and find freedom from that circle."

Equally significantly Yeats modified the traditional role of the epitaph as an address to a passing traveller. Professor Allen supports the view that the horseman in the epitaph is intended to be Yeats himself, hardly pausing after death to continue the journey. In the most substantial section of his book, he sets out in detail the complexity of allusion underlying the central image of the horseman. Drawing upon Yeats's poems, plays and essays, Yeats's work with Lady Gregory on the legends of Western Ireland and Yeats's knowledge of comparative mythology, Allen's discussion moves from the familiar images of aristocratic horsemen and the legendary heroes, Oisin and Cuchulain, to the legends associated with the sacred mountains of the west coast of Ireland. From beneath those mountains ride the host of the Sidhe accompanied by the legendary heroes and, as Yeats believed, the souls of the Irish poets and those other "primary" characters in *A Vision* who are out of phase with the current age. Allen gives a convincing account of the correspondences Yeats drew between those ghostly horsemen riding out from under Ben Bulben and his apocalyptic version of history in which the return of the Sidhe heralds the future age. This account is a direct challenge to the view that Yeats's work is nostalgia for a past age, and it sets Yeats's view of his own contribution to Ireland in dialogue with the future as well as the past. Though he draws attention to Yeats's impressive knowledge of comparative mythology, Professor Allen goes on to remark upon the "amazing" number of analogues to the image of the horseman. His lengthy excursion into Celtic, Greek, Roman and Indian Asvin images, and his use of handbooks, encyclopaedias and of more recent studies in comparative mythology may strike the reader as reductive. Perhaps a discussion of the books on comparative mythology known to have been in Yeats's own library might have given a clearer sense of the poet's own interests.

Professor Allen does not comment on the frequently cited similarity between Yeats's epitaph and that of Timon of Athens (see, for instance, the editor's note in the Arden Edition, p. 140). Both Shakespeare and Yeats used the conventional "pass by" though there seems to be little similarity beyond this verbal echo. Yeats was drawn chiefly to Timon as a figure of tragic joy as he "contemplates his own end, and orders his tomb by the beached verge of the salt flood" (*E&I* 255). In Shakespeare's verse, "Graves only be men's works, and death their gain". The figure of Timon reappears in Yeats's poem. "An Acre of

Grass", one of a series of late poems contrasting Yeats's fear of mortality with his beliefs in the continuation of his spirit and the permanence of works of art.

This opposition in Yeats's late poems between mortality and permanence is also the theme of Stanley Sultan's book, *Yeats at his Last* (Dolmen Press, 1975). Sultan's discussion of Yeats's interest in Pythagorean measure and proportion, though not cited by Allen, complements Allen's own explication of the image of the "cold eye" in the epitaph. Sultan too takes the "I" of "Under Ben Bulben" (which includes the epitaph) to be the poet speaking from beyond the grave. Basing his argument in part on the "manuscript table of contents" discovered by Curtis Bradford, Sultan shows that Yeats planned "Under Ben Bulben" as the introductory poem for the volume, *Last Poems*, in which Yeats courageously confronts his own approaching death. Sultan's book can be seen to give further arguments to support Professor Allen's study, which throws new light on the way Yeats modified the conventional art of the epitaph to give expression to his belief in the journey of the soul after death, the soul imagined as a horseman riding out from under the tomb.

A general point could be raised about the production of this book. The text has been printed, photographically, directly from typescript with an unjustified right-hand margin, an economical procedure, no doubt, which puts a strain on the reader but which seems to be used increasingly for academic monographs. Professor Allen's study, an illumination of a central image in Yeats's poetry and life, would have been better served by a more readable text.

David R. Clark, *Yeats at Songs and Choruses* (Gerrards Cross: Colin Smythe, 1983) pp. xxiv + 283.

Ian Fletcher

The pure volume of Yeats's manuscripts partly accounts for much editorial activity over the past twenty years since Jon Stallworthy produced his pioneering *Between the Lines* in 1963. There have been sensitive decipherings and criticism of individual poems from Thomas Parkinson; Curtis Bradford provided useful chunks of material (1965) and Stallworthy returned to the scene bearing some of the drafts for *Last Poems* (1969). Yeats scholarship was already an industrial complex by the late sixties and alarming piles of manuscript and photostats of manuscripts have since faced the veteran corps of scholars and the raw infantry of Ph.D. hopefuls.

The manuscripts are not only like the sands on Rosses' level shore, they frequently offer a sequence of composition from the first, ragged notion of a possible topic: Yeats tended to attack a poem very early in its career. If it succeeds triumphantly, the manuscript will also display a sudden leap from mere "sedentary toil" over lines, rhythms, syntax, to an insight that alters the direction of the draft: grace beyond the reach of art. Or if one prefers a chemical, or even alchemical metaphor: "the heat and pressure of genius which causes elements not merely to coalesce but to be transformed into something new". That leap may not be made in the only possible direction: a successful poem may well represent the suppression of other possibly successful poems.

The transcriber of Yeats's manuscript has also to wrestle with what David Clark aptly calls Yeats's "demonic" hand: the occultist poet often appears to preserve the *grimoire* aspect of his own writings. One of the master's pointed habits is to mass together or simply omit individual letters so that one may be thrust back on rational hunches. The trouble really begins when one proceeds, as all transcribers with any *macho* pretensions proceed, from transcription to interpretation and criticism.

David Clark is expert in this hard field and his essays on the manuscripts of seven poems principally from *The Winding Stair* are a valuable addition to our studies. The poems discussed extort different approaches: "Crazy Jane on the Day of Judgment"; "Three Things"; "After Long Silence"; "Michael Robartes and the Dancer" along with "Her Triumph"; three essays in translation: "Colonus' Praise", "A Gay Good Night" (both from *The Tower*) and "Sing I

258

Must", all from Sophocles. One of the impressive features of Clark's book is the manifold nature of his approach: transcriptions, photographs of manuscripts; literary and visual source material; close critical comment and a keen watch on the drama of the "leap". The aesthetic shudder this last produces is unfortunately muted by Clark's sense that such a ritual moment requires an equally ritual term. He coins the word "saltation", but either from modesty or failure of conviction does not set it in Bloomian hypostasised capitals; often, indeed, dropping it in favour of the swift clear unpretentious monosyllable: it has ponderously usurped. The word "leap" consorts after all far more amicably with Clark's own swiftness and clarity of prose and line of argument.

Clark's interpretation of the manuscripts is governed by two presuppositions: the importance of the revisions of the 1925 *Vision* that Yeats was accomplishing about the time of the making of most of these poems and his approval of a formula devised by Marjorie Perloff: "the reader must be wary of concluding from Yeats's own extreme statements that there is a pervasive presence of the sexual theme in the later poetry". Yeats worked, to be sure, well within that mystical tradition of using sexual metaphors for the loves of the ghost, but the ambiguities (Clark is well aware of those) and the bawdy puns in the Crazy Jane pieces and elsewhere remind one that the accent falls equally on sex and ghost. And Professor Perloff's high minded statement presumably falters in the presence of the speaker of a good many of the *Last Poems*, one who tells us how nasty it is to be an old feller, reliving lost sexual opportunities in a world awash with muck and blood and sperm. For Clark, the *Winding Stair* poems metaphysically as well as physically yearn and the notion of perfect congress beyond time opens a flank to the revision of *A Vision*. *If* Time were but gone, but poems are made in time. At all events Clark's interpretations of the Crazy Jane Judgment poem and of "After Long Silence" are strongly affected by his presuppositions. His critical method is inductive but cannot work without deducing insights from his postulates. Criticism of Yeats has its own circus animals: these days *A Vision* and Maud Gonne have a place reserved in interpretation; but Clark evades using the poems as vivacious footnotes merely to the "system". And before all the fine detailing of his essays, one can only pause and admit that justice is not possible in a moderately huddled review.

Before engaging with what is the triumph of the volume, the analysis of "After Long Silence", a few small comments can reasonably be offered. On page 55 we hear that "The Gift of Harun-Al-Rashid" (1924) tells the "true story" of *A Vision* through a parable of Yeats's own marriage night. Wisdom speaks through the bride who remains "in childish ignorance" of all the gaudy spiritual goings on. The poem is not one of Yeats's best but it works all right without having to be spliced to the "system". Does criticism of the old boy always have to be so hushed? There is that amusing story that when W. B. was depressed on his honeymoon, Mrs W. B., a lady of resource, tried faking spirit messages and then found herself to her own surprise "taken over". Ignorance, perhaps; childish, no.

Clark is free from the notion that only painters approved of by the art histories of yesterday can be promoted to "sources": so we find Puvis de Chavannes,

Gustave Moreau and Burne-Jones contributing to the "Michael Robartes and
the Dancer" and "Her Triumph" chapter. But we are also told that Yeats was
always a little ashamed of his admiration for Burne-Jones. The evidence for this
is a sentence that Yeats wrote: "is it because of some change in the weather that I
find beauty everywhere even in Burne-Jones's *King Cophetua*, one of his later
pictures and find it without shame?" Yeats may well have preferred the early
Rossetti-flavoured work or more likely he felt that *King Cophetua and the Beggar
Maid* was sentimental allegory, unlike some of Burne-Jones's later symbolist
images. It is Dr Clark, not Yeats, who is ashamed of Burne-Jones. Still, we have
advanced well beyond the notion that one picture lies behind a poem towards
more sophisticated uses of visual material. In the discussion of the two "dragon"
poems there is some plodding application of *A Vision* but fortunately a
recognition that the poems shift away from that matrix. Dr Clark also worries
about isolating a source for the sharply lit image of the conquering hero standing
among the dragon rings. Plenty of that detail can be found in late nineteenth
century painting and illustration and there is also Wagner. Morris's *Sigurd the
Volsung* might be thought to be a likely source, but the nearest analogue is not
very near: "his heart by the Work was folded, and the bonds of the Ancient Ill".
It is Regin not Sigurd who stands among the coils. Beardsley's *Third Tableau to the
Rheingold* is no help either; but I have no doubt that Clark has travelled this way
and further.

Moreau's splendid machine *Jupiter and Semele* is duly praised in the discussion
of "Colonus' Praise". Here Clark deals with a Sophoclean original almost closed
to Yeats, since apart from thrill words like *Daimon*, *hylic* and *Psyche*, he knew no
Greek at all. In the interest of actable drama Yeats deliberately omitted the
image clusters in Sophocles' tragic poems, but saw in the choruses an
opportunity for composing freeish later Yeatsian lyrics tied to the originals by a
pretty loose umbilical. Clark claims that Yeats breaks with the surface (the
surface that is of Jebb's and Paul Masqueray's versions and notes) but keeps
faith with the depth of the texts. But the Yeatsian view of the chorus is far from
that of Sophocles; Sophocles' choruses are fully integrated with the action and
indeed carry it forward. It is Euripides with his "refreshment" view of the choric
ode that Yeats follows. Here Clark commits himself to the hoarse hyperbole that
the dedicated Yeats scholar is always prone to enounce. It is not, to be fair,
prominent in *Yeats At Songs and Choruses*, though we are reminded that *The Winding
Stair* is "one of Yeats's very greatest volumes". If we are not floored by the double
superlative we might have breath enough to ask: "how many *very* great volumes
of verse did Yeats produce?" One is my reckoning, and the important value
judgement on *The Winding Stair* is that though it contains a good number of fine
poems, it contains one or perhaps none of Yeats's very greatest and represents a
decline from *The Tower*. In any case the total book of the *Collected Poems* is what
matters and this is shown by the need to refer backwards and forwards through
most of Yeats's *oeuvre*, when one is discussing a poem of any substance.

The chapter on "After Long Silence" will certainly be a point of departure for all future discussion. The poem had its genesis in a visit Yeats paid to Olivia Shakespear, his former mistress and long time friend. It contains cruces and ambiguities. The first lies in the nature of that "long silence". Does this, as Brooks and Warren suggest, imply an absolute pause in the conversation between "descant" and "yet again descant"? Clark comments "I do not feel such a break in the talk." The "yet again" then is intensification. Rather, Clark argues, the "long silence" must be one of years. Here we move rapidly from poem to biography. Yeats had certainly seen Mrs Shakespear on several occasions over the previous months; he had been writing to her for years.

Brooks and Warren also read "the supreme theme" as being "art and song", a twinge of the Walter Paters. This is indeed the simplest and most obvious grammatical and pointed interpretation, though any argument from punctuation in Yeats needs to be stated with severe reserve. Parkinson reads the theme as "love". John E. Parish suggests an entertainingly sour reading in a libertine mode: "being good for nothing else, we will be wise". The sixty-year-old smiling ex-public man as "Maimed Debauchee". "And indeed we are wonderfully wise now we are incapable of physical love." A nicely astringent reading; not the truth; better certainly than bang on to the Dreaming Back. So bodily decrepitude may be wisdom or it may be wisdom but still bodily decrepitude. The direction of Clark's interpretation via Perloff and *A Vision* is towards wisdom and the soul and away from all sensual irrelevance. This is not what "A Dialogue of Self and Soul" tells us: its final "sweetness" recalling, as it does, that "sweetness" which flows "up from the heart's root" in "Friends" is the crucial link with "blessedness".

But to return to that long silence. The silence, Clark believes, is a silence of many years, a silence that hangs between youth and bodily decrepitude.

Was there such a silence in Yeats's life which may have suggested the line? I suppose there were many, as there are in any life. A reunion with Mrs. Olivia Shakespear, his mistress during a brief period in the nineties, apparently seems a sufficient explanation to other critics. But I cannot think that the intensity of the line is sufficiently explained by the fact that Yeats had not seen Mrs. Shakespear for the duration of an entire summer in 1929.

This is vicious reductionism. Mrs Shakespear and Yeats *were* estranged and dramatically so for some years after 1897. She is among the women he praises in "Friends", and he evidently felt strongly enough about their early years to destroy a number of his letters to her when they were returned to him after her death in 1938. And it is possible Clark is inaccurate in declaring that Olivia was only "his mistress during a brief period in the nineties". The fact remains that of all his women friends Olivia Shakespear was the one who would most reciprocate a descant upon supreme themes. Even the talented Florence Farr hardly measured up. Mrs Yeats – perhaps she was teasing the Sassenach – once said to me "W. B. despised Florence's intellect!" And just imagine an evening under the lamplight with Maud discussing the supreme themes of art and song. The aim of Clark's superior induction is to edit poor Mrs Shakespear out of the poem and to smuggle *A Vision* and Maud Gonne in.

The earliest draft has nothing about "long silence", leaving aside whether the "long silence" in the room might be an echo of the "long silence" of biography. Why seeing Mrs Shakespear should be so severly devoid of memories, regrets and compensations is beyond conjecture. Yeats echoes in that "estranged or dead" a phrase of his own dedication to "Vestigia" of the 1925 *A Vision* where he gestures to "other students who were once friends or friends' friends [and who] were dead or estranged" (*AV*[*A*] ix). Clark, seizing upon this, and discovering that Yeats had been estranged from Mina Mathers for thirty odd years by a "long silence", uses "All Souls' Night", that summoning of ghosts, to reinforce his view that the "supreme theme" of "After Long Silence" is "wisdom". But could real friendship, friendship of equals that is, have been possible with the eccentric and dominating Mathers despite all Yeats's magnanimity in "All Souls' Night"? The reconstruction here is one if not of free then of zig zag association. To justify this, we are reminded that Maud had been associated with the Golden Dawn in the 1890s and so Mina was somehow involved with a more passionate association entering the poem.

Clark reads the first line of draft 2 of the poem as "Your other lover being dead & gone" and observes that Yeats "thought of his widowed mistress's late husband": Henry Hope Shakespear was an amiable old buffer but the line would have been such a pungent anticlimax if it had really possessed that meaning that it is no wonder that Yeats hastily scrubbed it. And in suggesting that Mrs Shakespear had rationed herself so acutely Yeats was no doubt indulging in the courtly idiom of "kissing her hand" that opens draft 3. "Those other lovers" in draft 2 appears to be written over "Your other lover": the first correction is straightforward; the second could merely be clarifying the word "lovers" which had appeared in hastier handwriting with the last letter docked. I do not suggest this is the case but it is an example of the difficulty of basing arguments on orthography. The substitution of "Those" for "Your" Clark sees as deliberately expanding the appeal of the poem beyond the narrow circuit of Mrs Shakespear's boudoir. I have no notion, nor do I suppose has Dr Clark, of how many lovers Mrs Shakespear had. She was a devotee of Shelley and free love in her earlier years – though that no doubt was mostly literature. In short, his relationship with Mrs Shakespear, both lover and friend, is enough to underwrite the passion of the poem and Yeats was perfectly capable of generalising an emotion without dragging in Mina, "All Souls' Night", Maud and Auntie Maeve and all. None of this of course affects the patient transcription, the discussion of the technical development of the poem. Dr Clark has lived with these manuscripts. His responses are based partly on "feel" as he admits and he also admits that once one passes from transcription to interpretation differences may well ensue.

Two brief cavils. Where visual sources are being called on – even if in a number of cases they are properly dismissed – it remains essential to provide highly defined images. In the photographs of the older masters here the effect is dark and blurred. The pencil of the manuscript reproductions is also on ocasion hard to distinguish. And the publishers have placed all the notes at the back in the worst modern way so that one spends much time reading with one finger stuck in the text and the others paddling at the back of the book like a novice half strangled by an archlute.

In discussion of "After Long Silence" I have been devil's advocate and nothing of what I've written can alter the fact that *Yeats at Songs and Choruses* is consistently challenging, enterprising in its range of sources, ingenious in its interpretations, nearly always faithful to its declared aim of "reconstructing" the original vision behind the poem. What is in doubt is the validity of this method, the dangers of the proceeding, however sensitively and learnedly accomplished.

Cairns Craig: *Yeats, Eliot, Pound and the Politics of Poetry: Richest to the Richest* (London: Croom Helm; Pittsburgh: University Pittsburgh Press, 1982) pp. 323.

Richard Burton

Cairns Craig has ably demonstrated in this study that "the open poem demanded as its counterbalance the closed society". Yeats's belief that poetry "cannot be understood without a rich memory" ("Certain Noble Plays of Japan") is a justification for reworking, and to some extent recreating, Celtic legendary material. At the same time it emphasises the heroic stature of the bard: "The power of memory was also a memory of power". The point, though a little glib, is taken, but we should remember that at least one Yeats persona, Paul Ruttledge, comes out strongly against memory in that anarchic early play, *Where There Is Nothing* – along with "hope" and "thought" it is no part of the "measureless eternal life" (*VPl* 1139). The power, then, is in the hands of those who possess the longest memories – being the custodians of the folk tradition, the peasantry, and the makers of history, the aristocracy. These classes were interdependent, culturally as well as economically, and together the aristocrat and the peasant furnish the nation's art with its images. The middle class, because devoid of tradition, or of the memory of tradition, is excluded and cannot contribute to the aesthetic growth of the race. Craig sees Yeats as coming to hate democracy, mass education and industry because they are hostile to the notion of "richest to the richest", and therefore to memory and to Associationist art. These are the bones of Craig's argument.

The imagination, Hazlitt claimed in his essay on *Coriolanus*, is

> an exaggerating and calculating faculty; it takes from one thing to add to another; it accumulates circumstances together to give the greatest possible effect to a favourable object. The understanding is a dividing and measuring faculty: it judges of things not according to their immediate impression on the mind, but according to their relations with one another (quoted Craig, p. 23)

The assumption that poetry springs from such an imagination is at the root of Hazlitt's belief that poetry is necessarily a "very anti-levelling principle", actively promoting "inequality and disproportion". Inherent in the neo-classical doctrine of Associationism, however, is just such a taking and adding, an accumulation of circumstances, and if the discovery of Yeats's poetic as a modern translation of this pre-Romantic doctrine is unexpected, it is largely because Associationism seems a most "democratic" rationale. It argues that all intellects begin, equally, as non-associative, and that they develop according to conditioning, according, as Locke puts it in *An Essay Concerning Human Understanding*, to "Education, Custom, and the constant din of their Party" (2.33.18). Does not Hallam himself, whose Tennyson essay Yeats read and admired (and which Craig makes the *sole* link between Yeats's poetic and eighteenth century psychological speculation), claim that complete identification with the artist's "leading sentiment" is "never *physically* impossible, because nature has placed in every man the simple elements, of which art is the sublimation"?[1] The discovery of an affinity between Yeats and the Associationists is unexpected, too, because it involves one of the last Romantics in a doctrinal split from one of the first.

By failing to account for the dichotomy of neo-classical and Romantic impulses in the tradition, and by choosing to compare Yeats's philosophy with that of a relatively obscure Scottish Associationist, Archibald Alison, whose work Yeats patently had not encountered, Craig blunts the point of the comparison. The connection between eighteenth century criticism and psychology and Yeats's poetic, via the slender reed of Hallam's essay, is implausible. There is no evidence to suggest that Yeats was interested in, or even aware of such a tradition, particularly at the outset of his career when he was supposedly already writing "Associationist" verse ("The Madness of King Goll", "Fergus and the Druid"), or that he saw Hallam as that tradition's heir. Craig, unaccountably, fails to deal adequately with Coleridge, however. Yeats knew of Coleridge's relationship with the mechanistic theories of the eighteenth century (*Au* 358), and it is likely that what he knew of Associationism came from Coleridge rather than from Hallam's rather nebulous account. It may well be that further examination of the chronology of Yeats's acquaintance with Coleridge would result in some reassessment of their poetic relationship. If "Frost at Midnight" is an "Associationist" poem, then so is "A Prayer for my Daughter". It would seem that Craig has exaggerated Hallam's importance as Yeats's stepping-stone to the eighteenth century. A rigorous investigation of Coleridge's role might have rendered Craig's thesis more credible.

On Yeats himself, however, Craig is considerably more compelling. It is clear that the poet's "psychological empiricism" is more than an acidental throwback to Associationism, for his poetic is intensely associative. Craig quotes from "The Symbolism of Poetry" to illustrate a Romantic (Wordsworthian) impulse that sets in motion Yeats's accumulation of images:

> If I watch a rushy pool in the moonlight, my emotion at its beauty is mixed with memories of the man I have seen ploughing by its margin, or the lovers I saw there a night ago; but if I look at the moon herself and remember any of her ancient names and meanings, I move among divine people, and things that have shaken off our mortality, the tower of ivory, the queen of waters . . .

and in "The Philosophy of Shelley's Poetry" Yeats explains that those processes bring him from Shelley's debt to Porphyry to Oisin's vision of the hound and the deer, to the woman with the golden apple, to Niamh, and finally to a friend's vision of "The Meeting of the Suns". As Craig says, Yeats experiences Shelley's imagery not so much as Shelley's, but in the context of his own "associational potentialities" (p. 39), and some of the tensions of the earliest verse are explained by that context. Fergus and Goll, for instance, seek to express a Romantic conception of nature but are trapped within Time as an associational model:

The romantic demand that art, through the spiritual power of the imagination, should save us from the world of time is undone by the knowledge that art works only through memory and is devoted to the endless recall of the events of time (p. 82).

The great value of this book is that it once again puts into perspective Yeats's claim to be one of the last Romantics, his commitment to Romantic models. Craig begins by accepting, with some justification, Hartley's attribution of mechanical psychological associationism to Locke's account of the irrational linkage of otherwise unrelated ideas and sensations. To Locke the association of ideas was a *madness*, because in "opposition to Reason" (op. cit., 2.33.3–4), and correspondences were due solely to "Chance and Custom" (ibid. 5). The "error" of this "unreasonableness" merely gave rise to trivial associations that should be regarded as little more than pleasant oddities – the inability of a certain man, for instance, to dance in a room that does not contain a trunk at its centre, because of the circumstances and irresistible conditioning of his early dance lessons (ibid., 16). The associations, for Locke, since not fixed by a rational structure, were inconsequential. Certainly, as both Coleridge and Hartley noted, the notion of association long preceded Locke, but since it was he who first used the word in "the particular Sense here affixed to it",[2] and since eighteenth century Associationists generally regarded Locke as the father of their doctrine, his examination of the "unnatural" linkage of ideas is as good a place as any to begin. We should perhaps remind ourselves, however, that, half a century earlier, Thomas Hobbes had demonstrated the principles of contiguity and causality, had applied the psychology critically, had regarded associational modes of thinking as entirely rational and natural (unlike Locke), and had insisted on the importance of *memory*. Indeed, since memory is to play so vital a role in Craig's thesis it is surprising that he ignores Hobbes's confirmation by the theory of the perception of the Ancients, that "memory" is the "Mother of the Muses".[3]

Hume's rejection of Locke's ultrarational psychology, his normalisation of the associative rationale, is clearly, as Craig suggests, a complete reversal of Locke's metaphysic, but it is a reversal that stretches back to Hobbes (and arguably to Aristotle), and it can be seen as an aspect of a distinct pro-associative tradition. Hume's observation in his *Treatise of Human Nature* ("Of Knowledge and Probability") that the definition of cause and effect is empirical, rather than rational or reflective, is picked up in the (still) mechanical associations of David

Hartley. Craig contracts the genesis of the Associationist theory of *Art*, however, by attributing it to Hume's reversal of Locke, and in seeing the crowning glory of associative art criticism in the Humeian tenets of Archibald Alison. At this point Yeats intrudes like an embarrassed gatecrasher, and we should regard the long comparison of Yeats with Alison, since it is closed with the announcement that, of course, Yeats had not read Alison, as something of an irrelevance. Yeats did come to read Berkeley, who promoted an associationist theory of language in the introduction to his *Principles of Human Knowledge*, but that hardly explains the "Associationism" of the poems on Fergus and Goll. We might conclude that Yeats was an independent Associationist, in spite of, and not because of the eighteenth century. This does not remove, however, the problem of Yeats's Associationism, and in spite of certain proto-Romantic elements in the tradition the application of psychology to critical theory inevitably carries the burden of the neo-classical rationale. For Associationists the systematisation of the psychology, and the analysis of the aesthetic were governed by the mechanics of reason. Craig's study serves to distance Yeats a little from the Romantic reaction that sought to overthrow such devotion to the rational mind.

It is in the attempt to relate the aesthetic to fascist political practice that this study begins to falter seriously. The connection, for Craig, swings on the conviction that both Fascism and Yeats's poetic depend on the irrational response of the multitude to specific images. This leads Craig to the assumption that "Yeats's turning to Fascism . . . is the result of his bitter realisation that the Anglo-Irish aristocracy was being destroyed as the peasants had been" (p. 197). It is a rather brittle argument. Craig demonstrates forcibly that Yeats's Associationist aesthetic was retrospective, and that it would have had a reactionary, and generally deliberalising effect on his political stance. Fascism, however, is a technical term that requires careful handling.[4] Partly we are, as Craig suggests, so horrified by the brutal excesses of inter-war Fascist machines that there is a feeling that to treat the subject as suitable for serious scholarly debate is to invite its reappearance in the political arena. Partly also, the prevalence of Marxist critiques of modern political history has debased the term. The problem of assimilating into the Marxist system a proletarian based revolution that, ideologically at least, is the antithesis of that system has resulted in the reduction of Fascism to little more than paramilitary capitalism. Because of its disturbing associations the term is retained, but its all-inclusiveness has rendered it virtually meaningless. Fascism is not easily isolated, and Craig's examination of various different attitudes to, and definitions of the ideology is interesting. As it develops into a personal statement, however, his analysis focuses, perhaps inevitably, on an aspect that is particularly germane to his thesis, but hardly the whole story. Without doubt Fascism was, and is, a movement that combines, paradoxically, extreme reaction with revolutionary "progress". Ideologically Fascism is committed to continual renewal and to continual preservation, fusing past and future, (another way of putting it is that it is, as Stanislav Andreski has demonstrated, both the "extremism of the centre" and the "centrism of the extremists"[5]). Although it *is* a "bizarre and horrendous combination of constructive and destructive forces"[6] those forces are, however, clearly classifiable. Fascism is founded on a strong sense of racial and national identity, an urgent militarism that expands that racism and nationalism into foreign affairs, a violent antipathy to socialism (though not, as Craig points out, to a number of significant socialist principles), and a clearly defined ruling elite, supporting a charismatic leader, whose presidency over a totalitarian state is uninterrupted.

Although Craig does not account for Yeats's relation to the entire Fascist phenomenon, or to the Associationist tradition, his point stands. There is a link between the *poetics* of Yeats, Eliot and Pound and the ideologies of extreme reaction, because both seek progress in a radical way that is firmly controlled by events and images of the past, and both seek this paradoxically dynamic stasis in the irrational motivation of men through images. Such a motivation is at the heart of the Associationist aesthetic, and Craig's perception of a link is an insight to be valued.

It may be possible to go further than Craig is prepared to go, and direct comparison of the three poets – of which there is surprisingly little in this account – is revealing. Yeats could not have written "The Waste Land" or the "Cantos" and, clearly, whatever the nature of the society demanded by the open poem, not all "open" poems are the same. It is a question of syntax, and in a study of poetics more attention should perhaps have been paid to this. As Rosemund Tuve has said, "there are few difficult images in Yeats in which the syntax does not repay study; syntax is the most unobtrusive of all methods of clarification, the closest one can come to the paradox of saying something tacitly".[7] It *is* difficult, as Donald Davie points out in *Articulate Energy*, "not to agree with Yeats that the abandonment of syntax testifies to the failure of the poet's nerve, a loss of confidence in the intelligible structure of the conscious mind, and the validity of its activity".[8]

This, of course, did not worry Pound. We might recall, for instance, his denigration of those translators of Homer who were "deaved with syntax"[9] (*Literary Essays of Ezra Pound*, p. 273). It was of some concern, however, to Yeats. In his introduction to the *Oxford Book of Modern Verse* (and we might note, in passing, his selections from Pound and Eliot) he writes of Pound that

> plot, characterization, logical discourse, seem to him abstractions unsuitable to a man of his generation, (pp. xxiii–xxiv)

that, indeed, his style is

> constantly interrupted, broken, twisted into nothing by its direct opposite, nervous obsession, nightmare, stammering confusion; he is an economist, poet, politician, raging at malignants with inexplicable characters and motives, grotesque figures out of a child's book of beasts. This loss of self-control . . . is rare . . . among men of Ezra Pound's culture and erudition.

Style and its opposite can alternate, but form must be full, sphere-like, single. Even where there is no interruption he is often content, if certain verses and lines have style, to leave unbridged transitions, unexplained ejaculations, that make his meaning unintelligible . . . (p. xxv)

This clear call for logical, systematic literary structures, for "self-control", may seem strange coming from Yeats. Does he not, after all, consistently rail against "logical" literature, science, realism? It would seem that Yeats's attitude to these needs some reassessment, for the railing is part of the mask. When Yeats turned from Huxley and Tyndall, insisting in a rather self-conscious "Axëlism" that he "did not care for mere reality" (Au 82–3), he was nevertheless unable to escape the influence of the scientific rationale. By his own admission he had failed to avoid the fascination of what he loathed (Au 88). If we regard Yeats as merely contemptuous of Huxley and Tyndall, and their irrepressible logic, we miss the essential emphasis of Autobiographies. Neither they, nor their literary representatives, Ibsen and Shaw, are rejected without qualification. Ibsen's influence was inescapable, and Yeats travelled with his works (Au 279). Shaw's "athletic wit" had made him "the most formidable man in modern letters", and, although repelled by Shaw's realism, Yeats "delighted" in him, and "stood aghast" before the energy of Arms and the Man (Au 281–3). Paradoxically Shaw was a sewing-machine, functional and utilitarian, yet possessed at the same time of a unique charm, powerful and irresistible. It is quite remarkable how similar are Yeats's description of Shaw and Huxley's description of a man of "liberal education":

so trained in youth that his body is the ready servant of his will, and does with ease and pleasure all the work that, as a mechanism, it is capable of; whose intellect is a clear, cold, logic engine, with all its parts of equal strength, and in smooth working order; ready, like a steam engine, to be turned to any kind of work . . . ('A Liberal Education', 1868).

Yeats admired Wilde, similarly, in spite of what Lionel Johnson regarded as his "cold scientific intellect" (Au 285) and, whilst disliking Eliot's realism, he was "forced to admit its satiric intensity" (E&I 499). Yeats could not avoid science and logic, so he demanded that literature learn from them and expect the same "right of exploration of all that passes before the mind's eye" (Au 326). Rationalism is deplored but its value is not denied, and it was the generalisations of popular science rather than the spirit of genuine scientific research that "cowed (his) boyhood" (Au 143). The expression of that spirit as precise syntax is a stepping-stone to a colder, harder and less sentimental poetic. J. I. M. Stewart considered Yeats to be "at least as shrewd as he was mystical"[10] and it would appear that what Conor Cruise O'Brien referred to as "cunning", the quality that I think is implied in Hazlitt's "understanding", can be as anti-levelling a principle as the notoriously imperious imagination. Yeats knew this well, and in his essay on "The Philosophy of Shelley's Poetry" he agrees that "the rich have become richer, the poor have become poorer, . . . such are the effects which must ever flow from an unmitigated exercise of the calculating faculty" (*E&I* 68). One wonders if Yeats ever really recovered from his deep immersion in the works of Darwin, Tyndall, Huxley, Haeckel and Wallace during his formative years.

Cairns Craig has produced a curious, provocative and demanding book. He does not demonstrate a credible connection between Yeats and Associationism, or between Yeats and Fascism, a great deal of the information is marginal to an interest in Yeats, and at the end one is left wondering if the argument might have been extended, and its implications pursued more rigorously. In spite of this much of the material is useful and suggestive, attesting to a degree of calculation that we may not normally associate with Yeats. Finally, though, the crucial question might not be so much Craig's – "how are we to read a poetry that tells us we ourselves are the destroyers of culture, part of the philistine modern world, 'Base-born products of base beds'?" (p. 5) – as that of how we are to respond to, say, the Irish Airman's "lonely impulse of delight" when we know that it is in his nature, in so un-Romantic a way to have "measured all, brought all to mind", and to have balanced so very carefully life and death.

NOTES

1. Isobel Armstrong (ed.), *Victorian Scrutinies* (London: Athlone, 1972) p. 89.
2. David Hartley, *Observations on Man* (London: 1749) I, p. 65.
3. Thomas Hobbes, *English Works*, Molesworth (ed.) (London: 1839 etc.) IV, p. 449. See also *Myth* 342 for Yeats's quotation of Landor on the same point.
4. A. James Gregor, *The Ideology of Fascism* (New York: Freeborn, London: Collier-Macmillan, 1969) p. 23.
5. S. U. Larsen (ed.), *Who were the Fascists?* (Bergen: Universitetsforlaget, 1980) pp. 52–5.
6. Paul Hayes, *Fascism* (London: Allen & Unwin, 1973) p. 119.
7. Rosemund Tuve, *Elizabethan and Metaphysical Imagery* (Chicago: Chicago University Press, 1961) p. 177.
8. Davie, op. cit., (London: Routledge & Kegan Paul, 1955) p. 129. See also Geoffrey Hill, " 'The Conscious Mind's Intelligible Structure': a Debate" in *Agenda*, 9:4 (Autumn–Winter, 1971–2).
9. Ezra Pound, *Literary Essays*, ed. with an intro. by T. S. Eliot (London: Faber, 1954, repr. 1960) p. 273.
10. J. I. M. Stewart, *Eight Modern Writers* (Oxford, Clarendon Hist. of English Literature, 12, 1963) p. 326.

Terence Diggory, *Yeats & American Poetry, the Tradition of the Self*,
(Princeton: Princeton University Press, 1983) pp. 262.

Marjorie Perloff

Until the late sixties, it was customary to think of Yeats in terms of *The Modern Tradition*, as Richard Ellmann and Charles Feidelson, Jr. called their important sourcebook of 1965. In Modern Poetry courses in the universities, Yeats functioned as a kind of origin: the poet who dismantled Victorian rhetoric and *fin-de-siècle* languor to become the great Symbolist and myth-maker of the Byzantium poems, the poet of "the natural words in the natural order", of rapt, impassioned speech. Out of Yeats, so we learned it at school, came Auden, the early Pound (before he succumbed to the *Canto* structure of "exquisite or grotesque fragments", thus failing to get "all the wine into the bowl"),[1] and Frost. Indeed, Yeats was held to be the greatest Modernist of them all in that, as Richard Ellmann and Donald Davie argued, he was the only member of the "post-symbolist generations" who remained "stubbornly loyal in his art to the conscious mind's intelligible structure" – to "authentic syntax."[2]

This reading of twentieth-century poetry was challenged as early as 1957 by critics like Robert Langbaum and John Bayley, who saw in Yeats a "romantic survival" at least as marked as his seeming Modernist "difference".[3] But it was probably Harold Bloom's *Yeats* (1970), that made the strongest case for Yeats's "belated" romanticism – his derivation from Blake, Shelley, and Pater – and this view has largely prevailed. Indeed, in 1972 Donald Davie declared that "in British poetry of the last fifty years (as not in American) the most far-reaching influence, for good and ill, has been not Yeats, still less Eliot or Pound, not Lawrence, but *Hardy*".[4]

What then of twentieth-century American poetry? Where does it stand *vis-à-vis* Yeats? This is a complicated issue, one well worth writing a book about, and Terence Diggory has now addressed himself to the subject, discussing both those American poets, like Emerson and Whitman, who preceded Yeats, and those that came after, from Eliot and Stevens down to Roethke, Berryman, and Lowell.

Diggory's thesis can be simply stated. His starting point is Yeats's well known statement (*Au* 463), "To oppose the new ill-breeding of Ireland, . . . I can only set up a secondary or interior personality created out of the tradition of myself." Diggory writes:

The view that personality is *created* distinguishes the tradition of the self from its origin in the romantic theory of artistic self-expression. . . . For Wordsworth, the self was given or, at most, discovered; for Yeats, the self was created. In the process of being created, the self becomes distanced or externalized. It is literally *ex-pressed*, but not as in romantic expression, because Yeats's externalized self differs from the internal self where it originated. (p. 5)

These are, at best, facile generalizations. "For Wordsworth," Diggory tells us, "the self was given or, at most, discovered; for Yeats the self was created." (p. 5); or again, "Because a poet in the tradition of the self creates a self when he writes, the act of writing extends his experience as well as that of the reader, whereas the romantic poet, in expressing a self that already exists, merely records preexisting experience." (p. 6). Does he indeed "merely" do so? One would think that Nietzsche and Freud, Lacan and Foucault, or, for that matter, Yeats scholars from Ellmann and Henn down to David Lynch (*The Poetics of the Self*, 1979) and Daniel O'Hara (*Tragic Knowledge: Yeats's Autobiography and Hermeneutics*, 1981) had never written on the question. Where, one wonders, would Byron fit into Diggory's simplified scheme? Or Goethe or Heine or, closer to Yeats's own time, Wilde? Such questions are not addressed: the "duality of the self" is taken to be Yeats's invention (p. 8) and this "tradition" is now to be traced from Yeats to Robert Lowell, in whose poetry, we read, "there are signs that the tradition has come to an end".

That this thesis can only pose problems for its author is evident from the brief Introduction. For one thing, Diggory never discusses Yeats's poetics of the self, his doctrine of the mask. It is therefore extremely difficult to determine whether, indeed, Yeats's "tradition of the self", is or is not an advance over the Adamic self of Emerson and Whitman, as Diggory argues it is (Chapter II). But, more importantly, the narrow focus on self and mask makes it impossible to assess Yeats's influence on later poets, poets who might well be influenced by Yeats's rhetoric or his imagery, his renewal of genre or his treatment of history – areas that inevitably fall outside Diggory's perimeters.

The focus of *Yeats & American Poetry* is, then, both too broad and too narrow. Too broad because we don't know what Diggory really means by the word *Self*, too narrow because the larger spheres of influence are ignored. Fortunately, Diggory's practice does not always follow his thesis. On the last page of the Introduction, he remarks (with a theoretical naiveté quite in keeping with his discussion of selfhood) that "The opinion of Yeats and other poets, as expressed in their prose and implied in their poetry, will be attended to closely, because in a historical study it is just as important to know what poets thought they were doing as it is to analyze what they were actually writing" (p. 10). What this means, in practice, is that Diggory takes one American poet at a time and diligently records his response to Yeats, as that response occurs in letters, essays, and so on. Occasionally, he set two poetic passages side by side, noting thematic or stylistic parallels that have, in fact, little to do with the whole question of Self and Anti-Self. The method is reminiscent of René Taupin's *L'Influence du symbolisme français sur la poésie américaine* of 1929. But where Taupin observed a scrupulous neutrality, Diggory regularly measures later poets against the Yeatsian model and finds them wanting.

Consider his chapter on Pound. The first two-thirds of this chapter reviews material familiar to readers of Hugh Witemeyer's *Ezra Pound: Forms and Renewal*, Thomas Jackson's *The Early Poetry of Ezra Pound*, and Thomas Parkinson's numerous studies of the Yeats-Pound relationship. But although Diggory understands that "the process of dissociation from Yeats began as early as 1913" (p. 49), he seems to regard Pound's apostasy as motivated by his fear that the strength of the older and stronger poet would stifle his own accomplishment. That Pound had a central poetic of his own, and that this poetic (for many of us at least as influential as Yeats's) is *not* equivalent to the "tradition of the self" does not seem to occur to Diggory; on the contrary, he praises the *Pisan Cantos* for their "new understanding of subjective vision" (p. 55): "The self. . . is objectified, it is a *persona*, and yet it remains, as a self, subjective" (p. 56). In order to come up with this reading, which happily lines up Pound with Yeats, Diggory has to ignore almost everything in the cantos in question – the use of "found objects" (documents, letters, snatches of conversation), the narrative portions, the network of allusions – all the features that make the speaking subject of the *Cantos* what Michael A. Bernstein has called in *The Tale of the Tribe* (Princeton, 1980), a "marginalized presence". And indeed, Diggory's distaste for the real momentum of the *Cantos* becomes increasingly obvious in the course of the chapter: he concludes that "In Pound's case the subjective vision gave way, though he retained a sense of the value of what he had lost" (p. 58).

A similar stacking of the deck occurs in the later chapters. Frost wanted to follow the Yeatsian model but "Yeats's scepticism was affirmative, Frost's negative. . . . Yeats uses silence to protect belief, whereas Frost uses it to disguise unbelief . . . Yeats's silence is less restricting than Frost's" (p. 72). Williams (whose earlier experimental poetry Diggory passes over) comes to the Yeatsian model late in life, specifically in *Paterson*, "the *persona* having gained in particularity as his circumstances registered a similar gain" (p. 85). Indeed, the main interest Williams has in this study is that he forms a kind of bridge from Yeats to Lowell (p. 86). Williams's own seminal poetic, a poetic that has, of course, influenced the course of later American poetry much more decisively than has Yeats's, is evidently not considered relevant.

If poets like Frost and Williams are not Yeatsian enough, others, like Roethke, are too imitative. Roethke, so Diggory posits, "calls on Yeats because he does not feel strong enough to rely on himself, and he rejects Yeats because he fears that the stronger presence might obliterate his identity altogether" (p. 182). What happens in the latter case (in Roethke's best poems, collected in *The Lost Son* and *Praise to the End*) is passed over quickly; rather, Diggory focuses on the early poetry and the late *The Far Field*, in both of which, as Jenijoy LaBelle and other critics have noted.[5] Yeats is a largely unassimilated presence: "Roethke's attempt to become Yeats in his poetry was his attempt to usurp the role of a natural father who was too awesome, but his choice of a poetic father presented an obstacle equally insurmountable" (p. 196).

This strikes me as a very curious way of tracing influence. Roethke's poetry is memorable, so Diggory admits, when he is least Yeatsian; why, then, not trace the tradition that *is* found in his important work (the vegetal animism, say, of Smart and Cowper, and its later version in Whitman), rather than the one that is a sideline? A similar process occurs in Diggory's discussion of Lowell, who, we are told, "chose to follow neither the example of his father nor of Yeats. On the one hand, he disdained his father's ineffectuality; on the other, he distrusted the potency of any literary influence" (p. 212).

How any poet's work can altogether escape the anxiety of influence remains a mystery, the irony being that Lowell's is an especially conventionalized poetry. redolent with echoes from Melville and Baudelaire and Eliot. Be that as it may, Diggory tells us that Lowell replaces what was once "tradition" with a "self" that is purely personal. Accordingly, although Lowell carries on, to some extent, Yeats's dynastic theme, he finally fails to incorporate the "dualistic self, both object and subject, real and imagined, man and mask, private and public, son and father" (p. 224). Indeed:

> Lowell *felt* that duality, but, unlike Yeats, he had no system that would allow him to accept it intellectually, so his public world reduces to a private world, and fathers can be no more than sons. The duality that Yeats understood in terms of Blake's positive contraries, Lowell could only record, in his "Epilogue," as "misalliance," echoing Pound's despairing confession in the *Cantos*: "I cannot make it cohere" . . . (p. 224).

The "tradition of myself" is thus played out, Yeats's poetry providing the yardstick against which the American poets of the twentieth century are measured and found wanting. The fallacy in such a one-dimensional view of influence, Yeats's or anyone else's, is that it assumes that there is only *one tradition* coming down to contemporary American poetry, that indeed the identity of poet x or y is to be established by his preservation (or lack thereof) of the Yeats model. Again, Diggory treats poetry as if it were written in a social and political vacuum, as if, somehow, the later poets might have "kept up" the Yeatsian standard, had they been more talented and less misguided.

The notable exception seems to be the poetry of the Southern Agrarians – Tate, Ransom, and Warren – and Diggory's best chapter deals with these poets. For here at least the parallels are real parallels – Yeats's "Second Coming" and Tate's "The Eagle," Yeats's "In Memory of Major Robert Gregory" and Tate's "Winter Mask," Yeats's "The Man and the Echo" and Ransom's "Birthday of an Aging Sear," Yeats's "Dialogue of Self and Soul" and Warren's "The Mango on the Mango Tree," which ends with the stanzas:

> And I could leap and laugh and sing
> And it could leap, and everything
> Take hands with us and pace the music in a ring,

And sway like the multitudinous wheat
In a blessedness so long in forfeit –
Blest in that blasphemy of love we cannot now repeat.
(p. 155).

Such parallels are not coincidental: the Agrarians of the forties, as Diggory shows, were in accord with Yeats's political conservatism, his hunger for truth matched by an inability to adhere to religious orthodoxy, his faith in Unity of Being. Not surprisingly, it is in the essays of these New Critics (and such related figures as Horace Gregory and Archibald MacLeish), that Yeats's poetry became a touchstone.

Diggory draws no larger conclusions from the linkage he establishes in Chapter VI, but perhaps we can draw them for him. Surveying the American scene from Frost to Lowell (and of course many other contemporary poets should be included – for example, Ginsberg, O'Hara, Ashbery, Plath, Bishop, Zukofsky, Oppen, Merrill), in search of Yeatsian echoes, we find not one tradition of the self, as Diggory suggests, but a curious splintering. Academic poets, of whom Ransom might be the epitome, followed the Yeatsian model. The others – poets as different from one another as Eliot and Williams, Stevens and Pound, Roethke and Lowell – on the whole, did not. Indeed, if Diggory's study convinces me of anything, it is that the major American poets, having paid respectful homage to Yeats in one form or another, have finally turned elsewhere. The reasons for this distance are complex and interesting. But it would take a book less theoretically and historically naive than this one to explore them.

NOTES

1. See Yeats, *The Oxford Book of Modern Verse 1892–1935* (Oxford, 1936) pp. xxiv–xxvi.
2. See *Articulate Energy: an Inquiry into the Syntax of English Poetry* (1955; London: Routledge & Kegan Paul, 1976) p. 151.
3. Bayley, *The Romantic Survival* (London: Constable, 1957); Langbaum, *The Poetry of Experience* (New York: W. W. Norton & Co., 1957).
4. *Thomas Hardy and Modern British Poetry* (New York: Oxford University Press, 1973) p. 5.
5. See Jenijoy LaBelle, *The Echoing Wood of Theodore Roethke* (Princeton: Princeton University Press, 1976) pp. 109–17.

R. A. Gilbert, *The Golden Dawn: Twilight of the Magicians* (Welling-borough: The Aquarian Press, 1983) pp. 144.

Ellic Howe

According to its sub-title *The Golden Dawn: Twilight of the Magicians* is "a concise history, drawing on new material from privately printed and manuscript sources". At the present time (October 1983) it is the only available (and reliable) account of what its author describes as "the cornerstone of all modern occultism". Perhaps Mr Gilbert claims too much, because there is no evidence that the GD had any noticeable influence on French, German or other European occultists during the era of its heyday, i.e. during the 1890s. Indeed, it never served as a model for any continental occult Order and while it gained a modest foothold in the USA little is known about its existence there. Indeed, were it not for W. B. Yeats's membership I doubt whether any outside the occultist milieu would be interested in the annals of a mildly extraordinary *fin de siècle* phenomenon. The GD evidently played a role in Yeats's early life or he would not have been so active in trying to revive its corpse when it was close to complete collapse after a ludicrous imbroglio in 1900.

Dr Francis Israel Regardie, of Sedona, Arizona, has contributed a Foreword to Mr Gilbert's book. Once close to the ineffable Aleister Crowley, Dr Regardie was a member of a latterday Stella Matutina Temple – the latter was an offshoot of the original Golden Dawn – and in 1937–40 published *The Golden Dawn: An Account of the Teachings, Rites and Ceremonies of the Golden Dawn* (Chicago, Aries Press, 4 vols, revised edition Llewellyn Publications, St Paul, Minnesota, USA, 1971). Dr Regardie's *The Complete Golden Dawn System of Magick*, apparently a recension of his earlier book, has been announced for publication in the USA and I assume that in Great Britain copies will be available from the Atlantis Bookshop, 49 Museum Street, London WC1. One or other edition must be regarded a prescribed reading for those who are interested in Yeats's preoccupation with occultism and ritual magic, while Mr Gilbert's book will tell them sufficient about the Order's rise and collapse, also about its teachings.

In his Foreword Dr Regardie wrote: "Mr Gilbert's book is written more in sympathy and sorrow for the Order's follies than with cynicism or contempt" and continued "the Story of the Golden Dawn is one of vanity, gullibility and deception; and yet there adheres in it an impressive nobility, a breadth of concept and magnanimity of both stature and structure that will persist and which is still worthy of our attention". The reference to "cynicism and contempt" is probably a reference to my ill-concealed laughter when, on the basis of a large and unknown collection of original documents, I was writing *The Magicians of the Golden Dawn: a Documentary History of a Magical Order, 1888–1923* (London, Routledge & Kegan Paul and New York City, Samuel Weiser, 1972, with a reprint announced by Aquarian Press for 1984–5). Considering that the Golden Dawn was founded on a basis of fraud and forgery, and yet taken so seriously by Yeats and Dr Regardie was I expected to weep sorrowful tears? Mr Gilbert (not an occultist as far as I know) was either more tolerant or more tactful and escaped Dr Regardie's opprobrium.

The story of Yeats's connection with the Golden Dawn and occultism has kept academics innocently occupied ever since Joseph Hone published his official biography in 1942. Here I need only mention Richard Ellmann's *Yeats: The Man and the Masks*, 1949; A. Norman Jeffares, *W. B. Yeats, Man and Poet*, 1949; Virginia Moore, *The Unicorn: William Butler Yeats' Search for Reality*, 1954, and H. R. Bachnan, *W. B. Yeats and Occultism*, Delhi (of all places), 1965. Finally there is George M. Harper's *Yeats's Golden Dawn*, 1974, in which the "Great Row" of 1900 was dissected with scholarly *Akribie* and a ludicrous farce was presented as something far more important than was actually the case. Personally I prefer to think of the Golden Dawn as a relatively minor episode in Yeats's life even if a handful of industrious academics have extracted the maximum mileage (and paper and print) from it. Indeed, I shudder to think of what the results will be when an industrious Herr Professor inflicts the results of his investigation of the automatic scripts (collected by Yeats in the course of seances with a spiritualist medium or mediums) upon a prospectively bored public.

Mr Gilbert, who is not a Professor (with or without tenure) has contrived to write a mercifully short book about the Golden Dawn, without perpetrating any of the usual legends and without offending Dr Regardie. Thus I gladly commend it to the attention of readers of *Yeats Annual* who are unlikely ever to manufacture or consecrate their Magical Instruments.

[R. A. Gilbert's *A. E. Waite: a Bibliography*, (with a foreword by Geoffrey Watkins) has recently been published by The Aquarian Press, Wellingborough, and is an invaluable research work. The same press and author have recently produced the first two volumes in a new series, "Roots of the Golden Dawn". Mr Gilbert has edited *The Magical Mason: Forgotten Hermetic Writings of William Wynn Westcott, Physician and Magus*, with a brief introduction, and sections devoted to Westcott's Rosicrucian, Kabalistic, Masonic, Miscellaneous and Divinatory works. Published simultaneously is Gilbert's edition of *The Sorcerer and his Apprentice: Unknown Hermetic Writings of S. L. MacGregor Mathers and J. W. Brodie-Innes*. A feature of both these collections is the large number of hitherto unpublished papers and lectures read to meetings of the *GD*, or used as instructional papers for its adepts. In so far as it is possible to do so, Mr Gilbert gives the dates of these papers and the names of order members who transcribed them, (e.g. from Florence Farr's MS copy of *The Book of the Concourse of the Forces*, transcribed 12 October 1893). Other papers are reprinted from fugitive publications. Further titles in this series which will be noticed in *Yeats Annual* upon publication, include Ellic Howe's *The Alchemical Secrets of the Golden Dawn: the Letters of W. A. Ayton to F. L. Gardner 1889–1904* and John Hamill's *The Rosicrucian Seer: the Magical Work of Frederick Hockley*.

–Ed.]

Eric Warner and Graham Hough (eds), *Strangeness and Beauty: an Anthology of Aesthetic Criticism 1840–1910*, 2 vols (Cambridge: Cambridge University Press 1983), vol. 1, *Ruskin to Swinburne*, pp. xii + 285; vol. 2, *Pater to Symons*, pp. xii + 303.

Patrick Parrinder

In 1942 Graham Hough found himself a prisoner of the Japanese. With him during the next three years of enforced meditation was a copy of Yeats's poems. The results were to be seen in *The Last Romantics* (1949):

> Continuing to ruminate on these matters, in pleasanter circumstances later on, I became interested in the genesis of Yeats's ideas from those of the small poetic circle with whom he associated in the nineties. They in turn seemed to owe almost everything to Pater and the pre-Raphaelites, and from them I was inevitably led back to Ruskin. . . . The new ideas about the arts and their relations to religion and the social order all seemed to originate somewhere in the dense jungle of Ruskin's works.

The Last Romantics was a masterful guide through the jungle of Ruskin and his successors. In subsequent books and essays Hough continued to inveigh against the "mistaken belief" – as the introduction to *Strangeness and Beauty* has it – "that the lessons of modernism were largely self-taught". Now Hough and Eric Warner have set out once again to trace the critical path from Romantic to modernist poetry.

When Arthur Symons wished to record his admiration for Pater, he called *The Renaissance* "the most beautiful book of prose in our literature". For Wilde (quoting Swinburne on *Mademoiselle de Maupin*) it was "the holy writ of beauty". For us, perhaps, it is something different. The continuities which interest Warner and Hough are continuities of ideas rather than of beautiful prose. They aim to demonstrate the genesis of modernism in a particular nineteenth-century "critical tradition".

A tradition is defined by continuities and exclusions. Warner and Hough tell us that Pater "must be considered in most important respects as Ruskin's disciple, and the continuator of his aesthetic gospel". It was Pater, to all intents, who coined the term "aesthetic criticism", and his preface to *The Renaissance* is its principal manifesto. Yet Warner and Hough sidestep the inconvenient fact that

Pater professed himself not Ruskin's but Arnold's disciple. Matthew Arnold is not represented in *Strangeness and Beauty* (though of course it may be argued that he has been over-represented elsewhere). The first volume of this anthology seems better balanced than the second, where a broad sampling from the nineties is foregone in favour of a triumvirate of Wilde, Yeats, and Symons. Symons, "one of the ghosts of literary history", gets sixty pages of attempted redress. Much is made of the rooms he shared with Yeats in Fountain Court. Oddly enough, the pioneering criticism of another of Symons's roommates – Havelock Ellis – goes unmentioned in this anthology. On a broader view, with 1910 as terminal date one wonders what disqualifies such diverse figures as Bernard Shaw, A. C. Bradley and the Roger Fry of "An Essay on Aesthetics".

Is it that in these critics the "aesthetic" component is adulterated with ideas from other, perhaps incompatible sources? Yet there is no single stream of aesthetic ideas, and hardly anything said by one critic in this anthology is not contradicted by someone else. The "didactic heresy", the sacredness of art, the relations of art to nature and of art to society are all subjects of sometimes languid, sometimes passionate dispute. The most public and passionate of these arguments – the Whistler/Ruskin trial – could perhaps be seen in retrospect as a family quarrel, and it could be said that the concept of family resemblances is broad and vague enough to cover the contents of the anthology (though not to justify all its exclusions). Perhaps the one thing the "aesthetic critics" have in common is their belief that the visual arts (and, increasingly, music) draws on a similar fundamental inspiration and offer a comparable experience to that of literature.

Symons, one of whose volumes was entitled *Studies in Seven Arts*, was self-consciously in this tradition. Moreover, *The Symbolist Movement in Literature* served as a crib for Eliot and Pound. To Hough and Warner he is thus "the man who helped bring the modern aesthetic into being". Yet Symons was an opportunist whose hour came and went and it is easy to see why the next generation contrived to forget him. His "Symbolist Movement" had been – before the hue and cry of 1895 – a "Decadent Movement". He moved on to Wagner, drawing "The Lesson of *Parsifal*" (1898) before he had read any of Wagner's theoretical writings; later he not only read, but paraphrased them at great length. His *Blake* (1907) was seen in the light of Nietzsche, yet another man of the hour. The rhetoric of modernity is a recurrent, and predictable, feature of his essays. Laforgue's art has "all the restlessness of modern life", Mallarmé shows the "lines . . . [on which] literature must now move", and so on. Symons's importance as a critic vanishes once you reject the Whig interpretation of history.

Which – it should not be forgotten – is what the great modernists did. Yeats, who figures prominently in *Strangeness and Beauty*, is on one occasion terribly misquoted:

Did that song of mine send out
Certain men the English shot?

(Which prompts the editors' bluff verdict, "Very unlikely".) The idea of tradition implicitly endorsed by Warner and Hough – tradition as evolution, a process of modernisation – is that of Symons, by and large, rather than Yeats. "The Symbolism of Poetry", it is true, looks forward to "the new sacred book . . . of which all the arts . . . are beginning to dream". A few sentences later, however, Yeats wrote "What change should one look for in the manner of our poetry? A return to the way of our fathers, . . .". This is not tradition as modernisation but tradition as the repository of ancient and permanent truths.

The abridged texts and mercilessly informative editorial matter of *Strangeness and Beauty* are evidence that it is mainly intended as a pedagogic tool. As such, it is both useful and welcome. If it is to succeed in its aims, however, it must find readers for whom the editorial apparatus is "but as the lyres and flutes" – readers who will respond to the extracts for their beauty, to the tradition for its truths.

Douglas Archibald, *Yeats* (Syracuse, N.Y.; Syracuse University Press, 1983) pp. 254.

Richard Taylor

The basic premise which animates this thoughtful and perceptive series of essays or meditations is made explicit in the final paragraph. "No matter to what school of critical theory we subscribe, or fashion we endorse, we generally agree that 'the text' – poems and stories, plays and essays – has a life of its own. Most of us believe that behind the text is a buried life that we can discover, intuit, approximate." Be that as it may, it does not necessarily follow that the recreation of that lived life, however well it might be done, constitutes either the most illuminating or exciting critical approach to Yeats's poetry in the 1980s. But rather than an argument for the road not taken, attention to Professor Archibald's actual achievement is more to the point.

The recovery of a lived life behind the text is largely predicated on the poet's involvement with family and friends, nation and cultural heritage, religion and philosophy. Joycean comparisons and contrasts leap to mind, and although they suggest a wider and more complete context of actual Irish realities during that period, Archibald's conclusions still hold good. The central ground of Yeats's experience was intimately bound up with his identity as an Anglo-Irishman and with his avowed aspiration to an established and hereditary ruling class. The word, "aristocracy", which is used frequently throughout the work is perhaps better taken figuratively than literally; at most, upper-class landed gentry is in question. The essential relationship between Yeats's ideal of nation or politics and his need to mythologise his own life and loves as well as those of his friends and even members of his (mother's) family is, however, definitively handled. The idea is not exactly new but it is very subtly and persuasively argued. What we do not get, however, is an equal emphasis on those wilful distortions and conscious reworkings of Celtic mythology according to either ascendancy or artistic values which even further underline Yeats's estrangement from a truly national unity of culture.

Archibald is perhaps at his most engaged and engaging in chapter 5, "Politics and Political Life", where he judges *On the Boiler* to be silly, repetitious, and dull; and lines from "Under Ben Bulben" to be a parody of late Yeats, self-indulgent ranting and old fashioned snobbery. Best of all is the final section of that chapter in which he confronts Yeats's Fascism directly and refuses to dodge any of its implications.

It is dangerous . . . to see politics from the point of view of art, to claim, as Yeats often does, that the primary function of politics is to foster conditions of artistic achievement and appreciation. It is even more dangerous to impose aesthetics on politics, and some of the central assumptions of modernism, when translated into political terms, do have an authoritarian thrust: the superiority of art and artist to ordinary life; the autonomy of art and the overriding power of individual vision; the primacy and imperialism of the imagination; the idealization of a mythic past; the driving thirst for commitment in the absence of fully realized belief.

At this point the thesis being pursued becomes a seamless garment and the authoritarian imperative of the age also serves to explain Yeats's deep-seated involvement with the Occult and the system of thought which found its ultimate expression in *A Vision*. The exposition of that very complicated construct is certainly one of the most lucid I have yet come across, but it does not seem to have prompted much practical application. Besides the four obvious examples which are discussed here, there are a number of other important poems which gain a good deal by being read in the light of Yeats's system.

In addition, Archibald finds it remarkable and instructive that only after working out his ideas on history, personality, and metaphysical order was the poet able to celebrate whole-heartedly and affirm the human condition. Yeats's statement of 1938 while working on a play – "that I might write lyrics out of dramatic experience, all my personal experience having in some strange way come to an end" – is twice commented upon with evident astonishment and incomprehension. Archibald sees the situation as a crisis for so autobiographical a poet and in all three cases forgets that the whole point of Yeats's occult studies was in creating,

> Those images that yet
> Fresh images beget.

The rituals of art served to slake his driving thirst for commitment in the absence of a fully realised belief.

By the same token, the last two chapters offer elegant and sometimes illuminating readings of major works from *The Tower* to *Last Poems*, but the discussion neither extends nor elaborates upon the author's thesis all that much. In fact, the volume ends as it began, with a slightly uneasy sense of disjunction. Throughout, the critical approach is biographical, but where the central chapters advance a coherent and considered analysis, the opening and closing chapter-pairs present other and largely miscellaneous aspects of the subject.

I am not at all convinced by the assertion of chapter 2, for example, that the relationship between the poet and his father was quite so simple and straightforward. The evidence for direct and uncritical assimilation of J. B. Yeats's ideas on history and personality or art and religion is rather inconclusive and there are any number of contradictions in the poet's work. Archibald himself raises the question of *Purgatory* at great length in a later chapter, emphasising the obsessive violence of the play and the sexual guilt that impels the protagonist.

> The Old Man hates his father, hates him many years after killing him, for his vulgarity, selfishness, and opportunism; but mostly hates him for his virility, for the desire he excited in his wife. . . . He loves and loathes his mother for her sexuality and her pliability. He hates his son for being the consequence of his own and his parent's sexuality, for his recent virility, and for his recognition that "now I am young and you are old."

Biographical criticism could well make something of all that with reference to the material in chapter 2 before turning to a reading of the play as an historical parable, the decline of the Anglo-Irish gentry. After all, the only other plays to be discussed in such detail are *The Countess Cathleen* and *The Death of Cuchulain* in both of which Archibald sees a strong autobiographical element in the projection of female characters and their relationship to either poet or warrior-hero. *The Only Jealousy of Emer* would have been equally relevant in that Eithne Inguba, Emer, and Fand can also be seen as various women in the poet's life, but there is an earlier play which offers a very interesting variant on the father-son relationship. The Old Man of *Purgatory* (1938) murders his son in order to keep pollution from being passed on while the Cuchulain of *Baile's Strand* (1903) kills his son in heroic combat unaware of his identity even though the hero of the original epic cycle knows full well who his challenger is. There is a good deal more to be said on the subject of youth versus age and father versus son than we find in the present study.

On the other hand, the opening chapter which defines Yeats's romanticism by comparison with Coleridge is very complete and even self-contained. Perhaps it, like the chapter on JBY and the readings of the major poems in the last two sections, was conceived separately and only now collected together. A glance at the bibliography shows that the greater share of the background reading was done some time ago and it is not always easy to rationalise the omission of more recent titles.

The book itself is well produced but one must point out that the dust jacket sports the world's worst portrait of WBY. There are remarkably few typographical errors for which may we be truly thankful, but those that remain tend to transform one word into another, doing much violence to the syntax. The student at whom the work is presumably aimed, will have some trouble with uncited or unexplained references to Dante's *Convito* [sic], Bran Boru [sic], and especially Therisites [sic] who drops unannounced from a clear blue sky into the discussion of *Purgatory*. I also find the system of endnotes unnecessarily nightmarish in that the onus of discovering what has been noted and what hasn't, falls unfairly to the reader. Most will just give up the unequal struggle. Whatever has been saved on production costs cannot outweigh the frustration thus engendered.

Editorial Miscellany

Shirley Neuman's *Some One Myth: Yeats's Autobiographical Prose* (Mountrath: Dolmen; Atlantic Highlands: Humanities, 1982) is the nineteenth "New Yeats Paper", and, with the exception of Liam Miller's own *The Noble Drama of W. B. Yeats*, the longest, at 160 pages. It is too long, and it is not easy to follow its argument through the maze of quotations and spongy paraphrase of Yeats. This latter habit is at its most annoying in the early pages, devoted to the early prose and *A Vision*, where more important aspects crowd out the autobiographical content. The core of Professor Neuman's case is that

> When the writer simultaneously creates literature and is created by that literature, his autobiography becomes a reversible garment: it remains the expected portrait of the artist and, therefore, of the genesis of his works, but turned, it reveals the author shaping himself through his works and in their image.

Metaphor lets Professor Neuman down here, but it is clear that at moments of stress in the work she is able to have things two ways. Though this is indeed the case in the account of *Dramatis Personae*, she is also at her best in that section of the book, which charts Yeats's response to Moore. For Professor Neuman, "In Yeats's view, Moore's real failure lay in his unrealizable desire to be Yeats", and she registers well Yeats's changing reaction to Moore following the publication of *Ave* – "a stranger's impression" he called it.

Aedh O'Connor was a lad who hid in the necessary house of the Abbey Theatre during the Playboy riots: now translated to a Chair at Johns Hopkins he can assure us, *in propria persona*, that no member of the audience at Synge's play, on the Tuesday night heard "more than half a dozen consecutive sentences".

Yeats declared that Aedh was a symbol of "the myrrh and frankincense that the imagination offers continually before all that it loves", but the homage that Hugh Kenner brings to the Irish Writers is dubious. A "cold eye" was good enough for Yeats, but it won't do for Professor Kenner. *A Colder Eye* (New York: Knopf; London: Allen Lane, 1983) seeks to disguise its apparent motivation, envy of creativity, with jocose familiarity.

Tuesday night now, the boyos in place again in the pit, someone had even
brought along a bugle, and for the honor of God and was that Holy Willie? All
black like an old jackdaw it was himself, with the eyeglasses on the ribbon and
the necktie on him like a poodle-dog's ruffle. Ireland's poet, back at last from
Scotland. Get on, he was no kind of poet at all. A notable gluggerabunthaun.
The very word. Whisht, here he is now.

One does not need to summon Sigmund Freud to explain what is concealed
under this Stage Irishry: Hugh Kenner's hostility to his subject seems deep. His
vade mecum to the Irish Literary Renaissance presumes that his audience will be
familiar with Irish Culture only in a vague, sentimental way and with Irish
Literature, hardly at all. The voice of the tour guide is unstoppable and
interposes a "personality" between reader and subject. The book is ingratiat-
ingly dedicated to "L. P. B., Citizen, Husband, Father, Wanderer and" (for the
obtuse) "Reincarnation of Ulysses".

"You have to hear his kind of talk", says Kenner, of a Dublin informant: this
book, under the authority of an epigraph, tries to pretend to be informal, oral
discourse and thus to imply that formal, written discourse is untrustworthy. Yet
the book has a familiarity and false directness, which is itself untrustworthy: one
expression of "orality" is the persistent use of idiomatic contractions; "you'd",
"they'd", "he'd", "we'll". The untrustworthiness is also displayed in the realm
of fact: Arthur Symons would not recognise himself in the "fey Welshman"
Kenner makes him out to be, *The Savoy* was not published in 1897 and Olivia
Shakespear had not "moved in with Yeats a while in 1895".

On first name terms with most of his writers, Kenner at least gets no fresher
with Lady Gregory than calling her "Augusta Gregory", in imitation of Yeats's
two poems which approach such familiarity with better credentials. He gets the
better of her, however, in his account of her family's decline, where he gloatingly
deploys hindsight. So intimate is Kenner with his writers that he feels free to
borrow other men's words without acknowledgement:

He was Cuchulain, fighting the waves: cold in his frenzy, defying the
ungovernable sea. . . . His beautiful mischievous head was thrown back.

More worrying are the phrases saturated with unacknowledged quotation: "In
Stephen's version lyric is no complex flower but early man's primitive cry".
Joyce is the source for the latter part of the sentence, but the first part is a
misremembered and unacknowledged adaptation of Yeats's statement that the
lyric poet's work "is no rootless flower but the speech of a man".

What is the reader to make of this? Does he congratulate Kenner for so many
fine phrases? Does he congratulate himself on his ability to identify quotation
and allusion? It is clear that, if Kenner *is* addressing the readership that his
discourse seems to assume, the former might be the case: yet it does also seem
that part of Kenner's motive is to share a joke with some of his admirers.

Buried in this chatter are flashes of Kenner's former acuity, as when he considers a textual change in the *Collected Poems*, 1933. Here Yeats has changed line 6 of "Who Goes With Fergus?" so that "fears" becomes "fear". The latter version, with its inevitable echo of "Fear no more the heat o' the sun" introduces a new possible reading, which Kenner rightly calls "disorienting". However, we are not compelled to follow that arm of the ambiguity: we can discount it, as any Oona chanting it would surely decide to do. That singular "fear", so much larger than any number of "fears", is quite congruent with what is clearly a consoling song, which seeks to prevent the Countess from dropping "down again into [her] trouble".

Other apparent insights are pure sleight of hand, the more alluring for exhibiting academic ingenuity in a shoddy context. Professor Kenner describes a German invention, a "painted toy", which demonstrated to children the way in which the colours of the spectrum combine into white light. By bending the argument slightly, one apparently arrives at the "grey truth" of "The Song of the Happy Shepherd".

This argument is sheer speculation and no documentation of any such toy's being available prior to 1885 is given. It also ignores the force of the "*now* her painted toy". The source is much less likely to be in a literal toy, than in the fabric of Yeats's own images. In 1899, he replied to critics of his Celtic studies who thought that he was "merely trying to wave a forlorn piece of gilt thread into the *dull grey worsted* of this century" (*UP1* 175). The imagery of course returns in "A Coat". Paradoxically Kenner's ingenuity at times fails him: he sneers at Yeats's "atrocious" spelling – "distains" in the first printing of "Byzantium" – forgetting the separate meaning of this word, to dim, to outshine, as well as its echo of Shelley's "stains the white radiance of Eternity", which Yeats possibly attempted to obliterate with the subsequent "disdains". Equally, the apparent sharpness of a comparison between Yeats and Tennyson in the service of a distinction between "English evasiveness" and Irish precision in the use of "dictionary words", such as "turbulence", is blunted by Kenner's choosing to ignore the Tennyson of "immemorial elms" from whom Yeats learned something of the use of the "arresting abstraction" or latinate word. An apparent "English conviction" that "strong Saxon words" are the "bone and muscle of discourse" is eccentrically illustrated with reference to Doughty, Barnes, Hopkins and *Hemingway*: where are Coleridge, Tennyson and Hardy?

What is it that Professor Kenner seeks? Perhaps the mantle of the George Moore of *Ave Atque Vale*. Envious, untrustworthy and intimate, Moore was, however, *one of the actors* in the history which he presents: this is its defence and part of its value. Kenner merely interposes his "Chautauqua" between the Irish Writers and an audience upon whose imperfect knowledge he relies.

It is a pleasure to turn to a serious book, Richard Ellmann's *James Joyce* (New York; Oxford, Toronto: Oxford University Press, 1982) and one singularly free from the vices of Kenner's work. Mr Ellmann does not suffer from a desire to rival his subject, and his main concern in this revised edition has been to add new material. So far as Joyce's relations with Yeats are concerned, much remains unchanged from the 1959 edition, including, unfortunately, a confusion between

"The Tables of the Law" (which does not contain an "orgiastic dance") and "Rosa Alchemica" (which does.) New depth of detail is added to the account of Joyce's first meeting with Yeats, and this is generally the pattern whenever Ellmann has come across material which casts new light on their association. In the 1959 edition Ellmann noted that Joyce had read the account of himself in *AV(A)*. Now, Ellmann feels Joyce "Probably did not see" that attack upon himself. The point, of course, qualifies our reading of the parody of *AV* in *Finnegan's Wake*, which was surely done with no desire for revenge.

Wisely, too in places does the original account resist recent error. Ellmann has always followed Stanislaus Joyce in averring that James Joyce was "the young man" of the note in the 1904 edition of *The Tables of the Law and The Adoration of the Magi*, who "liked them very much and nothing else that I have written". The *canard* raised by Robert O'Driscoll in *Yeats Studies: an International Journal No. 1* (Bealtaine 1971) (p. 99) that the young man was P. S. O'Hegarty is ignored. A letter from Arthur Symons, of 9 October 1906, now in Princeton, to Elkin Mathews, recommending Joyce for the Vigo Cabinet Series (in which Yeats's volume had appeared), supports Ellmann's view that Joyce is the "young man" of that volume's dedication.

One episode which might have been amplified is the account of Joyce at the first night of *The Countess Cathleen* in 1899, given that Joyce later *chanted* "Who Goes with Fergus" to his dying brother George, and to his dying mother. The Dublin *Daily Express* account (9 May 1899) of the first night stresses the extraordinary impression made by both Florence Farr and Anna Mather as they chanted "Impetuous Heart, be still, be still" and "Who Goes with Fergus" respectively. Farr's manner

> which approaches very nearly to singing, is perfectly natural, however, and for that reason much more convincing than singing. . . . The best example of her admirable talent was shown, perhaps, in her delivery of the beautiful lyric: –
>
> Impetuous heart, be still, be still,
>
> where the effect of music was produced, without its unreality, by the manner in which Miss Farr brought out the beauty of the rhythm and the vowels sounds. Indeed, the deception was so complete, as to leave on the mind of the audience a firm impression that the lyric had been really sung. . . . The effect [of Miss Anna Mather as Oona] . . . was that of singing, and of a beautiful kind of singing, which suited thoroughly the dreamy atmosphere of the play. A musician might easily have written down the beautiful rendering of "Who will go drive with Fergus now?" chanted, like the song of Aleel, to harp and violin music.

Augustine Martin's *W. B. Yeats* in the Gill's Irish Lives series (Dublin: Gill & Macmillan, 1983, pp. 146) sets itself modest limits and is intended as an introduction to the life. There are signs that the necessary compression has produced some distortions, as in the section upon the 'nineties, where in a paragraph we move from the Rhymers' Club to the death bed of Mabel

Beardsley. Also confusing is the treatment of Yeats's occult, philosophical, and mystical career. Professor Martin is preoccupied with developing an idea first propounded by Phillip L. Marcus in *Yeats and the Early Irish Renaissance* that *The Secret Rose* has an "apocalyptic" structure, and his treatment throughout the book of themes millenial and apocalyptic comes to seem repetitive and ûnder-defined: the volume's brevity imposes too severe a limitation on the necessary complexities of discussion.

Perhaps the facts of the life, with fewer intrusions of critical commentary upon the work, would have resulted in a more balanced book, but one sympathises with the problems of trying to write an introductory study. The book is at its best – perhaps because at its most personal – in the account of Yeats's years in the Irish Senate, and an economical last chapter explores Yeats's "close companions" through the poems, with a brisk attention to the essentials of biographical detail.

Richard J. Finneran has edited *Recent Research on Anglo-Irish Writers: A Supplement to "Anglo-Irish Literature: a Review of Research"* (New York: MLA, 1983), as well as contributing the Yeats chapter to that volume. The coverage, though monoglot, is impressive. There seems to be no discernible policy towards reviews which contain independent contributions of scholarly information. The citations are accurate, (allowing that a reference to *The Parliament of Fools* is the editor's own joke), but a certain jaundice settles over the compilers of such lists – with the honourable exception of the compilers of the Wilde survey – and there are signs that Professor Finneran is a sufferer. He chides those who write in blissful ignorance of all previous thought, and a certain sameness attends his dismissal of much (doubtlessly ephemeral) material. It is not always possible to tell whether an article which fails to acknowledge previous work has independent value and originality. Most critics abide Professor Finneran's question, but he is cautious with the bigger names. There is, too, an apparent isolationism in his approach, and a tendency to stamp firmly on comparatists who query Yeats's supremacy over other modern poets.

One of the most welcome new editions of recent years must surely be Ian Fletcher's second and revised edition of *The Collected Poems of Lionel Johnson* (New York & London: Garland, 1982). The title reflects a degree of editorial caution: the 1953 first edition, now very scarce – only 1000 copies were printed – announced itself as *The Complete Poems*. Having added eighteen new poems, and a larger selection of Johnson's *Juvenilia*, the editor is now not so sure. The larger introduction, drawing as it does upon work done in the intervening period, is now the definitive account of Johnson's life and works: at 61 pages it is invaluable, the textual notes and bibliography have been enlarged and are also indispensable.

One hopes that Mr Fletcher will be able to offer us Johnson's letters at some future stage, and one hopes too, that it will not be necessary, as Garland have found it to be with this volume, to print them in unjustified "camera-ready" typewriter face. Poor Johnson! The handsomeness of the typefaces and design of his books is legendary, and the 1953 edition preserved on its title the Wykehamist woodcut which had become his sigil. But it is better to have the poems in this form than not at all.

Fr. Brocard Sewell's *In the Dorian Mode: a Life of John Gray: 1866–1934* (Padstow: Tabb House, 1983) is a full-length study of the *fin-de-siècle* poet, and later, priest. Its few references to Yeats are not accurate, and it is a partisan perspective upon the period from the Gray-Raffalovich corner, but it provides a wealth of background material, and a touching account of Gray's rise from a working-class background to the Foreign Office. The life is Sewell's subject, and he does not make strong enough claims for Gray's short fiction, which reads illuminatingly alongside Yeats's of the same period. R. K. R. Thornton's *The Decadent Dilemma* (London: Arnold, 1983) offers an excellent discussion of the term, the period, and the individual authors of "the literature of failure". The book should not be judged by the short chapter on Yeats, which rather refuses the jump: in the context of Thornton's wise decision to concentrate upon the less well-known figures, there are plenty of fresh insights into Yeats for the discerning reader.

Several large anthologies of criticism (all described more fully in our bibliography below) reflect a new level of interest in Yeats and Anglo-Irish Literature in various countries. Heinz Kosok's *Studies in Anglo-Irish Literature* offers revised versions of 55 papers by scholars from 15 countries, first delivered at the Wuppertal symposium of 1981; there are very varied levels and lengths of treatment represented here. The French interest in Yeats, manifested in the various translations of the prose works emanating from Caen under the direction of Professor Jacqueline Genet, is represented in distinguished form in her *William Butler Yeats* collection in the series *Les Cahiers de l'Herne*. This volume is fully described in our bibliography: it is a wise choice of articles and translations of key texts, such as "A General Introduction for My Work" and the "Introduction" to *The Resurrection*, as well as translations of many poems and two plays. While I don't feel qualified to comment in detail upon the translations, which vary considerably in style, one glance at "Le Second Avènement" might alert the reader to the problems a translator faces in preserving meaning. "La brutale anarchie", "A l'oeil vide et cruel comme l'oeil du soleil" and, perhaps most worrying of all, "Que pour un berceau, vingt siècles d'un sommeil de pierre/Ont dû connaitre enfin le tourment du cauchemar," the last of which shows a reconstruction of two lines, and which does not seem to find any precise French equivalent for the "vexing" to nightmare of that "rocking cradle". Professor Genet includes a very useful bibliography of French studies of Yeats, and the volume includes a French perspective on "les autres" (including Mallarmé).

With *Irish Renaissance Annual No IV*, Zack Bowen's collections come to an end. The entire series is available from the University of Delaware and Associated University Presses. The concentration of the series was heaviest on Joyce. *Irish Culture and Nationalism 1750–1950* edd. Oliver MacDonagh, W. F. Mandle and Pauric Travers (London: Macmillan, 1983) is the result of a conference in Canberra in 1980: the late F. S. L. Lyons's piece, "Yeats and the Anglo-Irish

Twilight" is the most central, while Vincent Buckley's "Poetry and the Avoidance of Nationalism" is also valuable. An emphasis upon Irish-Australian cultural connections (including Sir Charles Gavan Duffy himself) offers the wider perspective.

Nicola Gordon Bowe's *Harry Clarke: His Graphic Arts* (Mountrath: Dolmen; Los Angeles: H. Keith Burns, 1983), is both full-length study and *catalogue raisonnée* of the graphic work of the stained glass worker Yeats declared to the Irish Senate to be "the maker of some of the best stained glass in the world today" (*SS* 65). Micheál OhAodha's *Pictures at the Abbey: The Collection of the Irish National Theatre* (Mountrath: Dolmen, 1983) contains Lennox Robinson's *Conversation Piece* and sixty-four illustrations, twenty-eight of which are in colour. Both books are useful visual guides to the period, though perhaps lovers of Clarke's glass at the Municipal Gallery will still feel that his best work was in that medium.

Set against a conventional sense of Yeats's poetic development (from the "vague, poetic shadows" of "The Wanderings of Oisin"), William H. O'Donnell's *A Guide to the Prose Fiction of W. B. Yeats* is the first in a series of Studies in Modern Literature which will appear from UMI Research Press in Ann Arbor. Further titles in the series, which aims to publish revised dissertations of distinction, will be noticed in subsequent issues. Professor O'Donnell's study revises a thesis completed some years ago, and textually updates it: however it has not been possible for him to incorporate revisions which more recent criticism might have seemed to necessitate. However the guide is modest and useful, and takes us chronologically through Yeats's prose writing career. The story by story approach, in which sources, details of composition and publication and revision are given with economy, has its obvious virtues as commentary. Less obvious, however, are the problems which such an approach brings in its train. It is never really possible, for example, for Professor O'Donnell to discuss the Hanrahan stories as a group; but then their career was quite Protean, and the sort of study I miss here might well be a long one. It is unfair to criticise Professor O'Donnell's book for not being the study of the textual changes of *The Secret Rose* we need in the wake of the *Variorum* edition of that work, but it does show the need for such a study.

Professor O'Donnell sketches in rapidly an account of the short story genre in the late 1880s and 1890s, without, it seems to me, saying enough about the experiments with romance and its various prose styles which were going on in the avant-garde periodicals. He is most forthright on *John Sherman*, where his judgement seems sound, elsewhere there are some severe value judgements, on "The Rose of Shadow" for instance, and "The Heart of Spring". It is a pity that the editor of *The Speckled Bird* should allow himself so little space on that work, and he seems to be temperamentally out of sympathy with certain other works such as the "Stories of Michael Robartes and His Friends".

These last earn his severe censure for the casualness of their execution. Yet surely they are Yeats's most "agreeably *Arabian-Nightish*" adventures – the phrase is Saintsbury's description of Balzac's *Les Comediens sans le savoir* in the edition in which Yeats read that favourite piece. This brings me to the matter of style. Has anyone really *tested* Yeats's claim that the extravagance of his three occult romances was "learned from Pater"? Paterian the stories are, and Paterianism is one of the modes of existence they reject, but their style is too complicated by what Todorov calls "the formula of alternate possibilities" to be Paterian, and one must follow the clue offered in "Rosa Alchemica" and go to Poe (and Hawthorne) to find Yeats's models. I am out of sympathy with Professor O'Donnell in many matters raised by these three stories, including their dating, sources and interpretation, but his account does suggest how important and exacting they are, and their stylistic formula is in many ways the key to their problems.

The Secret Rose blurs the crucial distinction between Magic and Mysticism discussed by Mr Gilbert (see pp. 3 & ff. above), and the matter was by no means as clear for Yeats in 1897 as it became in the period following the split in the Golden Dawn. But there are signs that Professor O'Donnell has not clearly grasped the issue of sanctity (as opposed to adeptship). This leads, I think, to his undervaluing of "The Heart of Spring", "The Adoration of the Magi" and "The Tables of the Law".

There is another tangle when Professor O'Donnell suggests that too much might be claimed of the connection between "Where there is Nothing There is God" and the later plays, *Where there is Nothing* and *The Unicorn from the Stars*. Yeats's 1908 letter to Bullen, affirming the connection between this last work and the "central idea" of *The Secret Rose*, is awkward for O'Donnell's thesis: the whole matter can be simplified when we note that both the later plays and the stories have a common pressure – an element of satirical rebuttal of Tolstoy, as Yeats hints in his note to "The Unicorn from the Stars".

"Where There is Nothing There is God" clearly derives its title not just from the Cabala, but also from an energetic tilt at the title of Tolstoy's studiedly simple story of the mystical shoemaker, Martuin Avdyéitch, "Where Love is, There God is Also" (as it is entitled in the Walter Scott edition of *Iván Ilyitch*, translated by Nathan Haskell Dole, 1889). In just such a fashion, "The Adoration of the Magi" gives a startling new thrust to the theme of Tolstoy's "The Three Mendicants" from the same collection. (The same trio are transformed in quite another way in "The Three Hermits" of *Responsbilities*). The ending of Yeats's story, delicately manoeuvres around the problem of heresy, (which dogged the publication of both "The Tables of the Law" and "The Adoration of the Magi" by Bullen) by means of an ambiguity. Where Tolstoy's three simple saints leave some "shining" evidence of their visit to the Bishop's ship across the surface of the sea, Yeats's three magi leave no tracks in the snow. Their status – avatars or demons – is left open to question.

All art is dream, and what the day is done with is dreaming-ripe, and what art has moulded religion accepts, and in the end all is in the wine-cup, all is in the drunken fantasy, and the grapes begin to stammer. (*E&I* 285)

Geoffrey Thurley's *The Turbulent Dream* (St. Lucia, London, N.Y.: University of Queensland Press, 1983) nowhere quotes this passage, which is however an epitome of its argument. For Mr Thurley, "Yeats . . . regard[ed] all human behaviour as inherently and necessarily historical and dialectical, taking place in a process which brings it into being, and is then affected by it . . . for Yeats all behaviour was more or less dreamlike, carried out with the curiously blind purposefulness of the somnambulist." Such a "vision of reality" involves a withdrawal, according to Mr Thurley, which Yeats learned from Tennyson, who was the "major direct influence" upon Yeats and who "articulates his withdrawal" in a number of "brilliant allegories" such as "The Lady of Shallott" [sic]. No wonder Tennsyon withdrew.

The "concern with dreaming is the identifying feature of Yeats" and entails "a more serious estimate of dream (fantasy) than is often assumed". Enter Nietzsche, the blunt instrument who, in Mr Thurley's hands, flattens the daring beginnings of ideas, fine distinctions in the reading of poems, into an opinionated sprawl of impatient generalisations. Mr Thurley has some very interesting things to say about fixity and obsession and the consequence of being "wrecked", in Yeats's phrase, "among dreams". (How curious that he should ignore "The Wanderings of Oisin"). The "paradox of enchantment" leads to a valuable, if diffuse, reading of "The Magi". Life, avers Mr Thurely "never escapes the vassalage of dream . . . [m]etaphysically this emerges in Yeats's conception of as the dream of a great dreamer, (History or Time or whatever)". That "whatever" is the giveaway. Elsewhere, in an aside upon "character isolated by a deed", Mr Thurley sees "isolation" as freezing by obsession. His own character as a writer seems frozen by a single obsession, to hustle, without pause or question.

The Turbulent Dream proceeds as a highly eclectic reading of Yeats's *Collected* lyrics – for the narratives are brushed aside in pursuit of the thesis, dream; antithesis, terror; synthestis, gaiety. The freshness and verve of Mr Thurley's approach are vitiated by carelessness and wilful ignorance. Confronted with only ninety-one notes in a full length study, readers will not be surprised to discover that Mr Thurley seems to have read nothing but Bloom and Leavis and Snukal since Joseph Hone's biography. An interesting, but brash discussion of Wordsworth as a source for "The Second Coming" is conducted in a vacuum. He "neither knows nor cares who Jacques Molay was", and "cannot fathom" why anyone "should be expected to be interested in" Robert Artisson and "someone called Lady Kyteler".

This book is therefore an unfinished sketch of the stimulating study its insights might have presaged. The best things in it are sensitive accounts of what Mr Thurley calls "Yeatsian root-words" and of Yeats's metrical tricks and apothegmic style. The worst things are quite astonishing lapses of taste and blind-spots. Five times (following Bloom) we are told that W. B. Yeats did not write a love lyric as fine as Dowson's "Non sum qualis eram bonæ sub regno Cynaræ", which Mr Thurley misreads to the extent of assuming that Dowson's harlot of "yesternight" is his Cynara. The "finished" man among his enemies is for Mr Thurley only done for, with no sense of being compleat. The last stanza of "Byzantium" "ends with chaos. . . . The well armed scholar and exegete

> can hunt down Yeats's bizarre imagery to its source in arcane lore easily enough. What he cannot do is show that this is good poetry. What use does Yeats makes of his sources here? He has, I suggest, produced a sick-bed poem, which may have had a therapeutic value . . . but which amounts to no more than a series of hallucinations that testify impotently to a craving for release. This is psychologically interesting but does not make for good poetry.

"News for the Delphic Oracle" is "ugly" because of the "insistence on foulness . . . the brutality, the foulness, even the use of the word 'bum' . . . I see no exception in the last line of Yeats's poem to the general rule that great writers tend to use the word *copulate* and its derivatives in moods of disguist [sic] . . . Yeats transmits his own inward resistance and distaste – that distaste which his renewed sexuality had opposed. 'News for the Delphic Oracle' is a Tennysonian scenario directed by Luis Buñuel, and it urinates upon the Poussin picture it was 'inspired by'. It is a saddening spectacle".

The truth is that Mr Thurley is wholly out of sympathy with Yeats's last poems, and has not really come to terms with them, or their tragic gaiety or the impact of that notion upon the whole of his work. Far from "urinating", upon the "Acis and Galatea" attributed to Poussin, Yeats's poems animates that splendid picture's "cold pastoral" and brings it closer to the Titianesque model for Poussin's mythologies.

Mr Thurley, then, has isolated himself in a headlong rush. Remote from the promptings and questionings of other minds, he hastens "unrememberingly", and therefore unmemorably, for the most part over great poetry.

Warwick Gould

LOCATION REGISTER
OF
TWENTIETH-CENTURY ENGLISH LITERARY MANUSCRIPTS AND LETTERS: CURRENT YEATS LISTINGS

The national Location Register of Twentieth-Century English Literary Manuscripts and Letters has been in operation in the University of Reading Library since October 1982. It is a project of the Standing Conference of National and University Libraries, funded by donations from cultural organisations and charitable trusts, and initially scheduled to run for five years, with a staff of three. The aim of the project is to create a computerised list, on microfiche, of all twentieth-century literary manuscripts (interpreted in a broad way) that are available for public consultation in the British Isles.

The work of collecting information is still at a very early stage, and the following items should be regarded as a "sampler" of the sort of details that the Location Register will include, rather than any sort of systematic attempt to describe Yeats's surviving manuscripts and letters.

David C. Sutton

YEATS, John Butler, 1838–1922
    Dublin. National Library of Ireland (Public). MS. 2064
        Copies, with annotations, made by Lily Yeats, of 7 letters from John Butler
        Yeats to Susan Yeats of Sligo. – 1872–1873
        On deposit
        Manuscript sources for the history of Irish civilisation/edited by Richard J.
        Hayes (1965), v. 4, p. 927. – [Mar 1983]   re00013285

YEATS, W. B., 1865–1939
    While most of W. B. Yeats's dramatic manuscripts have been deposited in the
    National Library of Ireland, most of the poetic manuscripts remain in the
    possession of Michael B. Yeats in Dublin. There are collections of W. B. Yeats
    papers in the following North American libraries: Henry E. Huntington
    Library, San Marino – Princeton University Library – Harvard University
    Library. – W. B. Yeats papers from the library of Lady Gregory were sold at
    Sotheby's, 23/24 July 1979   rx00000124

YEATS, W. B., 1865–1939
    Birmingham. Birmingham Reference Library (Public). MS. 434
        Letter from W. B. Yeats to A. H. Bullen. – [19–?]. – 4 pages, 2 blank
        Autograph. – Owned. – Undated letter from the Nassau Hotel, Dublin: a
        covering note for a letter to A. H. Bullen from a man writing a thesis on
        Yeats at the Sorbonne. – [Mar 1983]   re0000703x

YEATS, W. B., 1865–1939
  Canterbury. The King's School (Private)
    The isle of statues: an Arcadian fairy-tale in two acts / by W. B. Yeats. – 49
    pages, bound
    Autograph. – Owned. – Published in the "Dublin University Review" in
    1885
    Access: by appointment. – [Feb 1983]   re00002097

YEATS, W. B., 1865–1939
  Dublin. National Library of Ireland (Public). MS. 3726
    3 manuscripts of W. B. Yeats. – [188–?]
    Autograph. – On deposit. – Contents: "The wanderings of Oisin": a version
    of Part I, 1886 – "The wanderins of Usheen", Books I–III – A 6-page
    fragment beginning "Enter a fawn holding a shell"
    Manuscript sources for the history of Irish civilisation/edited by Richard J.
    Hayes (1965), v. 4, p. 928. – [Mar 1983]   re00005142

YEATS, W. B., 1865–1939
  Dublin. National Library of Ireland (Public). MS. 8758
    The Countess Cathleen: various versions, including several partial ver-
    sions, of the play / by W. B. Yeats. – 9 notebooks and 146 ff. in 9 folders
    Autograph. – On deposit. – Published in 1895; a revised version appeared in
    1912, and a further revision in 1913
    Manuscript sources for the history of Irish civilisation/edited by Richard J.
    Hayes (1965), v. 4, p. 927. – [Mar 1983]   re0000510x

YEATS, W. B., 1865–1939
  Dublin. National Library of Ireland (Public). MS. 8772
    The death of Cuchulain: [the play] / by W. B. Yeats. – 113 ff. in 7 folders
    Revised TS. – On deposit. – Published in 1939
    Manuscript sources for the history of Irish civilisation/edited by Richard J.
    Hayes (1965), v. 4, p. 927. – [Mar 1983]   re00005010

YEATS, W. B., 1865–1939
  Dublin. National Library of Ireland (Public). MS. 8760
    Deirdre: materials, including revisions, for the play / by W. B. Yeats. – 260
    pages of TS & 185 pages of autograph MS, in 20 folders
    On deposit. – Published in 1907
    Manuscript sources for the history of Irish civilisation/edited by Richard J.
    Hayes (1965), v. 4, p. 927. – [Mar 1983]   re00005096

YEATS, W. B., 1865–1939
  Dublin. National Library of Ireland (Public). MS. 8770
    The herne's egg: a stage play: text and revisions / by W. B. Yeats. – 53 ff. in 2
    folders
    On deposit. – Published in 1938
    Manuscript sources for the history of Irish civilisation/edited by Richard J.
    Hayes (1965), v. 4, p. 927. – [Mar 1983]   re00005037

YEATS, W. B., 1865–1939
  Dublin. National Library of Ireland (Public). MS. 8763
  The hour-glass: typescript with many extensive MS variants and one complete MS copy of the play / by W. B. Yeats. – About 100 ff. in 2 folders
  Autograph & TS. – On deposit. – "The hour-glass" was first published in 1907; a new version appeared in 1913
  Manuscript sources for the history of Irish civilisation/edited by Richard J. Hayes (1965), v. 4, p. 927. – [Mar 1983]   re00005088

YEATS, W. B., 1865–1939
  Dublin. National Library of Ireland (Public). MS. 8769
  The king of the great clock tower: text and revisions of the play / by W. B. Yeats. – 25 ff.
  On deposit. – Published in 1934
  Manuscript sources for the history of Irish civilisation/edited by Richard J. Hayes (1965), v. 4, p. 927. – [Mar 1983]   re00005045

YEATS, W. B., 1865–1939
  Dublin. National Library of Ireland (Public). MS. 13,585
  The lake isle of Innisfree / by W. B. Yeats
  Autograph fair copy. – On deposit. – First published in "The National Observer" in 1890
  Manuscript sources for the history of Irish civilisation/edited by Richard J. Hayes (1965), v. 4, p. 928. – [Mar 1983]   re00005134

YEATS, W. B. 1865–1939
  Dublin. National Library of Ireland (Public). MS. 13,572
  Lecture given in Manchester on the Abbey Theatre [by one of the Fay brothers?] / with corrections by W. B. Yeats. – [19—]
  Revised TS. – Owned
  Manuscript sources for the history of Irish civilisation/edited by Richard J. Hayes (1965), v. 1, p. 2. – [Mar 1983]   re00005398

YEATS, W. B., 1865–1939
  Dublin. National Library of Ireland (Public). MS. 13,576
  Notebook of W. B. Yeats begun April 7, 1921, containing material for "A vision" and diary entries, including the theme for "Among schoolchildren". – [192–]. – 1 notebook
  Autograph. – On deposit
  Manuscript sources for the history of Irish civilisation/edited by Richard J. Hayes (1965), v. 4, p. 929. – [Mar 1983]   re00005150

YEATS, W. B., 1865–1939
  Dublin. National Library of Ireland (Public). MS. 13,577
  Notebook of W. B. Yeats, containing stories of Michael Robartes. – [192–]. – 1 notebook
  Autograph. – On deposit. – Fol. 1 is headed "May 1924"

Manuscript sources for the history of Irish civilisation/edited by Richard J.
Hayes (1965), v. 4, p. 929. – [Mar 1983]   re00005169

YEATS, W. B., 1865–1939
  Dublin. National Library of Ireland (Public). MS. 13,574
  Notes on Irish gods and legends / by W. B. Yeats. – [19—?]. – 2 notebooks
  Autograph. – On deposit
  Manuscript sources for the history of Irish civilisation/edited by Richard J.
  Hayes (1965), v. 4, p. 928. – [Mar 1983]   re00005118

YEATS, W. B., 1865–1939
  Dublin. National Library of Ireland (Public). MS. 13,575
  Notes on Lady Gregory's "Visions and beliefs in the west of Ireland"; and,
  Swedenborg, mediums and the desolate place: MS and TS texts / by W. B.
  Yeats. – 1 notebook & 3 folders
  Autograph & TS. – On deposit. – "Swedenborg, mediums and the desolate
  places", was first published in "Visions and beliefs in the west of Ireland",
  second series, 1920
  Manuscript sources for the history of Irish civilisation/edited by Richard J.
  Hayes (1965), v. 4, p. 928. – [Mar 1983]   re00005126

YEATS, W. B., 1865–1939
  Dublin. National Library of Ireland (Public). MS. 8764
  The player queen: various partial and complete versions, with numerous
  variants and revisions, of the play / by W. B. Yeats. – 585 ff. & 13 notebooks,
  arranged in 12 packets
  On deposit. – Published in 1922
  Manuscript sources for the history of Irish civilisation/edited by Richard J.
  Hayes (1965), v. 4, p. 927. – [Mar 1983]   re0000507x

YEATS, W. B., 1865–1939
  Dublin. National Library of Ireland (Public). MS. 8771
  Purgatory: scenario and various versions / by W. B. Yeats. – [1938]. – 74 ff.
  in 8 folders
  Autograph & TS. – On deposit
  Manuscript sources for the history of Irish civilisation/edited by Richard J.
  Hayes (1965), v. 4, p. 927. – [Mar 1983]   re00005029

YEATS, W. B., 1865–1939
  Dublin. National Library of Ireland (Public). MS. 13,578
  Rapallo note-book A / by W. B. Yeats. – [192–?]. – 1 notebook
  Autograph. – On deposit. – Contents: Rewritten sections of "A vision",
  including comments on "The cat and the moon" – Passages of "The player
  queen" – The irish censorship – A letter about Wagner
  Manuscript sources for the history of Irish civilisation/edited by Richard J.
  Hayes (1965), v. 4, p. 928. – [Mar 1983]   re00005185

YEATS, W. B., 1865–1939
  Dublin. National Library of Ireland (Public). MS. 13,579
    Rapallo note-book B: notebook containing materials for "A vision" / by W.
    B. Yeats. – [192–?]. – 1 notebook
    Autograph. – On deposit
    Manuscript sources for the history of Irish civilisation/edited by Richard J.
    Hayes (1965), v. 4, p. 928. – [Mar 1983]   re00005193

YEATS, W. B., 1865–1939
  Dublin. National Library of Ireland (Public). MS. 13,580
    Rapallo note-book [C] / by W. B. Yeats. – [192–?]. – notebook
    Autograph. – On deposit. – Contents: Diary of thoughts. [finished June or
    July, 1929]. – Material for "A vision" – "The winding stair": drafts of
    poems – "Words for music perhaps": drafts of poems, including the
    Cracked Mary (later Crazy Jane) poems
    Manuscript sources for the history of Irish civilisation/edited by Richard J.
    Hayes (1965), v. 4, p. 929. – [Mar 1983]   re00005177

YEATS, W. B., 1865–1939
  Dublin. National Library of Ireland (Public). MS. 13,581
    Rapallo note-book [D] (Diary): notebook containing, inter alia, many
    versions of poems in "The winding stair" / by W. B. Yeats. – [192–?]. – 1
    notebook
    Autograph. – On deposit. – Fol. 3 is headed "Dublin August 1929"
    Manuscript sources for the history of Irish civilisation/edited by Richard J.
    Hayes (1965), v. 4, p. 929. – [Mar 1983]   re00005207

YEATS, W. B., 1865–1939
  Dublin. National Library of Ireland (Public). MS. 13,582
    Rapallo note-book E / by W. B. Yeats. – [192–?]. – 1 notebook
    Autograph. – On deposit. – Contents: The resurrection – A vision: drafts –
    The words upon the window-pane: drafts
    Manuscript sources for the history of Irish civilisation/edited by Richard J.
    Hayes (1965), v. 4, p. 928. – [Mar 1983]   re00005215

YEATS, W. B., 1865–1939
  Dublin. National Library of Ireland (Public). MS. 8766
    The resurrection: versions and revisions of the play / by W. B. Yeats. – 86 ff.
    in 4 folders
    Autograph & TS. – On deposit. – First published in "The Adelphi", June
    1927. – A revised version was included in "Stories of Michael Robartes and
    his friends". 1931
    Manuscript sources for the history of Irish civilisation/edited by Richard J.
    Hayes (1965), v. 4, p. 927. – [Mar 1983]   re00005061

YEATS, W. B., 1865–1939
  Dublin. National Library of Ireland (Public). MS. 8762

[The shadowy waters]

Drafts of portions of successive revisions of W. B. Yeats's play "The shadowy waters", with a few fragments which may relate to "The land of heart's desire". – 31 folders

On deposit. – "The shadowy waters" was first published in 1900, "The land of heart's desire" in 1894

Manuscript sources for the history of Irish civilisation/edited by Richard J. Hayes (1965), v. 4, p. 927. – [Mar 1983]   re00013048

YEATS, W. B., 1865–1939

Dublin. National Library of Ireland (Public). MS. 13,565

[The shadowy waters]

Corrections by W. B. Yeats to the acting version of "The shadowy waters". – 1 sheet

TS. – Owned. – "The shadowy waters" was first published in 1900

Manuscript sources for the history of Irish civilisation/edited by Richard J. Hayes (1965), v. 4, p. 927. – [Mar 1983]   re00013056

YEATS, W. B., 1865–1939

Dublin. National Library of Ireland (Public). MS. 8765

[Sophocles' "King Oedipus"]

King Oedipus/ by W. B. Yeats. – About 80 ff.

Revised TS. – On deposit. – Published in 1928

Manuscript sources for the history of Irish civilisation/edited by Richard J. Hayes (1965), v. 4, p. 927. – [Mar 1983]   re0001303x

YEATS, W. B., 1865–1939

Dublin. National Library of Ireland (Public). MS. 8767

[Sophocles' "Oedipus at Colonus"]

Oedipus at Colonus: play / by W. B. Yeats; with some notes and corrections by Lennox Robinson. – About 145 ff. in 2 folders

TS. – On deposit. – Published in 1934. – with a prompt copy corrected by W. B. Yeats

Manuscript sources for the history of Irish civilisation/edited by Richard J. Hayes (1965), v. 4, p. 927. – [Mar 1983]   re00013021

YEATS, W. B., 1865–1939

Dublin. National Library of Ireland (Public). MS. 8768

The words upon the window pane / by W. B. Yeats; with the introduction to the play. – 105 ff. in 4 folders

Revised TS. – On deposit. – Published in 1934. – With a prompt copy, with notes by Lennox Robinson

Manuscript sources for the history of Irish civilisation/edited by Richard J. Hayes (1965), v. 4, p. 927. – [Mar 1983]   re00005053

YEATS, W. B., 1865–1939

London. University of London. Library (Public). A.L.203

Letters to Florence Farr/[from William Archer and 14 other writers]. – 1891–1911

Autograph. – Owned. – With a letter from Sir Herbert Beerbohm Tree to John Todhunter, 1891, arranging to meet Florence Farr. – [Dec 1982] re00000752

YEATS, W. B., 1865–1939

Oxford. Plunkett Foundation for Co-operative Studies (Private)

Letters to Sir Horace Curzon Plunkett/[from Arthur James Balfour & others]. – 1899–1931

Autograph & TS. – Owned. – Catalogued. – Correspondents include: Arthur James Balfour (6 letters), John Buchan (1 letter), Erskine Childers (collection), Lord Dunsany (7 letters), St John Ervine (2 letters), Darrell Figgis (4 letters), H. Rider Haggard (3 letters), George W. Russell "AE", (5 letters), Bernard Shaw (collection), Katharine Tynan (1 letter), H. G. Wells (1 letter), W. B. Yeats (1 letter) & Filson Young (collection)

Access: by appointment. – [Feb 1983] re00002089

YEATS, W. B., 1865–1939

Oxford. Somerville College. Library (Private). PW Misc

Collection of letters to Percy Withers and his family. – 1891–1959

Owned. – Catalogued. – There are about 40 literary figures among the correspondents. – With 2 MS poems by Laurence Binyon & 1 MS poem by Ralph Hodgson

Access: by appointment. – [Feb 1983] re00001554

YEATS, W. B., 1865–1939

Stratford-upon-Avon. Shakespeare Birthplace Trust. Records Office. ER136/63

John Sherman; and, Dhoya/ by W. B. Yeats. – [1891?]. – Sheets of the 2nd ed., published by T. Fisher Unwin

Revised proofs. – Owned. – Corrected apparently for a new ed. by the Shakespeare Head Press. – Signed "W. B. Yeats, November 1891". – [Feb 1983]. re00002054

"Gasping on the Strand": a Yeats Bibliography, 1981–83

Warwick Gould and Olympia Sitwell

This, the first bibliography to appear in a *Yeats Annual*, attempts to include as many items as possible as have appeared since Richard J. Finneran's *Recent Research on Anglo-Irish Writers etc.* (see p. 289 above for review) went to press, as well as items overlooked by that survey. That work was reasonably complete (in English Language material) up until the end of 1980, and contained as many items from 1981 as possible. These have not been reproduced.

Reviews have been included when it has seemed that they have made some independent contribution to the subject: they have not, however, been consistently searched for. The compilers will be grateful to hear of all omissions or errors, (all due entirely to ignorance), which will be rectified in subsequent issues.

The format of this bibliography is based upon the larger subdivisions familiar to users of K. P. S. Jochum's standard *W. B. Yeats: a Classified Bibliography of Criticism*, with separate sections at the end for titles announced for publication and recent useful reprints. However, no attempt has been made at Jochum's more precise classifications, or at cross referencing, and only one section has been assigned to "The Irish Literary and Dramatic Revival". Inevitably, much of this bibliography was compiled from other listings (the authors of which have been thanked at the beginning of this volume), and it has not been possible to view every item listed. Hence there are some incomplete entries, and a large number of items have been somewhat tentatively assigned to the third section upon general coverage of Yeats's works. Items cited below from Japanese and Russian periodicals have been especially difficult to check: it is hoped in future that bibliographers resident in those countries will supply material. In the meantime it has been felt more urgent to give what information is to hand so as to indicate the breadth of activity in non-English-speaking centres.

In future the bibliography will shrink to an annual listing, with additional information from earlier years listed if it has been overlooked by Wade, Jochum, or Finneran. Naturally the editor is most interested to hear of material from prior to 1940, but is grateful to receive all information (which will be acknowledged). The editor values greatly receiving off-prints, review copies, and other information.

A. BIBLIOGRAPHIES, CATALOGUES, SPECIAL COLLECTIONS, AND ADDITIONS TO *WADE*, INCLUDING NEW EDITIONS OF YEATS'S WORKS WITH CRITICAL COMMENT, AND TRANSLATIONS

K. C. Bell, "Yeats", *Yeats Eliot Review*, VII, 1 & 2 (1982) 150–2.

Davies, Alistair, *An Annotated Critical Bibliography of Modernism* Brighton: Harvester Press, 1983). Reviewed by Edward Mendelson in "Picking through the Wreckage", *TLS*, 26 Aug. 1983, 901.

Feeney, William & O'Brien, Joseph, "Report on Current Research", *ACIS* (Checklist), IX, 1983.

Finneran, Richard J., "W. B. Yeats", in *Recent Research on Anglo-Irish Writers: A Supplement to "Anglo-Irish Literature: a Review of Research"*, ed. Richard J. Finneran (N.Y.: MLA, 1983) 85–153.

Ford, Jim, "Current Books of Irish Interest", *ACIS Newsletter*, XIII (Dec. 1982) 10–11.

Freeman, Ronald E. (ed.), *Bibliographies of Studies in Victorian Literature for the Ten Years 1965–1974* (N.Y.: AMS, 1981).

Genet, Jacqueline, "Bibliographie Francaise", in *William Butler Yeats* ed. Jacqueline Genet (Paris: Editions de l'Herne, 1981) 442–451. This volume is hereafter cited as *l'Herne*.

Gould, Warwick, " 'Fighting the Waves' " (Review of K. P. S. Jochum's *W. B. Yeats: a Classified Bibliography of Criticism*, *Antiquarian Book Monthly Review*, v:8 (52) (Aug. 1978) 341–2.

Jochum, K. P. S., "W. B. Yeats: a Survey of Book Publications 1966–1972", *Anglia*, 92 (1974) 143–71.

——, "A Yeats Bibliography for 1981", *Yeats: an Annual of Critical and Textual Studies*, ed. Richard J. Finneran (Ithaca & London: Cornell) I, 1983.

Kain, Richard M., "The Irish Collection: a Personal Account", *Library Review* (Louisville), XXXI (May 1981) 2–48.

Kosok, Heinz, "Anglo-Irish Studies in Germany, 1976–1979", *IASAIL News Letter*, XVIII (Autumn–Winter 1979/80) 9–16.

——, "Anglo-Irish Studies in Germany: a Bibliography 1979–1982", *IASAIL Newsletter*, XXIV (Autumn–Winter, 1982) 13–19.

——, (ed.) *German Studies in Anglo-Irish Literature 1972–1982* (An Exhibition presented by the Goethe Institute, Dublin, in association with the National Library, 1983, with a bibliographical checklist by H. K.).

Mikhail, E. H., *Lady Gregory: an Annotated Bibliography of Criticism* (Troy, N.Y.: Whitston. 1982).

——, *An Annotated Bibliography of Modern Anglo-Irish Drama* (Troy, N.Y.: Whitston, 1981).

——, *A Research Guide to Modern Irish Dramatists* (Troy, N.Y.: Whitston, 1979).

Murphy, Maureen, "Bibliography Bulletin for 1980", *IUR*, XI, 2 (Autumn 1981) 200–35, also for 1981, *IUR*, XII, 2 (Autumn 1982) 205–37.

——, "IASAIL Bibliography for 1982", *IUR*, XIII, 2 (Autumn 1983).

Rafroidi, Patrick, "The Year's Work in Irish-English Literature, Autumn 1980–Autumn 1981", *Études Irlandaises*, N.S. VI, 195–210.

Rafroidi, Anne & Patrick, "The Year's Work in Irish-English Literature Autumn 1981–Autumn 1982" *Études Irlandaises*, N.S. VII, 211–31.

Stanton, Michael N., *English Literary Journals, 1900–1950*: a Guide to Information Sources (Detroit: Gale Research, 1982).

Christie's: *Valuable Autograph Letters, Historical Documents and Music Manuscripts* (Sale 29 April, 1981).

Sotheby's: Parke Bernet, *Valuable Autograph Letters, Literary Manuscripts and Historical Documents* (Sale 17 Dec. 1981). *Valuable Autograph Letters, Literary Manuscripts and Historical Documents* (Sale 29–30 June 1982.) *English Literature Comprising Printed Books, Autograph Letters, and Manuscripts* (Sale 15 Dec. 1982).

Christie's: *Valuable Autograph Letters and Historical Documents* (Sale 20 July 1983). [Letters to Lady Dorothy Wellesley.]

Sotheby's: *English Literature comprising Printed Books, Autograph Letters and Manuscripts* (Sale 21–2 July 1983.)

Yeats, W. B., Review of George Sigerson's

Bards of the Gael and Gall etc., Illustrated London News (14 Aug. 1897).

Adams, Steve L. & Harper, George Mills (eds) "The Manuscript of 'Leo Africanus' ", *Yeats Annual No. 1* (1982) 3–47.

Finneran, Richard, J. (ed.), *The Poems of W. B. Yeats: a New Edition* (New York: Macmillan, 1983; London: Macmillan, 1984).

Marcus, Phillip L. (ed.), *The Death of Cuchulain: Manuscript Materials Including the Author's Final Text* (Ithaca and London: Cornell University Press, 1982). [Rev in *Irish Lit. Sup.* 1:2 (Fall 1982) 20, by James W. Flannery.]

Warner, Eric & Hough, Graham (eds), *Strangeness and Beauty: an Anthology of Aesthetic Criticism, 1840–1910*, 2 vols (Cambridge: Cambridge University Press, 1983). [Includes passages from *Au*, *E&I*, with intro. & notes, also Symons's "Mr. W. B. Yeats" (review of *The Wind among the Reed*).]

Breuer, Rolf & Althammer, Charlotte, *Anglo-Irish Literature: a Reader. I: Texte; II: Unterrichtsmodell.* Unterrichtsmodelle für die Sekundarstufe II (Frankfurt/M., 1981).

Imura, Kimie and Okubo, N. (trans.), *The Secret Rose* (Japanese) (Tokyo: Kokusho Kanko-Kai, 1980).

Sano, Tetsuro (ed.), *W. B. Yeats* (annotated edition) (Kyoto: Yamaguchi Shoten, 1981).

Sano, Tetsuro, Furomoto, T., Hirata, Y., Tanaka, M. & Matsuda, S (trans.) *The Collected Plays of W. B. Yeats* (Japanese), Kyoto: Yamaguchi Shoten, 1980).

Suzuki, Hiroshi (trans.) *The Collected Poems of W. B. Yeats* (Japanese) (Tokyo: Hokuseido, 1982).

Geschichten von Rot-Hanrahan (German trans. of *Stories of Red Hanrahan* (Leipzig: Insel, 1978).

Ierse Elfenverhalen (Dutch trans. of *Fairy and Folk Tales of the Irish Peasantry* and *Irish Fairy Tales*) (Den Haag: Uitgeverij Sirius en Siderius, 1981).

Fiabe Irlandesi (Italian trans. of *Fairy and Folk Tales of the Irish Peasantry* and *Irish Fairy Tales*, by Mariagiovanna Audreolli (Torino: Giulio Einavdi Editore, 1981).

Bonnefoy, Yves, "Dix poèmes", *Argile*, 1 (Winter, 1973).

De Bayser, Yves, *Le Cycle de Cuchulain* ("Le Heaume vert", "Sur le rivage de Baile", "La seule jalousie d'Emer", "La Mort de Cuchulain"), Collection "Théâtre Oblique", 1974.

Febvre, L., " 'The Sorrow of Love', – 'La Douleur d'aimer' ", *Présence Linguistique*, revue trimestrielle, Dec. 1973, IV.

Fouad, El. Etr., "Dix-septes poèmes", *La Delirante*, 1973, 48.

Frechet, René, *Choix de Poémes* (introduction, choix, commentaires et traduction) (Paris: Aubier-Montaigne, "Collection bilingue", 1975).

Garrier, G. Genet, J. & Zeini, P. (trans.), *Per Amica Silentia Lunæ*, (Lille: PUL, 1980).

Genet, Jacqueline *(et. al) Le Crépuscule Celtique* (Lille: PUL, 1982).

——, *Explorations* (Lille: PUL, 1981).

——, (ed.), *L'Herne* (op. cit.), which, in addition to items cited elsewhere, contains the following texts of Yeats, translated by Jean-Claude Castangt, Joël Dupont, Raymonde Popot, René Frechet, Jacqueline Genet, Elisabeth Hellegouarc'h, Jean Briat, Yves de Bayser, Sylviane Troadec, Michelle Morin; "Rosses et Drumcliff", "Il invite sa bien-aimée à être paisible", "Il souhaiterait posséder les voiles du ciel", "Petit sous brun", "Pas de seconde Troie", "Le Peuple", "Demon et Bête", "Introduction générale à mon oeuvre", "A l'Irlande future", "Pardon, pères anciens", "Les Cygnes sauvages de Coole", "À la mémoire du Commandant Robert Gregory", "Le Pêcheur", "Paques 1916", "Le second avènement", "Prière pour ma fille", "Meditations du temps de la guerre civile", "Voile vers Byzance", "Byzance", "Les Spires", "Introduction à mes pièces", "Le Seuil du Palais du Roi", "Le chat et la Lune", "Introduction à la Resurrection".

Gros, Léon-Gabriel, *Vision* (traduit de l'anglais) Paris: Fayard, 1979).

Jaujard, Francois-Xavier, "Sept poèmes", *Clivages*, 2 June 1974.

——, "Au puits de l'Epervier", *Empreintes, ecrits sur la danse*, June 1978, 2–9.

——, "An Acre of Grass", "What Then?", "The Great Day", "Parnell", "What was lost", "The Spur", "Those Images", trans. in *L'Alphée* (Nov. 1980) 90–118, which also contains "Pleine Lune de Mars" trans. Alain de Gourcuff.

B. BIOGRAPHIES AND BIOGRAPHICAL MATERIAL

Arnold, Bruce, *Orpen: Mirror to an Age* (London: Jonathan Cape, 1981).

Balliet, Conrad A., "Maud Gonne Mac-Bride: Violent Pacifist", *Irish Renaissance Annual*, ed. Dennis Jackson, III (1982) 93–105.

Beckson, Karl, "The Legends of the Rhymers' Club: a Review Article", *Victorian Poetry*, XIX:4 (Winter 1981) 397–406.

Dodds, E. R., *Missing Persons* (Oxford: Clarendon, 1977). ("I was not much of a favourite with Yeats . . .". Also Dodds's own account of "fabulous, formless darkness", p. 60.)

Eagle, Dorothy & Carnell, Hilary (eds), *The Oxford Illustrated Literary Guide to Great Britain and Ireland* (Oxford: Oxford University Press, 1981).

Ellmann, Richard, *James Joyce: New and Revised Edition* (Oxford, N.Y., Toronto: Oxford University Press, 1982).

Gilbert, R. A., *The Golden Dawn: Twilight of the Magicians* (Wellingborough: Aquarian, 1983).

Glendinning, Victoria, *Edith Sitwell: a Unicorn among Lions* (London: Weidenfeld & Nicholson, 1981). (Summary of unpub. corres. on *Oxford Book of Modern Verse*.)

Gould, Warwick, "The Biocritical Heritage" *English*, XXVI:126, (Augumn 1977) 240–54. (Review essay upon *W. B. Yeats: Reviews and Recollections* ed. E. H. Mikhail.)

——, "The Poet at the Breakfast Table", *English*, XXVII, 128–9 (Autumn 1978) 222–39. (Review essay upon *Letters to Yeats* and *The Correspondence of Robert Bridges and W. B. Yeats*.)

Holdsworth, Carolyn, " 'Shelley Plain': Yeats and Katharine Tynan", *Yeats Annual No. 2*, (1983) 59–92.

Ito, Hiromi, "W. B. Yeats and Iseult Gonne", *Eibungaku*, 51, Waseda Daigaku Eibungaku (Oxt 1979).

Jackson, Laura Riding, "Literary Mentioning", *Paris Review*, XXIII:79 (Spring 1981) 301–4. [Cf. interview with Stephen Spender in op. cit., XXII:77 (Winter–Spring 1980) 118–54.]

Jeffares, A. Norman, "Jeunesse à Dublin" *L'Herne* (op. cit.) 23–36.

Johnson, Josephine A., "The Music of Speech: Florence Farr and W. B. Yeats", *Literature in Performance*, II:1 (Nov. 1981) 56–65.

Jussim, Estelle, *Slave to Beauty: the Eccentric Life and Controversial Career of F. Holland Day Photographer, Publisher, Aesthete.* (Boston: David R. Godine, 1981.)

Martin, Augustine, *W. B. Yeats* (Dublin: Gill & Macmillan, 1983).

Phillips, Gary, "Lennox Robinson on the Dublin Drama League: a Letter to Gabriel Fallon", *ICarbS* (Carbondale, Ill.), IV:2 (Spring–Summer 1981) 75–82.

Pruitt, Virginia & Raymond D. "Yeats and the Steinach Operation", *Yeats: an Annual of Critical And Textual Studies*, ed. Richard J. Finneran (Ithaca and London: Cornell) 1, 1983.

Saddlemyer, Ann (ed.), *The Collected Letters of John Millington Synge*, (1, 1871–1907) (Oxford: Clarendon, 1983). [Rev. by Patricia Craig, "Ailing and Aislings", *TLS* (2 Sept. 1983) 937.]

Salmon, Eric, *Granville Barker: A Secret Life* (London: Heinemann, 1983).

Sassoon, Siegfried, *Diaries, 1920–1922*, ed. Rupert Hart-Davis (London: Faber, 1981).

Sewell, Brocard, *In the Dorian Mode: a Life of John Gray: 1866–1934* (Padstow: Tabb House, 1983).

Seymour-Smith, Martin, *Robert Graves: His Life and Work* (London: Hutchinson, 1982).

Sidnell, Michael J., Review of William M. Murphy's *Prodigal Father: The Life of John Butler Yeats*, in *University of Toronto Quarterly*, L:2 (Winter 1979/80) 180–3.

Stuart, Francis, "Rencontre", *L'Herne* (op. cit.) 441.

Walsh, Carolina, "In Search of Katharine Tynan", *Irish Times*, 29 Aug. 1981, 8.

Weintraub, Stanley, "Uneasy Friendship: Shaw and Yeats", *Yeats: an Annual of Critical and Textual Studies*, ed. Richard J. Finneran (Ithaca and London: Cornell) 1, 1983.

Wintle, Justin & Kenin, Richard, *The Pen-* guin *Concise Dictionary of Biographical Quotation* (Harmondsworth: Penguin, 1981). [First published as *The Dictionary of Biographical Quotation* (London: Routledge & Kegan Paul, 1978) this contains quotations by many figures upon W. B. Y., and by W. B. Y. on many figures and himself.]

Yeats, Michael, "Introduction" in *l'Herne* (op. cit.) 11–12.

C. THE WORKS (GENERAL SECTION)

(i) *Journals and Other Publications Devoted Wholly or Largely to Articles About W. B. Yeats*

Yeats Annual No. 1 (London: Macmillan; Atlantic Highlands, N.J.: Humanities, 1982). [Items are separately cited elsewhere except for reviews by Cleanth Brooks, George Mills Harper, James Kilroy, Patricia McFate, James Olney, Edward Partridge, Ronald Schuchard and Donald Stanford; and "Dissertation Abstracts, 1980", compiled by Carolyn Holdsworth.]

Yeats Annual No. 2 (London: Macmillan; Atlantic Highlands, N.J.: Humanities, 1983). [Items are separately cited elsewhere except for reviews by Michael André Bernstein, George Bornstein, Edward Engleberg, F. S. L. Lyons, Phillip L. Marcus, William H. O'Donnell, James Olney, Ann Saddlemyer and Ronald Schuchard; and "Dissertation Abstracts, 1981", compiled by Carolyn Holdsworth.]

Yeats Eliot Review, VII:1 & 2 (June 1982). [Items are separately cited, except for reviews by Herbert J. Levine and Shyamal Bagchee.]

Yeats: an Annual of Critical and Textual Studies, No. 1, ed. Richard J. Finneran (Ithaca and London: Cornell, 1983). [Items are separately cited except for the following: reviews by Michael André Bernstein, E. P. Bollier, George Bornstein, Mary Fitzgerald, Ian Fletcher, David Krause, F. S. L. Lyons, David S. Thatcher, Donald Torchiana and Hugh Witemyer; and "Dissertation Abstracts, 1982" compiled by Carolyn Holdsworth.]

Études Irlandaises, N.S. VII: (Dec. 1982). [In addition to items cited separately, this number contains reviews by Jacqueline Genet, Raymonde Popot, and Patrick Rafroidi of recent editions and studies, (including *Yeats Annual No. 1*).]

William Butler Yeats ed. Jacqueline Genet (Paris; Editions de l'Herne, 1981). [All items cited elsewhere in this list as being from "*l'Herne*".]

Bulletin of the Yeats Society of Japan. (Articles cited separately.)

(ii) *Articles and Longer Studies*

Adams, Hazard, *Philosophy of the Literary Symbolic* (Gainesville: University of Florida Press, 1983).

——, "The Seven Eyes of Yeats" in *William Blake and the Moderns*, ed. Robert J. Bertholf and Annet S. Levitt (Albany, N.Y.: SUNY Press, 1982) 3–14.

Albu, Rodica, "W. B. Yeats and Romanian Poetry: Suggestions for a Tentative Comparative Approach", *Analele Scientifice ale Universitatii Iasi*, XXVII (1981) 95–106.

Allen, James Lovic, "William Butler Yeats", *Critical Survey of Poetry* ed. Frank

N. Magill (Englewood Cliffs, N.J.: Salem Press, 1982) 8:3181–209.

Araki, Eiko, "Yeatsian Geometry", in *Bulletin of the Yeats Society of Japan*, XII (Oct. 1981).

Archibald, Douglas, *Yeats* (Syracuse: Syracuse University Press, 1983).

Armstrong, Alison, (ed.) "A Yeats Broadside", *Irish Literary Supplement*, II:1 (1983) 19–24.

Backés, Jean-Louis, "Mallarme", in *L'Herne* (op. cit.), 397–408.

Bain, Joseph, "W. B. Yeats", *Makers of Modern Culture*, ed. Justin Wintle (London: Routledge & Kegan Paul; N.Y.: Facts on file, 1981).

Balliet, Conrad A., "Yeats and His Bloody Repetition", *Studies in Anglo-Irish Literature*, ed. Heinz Kosok (Bonn: Bouvier, 1982) 214–26.

Bartlett, Donald R., "Maclennan and Yeats", *Canadian Literature*, LXXXIX (Summer 1981) 74–84.

Basile, Bruno, "Verso una Dinamica Letteraria: testo e avantesto", *Lingua e Stile*, XIV:2–3, (Sept. 1979), 395–410. [399–401 on Yeats and Leopardi.]

Bawer, Bruce, "Two on a Tower: Hardy and Yeats", *Yeats Eliot Review*, VII:1 & 2 (1982) 91–108.

Bedient, Calvin, "The Thick and the Thin of It: Contemporary British and Irish Poetry", *Kenyon Review*, III:3 (Summer 1981) 32–48.

Bohlmann, Otto, *Yeats and Nietszche: an Exploration of Major Nietzchean Echoes in the Writings of William Butler Yeats* (London: Macmillan; Totowa, N.J.: Barnes & Noble, 1982).

Boland, Eavan, "The Missing Shadow" *Irish Times*, 8 Dec. 1981, 8 [whole page "Padraic Colum, 1881–1981: a Tribute to the Centenary of His Birth" but Boland on influence of W. B. Yeats.]

——, "The Unknown Dimension of Padraic Colum", *Irish Times* 16 Sept. 1981, 12.

Bornstein, George, "Last Romantic or Last Victorian: Yeats, Tennyson, and Browning" *Yeats Annual No. 1* (1982) 114–32.

——, "Victorians and Volumes, Foreigners and First Drafts: Four Gaps in Postromantic Influence Study", *Romanticism Past and Present*, VI:2 (1982) 1–9.

Bötheroyd, Paul F., "Just who's in Hyde's Bag?" *Éire–Ireland*, XVI:2 (Summer 1981) 149–50.

Bradley, Anthony G., "Pastoral in Modern Irish Poetry", *Concerning Poetry*, XIV:2 (Fall 1981) 79–96. [Special Issue, *Concerning Irish Poetry since W. B. Yeats.*]

Bramsbäck, Birgit, "Allusions to Yeats in *Stephen Hero* and *A Portrait of the Artist as a Young Man*", *Nordic Rejoycings*, ed. Johannes Hedberg (James Joyce Soc. of Sweden & Finland, 1982).

Bruch, Hermann, *W. B. Yeats: Dichterische Theorie zwischen Isolation und Integration* (Bern: Herbert Lang; Frankfurt: Peter Lang, 1975).

Buckley, Vincent, "Poetry and the Avoidance of Nationalism" in *Irish Culture and Nationalism, 1750–1950*, eds Oliver MacDonagh, W. F. Mandle & Pauric Travers (London: Macmillan, 1983) 258–79.

Bush, Ronald, "The 'Rhythm of Metaphor': Yeats, Pound, Eliot, and the Unity of Image in Postsymbolist Poetry", *Allegory, Myth and Symbol*, ed. Morton W. Bloomfield (Cambridge, Mass.: Harvard University Press, 1981) 371–88.

Bushrui, Suheil Badi, "Images of a changing Ireland in the Works of W. B. Yeats", *Literature and the Changing Ireland*, ed. Peter Connolly (Gerrards Cross: Colin Smythe; Totowa, N.J.: Barnes & Noble, 1982) 103–32.

Cantor, Jay, *The Space Between: Literature and Politics* (Baltimore: Johns Hopkins University Press, 1981).

Carpenter, Humphrey, *W. H. Auden: a Biography* (London: Allen & Unwin, 1981).

Clark, David R., *Yeats at Songs and Choruses* (Gerrards Cross: Colin Smythe; Amherst: University of Massachusetts Press, 1983).

Clausen, Christopher, *The Place of Poetry: Two Centuries of an Art in Crisis* (Lexington: University of Kentucky Press, 1981).

Colbert, Judith A., "Masks of Ben Jonson in W. B. Yeats's *The Green Helmet* and *Responsibilities*", *Canadian Journal of Irish Studies*, VII:1 (June 1981) 32–48.

Cope, Jackson I., *Joyce's Cities: Archeologies of the Soul* (Baltimore: Johns Hopkins

University Press, 1981). [Yeats's occult interests as basis for Joyce esp. 74–8.]

Craig, Cairns, *Yeats, Eliot, Pound and the Politics of Poetry: Richest to the Richest* (London & Canberra: Croom Helm; Pittsburgh: University of Pittsburgh Press, 1982).

Cronin, Anthony, "William Butler Yeats: Containing Contradictions", *Heritage Now: Irish Literature in the English Language* (Dingle: Brandon, 1982).

Davenport, Gary, "Yeats and Belief", *Sewannee Review*, LXXXIX:3 (Summer 1981) 469–73.

Davie, Donald, "Poets on Stilts: Yeats and Some Contemporaries", *PN Review*, 30, IX, 4, 14–17.

Deane, Seamus, "Blueshirt" *London Review of Books*, III:10, 4–17 June, 1981, 23–4.

Denman, Peter, "Man into Myth: The Figure of Yeats in the Poetry of his Successors", *Gaéliana*, II, 1980, 11–22.

Diggory, Terence, *Yeats & American Poetry: The Tradition of the Self* (Princeton: Princeton University Press, 1983).

Doherty, Gerald, "The World that Shines and Sounds: W. B. Yeats and Diasetz Suzuki", *Irish Renaissance Annual*, IV (1983), 57–75.

El-Ghamrawi, Ahmed, *W. B. Yeats and the Culture of the Middle East* (Cairo: Anglo-Egyptian Bookshop, 1979).

Ellis, Stephen Paul, "Yeats and Dante", *Comparative Literature*, XXXIII:1 (Winter 1981) 1–17.

Ellis, Steve, *Dante and English Poetry: Shelley to T. S. Eliot* (Cambridge: Cambridge University Press, 1983).

Emmons, Jeanne Carter, "Hopkins and Yeats: Pre-Raphaelite Influence and Poetic Experience", *Hopkins Quarterly*, XIII:2 (Summer 1981) 75–83.

Farag, Fahmy F. "Yeats and the Irish Dialectic", *English Studies in Canada*, VII:4 (Dec. 1981) 402–13.

——, "The Ireland that sings: Yeats and the Heresy of Universal Education", *Studies in Anglo-Irish Literature* ed. Heinz Kosok (Bonn: Bouvier, 1982) 205–13.

Finney, Kathe Davis, "Crazy Jane Talks with Jonathan Culler: Using Structuralism to Teach Lyric Poetry", *CEA Critic* XLIII:3 (Mar. 1981) 29–36.

Foster, John Burt, *Heirs of Dionysus: a Nietzschean Current in Literary Modernism*

(Princeton: Princeton University Press, 1981).

Fowler, Alastair, *Kinds of Literature: an Introduction to the Theory of Genres and Modes* (Oxford: Clarendon, 1982).

Fraser, George S., *A Short History of English Poetry* (Shepton Mallet: Open Books, 1981).

Freitag, Hans-Heinrich, "Die Vision als Form der Wirklichkeitserfahrung bei Mangan und Yeats", in Hans-Heinrich Freitag and Peter Hühn (eds), *Literarische Ansichten der Wirklichkeit: Studien zur Wirklichkeitskonstitution in englischsprachiger Literatur: To honour Johannes Kleinstück*, Anglo-American Forum XII (Frankfurt, Bern, Cirencester: Lang, 1980) 173–90.

Funakura, Masanori, "W. B. Yeats and the Irish Renaissance", *Bulletin of Okayama University*, XVIII, Feb. 1982.

Gallagher, Brian, "About Us, For Us, Near Us: the Irish and Harlem Renaissance", *Eire–Ireland*, XVI:4 (Winter 1981) 14–26.

Garratt, Robert F., "Patrick Kavanagh and the Killing of the Irish Revival", *Colby Library Quarterly*, XVII:3 (Sept. 1981) 170–83.

Genet, Jacqueline, "La Dialectique de la nature et de l'esprit dans la poésie de Yeats", *Études anglaises*, LXVII 1975, 137–57.

——, "Les metamorphoses chez Yeats", *Actes du Colloque international de Valenciennes sur la Metamorphose*, 1981.

——, "La Poetique de l'eau chez Yeats" *Études anglaises*, LXV: 1973, 225–38.

——, "La Spirale Yeatsienne", *Études anglaises*, LXXV: 1975, 383–95.

——, "La symbolique de l'arbre chez Yeats", *Travaux et Mémoires* (Université de Limoges, 1974) 17–36.

——, "W. B. Yeats et Auden", *Trames*, Université de Limoges II, (avril 1979) 57–78.

——, *William Butler Yeats: Les Fondaments et l'Evolution de la Création Poétique* (Lille, Publications de l'Université de Lille III, 1976).

——, "Yeats et les problèmes politiques irlandais", *Cahiers des Pays du Nord et du Nord-Ouest* (Jan. 1979) 87–104.

——, "Yeats et la Revolution" in *L'Herne*, (op. cit.) 159–73.

Gould, Warwick, "A Misreading of Harold

Bloom" [Review Essay on *The Anxiety of Influence, A Map of Misreading, Kabbalah and Criticism*, and *Poetry and Repression*] *English*, xxvi:124 (Spring 1977) 40–54 [esp. 53–4 on Yeats and Gnosticism].

——, "W. B. Yeats's Dramatic Imagination" [Review Essay on Andrew Parkin's *The Dramatic Imagination of W. B. Yeats* and George Mills Harper & Walter Kelly Hood (eds) *A Critical Edition of Yeats's A Vision (1925)*] *Themes in Drama*, ed. James Redmond, iii (1981) 203–21.

Griffiths, A. R. G., "Finland, Norway and the Easter Rising", in *Irish Culture and Nationalism 1750–1950*, ed. Oliver MacDonagh, W. F. Mandle & Pauric Travers (London: Macmillan, 1983) 149–60.

Grünwald, Constance, "Yeats und die Versuchung des Ostens die Rolle der indischen transzendentalen Philosophie in Yeats' Dichtung seit seiner Begegnung mit Shri Purohit Swami, 1931" (Dis. München, 1979).

Harmon, Maurice, "Irish Poetry after Yeats", *Études Irlandaises*, n.s. ii, 1977, 45–62.

——, "Yeats et la jeune poésie irlandaise" in *L'Herne* (op. cit.) 425–40.

Harper, George Mills, " 'Out of a Medium's Mouth': Yeats's 'Theory of Transference' and Keats's 'Ode to a Nightingale' ", *Yeats: An Annual of Critical and Textual Studies*, ed. Richard J. Finneran (Ithaca & London: Cornell) i, 1983.

Harris, Daniel A., "The 'Figured Page': Dramatic Epistle in Browning and Yeats", *Yeats Annual No. 1* (1982) 133–94.

Heaney, Seamus, "A Tale of Two Islands: Reflections on the Irish Literary Revival", *Irish Studies*, i, 1980, 1–20.

Hegde, Narayan, "Yeats, India and Long Island", *The Recorder*, xl (1980), 86–93.

Heine, Elisabeth, " 'W. B. Yeats's Map in his own Hand' ", *Biography*, (Hawaii) i:3 Summer 1978, 37–50.

Hirschberg, Stuart, *Myth in the Poetry of Ted Hughes: a Guide to the Poems* (Dublin: Wolfhound, 1981).

Hönninghausen, Lothar, "Konservative Kulturkritik und Literaturtheorie zwischen den Weltkriegen: Yeats und Eliot", in Paul Goetsch and Heinz-Joachim Müllenbrock (eds), *Englische Literatur und*

Politik im 20. Jahrhundert (Wiesbaden: Athenaion, 1981) 95–110.

Ionkis, Greta, *Aesthetical Search of English Poets, 1910–1930* (Kishinev: 1979).

——, "Conception of History and its Application in the Poetry of W. B. Yeats", in *The Binding Thread of Times: Problems of Philosophy of History in the Works of Foreign Writers of the 17th-20th Centuries* (Kishinev, 1981) pp. 118–33.

Isato, Matsutoshi, "Yeats and the Dream of Tradition" in *Bungaku Ronshu* xxx (Aichi Prefectural University, 1981).

Izubuchi, Hisoshi, "Faulkner and Yeats: An Essay", *William Faulkner: Materials, Studies and Criticism*, iv: 1 (Dec. 1981) 1–16.

Jacquet, Claude, "Joyce" in *L'Herne* (op. cit.) 412–24.

Jeffares, A. Norman, *Anglo-Irish Literature* (London: Macmillan; Dublin: Gill & Macmillan; N.Y.: Schocken, 1982).

Jordan, John, "Austin Clarke, Theodore de Banville and Yeats" in *Poetry Ireland*, xvi, 3–6.

Kazmi, S. N. R., "Poetry and Politics: A Case Study of W. B. Yeats", *Studies in Anglo-Irish Literature*, ed. Heinz Kosok, (Bonn: Bouvier, 1982) 198–204.

Keane, Patrick J., "The Human Entrails and the Starry Heavens: Some Instances of Visual Art as Patterns for Yeats's Mingling of Heaven and Earth", *Bulletin of Research in the Humanities*, lxxxiv:3 (Autumn 1982) 366–91.

Kenner, Hugh, *A Colder Eye: The Modern Irish Writers* (N.Y.: Knopf; London: Allen Lane, 1983). [Review by Michael Mason, in "Watching for the Outsiders", *TLS*, 30 Sept. 1983, 1039.]

Khorolsky, V., "Symbolism of W. B. Yeats", in *Problems of Method and Genre in Foreign Literature* (Moscow) vi, 1981, 146–59.

——, "Traditions of English Romanticism in the World Views and Creative Method of W. B. Yeats", in *Transitional Aesthetic Phenomena in the Literary Process of the 18th-20th Centuries* (Moscow) 1981, 125–40.

——, "Yeats and Irish Folklore" in *Research Papers of Tumen University*, xxix, 1976, 49–65.

Kiely, Robert, "The Metaphysics behind

Yeats's Aesthetics", *Anglo-Irish Studies*, III, 1977, 19–34.

Kitadi, Sachiyo, "Yeats's View of Apocalypse", in *Bulletin of the Yeats Society of Japan*, XI, Nov. 1980.

Kline, Gloria, *The Last Courtly Lover: Yeats and the Idea of Woman* (Ann Arbor: UMI Research Press, 1983).

Kobayashi, Manji, "Another Reading of Yeats's Poetry", in *Bulletin of the Yeats Society of Japan* X, Nov. 1979.

Kobori, Ryuji, "On 'This or That' in Yeats", *Bulletin of the Yeats Society of Japan*, XI, (Nov. 1980).

Krajewska, Wanda, *William Butler Yeats* (Warsaw: Wiedza Poidszechna, 1978). Intro. profile, but n.b. 374–8 on "Yeats W. Polsce".

Krause, David, *The Profane Book of Irish Comedy* (Ithaca & London: Cornell University Press, 1982).

Kuch, Peter, "Mananaan Mac Lir as Monoglot-George Russell and the Irish Language", *Crane Bag*, V:2 (1981) 49–58.

Kusake, Ryuhei, "On Yeats's Interpretation of 'The Mental Traveller' ", *Jinbunkagaku Kenkyu*, XV: 2, (Momoyama Gakuin University, Dec. 1979).

Lahey-Dolega, Christine, "Brief Observations on the Life and Work of William Sharp (Fiona MacLeod)", *Ball State University Forum*, XXI:4 (Autumn 1980) 18–26.

Lenoski, Daniel S., "The Symbolism of Sound in W. B. Yeats: an Explanation", *Études Irlandaises*, n.s. III, 1978, 47–55.

——, "W. B. Yeats: God and Imagination", *English Studies in Canada*, VI:1 (Spring 1980) 84–93.

Levine, Herbert J., *Yeats's Daimonic Renewal* (Ann Arbor: UMI Research Press, 1983).

——, "Yeats's Ruskinian Byzantium", *Yeats Annual No. 2* (1983) 25–34.

Lipking, Lawrence, *The Life of the Poet: Beginning and Ending Poetic Careers* (Chicago & London: University of Chicago Press, 1981).

Lowery, Robert G., (ed.) *Essays on Sean O'Casey's Autobiographies*, (London: Macmillan, 1981).

McDiarmid, Lucy, "The Living Voice in the Thirties: Yeats, Eliot, Auden", *Yearbook of English Studies*, XI, (1981) 161–77.

MacDonagh, Oliver, *States of Mind: a Study of Anglo-Irish Conflict 1780–1980* (London: Allen & Unwin, 1983).

MacDonogh, Caroline, "Notes on MacDonagh and Yeats", *Gaéliana*, No. 4, 1982, 205–15.

——, "La notion de chant chez Yeats", *L'Herne* (op. cit.), 275–80.

McHugh, Roger & Harmon, Maurice, *Short History of Anglo-Irish Literature, From the Earliest Times to the Present* (Dublin: Wolfhound; Totowa, N.J.: Barnes & Noble, 1982).

MacInnes, Mairi, "Marvell in Yorkshire, Yeats in Sligo", *PN Review* 28, IX, 2, 29–33.

Magill, Frank N., (ed.) *English Literature: Romanticism to 1945* (Pasadena; Salem, 1981).

Mann, A. T., *The Round Art: The Astrology of Time and Space* (Cheltenham: Paper Tiger, 1979).

Marcus, Phillip L., "Incarnation in 'Middle Yeats' ", *Yeats Annual No. 1* (1982) 68–81.

Mendelson, Edward, *Early Auden* (London: Faber, 1981).

Metscher, Thomas, "Zur Entwicklung der bürgerlich en und socialistischen Nationalliteratur in Irland" in Dorothea Siegmund-Schultz (ed.) *Irland Gesellschaft und Kultur* (Halle, 1976).

Miller, J. Hillis, "The Two Allegories", *Allegory, Myth, and Symbol*, ed. Morton W. Bloomfield (Cambridge, Mass.: Harvard University Press, 1981), 355–70.

Morrison, Blake, *The Movement: English Poetry and Fiction of the 1950's* (London: Oxford University Press, 1980).

Naito, Shiro, "Hearn and Yeats: On 'A Bronze Head' ", in *Otani Gakuho*, LIX:3 (Otani University, 1979).

——, "The Mask of Yeats's Ballads: Narrative and Poetry", in *Festschrift for Prof. Suga and Prof. Ogoshi* (Kyoto: Apollonsha, 1980).

Norstedt, Johann, A., *Thomas MacDonagh: A Critical Biography* (Charlottesville: University Press of Virginia, 1980).

O'Brien, Conor Cruise, "What Rough Beast?" *Observer*, 19 July 1981, 28.

O'Hehir, Brendan, "Kickshaws and Wheelchairs: Yeats and the Irish Language", *Yeats: An Annual of Critical and Textual Studies*, ed. Richard J. Finneran (Ithaca & London: Cornell) I, 1983.

Otto, Erwin, "Tendenzen und Formen zeitgenössischer irischer Lyrik" in *Einführung in die zeitgenössische irische Literatur*, ed., J. Kornelius, E. Otto & G. Stratmann (Heidelberg, 1980).

Oura, Yukio, "Women around Yeats (2)", *Insight*, 13 (Notre-Dame Women's College, Mar. 1981).

Paley, Morton, D., "John Trivett Nettleship and the 'Blake Drawings' " *Blake: An Illustrated Quarterly*, XIV:4 (Spring 1981), 185–94.

Peterson, Richard F., "The Crane and the Swan: Lennox Robinson and W. B. Yeats", *Journal of Irish Literature*, IX:1 (Jan. 1980) 69–76.

——, *William Butler Yeats* (Boston: Twayne's English Authors, 1982).

——, and Phillips, Gary, "W. B. Yeats and Norreys Connell", *Yeats Annual No. 2* (1983) 46–58.

Picchi, Fernando, '*Esoterismo e magia nelle poesie di W. B. Yeats* (Firenze: Nordini Editore, 1977).

Powell, Grosvenor E., "Yeats's Second Vision: Berkeley, Coleridge, and the Correspondence with Sturge Moore", *Modern Language Review*, LXXVI:2 (Apr. 1981) 273–90.

Radford, Colin, and Sally Minogue, *The Nature of Criticism* (Brighton: Harvester Press, 1981).

Raine, Kathleen, "Ben Bulben fixe le décor", *L'Herne* (op. cit.) 44–59.

——, "Hades enveloppé de nuages", ibid., 240–61.

Reiman, Donald H., "Wordsworth, Shelley, and the Romantic Inheritance", *Romanticism Past and Present*, V:2 (1981) 1–22.

Rosenthal, M. L. & Sally M. Gall, *The Modern Poetic Sequence: the Genius of Modern Poetry* (N.Y.: Oxford University Press, 1983).

Sano, Tetsuro, "Current Yeats Studies in Japan" *The Rising Generation*, Mar. 1981.

——, "Current Yeats Studies Abroad", *Eibungaku Kenkyu*, 56, The English Literary Society of Japan (Sept. 1979).

——, "A Myth of a Woman: Yeats and Maud Gonne" *Josei to Eibeibungaku*, (Tokyo: Kenkyusha, 1980).

Sasaki, Mitsuru, "Preparation for Something that Never Happens: Yeats in his Middle Period", *Eibungakai-shi*, 21, Niigata University (Mar. 1982).

Schuchard, Ronald, "The Minstrel in the Theatre: Arnold, Chaucer, and Yeats's New Spiritual Democracy", *Yeats Annual No. 2* (1983) 3–24.

Sexton, Máire, "W. B. Yeats, Wilfred Owen and Sean O'Casey", *Studies*, LXX (Spring 1981) 88–95.

Shaw, Robert B., "Farewells to Poetry", *Yale Review*, LXX:2 (Jan. 1981) 187–205.

Smith, Stan, "Historians and Magicians: Ireland Between Fantasy and History" in *Literature and the Changing Ireland* ed. Peter Connolly (Gerrards Cross: Colin Smythe; Totowa, N.J.: Barnes & Noble 1982). [See esp. 144–150.]

Steinman, Michael A., "Yeats's Parnell: Sources of his Myth", *Éire-Ireland* XVIII:1 (Spring 1983) 46–60.

Stewart, James, "A Yeats Allusion", *Neuphilologische Mittellungen*, LXXXII:2 (1981) 214–16.

Suzuki, Hiroshi, "W. B. Yeats and the Gyre", *Kyoyo Shogaku Kenkyu*, 61, 1980.

Thomas, Edward, *A Language not to be Betrayed: Selected Prose of E. T.*, ed. Edna Longley (Manchester: Carcanet, 1981).

Thuente, Mary Helen, "W. B. Yeats and Celtic Ireland, 1885–1900", *Anglo-Irish Studies*, IV (1979) 91–104.

Timm, Eitel Friedrich, *William Butler Yeats und Friedrich Nietzsche* Würzburger wissenschaftliche Schriften, Reihe Literaturwissenschaft, 2 (Würzburg: Konigshausen & Neumann, 1980).

Toliver, Harold E., *The Past that Poets Make* (Cambridge, Mass.: Harvard University Press, 1981).

Ussher, Arland, *The Juggler: Selections from a Journal-being the Second Series of From a Dark Lantern, with a memoir by Mervyn Wall* (Mountrath: Dolmen, 1982).

Watanabe, Hisayoshi, "On Yeats's 'Terrible Beauty' " *Eibungaku Kenkyu*, 58, 2 [The English Literary Society of Japan, (Dec. 1981)].

——, "Poetry and Politics, or Solitude and Multitude in W. B. Yeats" *Eibungaku Hyoron*, 46, Kyoto University (Mar. 1982).

——, *Yeats* (Kyoto: Yamaguchi Shoten, Jan. 1982).

Ward, J. P., *Poetry and the Sociological Idea* (Brighton: Harvester Press, 1981).

Warner, Alan, *A Guide to Anglo-Irish Litera-ture* (Dublin: Gill & Macmillan, 1981).

Warner, Francis, "The Poetry of James Joyce" in *James Joyce: An International Perspective, Centenary Essays*, ed. Suheil Bushrui and Bernard Benstock (Gerrards Cross: Colin Smythe; Totowa, N.J.: Barnes and Noble, 1982) 115–27.

Watkins, Vernon, *Yeats and Owen: Two Essays* (Frome: Hunting Raven Press 1981). [Contains "The Poetry of W. B. Yeats" and "War and Poetry: the Reactions of Owen and Yeats".]

Wilson, Bruce M., " 'From Mirror after Mirror': Yeats and Eastern Thought", *Comparative Literature*, XXXIV:1 (Winter 1982) 28–46.

Windsor, Gerard, "Grafting Ireland onto Australia; some Literary Attempts" in *Irish Culture and Nationalism, 1750–1950*, ed. Oliver MacDonagh, W. F. Mandle & Pauric Travers (London: Macmillan, 1983) 194–211.

Wintle, Justin (ed.) *Makers of Nineteenth Century Culture, 1800–1914* (London & Boston, Routledge & Kegan Paul, 1982). (Yeats quoted *passim*.)

Wirrer, Jan, *Literatursoziologie, linguistische poetik: zur diskussion zwischen linguistik und literaturwissenschaft anhand zweier texte von W. B. Yeats* (München: Bayerische Schulbuch-Verlag, 1975). (On "The Countess Cathleen" and "Leda and the Swan".)

D. ON THE POEMS

Allen, James Lovic, "House, Horse and Hound: Emblems of Nobility in Yeats's 'The Curse of Cromwell' ", *Yeats Eliot Review*, VII:1 & 2 (1982) 69–77.

——, " 'Imitate him if you dare': Relations between the Epitaphs of Swift and Yeats", *Studies*, LXX (Summer/Autumn 1981) 177–96.

——, *Yeats's Epitaph: a Key to Symbolic Unity in His Life and Work* (Washington, D.C.: University Press of America, 1982).

Armstrong, Isobel, *Language as Living Form in Nineteenth Century Poetry* (Brighton: Harvester, 1982). (On "Among School Children", 210–18.)

Bagchee, Shyamal, "Sexual Passion and Nationalism *in extremis* in Yeats's 'The Statues' " *Canadian Journal of Irish Studies*, VI:2 (Dec. 1980) 18–33.

Bornstein, George, " 'Those Dancing Days are Gone' and Pound's 'Canto 23' ", *Yeats Annual No. 2*, (1983) 93–5.

Bötheroyd, Paul F., "The Years of the Travellers: Tinkers, Tramps and Travellers in Early Twentieth Century Irish Drama and Society", in *Studies in Anglo-Irish Literature* ed. Heinz Kosok (Bonn: Bouvier, 1982) 167–75.

Buchta, Norbert K., *Rezeption und ästhetische Verarbeitung romantischer Poetologie im lyrischen Werk William Butler Yeats* Forum Academicum Literaturwissenschaft, 52

(Königstein/Taunus: Athenäum, Hain, Scriptor, Hanstein, 1982).

Buckley, Vincent, "Yeats and 'Meditations' " in B. McFarlane (ed.) *Viewpoints 80* (Melbourne: Sorrett, 1980) 159–64.

Burns, Graham, "Yeats's City of Unageing Intellect: 'Sailing to Byzantium' " in B. MacFarlane *Viewpoints, 81* (Melbourne: Sorrett, 1981) 62–8.

Butler, Gerald, "Latent Content in 'Leda and the Swan' by W. B. Yeats", *Recovering Literature*, IX (1981) 30–41.

Chuto, Jacques, "Yeats's 'A Dialogue of Self and Soul' " *Études Irlandaises* III (1974) 33–7.

Clark, David R., Yeats's Fisherman & Samuel Ferguson's 'Willy Gilliland' " *Irish Studies*, I (1980) 73–83.

Dougherty, Adeline, " 'Traditional Metres' and 'Passionate Syntax' in the Verse of William Butler Yeats", *Language and Style* XIV:3 (Summer 1981) 216–25.

Dyson, A. E., *Yeats, Eliot and R. S. Thomas: Riding the Echo* (London: Macmillan; Atlantic Highlands, N.J.: Humanities, 1981).

Engelberg, Edward, "Absence and Presence in Yeats's Poetry", *Yeats Annual No. 1* (1982) 48–67.

Epstein, Edmund L., "Non-restrictive Modifiers: Poetic Features of Language" in *Studies in English Linguistics for Randolph Quirk*, eds Sidney Greenbaum, Geoffrey Leech and Jan Svartvik (London: Longmans, 1980) 221–34.

Erzgräber, Willi, "W. B. Yeats als Lyriker" in *Studien zur Englischen Philologie: Edgar Mertner zum 70 Geburtsstag* eds Herbert Mainusch and Dietrich Rolle (Frankfurt, Bern, Cirencester: Lang, 1979) 167–88.

Ezawa, Sokushin, "A Study of W. B. Yeats's Love Poems with Particular Reference to his Early and Middle Poems", *Bulletin of Kyushu University*, XVI, 1981.

Finneran, Richard J., *Editing Yeats's Poems* (London: Macmillan; N.Y.: St. Martins, 1983).

Fletcher, Ian, " 'Leda and the Swan' as Iconic Poem", *Yeats Annual No. 1* (1982) 82–113.

Frechet, René, "Sur Trois Poèmes de Yeats", *L'Herne* (op. cit.) 39–43.

Fujimoto, Reiji, "The Process of Mythologizing in the Poetry of W. B. Yeats: the Perfection of the Heroic Figures in the Easter Rising", *Gengobunka Kenkyu*, 5 (Hiroshima University, 1979).

——, "On the Swan Image of W. B. Yeats" in *Festschrift for Prof. H. Yoshida* (Tokyo: Shinozaki, 1980).

——, "W. B. Yeats's 'A Man Young and Old': The Wild Regrets for Youth and Love" *Hiroshima Studies in English Language and Literature*, XXVI (1981) 46–58.

Furomoto, Taketoshi, "A Dialogue of Self and Soul" *Kobe Miscellany*, XI (Kobe University, 1982).

Garab, Arra M., "Two American Sources of W. B. Yeats's 'The Second Coming' ", *Yeats Eliot Review*, VII:1 & 2 (1982) 117–19.

Genet, Jacqueline, "La Conception de l'Histoire dans la Poésie de W. B. Yeats", *Études Irlandaises*, n.s. I, 1976, 63–83.

——, "Du Mythe agraire de J. G. Frazer à la poésie de W. B. Yeats ou la recréation des mythes de Dionysos d'Attis" in Amalric, J.-C., (ed.) *Studies in Edwardian and Anglo-Irish Drama*, (9 & 10 of *Cahiers Victoriens et Edouardiens*, [Montpellier] Oct. 1979) 219–39.

Geniusiene, I., "Some traits of the Development of W. B. Yeats's Poetic

Diction", *Scientific Transactions of Tartu University*, 426 (Research Papers in Roman and German Philology VII: 1977, 14–31).

Ghiselin, Brewster, "The Tree of Knowledge, the Tree of Life", *Western Humanities Review*, 35:4 (Winter 1981) 297–303.

Grennan, Eamon, "Mastery and Beyond: Speech and Silence in Yeats's 'The Tower' ", *Études Irlandaises*, n.s. VII (Dec. 1982) 55–70.

Grove, Elisabeth, "Yeats and the Artist: 'Sailing to Byzantium' " in B. McFarlane (ed.) *Viewpoints 78* (Melbourne: Sorrett, 1978) 70–5.

Hassett, Joseph M., "The Meaning of the 'Cold Eye' in Yeats's Epitaph", *Éire–Ireland*, XVIII:1 (Spring 1983) 61–79.

Hirsch, Edward, " 'And I myself created Hanrahan': Yeats, Folklore, and Fiction", *ELH* (Winter 1981) 880–93.

——, "Yeats's Apocalyptic Horsemen", *Irish Renaissance Annual*, III (1982) 71–92.

——, "Yeats's 'Under Ben Bulben' ", *Explicator*, XXXIX:4 (Summer 1981) 21.

Hirschberg, Stuart, "The Shaping Role of *A Vision* on W. B. Yeats's 'The Double Vision of Michael Robartes' ", *Studies*, LXVIII (Spring 1979) 109–13.

——, " 'Under Ben Bulben': Art as Looking Glass", *Studies*, LXX (Winter 1982) 399–404.

Isato, Matsutoshi, "The 'Stone' of 'Easter 1916': the Revival of Irish Spirit", *Bungaku Hyoron*, XIX (Dec. 1982).

Jaynes, Joseph T., "A Search for Trends in the Poetic Style of W. B. Yeats", *Association for Library and Linguistic Computing Journal*, I:1 (Summer 1980) 11–15.

Jeffares, A. Norman, *A New Commentary on the Poems of Yeats* (London: Macmillan; Atlantic Highlands, N.J.: Humanities, 1983).

Joseph, Christiane, "Les Voyages d'Usheen", *L'Herne* (op. cit.) 129–45.

Joubert, J., "On setting Yeats's 'Byzantium' ", *Music Time*, 123: 1670 (1982) 249–50.

Kato, Fumihiko, "Reading 'The Dolls' the Sacrilegious Way" *Bulletin of the Yeats Society of Japan*, XI (Nov. 1980).

——, " 'Among School Children', or 'A Daydream of a School Inspector' " in

Eibungaku Ronso, xxv (Kyoto Women's College, 1981).

Khorolsky, V., "The Later Lyrics of W. B. Yeats: Subjects, Conflicts, Style", *The Problems of Creative Method* (Tumen, 1979) 110–19.

——, "The Poetry of W. B. Yeats in Soviet and Foreign Criticism", *Research Papers of Tumen' University*, LIII (1977) 56–71.

——, "Political Lyrics of W. B. Yeats in the First Decade of the Twentieth Century", *Problems, Method and Genre in Foreign Literature* (Moscow, 1978) 71–8.

Kishel, Joseph, "Yeats's Elegies," *Yeats Eliot Review*, VII:1 & 2 1982, 78–90.

Levine, Herbert J., "Freeing the Swans: Yeats's Exorcism of Maud Gonne", *ELH*, XLVIII:2, 411–26, Summer 1981.

Lucy, Sean, "Vers la maturité" in *L'Herne* (op. cit.) 146–58.

McFarland, Thomas, *Romanticism and the Forms of Ruin: Wordsworth, Coleridge, and modalities of fragmentation* (Princeton: Princeton University Press, 1981). ["The Wild Swans at Coole" discussed 282–3, "Sailing to Byzantium" discussed 414–16.]

Mallon, Thomas, " 'All Souls' Night': Yeats, Sassoon and the Dead", *Irish Studies*, I (1980) 85–99.

Marken, Ronald, " 'The Strange heart beating': Prosodic Considerations of Yeats's Poetry", *Studies in Anglo-Irish Literature*, ed Heinz Kosok (Bonn: Bouvier, 1982) 246–53.

——, "Yeats's 'Death': A Reading", *Irish Univeristy Review*, x:2 (Autumn 1980) 244–50.

Matsuda, Seishi, " 'The Wild Old Wicked Man': the Dream of the Beggar-Wanderer in Yeats's Poetry", *Kenkyu Ronso*, xv (Feb. 1982).

Meir, Colin, "À la recherche d'un language naturel" in *L'Herne* (op. cit.) 262–74.

——, "Narrative Verse in Yeats, Clarke and Kavanagh", *Gaéliana*, III (1981) 101–15

Miller, J. Hillis, "The Rewording Shell: Natural Image and Symbolic Emblem in Yeats's Early Poetry", *Poetic Knowledge, Circumference and Centre, Papers from the Wuppertal Symposium, 1978*, eds Joseph T. Swann & Roland Hagenbüchle. [Schriftenreihe Literaturwissenschaft der

Gesamthochshule Wuppertal, XVIII (Bonn: Bouvier, 1980) 75–86.]

Miura, Ikuyo, " 'Island' and 'Water' ", in *Bulletin of the Yeats Society of Japan*, x (Nov. 1979).

Miyauchi, Hiromu, "On the Later Poems of Yeats", in *The Rising Generation* (Oct. 1982).

——, "Rereading 'Among School Children' ", *Jinbun Kenkyu* (Osaka City University, 1979) 31–7.

Molnár, Ferenc A., "The Legend of Ferencz Rényi, a Hungarian Hero of Freedom, in English, Irish and Polish Literature", *Acta Litteraria Academiae Scientiarum Hungaricae*, XXI:1–2 (1979) 143–60.

Munch-Pedersen, Olé, "Some Aspects of the Rewriting of W. B. Yeats's 'Red Hanrahan's Song About Ireland' ", *Orbis Litterarum*, XXXVI:2 (1981) 155–72.

Myles, Ashley E., *Theatre of Aristocracy* (Salzburg: Institut für Anglistik und Amerikanistik, 1981).

Oda, Chie, "A Study of the Swan Symbol in the Poetry of W. B. Yeats", *Bulletin of the Yeats Society of Japan*, XII (Oct. 1981).

O'Donnell, William H., "The Art of Yeats's 'Lapis Lazuli' ", *Massachusetts Review*, XXIII:2 (Summer 1982) 353–67.

Okubo, Naoki, "Yeats's Poetry and the Flavour of Nō", *Hikakubungaku Kenkyu*, 35 (Todai Hikakubungaku-kai) Aug. 1975.

Pall, Santosh, "The Soul must Dance: Yeats's 'Byzantium' ", *Temenos, A Review devoted to the Arts of the Imagination*, II (1982) 25–44.

Parkin, Andrew, "Dramatic Elements in the Poetry of W. B. Yeats" *Anglo-Irish Studies*, II (1976) 109–28.

Pearce, Donald, "Ghostly Paradigms of Things in 'Among School Children' " *Yeats Eliot Review*, VII:1 & 2 (1982) 51–68.

Peskin, S. G., "W. B. Yeats & 'Adam's Curse' ", *Unisa English Studies* XIX:1 (Apr. 1981) 11–17.

Popot, Raymonde, "Lectures d'une poème de Yeats: 'The Two Trees' ", *Études Irlandaises* n.s. IV (1979) 67–88.

——, "Du refuge à l'envoi" in *L'Herne* (op. cit.) 189–239.

Pound, Ezra, "Yeats, 1914" in *L'Herne* (op. cit.) 408–11.

Pruitt, Virginia, "Yeats: A Major Theme

in a 'Minor' Poem", *Colby Library Quarterly*, xviii:4 (Dec. 1981) 197–200.

Pruitt, Virginia, "Return from Byzantium: W. B. Yeats and 'The Tower' " *ELH*, xlvii:1 (Spring 1980) 149–57.

Putzel, Steven D., "The Black Pig: Yeats's Apocalyptic Beast", *Eire–Ireland*, xvii:3 (Autumn 1982) 86–102.

Rajan, Tillottama, "The Romantic Backgrounds of Yeats's Use of Dante in 'Ego Dominus Tuus' " *Yeats Eliot Review*, vii:1 & 2 (1982) 120–2.

Rau-Guntermann, Mechthild, "Die Einheit von W. B. Yeats's 'The Tower' (1928): Zu einer Poetik des lyrischen Zyklus im Symbolismus" (Diss. Köln, 1974).

Rogers, Robert, *Metaphor, a Psychoanalytic View* (Berkeley and London: University of California Press, 1978). (Analysis of 'A Stick of Incense', 73–5.)

Schneider, Ulrich, "Yeats's Byzanz-Bild im Kontext seiner Zeit", *Anglia*, xcv (1977) 426–49.

Schricker, Gale C., *A New Species of Man: The Poetic Persona of W. B. Yeats* (Lewisburg: Bucknell University Press; London and Toronto: Associated University Presses, 1983).

Smith, Stan, "Writing a Will: Yeats's Ancestral Voices in 'The Tower' and 'Meditations in Time of Civil War' ", *Irish University Review*, xiii:1 (Spring 1983) 14–37.

Swann, Joseph T., " 'Where all the ladders start': Language and Experience in Yeats's Later Poetry", *Studies in Anglo-Irish Literature* ed Heinz Kosok (Bonn: Bouvier, 1982) 236–45.

Thomson, P., *George Sand and the Victorians* (London: Macmillan, 1977). [Yeats and

Sand, esp. on 'Meditations in Time of Civil War', 208–16.]

Thornton, R. K. R., *The Decadent Dilemma* (London: Edward Arnold, 1983). [Chapter 7; "W. B. Yeats".]

Thurley, Geoffrey, *The Turbulent Dream: Passion and Politics in the Poetry of W. B. Yeats* (St Lucia: University of Queensland Press, 1983).

Tsuji, Shozo, "On the Last Poem of Yeats", in *Festschrift for Professor Sugo and Professor Ogoshi* (Kyoto: Appollon-sha, 1980).

——, "Yeats in the *New Poems*: a Note on 'The Municipal Gallery Revisited' ", in *Bulletin of Kobe Shosen University* xxx: (July 1981).

Walcutt, Charles C., "Yeats's 'Crazy Jane and Jack the Journeyman' ", *Explicator*, xxxix:3 (Spring 1981) 40–1.

Welch, Robert, "Yeats's Crazy Jane Poems and Gaelic Love Song", *Studies in Anglo-Irish Literature*, ed. Heinz Kosok (Bonn: Bouvier, 1982) 227–35.

Wightman, Jennifer, "Yeats: Rough Passage to Byzantium" in B. McFarlane, (ed.) *Viewpoint 82* (Melbourne: Sorrett, 1982) 46–50.

Wright, George T., "Yeats's Expressive Style", *Yeats Eliot Review*, vii:1 & 2 (1982) 109–16.

Yasuda, Yoko, "Yeats's 'Old Man's Frenzy': His Last Struggle to Justify Himself", *Bulletin of the Yeats Society of Japan* (Nov. 1980).

Yoshino, Masaaki, "William B. Yeats and Maud Gonne – Revision of *The Wild Swans at Coole*" *Studies in English Language and Literature*, xxxiii (Jan. 1983) 15–39.

Zimmerman, Lee, "Singing amid Uncertainty: Yeats's Closing Questions", *Yeats Annual No. 2* (1983) 35–45.

E. THE PLAYS

Bushrui, Suheil, "Le poéte comme héros", *L'Herne*, (op. cit.), 318–35.

Cribb, T. J., Review of *Irish Myth and the Japanese Noh*, by Richard Taylor, *Anglo-Irish Studies*, iii: 1977, 123–5.

Duffy, William J., Jr., "Deirdre, Yeats and Synge" *Festschift José Cid Pérez*, ed.

Alberto Gutiérrez de la Solana and Elio Alba Buffill (N.Y.: Senda Nueva, 1981) 181–4.

Fitzsimons, Christopher, *The Irish Theatre*, (London: Thames & Hudson, 1983). [Includes "An Ancient Idealism 1898–1939: The Irish Literary Theatre, the National Theatre Society, Augusta Gregory, Edward Martyn, William Butler Yeats and others".]

Funakura, Masanori, " 'At the Hawk's Well': Drama of the Subconscious" in *Littera*, I, Okayama University (Mar. 1981).

Genet, Jacqueline, "Le Chat et La Lune: kyogen philosophique", *L'Herne*, (op. cit.) 365–78.

Halbritter, Rudolf, *Konzeptionsformen des modernen Anglo-Amerikanischen Kurzdramas: Dargestellt an Stücken von W. B. Yeats, Thornton Wilder und Harold Pinter*, Palaestra, 263 (Goettingen: Vandenhoeck & Ruprecht, 1975).

Hasegawa, Toshimitsu, "Yeats and the Noh: The Supernatural in Drama", *Eibungaku Hyoron* XLII, Kyoto University (Feb. 1980).

——, "Yeats in Irish Theatres", *Bulletin of the Yeats Society of Japan*, XII (Oct. 1981).

Hirata, Yashushi, " 'On Baile's Strand' " *Bulletin of Tachibana Women's College*, VII, (1979).

Hyakunari, Akira, "Yeats and Noh: a Memorandum on 'The Dreaming of the Bones' ", *Gaikokugo-bu Ronshu*, Komazawa University, (Mar. 1979).

Jeffares, A. Norman, "Three Plays by W. B. Yeats: 'The Land of Heart's Desire' (1894), 'The Words upon the Window Pane' (1930), 'The Herne's Egg' (1938)", *Gaeliana*, IV (1982) 57–74.

Jochum, Klaus Peter, "William Butler Yeats: 'The Land of Heart's Desire' " in *Das Englische Drama im. 18. und 19. Jahrhundert* ed Heinz Kosok (Berlin: Erich Schmidt, 1976) 308–17.

Kelly, John S., Review of *Yeats and the Theatre* eds O'Driscoll & Reynolds, *Anglo-Irish Studies*, III: 1977, 110–12. [same issue, 113–15, review by J. S. K. of T. R. Henn's *Last Essays*.]

Knox, David Blake, "Ideological Tactics in Yeats's Early Drama", *Anglo-Irish Studies*, I: 1975, 83–96.

Krivina, Theresa, "The Metaphorical Image of Ireland in the Plays of William Butler Yeats", *The Unity and National Originality in the Literary Process of the World*, II (Leningrad: 1977) 114–20.

Loiseaux, Elisabeth Bergmann, " 'Separating Strangeness': From Painting to Sculpture in Yeats's Theatre", *Yeats: an Annual of Critical and Textual Studies*, ed. Richard J. Finneran, (Ithaca and London: Cornell) I (1983).

Mahony, Christina Hunt, "The Influence of John Todhunter on the Plays of W. B. Yeats", *Studies in Anglo-Irish Literature*, ed. Heinz Kosok (Bonn: Bouvier, 1982) 262–8.

Mahony, Robert, "Some Problems in Editing Anglo-Irish Texts", *Studies in Anglo-Irish Literature*, ed. Heinz Kosok (Bonn: Bouvier, 1982) 490–6.

Martin, Heather, "Of Flood and Fire: A Study of 'The Player Queen' ", *Canadian Journal of Irish Studies*, VII:1 (June 1981) 49–60.

Matsuyama, Akio, "Yeats's Dance Plays and Nogaku", *Eibungaku*, LIII (Mar. 1980).

——, "Yeats and Kyogen" *Bulletin of the Yeats Society of Japan*, XI (Nov. 1980).

Meir, Colin, "Yeats and the Language of Drama", *Gaéliana*, 3 (1981) 101–15.

Murray, Christopher, "Three Sketches by Jack B. Yeats of the Camden Street Theatre, 1902" *Prompts*, IV (Nov. 1982) 3–7.

Myles, Ashley E., *Theatre of Aristocracy* (Salzburg: Institut für Anglistik und Americanistik, 1981).

Okunishi, Yoko, " 'On Baile's Strand' ", *Kenkyu Ronshu*, XIV (Tezukayama Gakuin College, 1980).

O'Muirithe, Diarmaid, "There's Broth in the Pot", *Éigse*, XVIII:2 (1981) 305–8.

Ono, Mitsuko, "From 'The King of the Great Clock Tower' to 'A Full Moon in March': Dramatic Unity and Noh", *Bulletin of the Yeats Society of Japan*, XII (Oct. 1981).

Parkin, Andrew, "W. B. Yeats's Stage Diction", *Studies in Anglo-Irish Literature*, ed Heinz Kosok, (Bonn: Bouvier, 1982) 254–61.

——, "Women in the Plays of W. B. Yeats", *Canadian Journal of Irish Studies*, VIII:2 (1981) 38–57.

Patsch, Sylvia, " 'The Countess Cathleen': The Irish Legend of Sin, Redemption, and Vicarious Self-Sacrifice as Interpreted by W. B. Yeats, Werner Egk and Oskar Kokoschka": *Proceedings of the IXth Congress of the International Comparative Literature Association*, ed. Zoran Konstantinovic (Innsbruck: 1981) III, 269–72.

Polyudova, T., "The Concept of Poetic Drama in the Work of W. B. Yeats" *Literary Theory and Creative Work* (Moscow: 1979) 117–34.

———, "The Concept of Tragedy in the Works of W. B. Yeats", *The Tragic and Comical in Foreign Drama* (Perm': 1979) 14–32.

———, " 'On Baile's Strand' by W. B. Yeats: the Analysis of the Dramatic Composition and Genre Aspect of the Play", *Problems of Method and Genre in Foreign Literature* (Moscow: 1978) 54–70.

Smith, Peter Alderson, " 'The Countess Cathleen' and the Otherworld" *Éire-Ireland*, XVII:2 (Summer 1982) 141–6.

Styan, John L., *Modern Drama in Theory and Practice*, Cambridge: Cambridge University Press, 1981) [vols I & II esp.].

Tanigawa, Fuyuji, "The Speakers and the Listeners in the Last Song: a Note towards the Interpretation of 'The Death of Cuchulain' " *Core* (Doshisha University, Mar. 1982).

Thilliez, Christiane, "L'apprentissage du Théâtre", *L'Herne* (op. cit.) 74–92.

Vlasopolos, Anca, "Thematic Contexts in Four of Yeats's Plays", *Modern Drama*, XXIV:1 (1981) 67–72.

Watanabe, Hisayoshi, "Will to Power in W. B. Yeats: On his Play 'Calvary' ", *Eibungaku Hyoron*, XLII (Kyoto University, Feb. 1980).

———, "The Will to Suffering: Structure of Religiosity in W. B. Yeats: An Essay on 'Purgatory' ", *Eibungaku Hyoron*, XLIV (Kyoto University, Nov. 1980).

Worth, Katharine, "A Meeting Place of the Arts", *TLS* (23 Oct. 1981) 1235.

F. THE PROSE

Dufour, Michel, "Le symbole de la Rose dans *La Rose Secrète* de W. B. Yeats", *Gaéliana*, III, 1981, 25–44.

Finneran, Richard J., "An omission in *The Secret Rose. Stories by W. B. Yeats: A Variorum Edition*", in Richard J. Finneran (ed.) *Yeats An Annual of Critical and Textual Studies*, I (Ithaca & London: Cornell, 1983).

Gould, Warwick, Review of *A Critical Edition of Yeats's "A Vision"* (1925), eds George Mills Harper & Walter Kelly Hood (London: Macmillan, 1978) in *Notes and Queries*, n.s. XXVIII: 5 (Oct. 1981) 458–60.

Henke, Suzette A., "Yeats's John Sherman: A Portal of Discovery", *Canadian Journal of Irish Studies*, VIII:1 (June 1982) 25–35.

Hirschberg, Stuart, "The 'Whirling Gyres' of History", *Studies*, Winter 1979, pp. 305–314.

Hood, Connie K., "The Remaking of *A Vision*", in Richard J. Finneran (ed.), *Yeats An Annual of Critical and Textual Studies*, I (Ithaca & London: Cornell, 1983).

Kearney, Richard, "Ces Images Magistrales" in *L'Herne* (op. cit.) 174–88.

Kinahan, Frank, "Armchair Folklore: Yeats and the Textual Sources of *Fairy and Folk Tales of the Irish Peasantry*" *Proceedings of the Royal Irish Academy* (Autumn 1983) 83, C, 10, 255–267

———, "Hour of Dawn: The Unity of Yeats's *The Celtic Twilight* (1893, 1902)", *Irish University Review*, XIII: 2, Autumn 1983, 189–205.

Kunne, Wolf, *Konzeption und Stil von Yeats' Autobiographies* (Bonn: Bouvier 1972).

Lickindorf, E. T., "W. B. Yeats's *Per Amica Silentia Lunae*" in *English Studies in Africa*, XXV, 39–53.

Neuman, Shirley, *Some One Myth: Yeats's Autobiographical Prose* (Mountrath: Dolmen; Atlantic Highlands: Humanities, 1982).

O'Donnell, William H., *A Guide to the Prose Fiction of W. B. Yeats* (Ann Arbor: UMI Research Press, 1983).

O'Hanlon, John, "Specific Use of Yeats's *A Vision* in *Finnegan's Wake*", *Wake Newslitter*, XVI:3 (June 1979) 35–44.

Osaka, Osamu, "Yeats: *John Sherman* reconsidered (2)", *Studies in English Language and Literature*, XXXIII (Jan. 1983) 41–63, [with English summary, 124–125].

Parkinson, Thomas, "This Extraordinary Book", [*A Vision*], *Yeats Annual No. 1*, (1982) 195–206.

Rankine-Galloway, Honora, "Mythologies" in *L'Herne* (op. cit.) 383–97.

Reilly, Kevin P., "Irish Literary Autobiography: The Goddesses that Poets dream of", *Éire-Ireland*, XVI:3 (Autumn 1981) 57–80.

G. REVIEWS OF WORKS BY YEATS

Boland, Eavan, "Yeats as Critic" [reviews *The Secret Rose, Stories by W. B. Yeats: A Variorum Edition* and Venod Sena, W. B. Yeats, *The Poet as Critic*], *Irish Times*, 8 May 1982, p. 12.

Clark, David R., "The Secrets of the Rose",

[reviews *The Secret Rose etc* (op. cit.)], *Irish Literary Supplement*, 1:1, (Spring, 1983) 13.

Martin, Augustine, Review of *The Secret Rose etc.* (op. cit.) and *The Celtic Twilight*, ed. Kathleen Raine, *Irish University Review*, XII:1, 1982, 113–16.

H. RECORDINGS, Etc.

Hirst, Désirée, and Mathews, Geoffrey, "W. B. Yeats, Poet of Love, Politics and the Other World" and "W. B. Yeats – Yeats's Interest in Politics, the Para-

normal and Old Age" on ELA 080 (Cassette with supplementary notes and bibliography), (London: Audio Learning, 1983).

I. POEMS, NOVELS, PLAYS AND PARODIES OF YEATS AND REFERENCES IN MORE POPULAR MATERIAL

Barker, George, "Ben Bulben Revisited", *PN Review*, XXXII:9:6, (1983), 39.

James, Clive, *Brilliant Creatures, a first novel* (London: Cape, 1983) 7, 282–3.

J. THE IRISH LITERARY AND DRAMATIC REVIVAL AND OTHER BACKGROUND MATERIAL

Bolton, G. C., "The Anglo-Irish and the Historians, 1830–1980" in *Irish Culture and Nationalism, 1750–1950*, eds Oliver MacDonagh, W. F. Mandle & Pauric Travers (London: Macmillan, 1983) 239–57.

Bowe, Nicola Gordon, *Harry Clarke: His Graphic Art* (Mountrath: Dolmen, Los Angeles: W. Keith Burns, 1983).

Clarke, Brenna Katz, *The Emergence of the Irish peasant play at the Abbey Theatre* (Michigan: Ann Arbor 1982).

Dalmasso, Michel, *Lady Gregory et La Renaissance Irlandaise* (Aix: University of Provence Presse, 1982).

Dalsimer, Adele M., "Players in the Western World: The Abbey Theatre's American Tours", *Eire-Ireland*, XVI 4, (Winter 1981) 75–92.

FitzGerald, Mary, "Some Problems of Nationality in the Early Irish Theatre", in *Studies in Anglo-Irish Literature*, ed Heinz Kosok (Bonn: Bouvier, 1982) 148–54.

—— *Selected Plays of Lady Gregory* (Gerrards Cross: Colin Smythe) 1983.

Flannery, James W. "A Financial Record of the Early Abbey Theatre", *Studies* (Autumn 1982) pp. 246–69).

Fletcher, Ian *The Collected Poems of Lionel Johnson*, 2nd & rev. edn (New York and London, Garland 1982).

Forster, John Wilson, "The Revival of Saga and Heroic Romance during the Irish Renaissance: the Ideology of Cultural Nationalism" in Heinz Kosok ed, *Studies in Anglo-Irish Literature* (Bonn: Bouvier, 1982) pp. 126–36.

——, "Yeats and the Folklore of the Irish Revival", *Eire–Ireland* (Summer 1982) 6–18.

Gabler, Hans Walter, "James Joyce and Ireland" in *Studies in Anglo-Irish Literature* ed Heinz Kosok (Bonn: Bouvier 1982) 74–9.

Gibbs, A. M., "Bernard Shaw's Other Island", in *Irish Culture and Nationalism 1750–1950*, eds Oliver MacDonagh, W. F. Mandle & Pauric Travers (London: Macmillan, 1983) 122–36.

Kelly, John S., "The Fall of Parnell and the Rise of Irish Literature: an Investigation" *Anglo-Irish Studies*, II, 1976, 1–23.

Kiberd, Declan, "The Perils of Nostalgia: A Critique of the Revival" in *Literature and the Changing Ireland* (Gerrards Cross: Colin Smythe, 1982) 1–24.

Kosok, Heinz, *Studies in Anglo Irish Literature* (Bonn: Bouvier, 1982).

Lyons, F. S. L., "Yeats and the Anglo-Irish Twilight" in *Irish Culture and Nationalism, 1750–1950*, eds Oliver MacDonagh, W. F. Mandle & Pauric Travers (London: Macmillan, 1983) 212–38.

Mandle & Pauric Travers (London: Association and Popular Culture, 1888–1924" in *Irish Culture and Nationalism, 1750–1950*, eds Oliver MacDonagh, W. F. Mandle & Pauric Travers (London: Macmillan 1983) 104–21.

Metscher, Priscilla, "Padraic Pearse and the Irish Cultural Revolution: The Significance of Pearse as an Irish Educationalist" in Heinz Kosok, (ed), *Studies in Anglo-Irish Literature* (Bonn: Bouvier, 1982) 137–47.

Metscher, Thomas, "The Genesis of Modern 'Anglo-Irish' Literature: Some Preliminary Remarks" in Dorothea Siegmund-Schulze (ed) *Ireland-Gesellschaft und Kultur II* (Halle/Salle, 1979) 86–102.

O'Brien, George, "In Search of an Audi-

ence: Notes on the Progress of Irish Literature, 1891–1941", *Yearbook of English Studies*, XI (1981) 117–26.

O'Driscoll, Robert, *The Celtic Consciousness* (Toronto: McClellan & Stewart; Dublin: Dolmen, 1981).

——, "The Aesthetic and Intellectual Foundations of the Celtic Literary Revival in Ireland" in Robert O'Driscoll (ed), *The Celtic Consciousness* (Toronto: McClelland & Stewart, Dublin: Dolmen, 1981) 401–25.

——, "Epilogue: The Celtic Hero" in Robert O'Driscoll (ed), *The Celtic Consciousness* (Toronto: McClelland & Stewart: Dublin: Dolment, 1981) 610–19.

Ó hAodha, Micheál, *Pictures at the Abbey: the Collection of the Irish National Theatre* (Mountrath: Dolmen, 1983).

Popot, Raymonde, "Mythes et Nationalisme: L'Example Irlandais" *Gaéliana*, 1980, 38–61.

Rafroidi, Patrick, Imagination and Revolution: the Cuchulain Myth" in *Irish Culture and Nationalism*, (eds) Oliver MacDonagh, W. F. Mandle & Pauric Travers, (London: Macmillan, 1983) 137–48.

——, "La Tradition Poetique" in *L'Herne* (op. cit.) 60–73.

Reynolds, Lorna, "The Irish Literary Revival: Preparation and Personalities" in Robert O'Driscoll (ed) *The Celtic Consciousness* (Toronto: McClelland & Stewart Dublin: Dolmen, 1981) 383–99.

Robinson, Lennox *Selected Plays*, intro. Christopher Murray (Gerrards Cross: Colin Smythe 1983). [Reviewed by Katharine Worth in "A Place in the Country", *TLS*, 2 Sept. 1983.]

Robinson, Paul N., "Synge's Aran Island Journals" in Heinz Kosok (ed), *Studies in Anglo-Irish Literature* (Bonn: Bouvier 1982) 161–6.

Saddlemyer, Ann, "James Joyce and the Irish Dramatic Movement" in *James Joyce: An International Perspective: Centenary Essays* (ed) S. H. Bushrui & Bernard Benstock (Gerrards Cross: Colin Smythe; Totowa, N.J.: Barnes & Noble, 1982) 190–212.

——, "National Drama and the Founding of Theatres" in *Theatrical Touring and Founding* (ed), L. W. Connolly (West-

322   *Yeats Annual No. 3*

wood, Conn.: Greenwood Press, 1982) 192–211.

Saddlemyer, Ann, "J. M. Synge on the Irish Dramatic Movement: an Unpublished Article", *Modern Drama*, XXIV (3 Sept. 1981), 276–81.

——, *Theatre Business: The Correspondence of the first Abbey Theatre Directors: William Bulter Yeats, Lady Gregory and J. M. Synge* (ed), Ann Saddlemyer (Gerrards Cross: Colin Smythe; Philadelphia: University of Pennsylvania Press, 1982).

[See review by Micheál OhAodha, "Plays and Controversies", *Irish Times* 5 June 1982, 12.]

St. Peter, Christine, "The Old Lady: In Principio" in *Denis Johnston: A Retrospective*, (ed) Joseph Ronsley (Gerrards Cross: Colin Smythe, 1981) 10–23.

Tapping, G. Craig, *Austin Clarke: A Study of His Writings* (Dublin: Academy Press, 1981).

Thuente, Mary Helen, "Lady Gregory and The 'Book of the People' ", *Éire–Ireland*, XV, Spring 1980, 86–99.

K. RECENT USEFUL REPRINTS

Ellmann, Richard, *The Identity of Yeats* (London: Faber, 1983).

Gogarty, Oliver, *It Isn't This Time of Year At All!* (Westport, Conn.: Greenwood, 1970).

Gonne (MacBride), Maud, *A Servant of the Queen* (Cambridge: Boydell and Brewer, 1983).

Gordon, D. J., *et al.*, *Images of a Poet* (Westport, Conn.: Greenwood, 1979).

Melchiori, Giorgio, *The Whole Mystery of Art: pattern into poetry in the work of W. B. Yeats* (Westport, Conn.: Greenwood 1979).

O'Connor, Frank, *W. B. Yeats: a Reminiscence* (Edinburgh: Tragara, 1982).

Reid, B. L., *William Butler Yeats: the Lyric of Tragedy* (Westport, Conn.: Greenwood, 1977).

Russell, George, *The National Being: Co-Operation and Nationality* (Blackrock: Irish Academic Press, 1982).

Ryan, Desmond, *The 1916 Poets* (Westport, Conn.: Greenwood, 1979).

Synge, J. M., *Collected Works*, 4 vols, (ed.) Robin Skelton (Gerrards Cross: Colin Smythe, 1982).

Unterecker, John, (ed.), *Yeats: A Collection*

of Critical Essays (Englewood Cliffs, N.J.: Prentice Hall, 1982).

Van Voris, Jacqueline, *Constance de Markievicz in the Cause of Ireland* (Gerrards Cross: Colin Smythe, 1982).

Weygandt, Cornelius, *Irish Plays and Playwrights* (Westport, Conn.: Greenwood, 1979).

Yeats, J. B., *J. B. Yeats, Letters to his son W. B. Yeats and others*, (ed.) Joseph Hone (London: Secker & Warburg, 1983).

Yeats, W. B., *The Celtic Twilight*, intro. Kathleen Raine (Gerrards Cross: Colin Smythe, 1982).

——, *Collected Plays* (London: Macmillan, 1982).

——, *Collected Poems* (London: Macmillan, 1982).

——, *The Letters of W. B. Yeats*, (ed) Allan Wade (New York: Octagon, 1980).

—— & Moore, Thomas Sturge, *Correspondence* (ed.), Ursula Bridge (Westport, Conn.: Greenwood, 1978).

——, *The Secret Rose and other Stories* (London: Macmillan, 1982). [*Mythologies* without *Per Amica Silentia Lunae*].

Young, Dudley, *Out of Ireland: the Poetry of W. B. Yeats* (Dingle: Brandon, 1982).

L. ANNOUNCED FOR PUBLICATION

Clark, David Ridgeley, *Visible Array* (Portlaoise: Dolmen, 1983).

Dorn, Karen, *Players and Painted Stage* (Brighton: Harvester Press, 1984).

Hough, Graham, *The Mystery Religion of W. B. Yeats* (Brighton: Harvester Press, 1984).

Innes, Christopher, *Edward Gordon Craig*

(Cambridge: Cambridge University Press, 1983).

Kinahan, Frank, *Yeats in Context* (London: Allen & Unwin, 1984).

Knowland, A. S., *W. B. Yeats, Dramatist of Vision* (Gerrards Cross: Colin Smythe, 1983).

Kohfeldt, Mary Lou, *Laughing in Black: the Life of Lady Gregory 1852–1932* (New York: Athenaeum, 1983).

Komesu, Okifumi, *The Double Perspective of Yeats's Aesthetic* (Gerrards Cross: Colin Smythe, 1984).

Kuch, Peter, *Yeats and AE* (Gerrards Cross: Colin Smythe, 1984).

Moore, George, *Collected Letters*, vol. ɪ (ed) Robert Becker (Gerrards Cross: Colin Smythe, 1984).

——, *George Moore on Parnassus: Letters (1900–1933)* (ed) Helmut Gerber (Newark: University of Delaware Press, 1984).

Naito, Shiro, *Yeats and Zen* (Kyoto, Yamaguchc, 1984).

O'Donnell, William H., *The Poetry of W. B. Yeats* (N.Y.: Unger, 1984).

Pyle, Hilary, *A Catalogue Raisonnée of the Paintings of Jack B. Yeats*, 2 vols (Gerrards Cross: Colin Smythe, 1984).

Quinn, John, *The Letters of John Quinn to W. B. Yeats*, (eds) Alan B. Himber & George Mills Harper (Ann Arbor, Mich.: UMI Research Pres, 1983).

Raine, Kathleen, *Yeats the Initiate: Essay on Certain Themes in the work of William Butler Yeats* (Mountrath: Dolmen, 1984).

Russell, George, *The Descent of the Gods* (Gerrards Cross: Colin Smythe, 1984).

Saddlemyer, Ann, *The Collected Letters of Synge*, vol ɪɪ (Oxford: Clarendon, 1984).

——, and Smythe, Colin, *Lady Gregory Fifty Years After* (Gerrards Cross: Colin Smythe, 1984).

Smythe, Colin, *A Guide to Coole Park, Home of Lady Gregory* (Gerrards Cross: Colin Smythe, 1983).

Steinman, Michael, *Yeats's Heroic Figures: Wilde, Parnell, Swift, Casement* (London: Macmillan, 1983).

Taylor, Richard, *A Reader's Guide to the Plays of W. B. Yeats* (London: Macmillan, 1983).

Vlasopolos, Anca, *The Symbolic Method of Coleridge, Baudelaire and Yeats* (Detroit: Wayne State University Press, 1984).

West, T. G., *Symbolism* (London: Methuen, 1984).